TEXAS POLITICS

TEXAS POLITICS

★ ★ ★ ★ ★ ★ ★ ★ ★ ★ ★ ★ ★ ★ ★

The Challenge of Change

Second Edition

John R. Todd

University of North Texas

HOUGHTON MIFFLIN COMPANY Boston New York

To Pat, for patience and encouragement during the writing of this book

Sponsoring Editor: Melissa Mashburn
Associate Editor: Katherine Meisenheimer
Project Editor: Rebecca Bennett
Senior Production/Design Coordinator: Carol Merrigan
Senior Manufacturing Coordinator: Priscilla J. Abreu
Senior Marketing Manager: Sandra McGuire

Cover Designer: Len Massiglia
Cover Image: Robert E. Daemmrich. Texas Independence Day Celebration at the Alamo. TSW

We would like to acknowledge and thank the following sources for permission to reprint material from their work:

Figure 3.1, Tables 3.5, 3.6: SOUTHERN STATE PARTY ORGANIZATIONS AND ACTIVISTS, Charles D. Hadley and Lewis Bowman (eds.), of SOUTHERN STATE PARTY ORGANIZATIONS AND ACTIVISTS. Copyright © 1995 by Charles D. Hadley and Lewis Bowman. Reproduced with permission of GREENWOOD PUBLISHING GROUP, INC., Westport, CT; **Table 3.2:** From John F. Bibby and Thomas M. Holbrook, "Parties and Elections" in *Politics in the American States,* 6/e, edited by Virginia Gray and Herbert Jacob. Copyright © 1996. Reprinted by permission of Addison Wesley Educational Publishers, Inc.; **Table 4.1:** Thomas, Clive S., and Ronald J. Hrebenar, "Interest Groups in the States," in Virginia Gray, Herbert Jacob and Robert B. Albritton, eds., POLITICS IN THE AMERICAN STATES: A COMPARATIVE ANALYSIS, Fifth Edition (New York: HarperCollins, 1990), p. 147. Used with permission; **Figure 5.6:** Adapted from *Dallas Morning News,* January 7, 1990, p. 9J. Used by permission; **Figure 6.4:** Figure p. 569 from "Legislative Workload Congestion in Texas" by Harvey J. Tucker from *Journal of Politics* 49:2, pp. 565–578; by permission of the author and the University of Texas Press. All rights retained by the University of Texas Press; **Table 6.2:** Harry J. Tucker and Gary M. Halter, eds., *Texas Legislative Almanac* 1997 (College

(Copyright page continues on page 392.)

Printed in the U.S.A.

Library of Congress Catalog Card Number: 98-72087

ISBN: 0-395-90612-1

3456789—CW—02 01 00

Contents

Preface

Any book on Texas government must certainly face the question, "What does this book offer that is not already provided by other texts?" The decision to write a book on this subject was based on the conviction that Texas is now facing a number of changes that challenge the way things have traditionally been done in the state's politics and government. The Texas of the future will be determined by the responses made to these changes. And so, change became the theme guiding the writing of *Texas Politics.* The text attempts to identify the major forces challenging the state and to discuss the responses to those challenges. It covers events through the 1998 gubernatorial election and the 1997 session of the legislature.

Thematic Framework

Some of the challenges facing the state have been economic. For example, the assumptions on which the state's economy have been traditionally based were profoundly shaken by the collapse of oil prices in the mid-1980s. This event forced the state government to look for new sources of revenue and to help plot a course toward a more diversified economic future. In another area, the state courts forced a reexamination of the way the state finances its public education system and paved the way for changes in the state's prison system and mental health services.

Politically, in recent years the Republican party has challenged the Democratic party for key positions and power within the state's political system. Candidates and parties, then, must try to adapt to these new realities. Changes in the party system have also begun to affect the way the political institutions, such as the legislature and the courts, function.

The state's socioeconomic framework is changing as well. Hispanics are rapidly becoming the largest minority group in the state and may one day become the majority. School districts in the largest metropolitan areas are already serving minority majorities. Adapting to this shifting racial/ethnic composition will pose challenges to many state institutions and policies.

Challenges and choices, then, are facing the Texas political system, and it is within this context that each of the major topics covered in this text is addressed. For example, the description of the executive branch highlights the efforts of governors to gain enough authority to actually direct and lead the state as it responds to change. Likewise, the chapter on political parties describes the changes in the Texas political system and assesses the impact of these changes on the various political institutions.

As might be expected, change produces resistance as well as adaptation. In many cases, then, chapters describe the stresses on the institutional and political systems and examine the reasons why change is resisted. In those cases, the emphasis is on examining that resistance and looking to the prospects for change.

Organization of the Book

This book is organized to help identify and analyze key changes. Chapter 1 introduces the theme of change and the challenges it presents to the political system and sketches out the contemporary context of Texas government. Chapter 2 identifies forces of change and the restraints that come from the state's legal setting. The influence of the federal system and the state's constitution are explored. The next three chapters (Chapters 3–5) examine changes in the key political processes (political parties, interest group activity, elections and voting). Major changes in all of these areas become apparent as these topics are analyzed.

Five chapters (Chapters 6–10) analyze the state's political institutions (legislature, governorship, bureaucracy, courts, and local government) and look for evidence of adaptive change or resistance. Each of these institutions has been challenged by change, but not all have responded adaptively.

The book closes with four policy chapters (Chapters 11–14) that examine four of the perplexing policy areas that have occupied the state's attention in recent years (public finance, social welfare, education, and the environment). Each chapter traces the major changes in policy development that have taken place in recent years.

The theme of change is brought into each chapter in several ways. Early in the chapter a preliminary section identifies the major forces of change that are relevant to the topic. Each chapter's concluding section summarizes the changes and talks about the prospects for further change. In addition, each chapter features a special interest box called "The Changing Face of Texas Politics." Boxes highlight a person or force typifying some of the key changes taking place, and topics include Governor George W. Bush, partisan change in the Texas Senate, charter schools and education reform, judicial reform, the Texas Lottery, the effects of federal highway policy, minority leadership in the major cities, and the role of judges in making policy. These organizational features as well as the analysis of forces of change throughout the text make the theme an integral feature of the book.

While a consistent effort has been made to address the theme of change throughout the book, the theme has not been allowed to filter out material that one would normally expect to find in a textbook for the Texas politics course. The major topics are addressed in a style that attempts to be informative and lively.

Since change will not stop and students need to keep learning after reading this book, Appendix A suggests resources for "Keeping Up with Texas

Politics." Appendix A includes a variety of print sources, but also suggests ways that up-to-date information can be gathered from the Internet. The resources listed were some of the most helpful to the writing of this book. Using these resources can keep the learning process from ending with this book or a particular college course. Appendix B provides exercises that give students practice in using Internet resources.

What's New in This Edition

As one would expect, part of the task of this revision was simply to update information to the latest source wherever possible. This includes a thorough updating of the public finance chapter to reflect the sources of revenue and the allocation of expenditures in the 1998–1999 biennium. It also includes election updates that cover the outcome of the 1998 state elections.

Some chapters have new sections or changed emphases. For example, Chapter 2 now contains more information about the federal system and its implications for Texas. The education chapter gives less space to school finance reform and more to the recent reforms focused on student performance. The judicial chapter gives less emphasis to structural reform, since the issue no longer seems to be central to the state's political agenda.

A chapter on social welfare reform replaces the chapter on economic development. The state's economy is no longer struggling as it was in the late 1980s and early 1990s; therefore, wrestling with poverty and welfare reform is now a more pressing concern. The new chapter explains the role of national government reforms, but it also emphasizes the distinctive approaches Texas is taking.

The Teaching Package

Texas Politics: The Challenge of Change, Second Edition, offers supplementary materials for both the instructor and the student.

The *Instructor's Resource Manual with Test Items,* written by the text author, provides teachers with material that relates directly to the thematic framework of the text. The Resources section includes learning objectives, lecture outlines, and suggested classroom activities for each chapter of the text. The Test Items section provides multiple-choice and essay questions for each chapter. A *Computerized Test Bank* for Windows is also available to adopters.

The *Study Guide,* written by David Garrison of Collin County Community College, contains learning objectives, chapter outlines, key concepts, multimedia resources, Internet exercises, multiple-choice questions, and essay questions for student practice and review.

New to this edition is a web site designed to help students get the most out of their text. The site offers chapter outlines, on-line practice quizzes, links to all the sites mentioned in the text, and a function allowing students to complete the Appendix B Internet exercises on line. The Todd, *Texas Politics* site can be accessed through the Houghton Mifflin College Division home page at **http://www.hmco.com/college.**

Acknowledgments

When one undertakes a task such as this, a number of debts of gratitude are accumulated along the way. The editorial staff at Houghton Mifflin must be praised for its encouraging manner and its determination to produce a good book. Developmental editor Katherine Meisenheimer's warm, encouraging manner helped keep the project moving or reinvigorated it when it periodically stalled. I also thank the reviewers who identified topics that had been left out, errors that had been made, and failures to address the theme consistently. They helped us keep the project honest. My thanks go to:

Kay Hofer, Southwest Texas State University
U. Lynn Jones, Collin County Community College
Eric Miller, Blinn College
J. D. Phaup, Texas A&M University–Kingsville

And, finally, I must thank my family for their patience.

John R. Todd

TEXAS POLITICS

1

The Context of Texas Government

Chapter Outline

Texans have a romantic view of life in their state, a view that the movies often have contributed to. But even a cinematic history of Texas reveals a state caught up in the throes of change. When the movie *Giant* came out in 1956, it depicted determined Texans battling the elements to make their fortunes in cattle ranching; it also depicted the impact of oil exploration and development on the lives of those Texans. The movie version of Texas novelist Larry McMurtry's *The Last Picture Show,* which came out in 1971, showed the death of a small Texas town. The closing of the town's movie theater symbolized the loss of its youth and vitality. When *Urban Cowboy* was released in 1980, young Texans were shown living a new kind of life: living in the city and working in oil refineries, yet clinging to the pretense of cowboy life by hanging out in honky-tonks and riding a mechanical bull. By 1990, *Texasville,* the movie based on McMurtry's sequel to *The Last Picture Show,* exposed the collapse of the oil patch and the desperation of the people who had based their hopes on big oil. Then in 1997, *Lone Star* explored the realm of ethnic tensions in Texas.

Texas is not what it used to be. People's lives are different, and so are their politics. Any understanding of contemporary Texas government must be based on an understanding of how the social and economic environment in the state has changed. This is the approach that this book takes. The traditional topics are covered here, but always in light of two questions: How has change altered the traditional workings of government and politics in Texas? And what challenges has change created?

This chapter sets the stage for an analysis of Texas government and politics. The text here addresses several questions:

- What is the purpose of government and politics?
- What is the political environment in Texas?
- How has change affected and how will it continue to affect Texas government and politics?

Government and Politics

Governments regulate the lives of their citizens. They decide how fast you should drive on the highways, whether you can carry a gun, and whether the parents of a minor must be notified before she has an abortion. Governments also produce and distribute services to their citizens. They decide what services to provide, at what level, and to whom. Because there always are more things that might be done than a state can afford to do, states must decide how to allocate their resources among public education, welfare, prisons, highways, and other competing services.

Politics is all of the processes by which citizens attempt to control or influence the decisions that are made by governments. Those processes include voting, joining interest groups, and demonstrating to protest govern-

The image of the cowboy is still romantically linked to Texas life despite the declining economic importance of cattle and ranching.

ment decisions. That individuals and groups are motivated to influence government decisions makes sense: governments do things that significantly affect people's lives. But some are better able to influence government than others. The more wealth, education, and income people have, the more influence they tend to have and the more active they tend to be.[1]

The Environment of Texas Politics

State governments operate in an environment that affects what they can and will do. That environment includes the land and natural resources in a state's territory, the economy, and the people.

The Land

The politics and culture of Texas have been strongly shaped by the land. One characteristic of that land is its vastness. Until Alaska became a state, Texas was the largest state in the nation in land area—about 276,000 square miles

Although the idling of Texas oil fields is often a modern reality, oil is still an important part of the Texas economy.

of land within the state's boundaries.[2] Texas is so large that fourteen of the fifty states could fit within its borders.[3]

In the early years, this land area created a frontier environment: land was readily available to those hardy enough to settle it. An early policy of the state was to put as much land into private ownership as possible. The state sold land to encourage settlement, to raise money for the government, and even to pay for the construction of the state capitol. In addition, the state gave land to settlers, to soldiers and their survivors, and to railroads. In 1899 the frontier essentially was closed. The state dropped its **homestead policy** and donated almost all of the remaining public land to the state school system. Because the state retained title to its public lands when it joined the Union in 1845, and because it promoted private ownership of land, 98 percent of the land in Texas is owned privately. By contrast, in many western states the national government owns as much as half of the land.[4]

At the time Texas joined the Union, land was the state's principal resource. The people of Texas were farmers and cattle ranchers, working large tracts of land. For example, the King Ranch covered 825,000 acres in South Texas. And after the state traded 3 million acres of public land in 1879 to finance the construction of a state capitol, the XIT Ranch stretched over nine counties in the Texas Panhandle.[5]

The physical size of the state created a challenge for its government: to provide a transportation system. Linking Texans together over a vast land space are more than 220,000 miles of roadways. The state government maintains about 183,000 miles of those highways.[6]

The Economy

From land to oil. Before Texas had an **oil-based economy,** it had a **land-based economy,** an economy that relied primarily on agricultural employment. At the turn of the century, about 70 percent of the jobs in Texas were in farming. But the discovery of large crude oil and natural gas reserves in the first decade of the twentieth century launched a fundamental overhaul of the state's economy. Over time, agricultural employment has steadily given way to growth in the mining (oil), manufacturing and construction, and services sectors. Although the percentage of earnings that comes from agriculture is still greater in Texas today than it is in the nation as a whole, that percentage has dropped toward the national average in recent years.[7]

The decline of oil. One of the most dramatic changes since the crisis of the 1980s has been the diminished role of the oil and gas industry in the Texas economy. Until 1981 that industry had been a growing part of the gross state product. But the share of the gross state product that came from oil and gas fell sharply between 1981 and 1991 (Figure 1.1). And despite increases in oil prices in the mid-1990s, oil prices plummeted again in 1998. Indeed, experts noted the differences in the Texas economy in 1998 that made it possible for the state to survive prices comparable to those that drove the Texas economy into recession in the 1980s.[8]

The loss of cheap labor. Economists traditionally identify labor, land, and capital as the basic assets on which wealth is built. A state's economic development often hinges on some special advantage it holds in one of these factors of production. In the past, Texas has depended on low labor costs to fuel its economic development. That advantage generally lasted into the post–World War II period. By the 1980s, however, labor costs exceeded the national average in the state's three major labor markets; and labor costs were still higher than average in the state's two largest markets in the 1990s (Figure 1.2). Future economic development in Texas, then, cannot be based on the assumption of low labor costs; the state is going to have to demonstrate other advantages to encourage economic development there.

In the absence of cheap labor, Texas needs a well-prepared workforce. Although the state does relatively well in providing workers with the advanced skills necessary to support an economy based on high technology (computers and electronics, for example), it has been less successful in meeting the demand for a labor force with basic skills. About one in five Texas workers is functionally illiterate, and many more workers would be considered illiterate if analytical and problem-solving skills were taken into consideration.[9]

The rising service sector. Another major change in the Texas economy is the growing percentage of jobs in the service sector. The proportion of jobs in

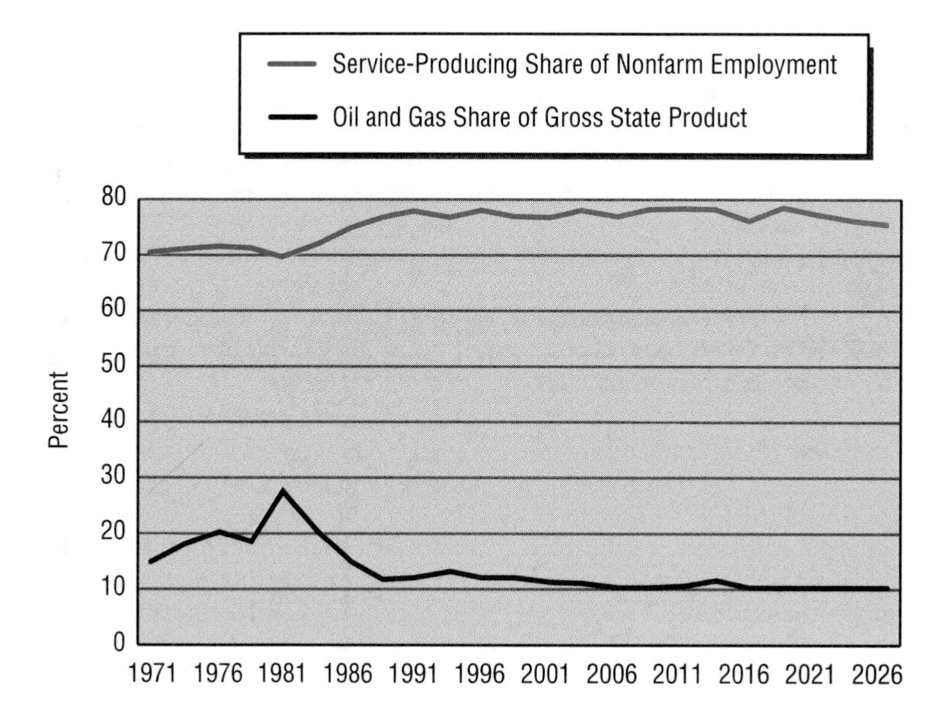

FIGURE 1.1 Diversification of the Texas Economy, 1971–2026
Source: Texas Comptroller of Public Accounts, The Changing Face of Texas: Texas Through the Year 2026 *(Austin, 1992), 5.*

the **service sector** jumped by almost 10 percent between 1981 and 1991 (see Figure 1.1); and by 1994 almost 90 percent of new jobs were in this sector, a trend that seems likely to continue.[10]

Economists often divide the service sector into two parts: the high-tech jobs that produce good income and offer good opportunity for advancement and the unskilled jobs that pay little and offer little opportunity. The growth of this sector in Texas, then, as in the rest of the country, can contribute to income inequality depending on whether an individual has the skills to work in the high-tech part of the sector or in the low-skill, low-pay part of the sector.

The People

In addition to being the second largest state in land area, Texas is now the second largest state in population, moving past New York in 1994.[11] Population grew rapidly in the early part of the century, with an average annual growth rate of 5.5 percent in 1900. The growth rate has slowed more recently.

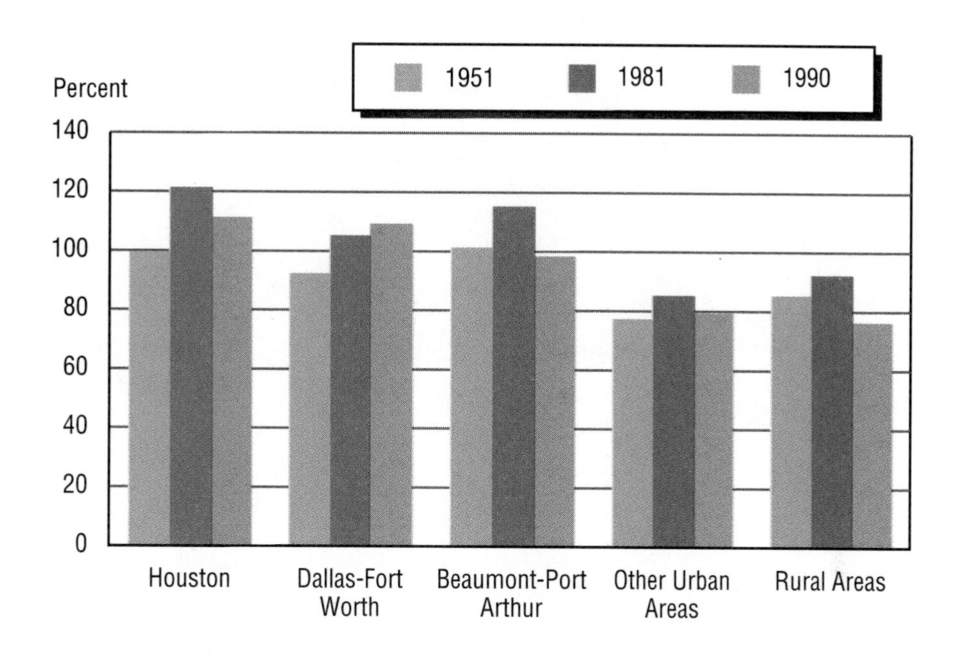

FIGURE 1.2 Texas Wages as a Percentage of the U.S. Average, 1951, 1981, and 1990

Source: Texas Comptroller of Public Accounts, Forces of Change *(Austin, 1994), 2: pt. 1, 131.*

Between 1980 and 1990 the state's average annual growth rate was 1.8 percent.[12] Growth rates have edged upward again in the 1990s. The growth rate was 2 percent between 1992–1993 and 1993–1994. The growth rate was 1.7 percent for 1994–1995.[13] Migration to the state has been an important source of population growth. During the 1970s net migration accounted for over half the state's population growth. In the 1980s and 1990s, migration has accounted for more than one-third of the state's population growth.[14]

The composition of the population is changing and will continue to change in the future. Several trends are noteworthy. First, the proportion of elderly people in the population is expected to increase. The segment of the population over age 59 has grown almost twice as fast as the state average since 1900. And the aging of the baby boomers (those born in the two decades following World War II), who are now between the ages of 37 and 51, will add significantly to the elderly population as the state enters the next century.[15]

Another change in the state's population distribution is occurring in racial and ethnic makeup. Whites have dominated the state's population through most of its history, but projections for the future depict a state with no racial

Racial and ethnic diversity is a major feature of Texas life today and will continue to be important in the future.

or ethnic majority (Figure 1.3). Whites made up almost 70 percent of the state's population in 1970; by 1990 they made up just over 60 percent; and by 2026 they are expected to make up less than 50 percent. Hispanics have expanded their share of the population and are expected to make up almost 40 percent of the state's population by 2026. Although African Americans in the population will grow in numbers, they will make up a slightly smaller share of the state's population in 2026 than they do now.

The final important **demographic trend** in Texas is the geographic concentration of the state's population. By 1950 most of the state's population was urban, and almost all of the state's population growth since 1950 has been in metropolitan areas. Today over half the state's population lives in the state's three largest metropolitan areas: Dallas–Fort Worth, Houston–Galveston–Brazoria, and San Antonio.[16] In fact the triangle shown in Figure 1.4 includes the state's largest metropolitan areas and about 60 percent of the state's population.[17]

The Regions

Molded by the land, its economy, and its people, Texas has become a state with several clearly differentiated **regions.** An understanding of those regions helps lay the foundation for understanding Texas politics.

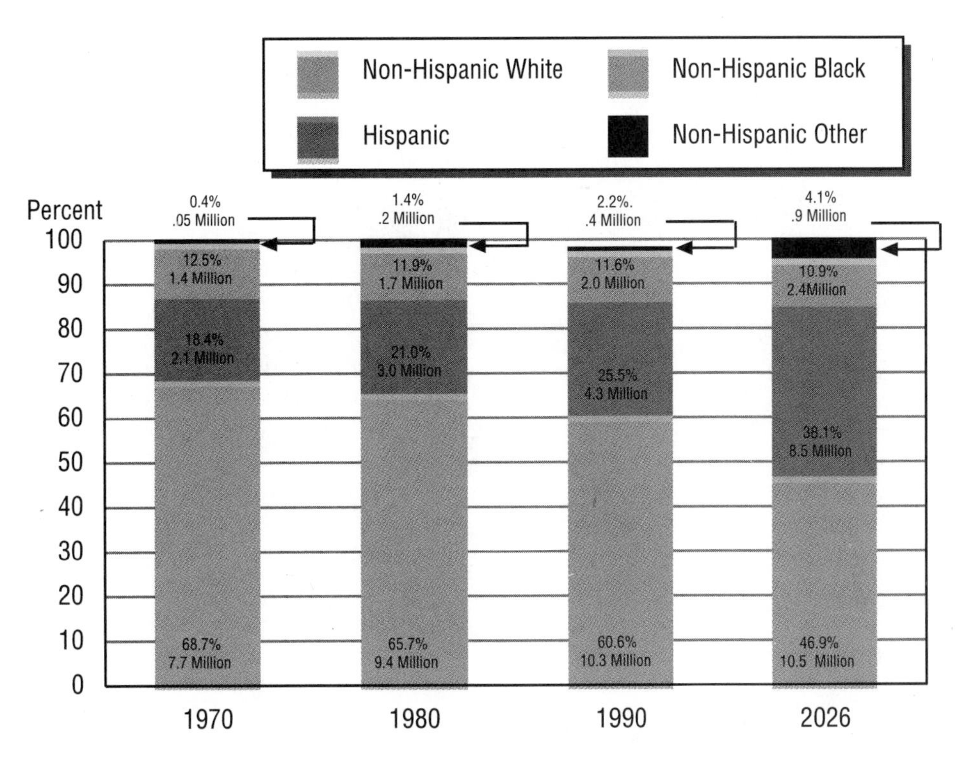

FIGURE 1.3 Texas Population by Race and Ethnicity, 1970–2026
Source: Texas Comptroller of Public Accounts, Forces of Change *(Austin, 1994), 2: pt. 1, 7.*

Economic regions. The Office of the Comptroller of Public Accounts divides Texas into ten economic regions (Figure 1.5). Two of the regions, *Upper East Texas* and *Southeast Texas,* run along the wooded border with Louisiana. Timber, oil, and gas are the key industries in these regions. The *Gulf Coast* region includes Houston, Galveston, and other cities that are linked together in a large metropolitan area. Oil and gas are important in this area too, along with the manufacturing of related products. Four major ports for ocean-going vessels open this area up to world trade. The *Metropolex* includes the Dallas–Fort Worth metropolitan area. Its economy includes high-technology electronics, trade, and transportation. The Dallas/Fort Worth Airport opens the region to trade and transportation. *Central Texas* includes the state's capital (Austin) and several high-technology computer-related industries. *South Texas* is a large geographic region that encompasses six metropolitan areas (including San Antonio) and forty-seven counties. Tourism, manufacturing, and government are important economic activities here. Thirty counties comprise *Northwest Texas,* and it includes the metropolitan areas of Abilene and Wichita Falls. The economy of the region depends on agriculture, oil, and gas. The agriculture of this region tends toward cotton and feed crops for cattle. In *West Texas,* where the economy

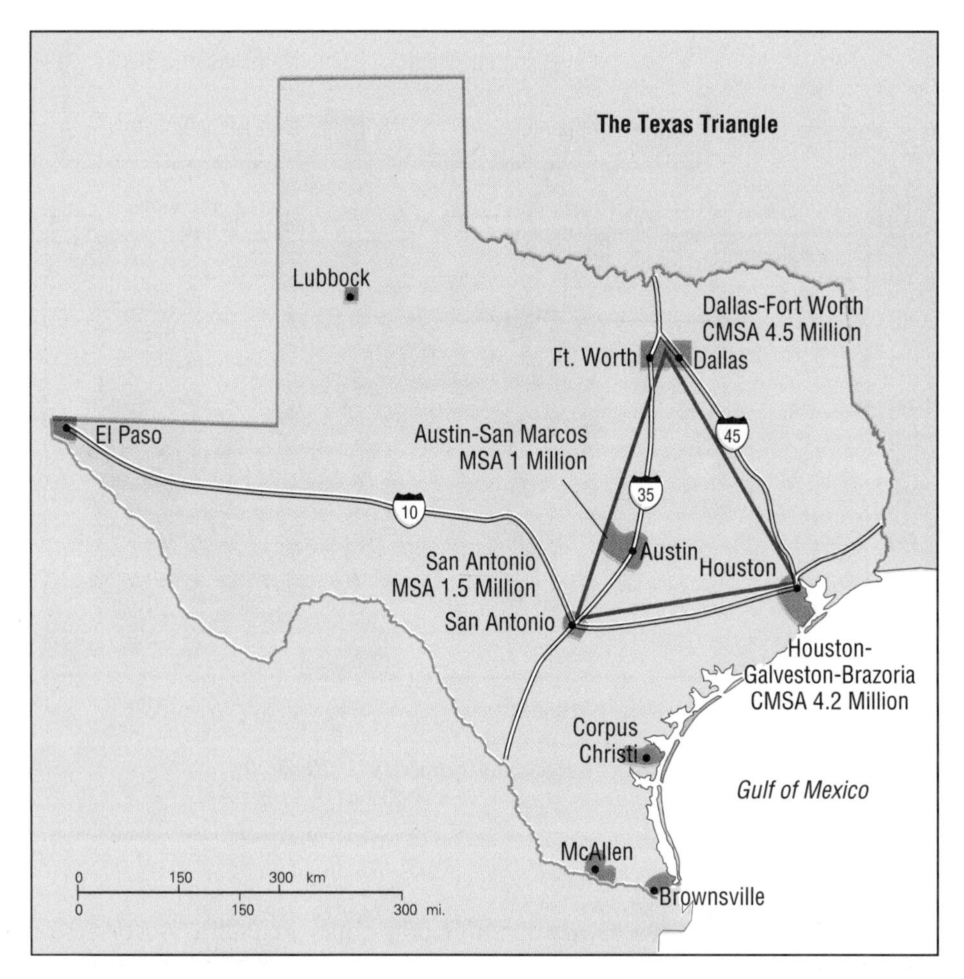

FIGURE 1.4 The Texas Triangle: Home of 60 Percent of the State's Population
Source: Texas Comptroller of Public Accounts, Forces of Change *(Austin, 1994), 2: pt. 1, 144 and* Texas Almanac 1998–1999 *(Dallas:* Dallas Morning News, *1997), p. 296.*

historically has been based on oil and gas extraction and agriculture, low oil prices have led to economic stress. The *Upper Rio Grande* includes several counties that are sparsely populated, as well as the city of El Paso, the region's economic center. The economy in El Paso is manufacturing-intensive. The *High Plains* region includes forty-one counties, with Lubbock and Amarillo the major urban centers. Agriculture dominates this region. Cotton and wheat are the major crops. Cattle also contribute to the area's economy.

Ethnic regions. The concentration of ethnic groups in some areas of the state also leads to regional differences. As Figure 1.6 shows, the state's Hispanic population is concentrated in counties along the Rio Grande Valley. In

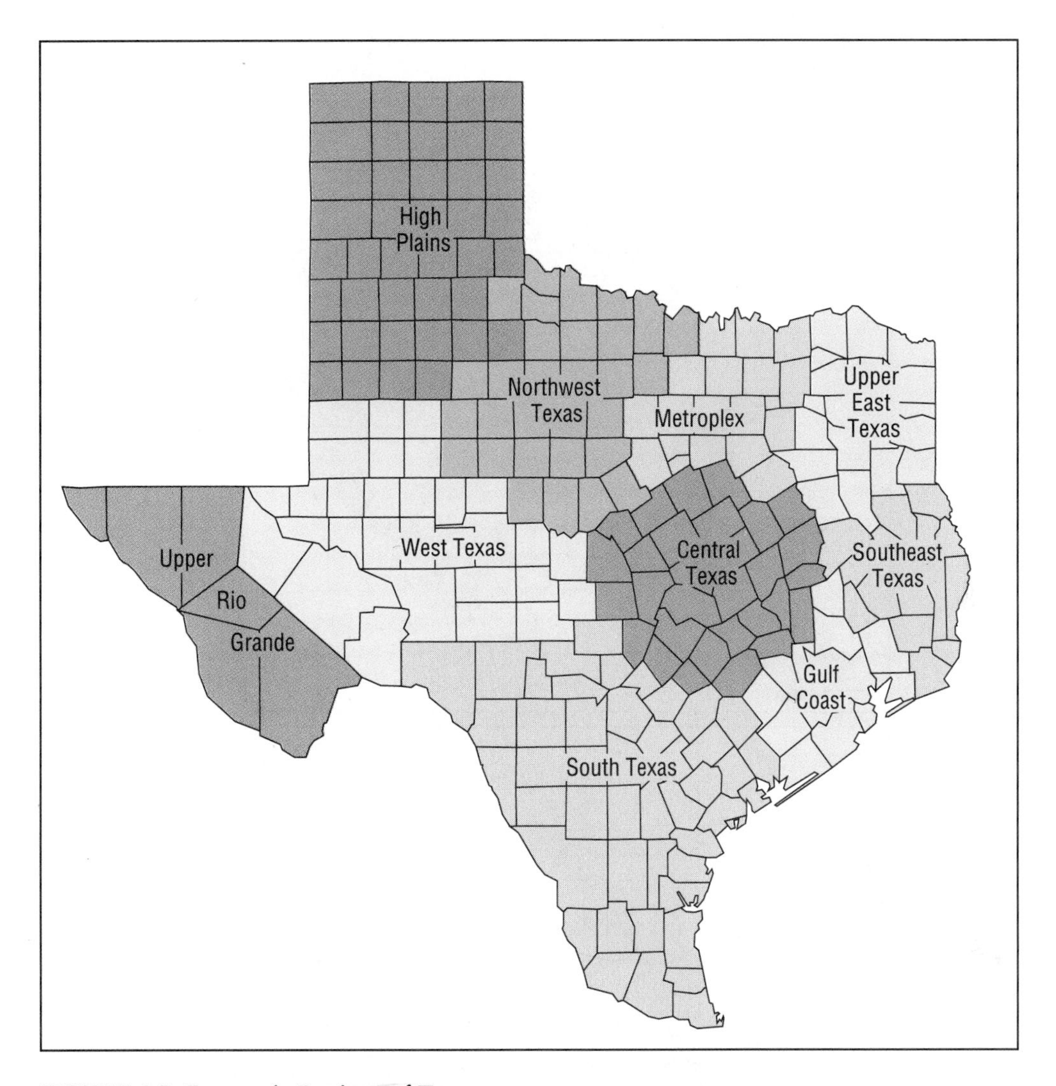

FIGURE 1.5 Economic Regions of Texas
Source: Texas Almanac 1994–95 *(Dallas:* Dallas Morning News, *1994), 442.*

contrast, the anglo population is concentrated in areas of East and Central Texas and in the Texas Panhandle. Areas of African-American concentration are in only a few counties of East and Central Texas.

The Challenge of Change

With changes in the environment of Texas politics come challenges for the government. One test of government and political institutions is their flexi-

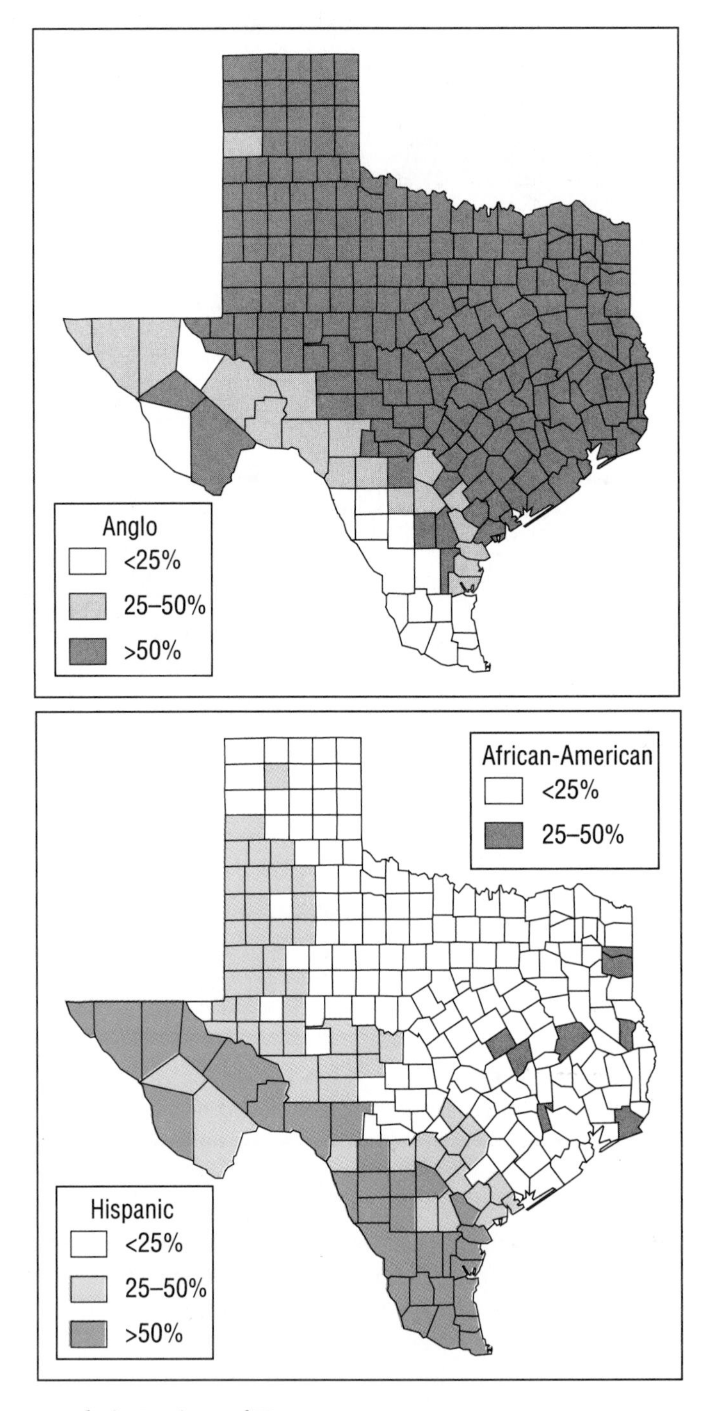

FIGURE 1.6 Ethnic Regions of Texas

Source: Texas Comptroller of Public Accounts, Forces of Change *(Austin, 1994), 2: pt. 1, 494, 497, 499.*

Texas life is an increasingly urban one. The Dallas skyline at night glitters with lighted highrises and towers.

bility, their ability to accommodate change. The challenge of governing is responding to and managing change. As elements of the environment change, problems often arise that call for new or more government action. For example, changes in the state's economy or in the state's ethnic or racial makeup can affect its capacity to provide services or lead to demands for new services. Aspects of the environment, then, also can become forces of change.

Several types of change—economic change, demographic change, and intergovernmental change—have posed challenges to Texas in recent years. Each of these was a force over which the state had little or no control. Yet they challenged the state to adjust policies and procedures to meet public needs and maintain the stability of the government.

Economic Change

Changes in a state's economy pose several types of challenges to the state's government. An economic downturn can reduce the state's tax collections, leave the state's budget unbalanced, and produce a demand for new revenue. The state must take action to encourage economic growth, both to promote jobs for its citizens and to increase revenues to support state services. Texas

The Changing Face of Texas Politics

Reading the Newspaper, Noticing Change

Some changes are trumpeted in newspaper headlines; the stories of other changes are tucked away on the inside pages of the newspaper. It can take practice and perspective to spot these kinds of stories.

In November 1992 a story appeared several sections into the *Dallas Morning News* under the heading "Can San Jose Find Its Way?" The article reported that about two dozen San Jose business leaders and boosters had just arrived in Austin "to find out why the capital of the Lone Star State keeps grabbing jobs from Silicon Valley."[1] Why was the story significant? Because it carried a message about change in the Texas economy and in the state's place in the national economy. The San Jose area is called Silicon Valley because of its pivotal role in the computer industry. That business leaders from San Jose were visiting Austin was a sign that things are changing and that Austin has become a major player in the industry. In fact the Californians' visit coincided with yet another company's announcement that it would leave California and move to Austin.[2]

Another story that signalled change was printed in the *Wall Street Journal* in January 1995.[3] The story, also on an inside page of the paper, reported that a number of new FM radio stations were appearing in major metropolitan markets in Texas. These stations use a bilingual (Spanish and English) format and emphasize a Hispanic-style music called *Tejano.* Until recently Hispanic stations tended to be smaller AM stations and to play Latino music. Why are the new stations cropping up? Because the Hispanic community in Texas has grown. Hispanics are already the second largest ethnic group in the state. And by early in the next century, their proportion of the population should nearly equal that of Anglos. That the stations broadcast on FM bands, in Spanish and English, and that they play Tejano music signal a recog-

went through a wrenching economic change in the mid-1980s, when the oil and gas industry collapsed. The stability of its government was jeopardized, and the livelihood of its citizens threatened. The response of the state to this challenge is analyzed in later chapters.

Demographic Change

As noted earlier, the size and makeup of the Texas population have begun to change and are expected to continue to change into the next century. Although population growth will level off, some groups will see their proportion increase, while others will see it decrease. The failure of any one group to emerge as a majority poses several challenges for the state's government. For example, as the Hispanic population grows, the state will need to incorporate that population into its political and economic processes. It will have to nition of the number of bilingual listeners who have been in the state for generations. Tejano music was born in the barrios of South Texas: it is Hispanic music with Texas origins. By focusing on that music, marketing experts and investors are acknowledging that Spanish-language radio no longer has to target newly arriving Hispanics. The largest cities in Texas have significant bilingual Hispanic populations, and those populations are the market the new-format stations want to capture. The success of KXTN-FM in San Antonio proved the strategy works; and investors in Dallas and Houston recognized an opportunity to cash in on it.

This story also tells us that the Hispanic community in the state's major cities has become large enough and stable enough to attract investors' dollars. This could well mean that the role of Hispanics is changing in other areas as well.

In 1997, another sign of change was evident in the announcement that Sea World, a major tourist attraction in San Antonio, had added a salute to Hispanic culture to its displays. Plaza Del Sol is a 4,300 square foot pavilion containing information about Hispanic contributions and achievements. This new pavilion demonstrates that profit-making businesses recognize the growing economic significance of the Hispanic population in Texas and want to profit from it.[4]

To recognize change, we have to learn to look for signs of change. When those signs make the front page, the process is relatively simple. It becomes more difficult when the evidence of change is buried in a story about a visiting group of businesspeople or new-format radio stations. Yet our understanding of life in Texas—in this case, the state's economy and changing ethnic roles—depends on our willingness to search out all indications of change. ★

[1]Steve Kaufman, "Can San Jose Find Its Way? Californians Come to Austin to Find Out Why So Many Firms Are Moving to Texas," *Dallas Morning News,* November 26, 1992, 1D.

[2]The company was Advanced Micro Devices, Inc., located in Sunnyvale, California. See ibid.

[3]Susan Warren, "Texas Journal: Stations Change Tune to Woo Hispanics," *Wall Street Journal,* January 25, 1995, 3T.

[4]Kathryn Straach, "New Sea World Exhibit Salutes Hispanic Culture," *Dallas Morning News* (September 14, 1997), p. 96.

provide educational services that can move Hispanics into the economic mainstream. How the state's political parties respond to demographic change may well determine the relative strength of each party. Whether the state responds to the needs of this growing minority will have much to do with whether the government lives up to the principles of democracy or whether a minority may come to dominate the system. Building party coalitions that bridge racial and ethnic differences will be critical to party success once the state has no racial or ethnic majority.

Intergovernmental Change

Texas also is challenged by changes in the national government. In the Reagan–Bush years, the level of help the states could expect from the national government fell. The Republican majority that took control of Congress after the 1994 elections brought more change. After early budget battles with the Clinton administration that brought the national government to a standstill, the Republican leadership was able to negotiate a balanced budget agreement in 1997. The trend toward delegating more to the states continued. Financial aid has been reduced in some areas, but the state's flexibility in handling services in some of those areas has increased. Texas, like the other states, must find new ways of providing certain services while making do with fewer resources.

Responding to Change

The challenge of change is to find ways to adjust state policies and procedures so that problems can be solved and public support maintained. Whether a state can pull off this feat depends on several factors. One is its quality of leadership. Solutions to problems depend on leaders who have a vision of how problems can be resolved and who can mobilize public support behind their vision. In the analysis of Texas government in this book, it is important to recognize whether government structures and policies make it easy or difficult for this kind of leadership to be exerted. This question is particularly important in the analysis of the governorship and key legislative offices.

Another factor that affects a state's ability to handle change is the appropriateness and responsiveness of its government institutions. Sometimes solving a problem can be easier if structures and policies can be designed from scratch. For example, as the problem of producing a fair system for financing public schools is examined in Chapter 13, it should become apparent that the problem could have been resolved more easily if the state's system for administering public schools could have been redesigned. Working with the structures already in place made solving the problem more difficult.

Another factor that influences the ability of the Texas government to meet the challenges before it is the limitations imposed on the state by the national government. Sometimes what Texas can do to solve a problem depends on what the national government allows it to do. Federal court orders certainly have shaped the policy options open to the state in coping with its growing prison population, for example. And the availability of federal funds often is contingent on the state's implementation of federal standards and programs.

Conclusion

This book focuses on change and how Texas has responded to it. Change by definition is unsettling. The ability of a government to manage change and to keep the support of its citizens is one of the real tests of effective government today. The environment described here is the raw material with which the state can work. The land, the economy, the people, all condition the state government's options and its evaluation of those options. The remainder of this book explores the ways that political processes, government institutions, and public policies in Texas—all products of the state's unique environment—respond to change.

Notes

1. See, for example, Sidney Verba and Norman H. Nie, *Participation in America: Political Democracy and Social Equality* (New York: Harper & Row, 1972), especially Chapter 8.
2. Texas Comptroller of Public Accounts, *Forces of Change* (Austin, 1994), 2: pt. 1, 394.
3. Texas Comptroller, *Forces of Change,* 2: pt. 1, 483.
4. Texas Comptroller, *Forces of Change,* 2: pt. 1, 394.
5. Texas Comptroller, *Forces of Change,* 2: pt. 1, 501.
6. *Texas Almanac, 1998–1999* (Dallas: *Dallas Morning News,* 1997), 576–579.
7. Texas Comptroller of Public Accounts, *Forces of Change* (Austin, 1994), 2: pt. 1, 57.
8. Jane Seabury, "Hitting a Rough Patch," *Dallas Morning News,* March 18, 1988, p. 11.
9. Texas Comptroller, *Forces of Change,* 2: pt. 1, 143.
10. "Texas Economic Outlook," *Texas Economic Quarterly,* December 1994, 5.
11. "Texas Adds 356,000 People, Tops NY's Population," *Dallas Morning News,* December 28, 1994, 8A.
12. Texas Comptroller, *Forces of Change,* 2: pt. 1, 14–15.
13. Steve H. Murdock et al., *The Texas Challenge: Population Change and the Future of Texas* (College Station: Texas A&M University Press, 1997), p. 11.
14. Texas Comptroller, *Forces of Change,* 2: pt. 1, 21.
15. Texas Comptroller, *Forces of Change,* 2: pt. 1, 23.
16. Texas Comptroller, *Forces of Change,* 2: pt. 1, 30.
17. Texas Comptroller, *Forces of Change,* 1: 144.

2

The Legal Environment of Texas Politics: Federalism and the State Constitution

Chapter Outline

When the Texas legislature met in 1991, estimates of state revenue fell over $4 billion short of the amount needed to maintain services at existing levels. In response to that crisis, the legislature eventually passed a lottery bill. But before the bill could be passed, the Texas Constitution had to be amended because Article II, Section 47, prohibited a lottery. The legislature proposed an amendment, which the voters ratified in 1991. Only after the amendment was passed was it possible for lawmakers to enact the lottery legislation.

In 1998, Texas followed the lead of the other forty-nine states by permitting its citizens to take out home equity loans. Home equity loans had become an important source of consumer credit in other states, allowing individuals to borrow at rates significantly below the rates charged by credit cards. Although most states could provide their citizens access to such loans simply by passing a law, in Texas the constitution prohibited such loans (Article VI, Section 50). Thus, the Texas Constitution had to be amended before the new types of loans could be made available. That made approval more difficult, because constitutional amendments require large majorities in the legislature and must be approved in a statewide referendum. In this case, such an amendment was proposed by the legislature and approved by the voters in 1997.

These are two examples of how the Texas Constitution limits the responses of the state's leaders to public problems. Sometimes, the constitution delays the solution of a problem. At other times, some solutions are prohibited altogether. And whenever amending the constitution is involved, solving the problem is made more difficult. The constitution, then, can have a significant effect on the choices lawmakers make.

The state constitution is one component of the legal environment in which Texas must operate. The other is the federal system of government. Both set out rules that limit what the state can do. This chapter will explore several key questions about the legal environment in Texas:

- How does the federal system affect Texas government?
- What forces shaped the Texas Constitution and produced the document that guides Texas government today?
- How is Texas government influenced by its constitution?
- What are the prospects for change in the Texas legal environment?

The answers to these questions should lead to a better understanding of the daily constraints under which Texas government operates.

The Legal Environment and Change

The topics considered in this chapter—the constitution and the federal system—are among the elements of government that are most resistant to change. They hold some of the answers to questions about the ability of a state like Texas to respond effectively to social and economic changes within its boundaries.

What is the relationship of a state's legal environment to change? Usually, the legal environment sets limits on policy actions. In fact, the legal environment itself tends to resist change. Constitutions are written to stabilize governments. They cannot do that if they are constantly changing. Certainly a constitution can become outdated, no longer providing a suitable framework for a contemporary government. But even here change comes slowly.

The federal system also operates under a constitution, the U.S. Constitution. So that system also is expected to help stabilize the operations of the governments that are part of the system. Of course federalism has changed to accommodate new circumstances—the economic problems of the 1930s and the national deficit problems of the 1980s and 1990s, for example.

The Implications of Federalism

Membership in the federal system is an important part of the legal environment in which Texas operates. **Federalism** is a system of government that divides governmental authority between a national government and a set of component regional governments (i.e., states in this country). In a federal system, both the national and the state governments have the right to act directly on the people.[1] That is, each can impose and collect taxes, provide services, and impose regulations on the people, without being required to seek the permission of the other level or to work through any other level of government. In the United States, this arrangement was devised to overcome the problems the national government experienced under the Articles of Confederation (1781–1788), when it lacked the power to tax the people to finance its operations.

A second defining characteristic of a federal system is the division of responsibilities between the two levels of government in the constitution. That is, the constitution provides a broad description of **national government powers** and **state powers.** In the U.S. Constitution, Article I, Section 8 lists powers that can be exercised by the national Congress. The Tenth Amendment to the Constitution stipulates that "the powers not delegated to the United States by the Constitution, or prohibited by it to the States, are reserved to the States respectively, or to the people." Although the boundaries have been changing, these two sections of the Constitution create a broad division of labor between the national government and the states, allocating certain powers to the national government and reserving others to the states.

Finally, in a federal system the constitution protects each level of government from "undue encroachment or destruction by the other."[2] In a federal system neither level of government is allowed to destroy or abolish the other. The United States Constitution protects even the **geographic integrity** of the states by prohibiting Congress from subdividing states or arbitrarily combining them, without the consent of the states.[3] It is also crucial in a federal system that one level not be able to take over all the significant powers of the other. As noted earlier, the Constitution attempts to protect the division of responsibilities between the two levels by defining the appropriate powers of each.

Although federalism is a practical way of governing a country that is geographically large and economically, ethnically, and racially diverse, operating within a federal system can impose a variety of constraints on the states. The states may find that their ability to act is limited by orders or restrictions imposed by the national government. Thus, because they must operate within the framework of national rules and policies, Texas and other states are affected by at least four types of actions by the national government: judicial decrees, legislative regulations, preemptions, and grant-in-aid conditions.[4]

Judicial Decrees

Judicial decrees are court decisions that require states to take certain actions. The due process clause of the Fourteenth Amendment to the U.S. Constitution has been the basis of many important decisions that limit the power of state governments.[5] That clause prohibits the states from depriving "any person of life, liberty, or property, without due process of law." In 1925 the Supreme Court began to use the due process clause to apply provisions of the Bill of Rights to the states.[6] The Bill of Rights defines individual rights that governments must respect and protect, including expressive rights (for example, freedom of speech, freedom of the press, and freedom of religion) and procedural rights (the right to trial by jury, the right to counsel in trials, and freedom from unreasonable searches and seizures). Today almost all of the provisions of the Bill of Rights apply to the states. As a result, Texas (and other states) must take the Bill of Rights into account in its laws and procedures.

The equal protection clause of the Fourteenth Amendment says that no state should deny equal protection of the laws to any person within its jurisdiction. This clause also has been the basis for judicial decrees that affect the states. For example, the courts used the equality standard to require southern states to open their primary elections to nonwhites[7] and to desegregate their schools.[8] In 1966 the Supreme Court based its finding that state poll taxes were unconstitutional on the equal protection clause.[9] (Texas was still imposing a poll tax at the time.)

Some judicial decrees directly involved Texas. In 1973, in *Roe* v. *Wade,* the Supreme Court struck down a Texas statute that allowed abortion only in cases where the mother's life is in danger.[10] Using the right to privacy derived from the Ninth Amendment and the due process clause of the Fourteenth Amendment, the Court limited the power of Texas and other states to regulate abortion. In 1981, in *Ruiz* v. *Estelle,* a federal judge concluded that the overcrowding in Texas prisons violated the prohibition of cruel and unusual punishment found in the Bill of Rights.[11] The court ordered Texas to reduce prison overcrowding, which meant that the state had to build more prisons and carefully manage its prison population.

Legislative Regulations

The right of the national government to control the affairs of state governments through **legislative regulations** has been a matter of dispute. Relying on increasingly broad interpretations of its powers by the Supreme Court, Congress expanded its regulatory activity under the U.S. Constitution's interstate commerce clause. The states traditionally relied on the national constitution to limit the regulations imposed on them by Congress. In 1985, the Supreme Court concluded in *Garcia* v. *San Antonio Metropolitan Transit Authority* that the states could no longer expect constitutional restrictions to limit the national government's regulatory power. In *Garcia* the Court argued that

> the principal and basic limit on the federal commerce power is that inherent in all congressional action—the built-in restraints that our system provides through state participation in federal governmental action. The political process ensures that laws that unduly burden the states will not be promulgated.[12]

In effect, the Court opened the door for the national government to regulate the states. The specific result of the Garcia case is that state and local governments were held responsible for paying their employees the federal minimum wage and for conforming to other requirements of federal wage and hour legislation. No longer would legal status in the federal system be held to protect the states from this regulation.

Although it appeared that the Supreme Court intended to open wide the doors for congressional regulation of the states, in more recent years it has delimited the scope of federal legislation once again.[13] One of those cases that set limits for the national government was a Texas case *City of Boerne, Texas* v. *Flores.*[14] This case involved a dispute between the city of Boerne and the St. Peter Catholic church. The church wanted to expand its historic building to accommodate a growing parish. The city objected that the expansion would violate the city's ordinance creating a historic district, which included the church. The church responded that the city's ordinance violated the national Religious Freedom Restoration Act of 1993, which prohibits a government from substantially burdening a person's exercise of religion unless the government can show that the restriction furthers a compelling governmental interest and is the least restrictive means of furthering that interest. The city, in turn, alleged that the Religious Freedom Restoration Act (RFRA) was unconstitutional because it exceeded Congress's legitimate authority. The Supreme Court found the congressional act unconstitutional. The court argued that RFRA was "a considerable congressional intrusion into the States' traditional prerogatives and general authority to regulate for the health and welfare of their citizens." Although there were many implications from this case, the significance for the federal system was that the court reasserted that Congress's power to intrude on the traditional powers of the states is limited.

Federal Preemptions

A **federal preemption** is the assertion of exclusive federal jurisdiction over a policy area previously overseen by the state. When the national government preempts an area, it either takes over the regulation of that area or imposes standards that the states must match if they want to remain active in the area. The latter kind of preemption has been prevalent in recent environmental regulations. One recent example is presented in the area of telecommunications deregulation. This type of legislation has been passed by a number of states in recent years, allowing long distance companies to enter the local telephone service market and allowing the local companies to enter the long distance market. After the Texas legislature struggled to produce such a bill in 1995, the national government passed a telecommunications deregulation bill in 1996. The national legislation, which was more favorable to the long distance companies than the Texas bill, was interpreted by the courts to have preempted the field, thus setting aside legislation enacted by the Texas legislature.

Grant-in-Aid Conditions

Just over 29 percent of the revenue in the 1998–1999 Texas budget came from the national government—much of it in the form of grants-in-aid. Most of the funds went to support health and human services programs, highway construction, and school lunch programs.[15] Since the 1930s, national and state governments have worked together on programs that were created and funded by the national government and administered by the states and their localities.

When the national government provides funds to the states to help them administer cooperative programs, it also makes requirements (**grant-in-aid conditions**) that the states must meet. For example, the national government sets standards for the construction of interstate highways and for the administration of welfare programs. Over the years, regulations have tended to become longer and more detailed. With the conversion of Aid to Families with Dependent Children (AFDC) to Temporary Assistance to Needy Families in 1996, Congress gave the states more flexibility in dealing with needy families. (See Chapter 12 for more information on this change.) At the same time, Congress imposed stringent reporting requirements on the states. Specifically, states are required to track every case across time, prohibit noncitizens and criminals from receiving welfare, verify school attendance for teenage mothers, and keep track of work participation rates. Data processing experts were complaining about the magnitude of the problem.[16]

Besides setting minimum program standards, the national government uses financial aid as leverage, to force states to adopt policies that meet the national government's needs. For example, the Nixon administration required the states to reduce speed limits on interstate highways or face the loss of funding for those highways. That requirement was in line with the national government's energy conservation policy, but it vexed Texans because of the great distances they have to travel to get around the state. It was especially irksome to those traveling through the western part of the state, where major towns are far apart and roads go through vast, sparsely populated areas. Texas officials spent years trying to find a loophole that would allow the state to raise speed limits. Finally, in 1987, the national government changed its policy and allowed speed limits to be increased on interstate highways in rural areas.

Another example of federal aid forcing a change in state policy came in 1984, when the national government required the states to increase the minimum age for drinking alcoholic beverages to twenty-one. Again federal highway funds provided the needed leverage. Texas, which had reduced the minimum drinking age to nineteen after an amendment to the U.S. Constitution lowered the minimum voting age to eighteen, raised it once again to twenty-one.[17]

State Constitutions: An Overview

A state constitution sets the legal framework for an individual state. The **constitution** organizes the government, setting forth its basic structures and operating principles. It limits government by protecting individual freedoms from government interference and by prohibiting specific actions.

State constitutions differ from the national constitution. State constitutions tend to be long and detailed; the U.S. Constitution is short and general. One scholar suggests that the people who write state constitutions take a different approach because those constitutions serve a different purpose in the American legal system.[18] The national government has delegated powers: it does not have the right to act unless the Constitution authorizes it to do so. The states have reserved powers—those powers not delegated to the national government nor reserved for the people by the Tenth Amendment to the U.S. Constitution. They have the right to act unless they are prohibited specifically from doing so. In the national constitution the failure to address an issue limits the government; in a state constitution it may give the state permission to act. Detailed restrictions, then, are necessary to limit the powers of state governments.

The detail found in many state constitutions today also was a response to the abuses of power by state officials in the second half of the nineteenth century. In southern states, Reconstruction—the transition period between the end of the Civil War and restoration of the full rights of statehood—was marked by harsh, abusive governments. And states in other parts of the country faced rampant corruption among public officials. Those experiences led to a distrust of government that was expressed through restrictive constitutions. The emphasis in state constitutions shifted from empowering government to limiting it.

The Texas Constitution

Its constitution shapes and constrains the government of Texas. This section will explain how that constitution came to have its distinctive qualities and assess both the document and its implications for politics in Texas.

A Series of Constitutions

Five constitutions have guided Texas government since the state's admission to the Union in 1845. (An additional constitution served Texas during its days as a republic—from 1836 to 1845.) The first constitution, adopted when the state joined the Union, was in place until the outbreak of the Civil War. The constitution of 1861 recognized the state's secession from the Union and its membership in the Confederacy. By 1866 the war was over, and another constitution was drafted to guide the state during Reconstruction. That constitution was rejected by a punitive Congress. So a fourth constitution was drafted in 1868. It was ratified in 1869.

The government under the constitution of 1869 had a profound effect on the constitutional history of Texas. Once elections were held under the new constitution, the U.S. military authority relinquished control of the state to **Governor E. J. Davis.** Davis, who governed the state from 1870 to 1874, pushed several pieces of legislation through a compliant legislature, giving himself enormous power.[19] The Militia Bill allowed the governor to declare martial law—to suspend the laws in any Texas county. The Enabling Act allowed the governor to appoint mayors, district attorneys, and city aldermen. Under its provisions Davis appointed over eight thousand public officials. The Printing Bill created an official public printer, established a state journal, and required that regional newspapers run official notices. In effect the bill created a state-controlled press.

To enforce his programs, Davis set up a state police force—some two hundred men strong—with unheard-of authority. These officers could act anywhere in the state, and they did, often under cover. The governor used his power to snuff out opposition and to reward his supporters. The state treasury was drained, and taxes soared.[20]

Davis literally had to be forced from office: he surrendered the reins of power only after President Grant refused to intervene to keep him in office. In 1874, the duly elected governor, Richard Coke, ordered the door to the governor's office broken down and assumed control of the state.[21] Davis was ousted, but he left a legacy: a fear of abuse that would underlie all of the provisions in the state's next constitution.

One step toward restoring orderly government in Texas was to call a constitutional convention. Congressman W. P. McLean set the tone of the 1875 convention when he proclaimed, "If future State Governments prove burdensome and onerous, it ought not to be the fault of this Convention."[22] The lesson learned from the Davis years was that the more the government did, the more harm it was likely to do. The safest course, then, was to design a government with limited powers. The new document was ratified and went into effect in 1876. It is still in effect today.

The Constitution of 1876

An overview. After a brief preamble, the Texas Constitution begins with a bill of rights that includes the major rights protected by the national constitution (Table 2.1). Although today that duplication seems unnecessary, it certainly was necessary at the time the constitution of 1876 was drafted. For much of this nation's history, the courts have interpreted the U.S. Bill of Rights as protecting individual rights and liberties from infringement by the national government, not by state governments. Guaranteeing individual rights in the state constitution, then, was important. Moreover, the current Texas Bill of Rights goes beyond the national bill of rights in some areas. For example, Texas adopted an equal rights amendment in 1972 that prohibits discrimination based on gender; a similar Equal Rights Amendment to the U.S. Constitution was not ratified.

Article II of the Texas Constitution defines the separation of powers. The national constitution does divide the powers of government, but it never uses the term **separation of powers.** The Texas Constitution explicitly allocates the three powers of government—executive, legislative, and judicial—to different institutions. It also specifies that one branch should not exercise the power of another except as expressly permitted in the constitution.

Articles III, IV, and V define the powers of the three branches of government: legislative, executive, and judicial. Compared with the equivalent articles in the national constitution, the articles in the Texas Constitution are very detailed. In the U.S. Constitution, each article is several paragraphs long; in the state constitution, each is several pages long.

Articles VI and VII deal with issues the national constitution leaves to the states: suffrage (the right to vote) and public education. The people who wrote the U.S. Constitution chose not to set a national standard for voter eligibility. Article VI of the Texas Constitution outlines voter requirements. Article VII, which is several pages long, deals with public elementary and secondary schools and universities.

In Article VIII the Texas Constitution sets forth rules on taxing and spending. A provision has been added to this section that commits the state to pay-as-you-go budgeting; the legislature cannot appropriate more money than is estimated to be available over a budget period.

Article XVI, "General Provisions," is a catchall. The various sections describe oaths of offices, marital community property, the creation of banking

Table 2.1 An Overview of the Texas Constitution of 1876

Article	Title	Provisions
I	Bill of Rights	Includes basic rights protected by U.S. Constitution; also includes an equal rights amendment that prohibits gender discrimination.
II	Powers of Government	Spells out concept of separation of powers.
III	Legislative Department	Outlines structure and powers of Texas legislature.
IV	Executive Department	Outlines structure and powers of executive officials, including governor.
V	Judicial Department	Outlines structure and powers of Texas courts.
VI	Suffrage	Lists requirements for voting.
VII	Education	Makes provisions for public schools and institutions of higher learning.
VIII	Taxation and Revenue	Sets limits on taxing power; includes balanced-budget provision.
IX	Counties	Allows for division of state into counties and designation of county seats; offers little information about county government.
X	Railroads	Authorizes state to regulate railroads and to create agencies to enforce regulations. Most original material deleted by amendment.
XI	Municipal Corporations	Outlines procedures for creating city governments and determining their powers.
XII	Private Corporations	Lists procedures for chartering private corporations.
XIII	Spanish and Mexican Land Titles	All provisions deleted by amendments.
XIV	Public Lands and Land Office	Creates a general land office to register land titles.
XV	Impeachment	Spells out procedures for removing public officials from office.
XVI	General Provisions	Includes diverse material such as oaths of office, homestead protection, terms of office for some officials.
XVII	Mode of Amending	Lists procedures for amending the constitution.

The constitution begins with a brief preamble invoking the blessing of God on this Constitution.

corporations, terms of office for the Texas Railroad Commission and boards of regents of state universities, and homestead protections. Finally, Article XVII describes how to amend the constitution.

Constitution of the State of Texas

Preamble

Humbly invoking the blessings of Almighty God, the people of the State of Texas, do ordain and establish this Const

Article I

Bill of Rights

That the general, great and essential principles of liberty and free government may be recognized and established,
Texas is a free and independent State, subject only to the Constitution of the United States, and the mainten
the preservation of the right of local self-government, unimpaired to all the States.
All political power is inherent in the people, and all free governments are founded on their authority, and in
the preservation of a republican form of government, and, subject to this limitation only, they have at all time
manner as they may think expedient.
All freemen, when they form a social compact, have equal rights, and no man, or set of men, is entitled
ation of public services.
No religious test shall ever be required as a qualification to any office, or public trust, in this State; nor
sentiments, provided he acknowledge the existence of a Supreme Being.
No person shall be disqualified to give evidence in any of the Courts of this State on account of his religious
shall be administered in the mode most binding upon the conscience, and shall be taken subject to
All men have a natural and indefeasible right to worship Almighty God according to the dictates of
port any place of worship, or to maintain any ministry against his consent. No human authority o
nce in matters of religion, and no preference shall ever be given by law to any religious society or
ch laws as may be necessary to protect equally every religious denomination in the peaceable

The current Texas Constitution was drafted in 1875. Unlike the national Constitution, it gives the Bill of Rights top priority by placing it at the beginning of the Constitution.

An assessment. Underlying the deliberations of the delegates to the 1875 convention was a commitment to limiting government. Every institution of government was subject to provisions limiting its powers:

- The **legislature.** Biennial sessions replaced annual sessions. The financial powers of the legislature were limited by restricting its power to incur debt and by limiting the tax rate it could impose on property.
- The **executive branch.** All offices were made elective (the governor would no longer be able to appoint department heads). And the terms of all executive offices were cut back to two years.
- The **judiciary.** All judges, including Texas Supreme Court justices, were made subject to popular election.

The constitution of 1876 was a decisive response to the abuse of power that marked Davis's term in office. It was well suited to its time. But was it well suited to shape the government of Texas for over a century? How has the Texas Constitution held up?

Critics point out that the constitution is poorly drafted. The document is too long and too detailed. The U.S. Constitution runs a few thousand words;

the Texas Constitution is the size of a small novel—over 60,000 words. Its length alone makes the document inaccessible: it is neither easy to read nor easy to understand.

Another indication that the constitution is poorly drafted is its organization. All provisions that relate to a single topic should be together in the constitution. Although the Texas Constitution uses logical titles for articles, some provisions are not where they should be. For example, the role of county officers is described in the judiciary article (Article V), not in the article on counties (Article IX). Article XVI, the general provisions article, is a catchall. Here are provisions about voting and elections that logically belong in the suffrage article (Article VI). Also here is a provision that prohibits the legislature from appropriating money for private purposes that should have been placed in Article VIII, the taxing and spending article. And a section on civil service systems in municipalities belongs in the article on municipal corporations (Article XI). This lack of organization makes it difficult to locate provisions in the document.

The way in which a constitution is drafted is more than a matter of style and composition; it also has political consequences. One by-product of a long, detailed document is that judges interpret that document strictly. They assume that if the writers specified one way of doing something, then they must have intended to prohibit any other way of doing it.

The details of a long, detailed constitution sometime allocate benefits to specific groups. Once such provisions make their way into a constitution, it is very difficult to change them, giving the beneficiaries an undue political advantage. One such provision in the Texas Constitution is the Permanent University Fund. That fund, which receives revenues from state-owned lands, is earmarked to support the University of Texas system and the Texas A&M University system. Two-thirds of the earnings from the fund go to the University of Texas system; one-third goes to the Texas A&M University system. Certainly creating an endowment for these university systems was a good idea, but the constitution plays favorites, providing benefits to some segments of higher education that are not available to others. The upshot is that one group has a special privilege. And because that privilege is spelled out in the constitution, it cannot be touched politically.

Constitutional Reform

If the Texas Constitution is excessively long, poorly organized, and too restrictive, why has the state not written another constitution? Many states, including Texas, have drafted new constitutions from time to time. Why not Texas? Answering that question requires an understanding of the politics of constitutional revision—the forces that lead states to undertake major constitutional changes and the forces that prevent states from making major constitutional changes.

The process of **constitutional reform** is threatening: it reopens fundamental questions about political power and how it should be organized. One study of constitutional reform concluded that before a state will start the constitutional revision process, two conditions must be met to some degree: a pressing issue and organized reform activity.[23]

The pressing issue can take the form of a major scandal. By discrediting the existing order, a scandal justifies a reexamination of the way a state organizes its business. Organized reform activity often followed the legislative reapportionment. Following the U.S. Supreme Court's *Baker* v. *Carr* decision in 1962, federal judges ordered many states, including Texas, to redraw their legislative districts to give fair representation to previously underrepresented urban areas.[24] The shift in power that accompanied the reapportionment created a group of reform-minded legislators—in Texas and in other states—who wanted to see their state government work in new ways.

Early Reform Efforts

Although the constitution of 1876 often was criticized and bills periodically were introduced in the legislature calling for a constitutional convention, few steps were taken toward revising the constitution before the late 1950s. In 1957 the legislature passed a resolution instructing the Texas Legislative Council (the research arm of the legislature) to study the constitution and suggest changes. The council finished its study in 1960. It concluded that except for revising the judicial article and deleting passages made obsolete by amendment or judicial ruling, no change was necessary.[25]

The next effort at revising the constitution came in 1967, when Governor John Connally asked the legislature to begin the constitutional revision process. The legislature established a commission to study the constitution and make recommendations in the next session. But when Connally chose not to run for reelection in 1968, enthusiasm for constitutional reform waned. The legislature ignored the new constitution the commission had recommended. Instead it proposed amendments to the constitution that removed obsolete material, including all of the provisions of Article XIII, which had dealt with Spanish and Mexican land titles.[26] The voters approved these amendments in 1969.

Launching Reform in the 1970s

In 1971, in the next regular session of the legislature, lawmakers proposed an amendment to the constitution authorizing the legislature to serve as a constitutional convention in 1974.[27] In November 1972, 61 percent of the voters in Texas cast their ballots in favor of the amendment.[28]

After several abortive efforts at major constitutional revision, what caused the constitutional reform effort to take off in 1971? Many believed that the **Sharpstown banking scandal** was the triggering mechanism. It was alleged that several political leaders were bribed by a Houston developer to get favorable banking legislation passed. That scandal rocked the government, leading to the downfall of the powerful speaker of the Texas house and to the rise of a reform-oriented group in the house, the "Dirty Thirty." This

THE CHANGING FACE OF TEXAS POLITICS

National Highway Transportation Policy: The Good News and the Bad News About Living in a Federal System

One of the battles ranging in Congress in the spring of 1998 was over renewal of the highway and transportation program called ISTEA (Intermodal Surface Transportation Efficiency Act). ISTEA (pronounced "ice tea") started a new course in national transportation policy when it was passed in 1991. A quick look at national highway policy will reveal that for Texas, there is good news and bad news about living in a federal system and that change brings benefits to some and losses to others.

The national government began assisting the states in highway construction in 1916. It expanded its commitment in the 1940s. In the 1950s, Congress made a commitment to the interstate highway system and committed the national government to paying 90 percent of the construction cost for the system. From the 1940s onward, the states came to depend on federal contributions to the building of highways.[1]

By the 1990s, with the completion of the interstate highway system, cities began complaining about the impact of highways on urban development and pollution. They felt that their efforts to meet national air quality standards were impeded by problems created from highway usage. Congress took a new approach in 1991 with the passage of ISTEA. Instead of focusing solely on paving more miles of highways, ISTEA designated funds for other transportation projects and allowed the states to divert traditional highway funds to other projects, including bicycle paths and mass transportation. The funds were allocated to the states through a fairly complex formula.[2]

For a state like Texas, ISTEA was a good news/bad news kind of story. The good news was the ISTEA continued the national government's commitment to helping the states fund transportation projects. Texas received about $1.1 billion per year from its ISTEA allotment.[3] The impact of that commitment became apparent when the bill came up for renewal in 1997 and Congress could not agree on new legislation. Suddenly states were faced with the prospect that funds were no longer available to complete important projects. To avert a crisis in 1997, Congress passed a temporary extension of the bill.

group of thirty house members, both Democrats and Republicans, was committed to bringing about reform in the Texas legislature. In fact, although the scandal may have opened the minds of legislators to the possibility of constitutional reform, the Dirty Thirty did not lead the movement for constitutional reform. Of the sixty-five sponsors of the amendment calling for the constitutional convention, only twelve were members of the Dirty Thirty.[29]

In the opinion of one close observer, legislative reapportionment had more to do with the push for a constitutional convention than did the Sharpstown banking scandal. The redrawing of district lines had led to the election of new

The bad news about ISTEA for Texas was that the state was a so-called donor state in the program. That is, it sent more money to Washington in taxes than it got back under the program. The principal funding source for ISTEA is the national highway gasoline tax (18.3 cents per gallon). In 1995, Texas got back 85 cents for every dollar it paid into the federal highway trust fund.[4] Although there is widespread agreement that some shifting of funds among the states is necessary to fund a truly national highway system, this degree of subsidy was not welcomed by a state like Texas, with thousands of miles of highways and hundreds of competing new projects.

By spring 1998, each house of Congress had passed its own version of a new transportation bill. The House version (called BESTEA) was more favorable to Texas than the Senate version (called ISTEA-II). It was estimated that Texas' annual allotment would be around $1.7 billion under BESTEA and about $1.5 billion under ISTEA-II.[5] As Congress worked toward a compromise version in May 1998, Texas sought to push its return from the highway trust fund above 90 percent of its contribution to the fund, thus reducing its role as a donor state. Texas was successful in the final bill. It guaranteed that the state would get back at least 90.5 cents of each highway tax dollar. The state could expect a total of about $11 billion in funding from the bill over the next six years.[6]

The fight over ISTEA in 1998 reveals that a change in national policy in a federal system produces benefits for some states and losses for others. Much of the fight in 1998 had to do with determining who those winners and losers would be. States that were getting back more than they were contributing to the federal highway trust fund obviously wanted to hold onto that subsidy. For Texas and the other donor states, an important part of the battle was to get back a bigger share of what they were contributing.

The fight over ISTEA also revealed how a sudden, unexpected interruption in a federal program could disrupt state projects. Texas and other states were suddenly faced with an impending crisis in highway construction when it appeared that ISTEA would not be renewed in 1997. The intertwining of federal and state policy was made glaringly apparent by the prospect of ISTEA's discontinuance in 1997.★

[1]See Chapter 6 of Thomas R. Dye, *Politics, Economics, and the Public* (Chicago: Rand McNally, 1966).

[2]Geoff Earle, "The Once and Future ISTEA," *Governing* (February 1998), p. 51.

[3]"Battle of the TEAS," *Governing* (February 1998), p. 57.

[4]Nancy Mathis, "$175 Billion Road Plan is Unveiled," *Houston Chronicle* (March 13, 1997), p. 1A.

[5]"Battle of the TEAS," p. 57.

[6]Greg McDonald, "Texas Gets $11 Billion in Transportation Bill," *Houston Chronicle*, May 23, 1998, p. A1.

members to the Texas house. The resolution proposing the constitutional convention originated with several of those newly elected members, who met privately to consider ways of improving government in Texas. Constitutional reform seemed ripe for consideration.[30]

The Constitutional Revision Commission

The constitutional amendment approved by the voters in 1972 called on the legislature to create a commission to study the constitution. When lawmakers met in 1973, they acted on that mandate and set up the thirty-seven-member **Constitutional Revision Commission.** The members were appointed by a committee made up of the governor, the lieutenant governor, the speaker of the house of representatives, the attorney general, the chief justice of the Texas Supreme Court, and the presiding judge of the Texas Court of Criminal Appeals. The legislature appropriated $900,000 to fund the commission's work.

The commission completed its work on schedule and submitted a report to the legislature on November 1, 1973. The report proposed a new constitution about one-fourth the size of the existing constitution (under 15,000 words) that strengthened the institutions of government by removing many limiting provisions.

The Constitutional Convention of 1974

In January 1974 the Texas legislature—the house and the senate—convened in Austin as a **constitutional convention.**

Early on there was hope that the job might be done in ninety days, but the convention's work dragged on into the spring, continuing until the constitutional deadline, July 30. Late that night, the last of many votes was taken on submitting a proposed constitution to the electorate. That vote was just three short of the two-thirds necessary to submit a proposal to the voters for ratification. A little after midnight, the convention adjourned. After months of work, it had nothing to submit to the people!

How had lawmakers allowed the opportunity for constitutional reform to slip through their fingers? One problem stemmed from the legislature's serving as a constitutional convention instead of turning the task of drafting a new constitution over to a citizens' convention. Legislators have standing political obligations, and most want to be reelected. Lawmakers in Texas faced political pressure as interest groups threatened to withdraw their support when their interests were threatened by proposals for the new constitution. Some legislators found it necessary to respond to that pressure or lose valuable sources of campaign funds. For example, labor unions lobbied hard during the session's closing days to prevent the inclusion of a right-to-work provision in the constitution.

The Postconvention Legislative Effort

However observers assigned the blame, many were shocked that the legislature had spent so much time and money and had made no progress on a new constitution. When the legislature convened for its regular session in 1975, it tried to recover from the disaster by establishing a constitutional revision committee in each house. In April 1975, the legislature approved the submission of a new constitution to the people of Texas. The proposal was packaged as eight amendments, a strategy that would allow the voters to approve some parts of the revised constitution, while rejecting others. Lawmakers knew that voters have a tendency to reject a new constitution if they find some part of it objectionable.

The proposed constitution was basically the same as that proposed by the constitutional convention the year before. It had eleven articles (the existing constitution had seventeen) that would have changed every part of the constitution except the bill of rights. (The amendment authorizing the constitutional convention had prohibited changes in the bill of rights.)

Although some experts thought the constitution did not go far enough in simplifying the constitution and streamlining the government, most thought it made significant advances over the existing document. It certainly would have strengthened the three branches of government in important ways.

The Electorate Speaks

In November 1975 the voters rejected all eight of the constitutional amendments by an overwhelming margin. The legislators' hope that the electorate might approve at least some of the proposed new constitution was dashed.

Once more analysts had to ask what had gone wrong. The lack of pro-revision leadership was certainly one factor. Studies of constitutional reform often find that success is more likely if the state's leaders—especially the governor—support the revision effort.[31] There was no real leadership in the reform effort. Governor Dolph Briscoe did not take an active part in promoting the call for a constitutional convention or in campaigning for the proposed constitution. Instead, after the legislature had completed its work and submitted the proposal for ratification, Briscoe announced his opposition to the constitution.

And those who opposed the new constitution did their work well, playing on people's fears. And the opposition of certain groups took its toll. Judicial officers, threatened by reform of the judicial article, opposed ratification. So did business interests, afraid that the new constitution would open the door to higher taxes.

Probably the biggest obstacle to ratification was the lack of interest on the part of the average citizen. Although the Constitutional Revision Commission had gone to extraordinary lengths to gather citizens' input, most people just were not interested. In the end, with no major selling point and no chief salesperson, the voters rejected the new constitution.

Changing the Constitution by Amendment

Although major constitutional revision has failed, a major overhaul is not the only way of changing the constitution. The more common way of changing a **constitution** is by **amendment.** The Texas Constitution stipulates that amendments to the constitution can be proposed by the legislature (by a two-thirds majority in each house) and are subject to ratification by the people in a statewide referendum. Although the requirement of an extraordinary majority in the legislature may make it easy to block amendments, it has not prevented amendments from becoming a routine feature of Texas politics. The Texas Constitution had been amended over 360 times by 1997, and new amendments are submitted to the voters at almost every election.

The booming business of home equity loans was not possible in Texas before a 1998 constitutional amendment.

Why has the constitution been amended so many times? In large part because the document is so detailed. Often an amendment is necessary simply to change one detail. For example, the article on counties is filled with amendments creating and eliminating local special district governments. Often the simplest changes require constitutional amendments.

Of course details are not the only subject of amendments to the Texas Constitution. At times the solution to a major policy problem has required amending the constitution. As noted in the introduction to this chapter, it has not been unusual for a constitutional amendment to be a necessary step in solving a major policy problem.

The difficulty with piecemeal change in the constitution is that it does not produce any real improvement in the constitution as a whole. The constitution just gets longer, more disorganized, and more unwieldy—problems only a major overhaul is likely to solve.

 Prospects for Change

This chapter has demonstrated that the state's constitution and the federal system set boundaries for Texas government. And those boundaries limit the choices open to lawmakers.

What is the likelihood that the legal environment in Texas will change? The prospects for constitutional reform are not good. Yes, there will continue to be piecemeal change, but a systematic overhaul of the constitution does not seem likely. At work here is the difficulty of a major constitutional revision. Two things probably would have to happen to open the door to comprehensive reform of the Texas Constitution. First, many people in the state would have to become convinced that the constitution is preventing the state from solving important problems. Second, a strong leader (probably a governor) would have to see some political advantage in championing constitutional reform. Neither of these things appears possible in the immediate future in Texas. Certainly there is no widespread consensus among voters that the existing constitution has serious problems that need to be fixed. And memories of the unproductive efforts of the mid-1970s are not likely to convince politicians that constitutional reform wins votes.

What about the federal system? That system has changed over the years. From the 1930s through the 1960s, the national government expanded the scope of its activities, imposing new constraints on the states.[32] In the 1980s, the so-called Reagan revolution challenged that centralization. Believing that the national government was bloated and overgrown, President Reagan introduced a program of decentralization. Many aspects of the Reagan program were rejected because state and local governments did not want to be saddled with huge administrative costs. So Reagan changed the direction of American federalism in a different way. By cutting the federal income tax, thereby reducing the flow of revenue to the national government, he forced the national government to change its role. The financial senior partner was gone. The states could no longer expect the national government to solve every domestic policy problem. Instead they had to face many of those problems on their own. Some observers believe this was a good thing: that as the federal government reduced financial support for the states, the states reemerged as policy leaders.[33] The election of a Republican majority to Congress in 1994 furthered the tendency to reduce federal aid to the states and use more block grants as the means of distributing funds to the states. Although many states, including Texas, could expect to lose some funding, the new block grants left more control to the states in determining how money should be spent.

With state constitutional politics dominated by the status quo, and federal policy dominated by concerns about balancing the budget, change in the legal environment in which the government of Texas operates does not appear imminent. The constitution will continue to limit the choices open to Texas leaders and limit opportunities to reorganize the government. The federal government is likely to continue its withdrawal of financial support for the states, while leaving them more flexibility in using remaining funds. Texas is likely to be left to work out its own solutions to policy problems with less help from Washington.

Notes

1. Richard H. Leach, *American Federalism* (New York: W. W. Norton, 1970), p. 1.
2. *Ibid.*
3. U.S. Constitution, art. IV, sec. 3.
4. Martha Derthick, "Federal Government Mandates: Why the States Are Complaining," *Annual Editions: State and Local Government,* 6th ed. (Guilford, CT: Dushkin Publishing Group, 1993), 30–33.
5. David B. Walker, *Toward a Functioning Federalism* (Cambridge: Winthrop Publishers, 1981), 137.
6. *Gitlow* v. *New York,* 268 U.S. 652 (1925).
7. *Smith* v. *Allwright,* 321 U.S. 649 (1944).
8. *Brown* v. *Board of Education,* 347 U.S. 487 (1954).
9. *Harper* v. *State Board of Elections,* 383 U.S. 663 (1966).
10. *Roe* v. *Wade,* 410 U.S. 113 (1973).
11. *Ruiz* v. *Estelle,* 666 Fed.2d. 854 (1982) and 650 Fed.2d 555 (5th Circuit, 1981).
12. *Garcia* v. *San Antonio Metropolitan Transit Authority,* 469 U.S. 556 (1985).
13. See for example *New York* v. *United States,* 505 U.S. 144 (1992) and *Printz* v. *United States,* 117 S. Ct. 2365 (1997).
14. 117 S. Ct. 2157 (1997).
15. Legislative Budget Board, *Fiscal Size Up: 1998–99 Biennium* (Austin, 1997), 2–1 and 2–8.
16. Tod Newcombe, "Welfare's New Burden: Feds Tie Down States with Data Reporting Requirements," *Government Technology,* XI (April 1998), p. 14.
17. Elaine S. Knapp, "21 or Else Mandate Angers States," in *State Government: CQ's Guide to Current Issues and Activities: 1985–86,* Thad L. Beyle, ed. (Washington, DC: CQ Press, 1985), 184–190.
18. Janice C. May, *The Texas Constitutional Revision Experience in the '70s* (Austin: Sterling Swift Publishing, 1975), 13–14.
19. T. R. Fehrenbach, *Lone Star: A History of Texas and the Texans* (New York: Macmillan, 1968), 416–417.
20. Fehrenbach, *Lone Star,* 418–419.
21. Fehrenbach, *Lone Star,* 432.
22. Quoted in Fehrenbach, *Lone Star,* 434.
23. Elmer E. Cornwell, Jr., et al., *State Constitutional Conventions: The Politics of the Revision Process in Seven States* (New York: Praeger, 1975), 193.
24. *Baker* v. *Carr,* 369 U.S. 186 (1962).
25. May, *Texas Constitutional Revision Experience,* 26.
26. May, *Texas Constitutional Revision Experience,* 28–29.
27. May, *Texas Constitutional Revision Experience,* 35–37.
28. May, *Texas Constitutional Revision Experience,* 46.
29. May, *Texas Constitutional Revision Experience,* 35.
30. May, *Texas Constitutional Revision Experience,* 35.
31. Albert L. Sturm, *Thirty Years of State Constitution-Making: 1938–1968* (New York: National Municipal League, 1970), 87.
32. Walker, *Toward a Functioning Federalism,* especially Chapter 3.
33. See, for example, David Osborne, *Laboratories of Democracy* (Boston: Harvard Business School Press, 1990).

3 Political Parties

Chapter Outline

Constancy—not change—was the rule in Texas party politics after the Democrats regained control of the governorship in 1874. The basic pattern was set. In the spring of each gubernatorial election year, a vigorous battle within the Democratic primaries would decide the Democratic candidate for governor. That person then would be elected by a large percentage of the vote in the November general election. The Republicans nominated candidates, but the winner of the Democratic primary always became the next governor of Texas.

No one expected 1978 to be a year of great political change. The party primaries in the spring proceeded normally. In the Democratic primary, the incumbent governor, Dolph Briscoe, was running for renomination against Attorney General John Hill and former governor Preston Smith. On the Republican side, Bill Clements, a wealthy oilman from Dallas, was running against the Republican party chair, Ray Hutchison. Hill won the Democratic nomination; Clements won the Republican nomination. It was unusual for the Democrats to deny renomination to an incumbent governor. Most analysts thought the vote was a response to Briscoe's personality and to the fact that reelection would have extended his tenure to ten years in office. Although a few Republicans had made a decent showing in the 1970s against their Democratic opponents, at this point no one expected a Republican to win the governor's race.

But when the general election was over, the voters had elected the first Republican governor since 1874. Bill Clements, the Dallas oilman, had won a narrow victory over the Democratic nominee, John Hill. Why? Postelection analysts had several explanations. The first had to do with money. Clements had set a record in campaign spending for his day, putting in much of the money himself. Second, the Democrats had been complacent. For generations the winner of the Democratic primary had been assured the win in the general election. Hill assumed that he did not have to campaign vigorously for the general election. He was wrong. Third was voter turnout. The turnout in Texas elections had dropped off sharply in the early 1970s. Clements's strategists used this information to target supporters. They relied heavily on operators in phone banks who called residents of known Republican precincts and urged them to go to the polls and vote for Clements. Democrats stayed home. All of these factors gave Clements 50 percent of the vote in November; Hill received 49.2 percent.

What did this unexpected Republican win mean? Initially it seemed a fluke, not a long-term change. After all, most analysts thought, if Hill had been less complacent and turnout had been higher, Clements never would have won. This thinking was reinforced by the Republicans' failure to win any other statewide office in 1978 and by Clements's loss to a Democrat in the very next election. Subsequent elections, however, have made it clear that something big had happened. A political era was ending. No longer could Democrats assume that they would win all of the important elections in the state. Texas had taken its first step toward two-party competition at the state level. The party system was changing.

Bill Clements surprised Texas politicos when he won the governor's election in 1978 and became governor in 1979.

As you read this chapter, the significance of the 1978 election should become clear, as should the answers to these questions about political parties and party systems:

- What is a political party, and what does it do?
- What kind of party system does Texas have, and how is it changing?
- How are political parties in Texas organized?
- What is the future of the political parties in Texas?

Political Parties and Change

According to one scholar, a **political party** is "any group, however loosely organized, seeking to elect government officeholders under a given label."[1] A political party, then, is a structured social organization whose objective is to elect its candidates to government offices. And the success of a political party, then, is measured by how many of its candidates win office.

Political parties want to elect their nominees to public office. This means they must be sensitive to changes taking place in the electorate. As social conditions and attitudes change, parties must alter their strategies in ways that will allow them to continue to win votes. Parties that fail to adjust run the risk of extinction.

The literature on political parties emphasize two kinds of change: realignment and dealignment. **Realignment** is a turning point at which one party gains support and the other loses support.[2] In a **dealignment,** all of the major parties lose support. Texas has experienced both kinds of change: a shift in support from the Democratic party to the Republican party and a general decline in support for political parties. The dominant Democratic party has been challenged by a revived Republican party, and the nature of the party system in the state still is being worked out. As competition between the parties grows, both parties are being challenged by an increasing unwillingness on the part of voters to make a strong commitment to any political party. Each party must compete in elections with a smaller pool of voters who can be depended on to support the party's candidates.

The History of Political Parties in Texas

In Texas, slates of candidates bearing the Democratic or Republican label regularly run for office, yet the party organizations in the state are weak. Why? The answer lies in the history of the parties' development in Texas (Table 3.1).

Statehood to the Civil War

When Texas became a state in 1845, political parties did not play an important role in state politics. Although candidates used the Democratic party label, the party had no local organization and it held state conventions only to select delegates to the national convention.[3]

In the 1850s the Democratic party began to organize at the state level. That activity was largely a response to the Know-Nothing party—a pro-American, anti-immigrant group. In 1855 the Know-Nothings won twenty seats in the state house of representatives and five seats in the state senate. The Democratic party responded by organizing seriously; in 1857 the party nominated candidates for statewide offices at a convention for the first time. With the party's new organizational strength behind him, Hardin Runnels, a former lieutenant governor and speaker of the Texas house, defeated popular hero Sam Houston in the governor's race.

Civil War and Reconstruction

The Democratic party controlled the state during the Civil War (1861–1865). When Union forces arrived in Texas in June 1865, the Democratic governor fled to Mexico to avoid possible prosecution. The Republican party, which had organized officially in Texas in 1867, won the governorship in the 1869 election. Republican E. J. Davis, who held office from 1870 to 1874, was one

Table 3.1 Party Development in Texas

Dates	Period	Characteristics
1845–1860	Statehood to Civil War	No real party organization until Know-Nothing party has some success in 1855. Democratic party organizes in 1857 and dominates until end of period.
1861–1873	Civil War and Reconstruction	Democrats dominate from 1861 to 1869; Republicans dominate from 1869 through 1874.
1874–1961	One-Party Dominance	Republican party collapses. Democrats dominate.
1961–1978	Republican revival	Republican party wins U.S. Senate seat in 1961, raising party hopes. Republicans win governorship in 1978 and increasingly challenge Democrats.
1979–present	Contemporary politics	Republicans contest more and more elections and have more success. Movement toward real two-party system.

of the most unpopular governors in Texas history (see Chapter 2). Taxes rose dramatically during his administration, and a militia and police force operating under his control used force to maintain order in the state. The Democrats regained control of the legislature in 1872 and of the governorship in 1874.

One-Party Dominance

When Reconstruction ended, party politics changed dramatically in Texas and other southern states. The memory of the abuses suffered under Republican leaders was an insurmountable barrier to Republican success in the post-Reconstruction era. The party virtually disappeared from the political landscape. Although the Republicans maintained a skeletal organization, they contested few elections and had little hope of winning. All politics became Democratic-party politics: Texas entered a long period of **one-party dominance.**

That dominance was interrupted briefly in the last decade of the nineteenth century, when a new political party was organized in the United States. The Populist party—a party of protest—was founded in 1891. Driving that party was the discontent of the farming community throughout the country. Economic conditions in Texas also had deteriorated for farmers, and the Democratic party did not seem to have solutions. In 1892 the Populist party in the state fielded a gubernatorial candidate, T. L. Nugent. The party did not capture the governorship that year, but it did run competitive candidates for a number of offices over the next six years. Eventually the party disappeared—the national Populist party had merged with the Democratic party in 1896—and the Democrats once again had the political playing field in Texas to themselves.

When one political party dominates, conflict moves from the general election to the party nominating process. The battles are waged, not between parties, but between factions within the dominant party. In the Democratic party in Texas, stable issue-oriented factions formed in the 1930s, as the national Democratic party adopted new social welfare programs to respond to the problems caused by the Great Depression. Texas Democrats split into two groups: a liberal faction that supported the positions taken by the national party and a conservative faction that rejected the New Deal. The liberal faction shared the national Democratic party's belief in social welfare programs, in programs to help people who are unable to earn enough income to care for themselves. They supported government regulation of business to protect consumers and prevent fraud. And they supported the national party's efforts to extend civil rights to ethnic and racial minorities. The conservative faction opposed social welfare programs, insisting they were wasteful and detrimental to individual initiative. They opposed regulation, arguing that it too stifles initiative. And the conservative faction was less enthusiastic, if not outright hostile, to civil rights laws.

When **factionalism** was at its strongest in Texas, the typical election began with several candidates running for major offices in the first primary. Usually, the field included a mix of liberal and conservative candidates. And usually the number of candidates in the first primary made it impossible for any one candidate to get a majority of the votes, thus necessitating a runoff election. In the runoff election between the two highest vote-getters, typically a liberal-faction candidate faced a conservative-faction candidate. When that happened, the conservative candidate won most of the time because the conservative faction had the larger bloc of voters. And whoever won the Democratic nomination won the office in the general election.

Republican Revival

In the 1960s the Republican party began to make a comeback in Texas politics. Several forces were at work here. First, there was growing dissatisfaction among Texans and other southerners with the direction the national Democratic party took under the leadership of Franklin Roosevelt and Harry Truman in the 1930s and 1940s. Roosevelt led the party to support a broad social welfare program to combat the widespread poverty of the Great Depression. Truman pushed the party toward a strong civil rights stand, defending the rights of African Americans—a stand that was not popular in the racially segregated South. In fact in 1948 many southern states, including Texas, found the civil rights plank in the Democratic national plat-

When Republican John Tower was elected to the U.S. Senate in 1961, a new era for the Texas Republican party began.

form so objectionable that they walked out of the party's national convention and backed Strom Thurmond, the Dixiecrat candidate for president. The pro–social welfare and pro–civil rights position of the national Democratic party made it difficult for Texans (and other southerners) to support the party's presidential candidates.

A second factor in the Republican revival in Texas was the presidential candidacy of Dwight Eisenhower in 1952. Eisenhower was a widely respected World War II military hero whose popularity helped the Republican party reach beyond its traditional base, to unhappy Democrats. In Texas the temptation among Democrats to vote for the Republican candidate was reinforced by Governor Allan Shivers's open support for Eisenhower. Eisenhower won in 1952 and again in 1956. In both years, Texas gave him its electoral votes. Texans may not have thought of themselves as Republicans yet, but they had learned that the world would not end if they voted for a Republican candidate for president.

Finally, in 1961, the Republican party captured a statewide office. According to one analyst, "The modern Texas Republican party was born in 1961 with the election of John Tower to the U.S. Senate."[4] In 1960 Lyndon Johnson, the new vice president of the United States, resigned his U.S. Senate seat. A special election was called for 1961. The Texas Election Code specifies that all candidates from both parties run in a special election and that no nominating primaries precede the election. If no candidate receives a majority of the votes cast in the first round of balloting, a runoff election between the two candidates with the highest vote totals decides the election. Seventy-one candidates took part in the 1961 special election. Republican John Tower made it into the runoff against Democrat William Blakley, who was so conservative that many liberal Democrats could not support him.[5] Tower won a surprise victory: he became the first Republican senator from Texas—in fact, from the South—since Reconstruction.

In the years following Tower's election, the Republican party in Texas made small gains. In 1962 two Republicans were elected to the U.S. House of Representatives, and seven were elected to the Texas house. But there was no breakthrough at the statewide level: the offices of governor, attorney general, and comptroller stayed in Democratic hands through the 1960s.

In the 1970s a minor party, **La Raza Unida** ("the united race"), formed in Texas. The party originated as a local protest movement among Hispanics in Crystal City, Texas, and its first successes were in local elections there. In the statewide arena it served notice on the major parties that Hispanics did not want to be taken for granted. In the 1972 gubernatorial election, La Raza Unida ran Ramsey Muniz as its candidate. The third-party strategy did not work in the statewide race, and the party had disappeared by the 1980s. Thus, the way was cleared for the development of competition between Democrats and Republicans.

Contemporary Politics

The presumption of Democratic victory in Texas is no longer valid. The 1978 gubernatorial election proved to be the next big turning point for the Republican party in Texas. With his surprise victory, Bill Clements became the first Republican governor of the state since Reconstruction. The Republicans won the governorship again in 1986, and they have begun to elect their candidates to other statewide offices, to the legislature, and to many county offices. Although the Democrats recaptured the governorship in 1990, the Republicans continued to expand the arena of Texas politics in which they were competitive. Republican Kay Bailey Hutchison won the treasurer's office that Ann Richards, the new governor, had just left. Republican Rick Perry captured the commissioner of agriculture's office. In 1992 the Republicans increased the number of seats they held in each chamber of the state legislature and defeated a liberal Democratic justice on the Texas Supreme Court. When Texas Senator Lloyd Bentsen was appointed to President Clinton's cabinet in 1993 as secretary of treasury, a special election in 1993 gave the Republicans an opportunity to win a second U.S. Senate seat. Kay Bailey Hutchison's defeat of Democrat Bob Krueger was another blow to Democratic dominance of Texas politics. In 1994, Republicans further demonstrated their ability to compete effectively in statewide races when George W. Bush defeated Ann Richards in the governor's race.

In 1998, the Republican party demonstrated its strength in Texas politics by winning all of the statewide offices that were up for election. Many thought the Republican party was on its way to dominance of Texas politics.

The Republican party of the 1990s has demonstrated the will and the ability to compete with Democrats in all elections. Although its goal of becoming the majority party in the Texas Senate was not met in 1992 or 1994, the Republicans did achieve a majority in the 1996 election. The Republican party has become a major player in contemporary Texas politics.

Factionalism still may affect both political parties. Some observers believe the liberal versus conservative factionalism within the Democratic party is eroding, that Texas Democrats are converging on a middle-of-the-road stance.[6] This trend probably has a lot to do with the revival of two-party competition in the state. Recent Democratic candidates for governor have assumed moderate positions to unify the party in its battles against Republicans in the general elections. Straying too far from the center can be a strategic error for a Democratic candidate in a state where the liberal label is still a heavy burden for politicians. To beat the Republicans, the factionalism that has marked the Democratic party in Texas may be coming to an end.

While Democrats are overcoming factionalism, Republicans are facing factional struggles. The Religious Right has been working to control the party organization, to see to it that the party adheres to very conservative positions, especially opposition to abortion.[7] Televangelist Pat Robertson coordinated the efforts in 1993 and 1994 of a group called the Texas Christian Coalition. This bloc of social conservatives, already successful at the precinct level, had enough votes to control the party's state convention in 1994. Anticipating conflict at the convention, the Republican party's state chair, Fred Meyer, chose not to seek reelection in 1994. Of the three remaining candidates for party chair, only one professed to be a moderate. A behind-the-scenes agreement to back a single candidate for party chair saved the convention from a bruising factional battle for control of that office, but votes on platform issues made it apparent that the Christian Coalition had the controlling bloc of votes at the convention.

The Party System in Texas Today

When we talk about the party system in a state, we are talking about the number of parties operating in the state and the level of competition among them. Political scientists commonly use three classifications to describe party systems: In a **one-party system,** a single party consistently wins all or almost all state offices. In a **modified one-party system,** a single party wins most offices most of the time. In a **two-party system,** two political parties compete and have a roughly equal chance of winning elections. Remember that this classification scheme focuses on state elections. Texas, like most

Table 3.2 States Classified According to Degree of Interparty Competition for Control of Government, 1989–1994

State	State	State	State
Modified one-party: Democratic			
Arkansas	Rhode Island	Georgia	Nebraska
Louisiana	Maryland	Mississippi	Oklahoma
Hawaii	Kentucky	Alabama	Massachusetts
West Virginia			
Two-party competition			
Tennessee	Washington	Delaware	Montana
New Mexico	Vermont	Indiana	Colorado
North Carolina	South Carolina	Connecticut	Michigan
Missouri	Nevada	Wisconsin	New Jersey
Texas	California	Pennsylvania	North Dakota
Virginia	Oregon	Iowa	Ohio
Minnesota	New York	Alaska	Kansas
Florida	Maine	Illinois	
Modified one-party: Republican			
Idaho	Arizona	New Hampshire	
South Dakota	Wyoming	Utah	

Source: John F. Bibby and Thomas M. Holbrook, "Parties and Elections," in *Politics in the American States.* 6th ed., Virginia Gray and Herbert Jacob, eds. (Washington, DC: CQ Press, 1996), 105.

other states, would look much more competitive if we focused on the outcome of presidential elections.

What kind of party system does Texas have? Table 3.2 classifies Texas as a two-party state. This is the result of a substantial amount of change in the 1970s and 1980s. An analysis based on the period from 1981 to 1988 put Texas in the modified one-party Democratic category.[8] A similar analysis of the years before the 1978 election placed Texas in the one-party Democratic category.[9]

The Nominating Process

One of the critical functions of political parties is nominating candidates for public office. The nomination process can have a profound effect on a party, encouraging loyalty and party unity.

Until 1905, candidates who ran with a party label usually were nominated at the state convention. The party activists selected to attend the state convention chose the party's candidates. Since 1905, the law (with a few exceptions) had required that parties in Texas use the direct primary to nominate their candidates. According to the Texas Election Code, the primary process begins with a first primary, held on the second Tuesday in March in even-numbered years.

Primaries can be open or closed. Any qualified voter can participate in an **open primary**; only party members can participate in a party's **closed primary.** Primaries in Texas are open.[10] Voters are not required to declare their party affiliation before the primary; they can choose the party's primary in which they want to vote at the time of the election. There are just two restrictions: voters must choose publicly between the two primaries, and each voter can participate in only one party's primary.

If no candidate receives a majority of the votes cast (that is, more than 50 percent) in the party's first primary, the top two vote-getters compete in a runoff election held on the second Tuesday in April. **Runoff primaries** are common in southern states, a product of one-party domination. Because the winner of the dominant-party primary is guaranteed election to office in a one-party state, making sure that primary winners have majority support is important.

Participation in runoff elections is more restricted than it is in first primaries. Those who voted in a party's first primary can only vote in the same party's runoff election. Those who did not vote in the first primary are allowed to choose the runoff election in which they want to vote.

What are the consequences of the nomination process used in Texas? One is that party organizations have little control over who their nominees are. This is true of all direct-primary systems. The open-primary system in Texas also allows a member of one party to vote in the opposing party's primary. During the period of Democratic dominance in Texas, Republicans often voted in the Democratic primary because it was the only election that mattered. Although crossover voting is less tempting when two parties actually are competing in elections, voters occasionally are drawn to the opposition party's primary by a particular candidate.

Finally, any primary system has the potential to destroy party unity. After a bitter primary campaign, it can be difficult for members of a party to work together in the general election. The 1990 primary battle to become the Democratic nominee for governor ended in a bitter struggle among Treasurer Ann Richards, former governor Mark White, and Attorney General Jim Mattox. Richards raised questions about White's honesty, suggesting that he might have enriched himself at the state's expense. As a result, many of White's supporters found it difficult, if not impossible, to get behind Richards in the general election battle against Clayton Williams. In 1993, when she had to choose someone to fill Lloyd Bentsen's unexpired U.S. Senate term, Governor Richards refused even to interview her old opponent Jim Mattox.

While the primary system puts party nominations in the hands of the people, it creates some problems for Texas political parties. It makes it difficult for them to recruit party workers because those workers have no say in choosing the candidates they are expected to support. Moreover, the system allows "outsiders" to influence the parties' choice of nominees. And, finally, the system invites conflict within the parties. Building and maintaining strong, cohesive parties is not easy when the nominating process is in the hands of voters.

Party Organization

A political party is part of a system that includes the party itself, the government, and the electorate. When we talk about the strength of a party, then, we are talking about three elements of the political system:[11]

- *Party organization*—how well the party is organized
- *Party and government*—how much influence the party has on the government
- *Party and the electorate*—what kind of support the party draws from the electorate

Here and in the next two sections, we examine these three elements of the political system.

Party Structures

Political parties are "seasonal" organizations: their form and function change with the stages of the electoral process. In the years between elections, a small cadre of party activists keeps the state party organization alive. Local party organizations are less active, and local party offices may be closed during these times. In election years, party offices are reopened, workers are hired, and volunteers are recruited.

The organizational structure of political parties in Texas also follows a seasonal pattern. Party organization consists of a set of temporary and permanent structures. The temporary structures are most important during election years. These structures form and then dissolve as they fulfill their special tasks. **Permanent party structures** are most important between elections.

The structure of party offices, the schedule of party conventions, and the procedures for choosing delegates and officials are outlined in the Texas Election Code. That is not unusual. State regulation of political parties began in the 1890s with the introduction of the Australian ballot, a secret ballot that identifies candidates by party label. In the late nineteenth and early twentieth centuries, many party organizations in this country were corrupt. State regulation of party organizations and procedures was part of the effort to clean up the political parties.[12]

Temporary party structures. The **temporary party structures** that come to life in election years are actually a series of party conventions. That series of

Table 3.3 Temporary Party Structures in Texas

Structure	Membership	Functions	Meeting Time
Precinct Convention	All who voted in party primary are eligible. Convention is made up of those eligible who return on the evening of the primary for the convention meeting.	1. Choose delegates to county or senatorial district convention. 2. Consider resolutions on public issues.	Every two years, on night of day primary election was held.
County or Senatorial District Convention	Delegates elected by precinct conventions.	1. Choose delegates to state convention. 2. Consider resolutions on public issues.	Every two years, on third Saturday after first primary election.
State Convention	Delegates elected by county or senatorial district conventions.	1. Certify list of party's nominees chosen in primary elections. 2. Adopt party platform. 3. Elect members of state executive committee. 4. Elect party chair and vice chair. 5. In presidential election years, elect delegates to the national convention, elect representatives to national party committee, and choose slate of presidential electors.	Every two years, in June.

conventions starts at the local precinct level and moves up to the state convention (Table 3.3).

A **precinct convention,** the lowest-level temporary organization, is held in each election precinct in every county in the state. Counties in Texas are divided into precincts to simplify the election process. The more populated a county, the more precincts it has. Precinct conventions meet in even-numbered years on the night of the day the primary election is held,

Although party precinct conventions are often small informal gatherings, they are the starting battleground for control of Texas party organizations.

usually in the polling places where people voted during the day. Only those who participated in their party's primary can attend.

The principal tasks of the precinct convention are to choose delegates to the county or senatorial district conventions and to consider resolutions on public issues. The number of delegates each precinct sends to its county or senatorial district convention is determined by the number of votes cast in the precinct for the party's candidate in the previous gubernatorial election. The current formula is one delegate for every twenty-five votes.

Who gets elected a delegate to the county or senatorial district convention (and ultimately to the state convention) depends on who shows up at the precinct convention. This means that the precinct conventions are an important battleground for control of the party organization. Anyone who wants to win the delegate elections at the county or senatorial district convention must get likeminded people to attend the precinct convention. Because the turnout is often low at precinct conventions, bringing along a few friends can be all that is necessary to get elected a delegate to the county convention. Adding a few more friends can be enough to elect a whole delegation! Regular party participants understand how the system works, so packing the precinct convention is a common strategy.

Televangelist Pat Robertson used organized efforts at the precinct level to gain control of the Republican party organization in Texas in the 1990s, when he launched "Operation Precinct." Potential recruits got a letter from Robertson describing the plan and asking them to take part. Workshops were held for those who were not familiar with party organization and procedures. The strategy worked, and the delegates elected by this effort controlled the Republican state convention by 1994.[13]

For many years those who wanted a Texas party to support a candidate at the national convention realized that it all started in thousands of precinct conventions. The candidate whose workers did the best job of packing precinct conventions across the state would have the largest number of supporters in the Texas delegation to the national convention. This changed in 1987, when a new state law went into effect. Now each party must allocate at least 75 percent of its delegates to the national convention on the basis of the voting in the presidential primary held in March in presidential election years.[14] So the role of the precinct conventions in presidential politics has diminished significantly.

The **county convention** or the **senatorial district convention** is the next step up the ladder of temporary party organizations. Counties that fall entirely within a single state senatorial district hold a county convention. Counties whose boundaries cross more than one state senatorial district hold a convention in each part of the county that is situated in a different senatorial district. The county or senatorial district convention meets in even-numbered years on the third Saturday after the first primary election.

The prize here, as it is at the precinct convention, is being elected a delegate to the next convention—in this case the state convention. The number of votes cast for the party's candidate in the previous gubernatorial election determines the size of each county's or senatorial district's delegation to the state convention—one delegate for every three hundred votes. This rule gives the county organization an incentive to work hard for the party's candidate. Increasing the number of delegates increases the county's influence at the state convention.

The delegates at county or senatorial district conventions also can involve resolutions on policy. Those resolutions are not binding; they are simply expressions of opinion by the convention, usually made in an effort to influence the state convention's decisions about a party platform.

The **state convention** is the highest-level temporary structure of political parties in Texas. By state law this convention meets every two years—again, in even-numbered years—in June. State party conventions are huge gatherings, with thousands of delegates. Little serious debate happens on the convention floor.

Basic business at state conventions includes (1) certifying the official list of the party's nominees chosen in the primary elections; (2) adopting a party platform; (3) electing the members of the party's state executive committee; and (4) electing the party's chair and vice chair. Certifying the nominee list is a formality: the convention simply approves the list of candidates who won nomination in the primaries. The adoption of the **party platform**—the statement of the party's position on key issues—and the election of members and officers of the state executive committee usually are hotly contested. For

State party conventions are bustling, noisy gatherings at which various groups struggle for control of the party organization and the party's platform.

example, Republicans in recent years have battled over the party's stand on abortion. And the members of the executive committee control the state party organization.

In presidential election years, important decisions linking the state party organization to the national party organization must be made. These choices center on electing delegates to the national party convention, electing the state's representatives to the national party committee, and choosing a slate of electors to cast the state's electoral votes (if the party's presidential nominee carries the state).

Permanent party structures. Between elections the permanent party organization tries to keep the party going and to plan for future elections. There are permanent party officials at each of the levels at which the temporary party structures function—precinct, county, and state (Table 3.4).

The **precinct chair** is the permanent officer at the precinct level. Precinct chairs are elected in the party's primary for two-year terms. Their role is to keep the party going at the local level between elections. They recruit candidates and prepare candidates and campaigns for elections in the precinct; target, register, and turn out voters in the precinct; and spend time on fundraising, media events, and gathering support.

The job of precinct chair pays no money and carries little prestige—both of which make it difficult to recruit precinct chairs. One recent study

Table 3.4 Permanent Party Structures in Texas

Office	How Chosen?	Responsibilities
Precinct chair	Elected in party primary for two-year term.	1. Administer primary election. 2. Campaign for party candidates. 3. Work to increase voter turnout in precinct. 4. Recruit candidates. 5. Raise funds.
County executive committee	All precinct chairs in county.	1. Campaign for party candidates. 2. Work to increase voter turnout in county. 3. Raise funds.
County party chair	Elected in party primary for two-year term.	1. Campaign for party candidates. 2. Work to increase voter turnout in county. 3. Raise funds.
State executive committee	One man and one woman from each state senatorial district, chosen by state convention delegates from that district.	1. Advise state party chair on party strategy. 2. Determine site of next state convention. 3. Canvass returns and direct party chair to certify names of candidates elected in party's primary.
State party chair and vice chair	Chosen by members of state convention. Party chair and vice chair must be of opposite sex.	1. Preside over meetings of state executive committee. 2. Call state convention to order. 3. Certify names of party's candidates.

estimated that the Democratic party had precinct chairs in about 77 percent of the state's nearly 7,238 precincts; the Republican party had precinct chairs in just 52 percent of the precincts.[15]

At the county level, the permanent organization is made up of the **county executive committee** and the **county party chair.** The county executive committee is composed of all the precinct chairs in the county. Participants in the party's March primary elect the county chair for a two-year term of office. The county chair performs the same functions the precinct chair does, but for the whole county.

Usually elections for precinct chairs and county chairs are low-keyed, with little competition; but they can become the arena for factional battles within a party. This was the case in 1992, in Harris County. A well-organized group described as the Religious Right in newspaper reports took control of the Republican party organization there. The leader of the group, Dr. Steven Hotze, was described as being antiabortion and antigay rights. The takeover began with the election of members of the Hotze faction as precinct chairs in the 1992 primary. The Hotze faction could not overthrow the duly elected county chair, Betsy Lake, but it could change the party rules to limit her power. In a meeting of the county executive committee in December 1992, the group created a new advisory committee and rewrote local bylaws to transfer power from the county chair to the advisory committee. Although leaders of the Republican party tried to downplay the importance of the organizational struggle in Harris County, some observers thought it would be the first of many similar struggles for control of the Republican party in Texas.[16]

At the top of the state party organization are the **state executive committee** and the **state party chair.** The state executive committee is composed of one man and one woman from each of the state's thirty-one senatorial districts. The members of the state executive committee are elected at the party's state convention. Delegates caucus by senatorial district and nominate a man and a woman from their district; then the state convention votes on the slate of candidates. The chair and vice chair of the state executive committee also are chosen by the state convention. The state executive committees ostensibly are the policymaking bodies of the political parties in Texas. But in reality the parties continue to be guided by the strong hand of the party chair.

The Strength of the Party Organizations

Indicators of party strength include (1) a permanent party headquarters, (2) professional leadership and staff, (3) an adequate budget, and (4) programs to maintain party structure, assist local party units, and support candidates and officeholders.[17] The last comprehensive study of state party organizations made in the early 1980s rated the Democratic party in Texas as moderately weak and the Republican party in Texas as moderately strong.[18]

How have the political parties in Texas fared since the early 1980s? Have they grown stronger? Although there have not been any comprehensive studies of state party organization since the early 1980s, a survey of local party activists in 1991 asked them what they thought about their party organization. The authors found that Republican activists were much more likely than Democratic activists to believe that their local party organization was stronger than it had been five to ten years before.[19] Table 3.5 shows that a majority of the Republican activists believed that their county party organization had improved in all of the areas listed except the use of public opinion polls. Among the Democrats, the only area in which a majority agreed that they had improved was in the use of computer technology. This study provides some support for the idea that the Republican party continues to have a stronger organization than does the Democratic party.

Certainly Republicans appear to be better organized in Texas. They have the resources to pay "party workers" to staff phone banks, to get out the vote, to be poll-watchers, and to do other necessary campaign jobs. In recent years, both the Democratic party in Texas and individual candidates have learned a lesson from the Republicans: volunteer labor may be the ideal, but volunteer campaign workers are less reliable than paid workers.

Table 3.5 Party Activists' Views of the Relative Vitality of Party Organization

	Percent Stronger		
Function	Democrats	Republicans	N
Overall organization	33.9	85.3	1,414
Campaign effectiveness	37.6	77.5	1,412
Ability to raise funds	25.7	67.3	1,396
Recruitment	27.8	68.2	1,393
Worker organization	33.5	58.9	1,385
Use of media	41.3	57.7	1,398
Use of opinion polls	29.2	43.1	1,375
Use of computer technology	51.5	63.1	1,368

Source: *Southern State Party Organizations and Activists,* Charles D. Hadley and Lewis Bowman (eds.), of *Southern State Party Organizations and Activists.*

Party Activists

Another way to evaluate party organization is to examine the people who are actively involved in that organization. There is a profile of precinct and county chairs from both parties in 1990.[20] A word of caution, though: Conclusions cannot be drawn about a whole party on the basis of how party activists think and behave. Studies usually find that **party activists** take more extreme positions on issues and ideology than those taken by rank-and-file party members.[21] This means that the ideological differences between Republican activists and Democratic activists tend to be greater than the differences between party supporters. Studies of party activists tell us about the party organization, not about the party as a whole.

Table 3.6 summarizes the social characteristics of activists from the two parties. The two groups differ notably in race and ethnicity, religion, and family income. Republican activists tend to be white Protestants and to earn more than do their Democratic counterparts. Democratic activists include more members of racial and ethnic minority groups and more Catholics than do Republicans. The two groups are not very different in terms of gender, age, education, and occupation. Both parties tend to rely on older, fairly well-to-do individuals working at fairly high status occupations.

Figure 3.1 compares the political philosophies of Republican and Democratic party activists. Republican activists are concentrated overwhelmingly at the conservative end of the ideological spectrum, with 46.2 percent classifying themselves as somewhat conservative and 39.8 percent classifying themselves as very conservative. Democratic party activists are distributed over the whole ideological spectrum, with most classifying themselves as moderate or somewhat liberal. It may seem surprising to find that many

Table 3.6 Demographic Characteristics of Texas Party Activists, 1991 (in percentages)

Demographic Characteristic		Total Sample	Democrats		Republicans	
			Chairs	Members	Chairs	Members
Gender	Male	57.7	71.8	50.7	67.4	57.1
	Female	42.3	28.2	49.3	32.6	42.9
Race/ Ethnicity	White	89.4	88.8	81.7	97.7	93.7
	Black	3.2	0.6	6.6	1.1	1.5
	Hispanic	5.1	9.3	9.7	1.1	1.2
	Other	2.3	1.2	2.0	0.0	3.6
Religion	Protestant	81.6	80.0	75.2	90.4	85.0
	Roman Catholic	15.0	15.8	19.6	7.9	13.0
	Jewish	0.8	1.2	1.2	0.0	0.7
	Other/none	2.6	3.0	4.1	1.7	1.0
Age	Under 40	16.9	16.7	14.3	15.5	19.6
	40–49	19.8	18.5	19.9	20.1	20.1
	50–59	22.6	25.9	21.5	28.2	21.1
	Over 60	40.6	38.9	44.3	36.2	39.2
Education	≤High school	15.2	12.0	23.4	5.1	11.9
	Some college	35.3	31.9	36.0	30.1	37.0
	College degree	23.7	19.9	14.6	33.5	29.7
	Graduate degree	25.9	36.1	26.0	31.3	21.4
Family Income	≤$30,000	24.8	18.9	33.4	12.1	22.9
	$30–59,999	33.8	51.7	45.8	44.0	47.3
	≥$60,000	41.3	29.4	20.9	43.9	29.8
Occupa- tion	Executive	21.5	20.3	17.9	24.7	23.8
	Professional	23.8	32.3	26.6	24.7	19.0
	Technical/sales	18.2	15.2	20.4	14.7	18.3
	Service	2.9	1.3	2.7	1.8	3.8
	Farm/forestry	7.1	12.7	6.4	12.9	4.3
	Skilled/ semi-skilled	7.5	5.0	9.3	5.3	7.5
	Other*	19.0	13.3	16.6	15.9	24.0

*Other includes those with "other" occupations, students, homemakers, and the unemployed.

Note: Some discrepancies in the numbers are due to rounding.

Source: *Southern State Party Organizations and Activists*, Charles D. Hadley and Lewis Bowman (eds.), of *Southern State Party Organizations and Activists*. Copyright © 1995 by Charles D. Hadley and Lewis Bowman. Reproduced with permission of Greenwood Publishing Group, Inc., Westport, CT.

Democratic activists call themselves liberal in a state where that label is not at all popular. But research shows that although activists from southern states are more conservative than those from other states, the most conservative

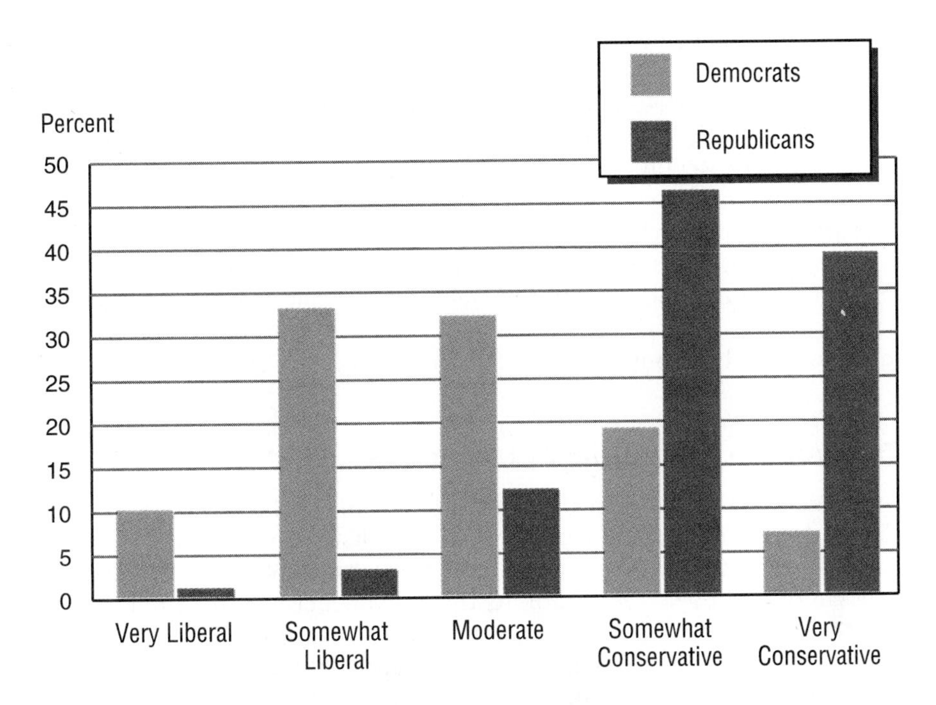

FIGURE 3.1 Ideology of Party Activists in Texas, 1992

Source: Southern State Party Organizations and Activists, Charles D. Hadley and Lewis Bowman (eds.), of *Southern State Party Organizations and Activists.* Copyright © 1995 by Charles D. Hadley and Lewis Bowman. Reproduced with permission of Greenwood Publishing Group, Inc., Westport, CT.

group of Democratic activists are more liberal than the most liberal group of Republican activists.[22]

 Party and Government

Political parties would be of little consequence if they had no effect on the structures that actually run the government. In this section we examine the influence of the political parties in Texas on the three branches of government: the executive, the legislature, and the judiciary.

Partisanship and the Governor

For much of Texas history, partisanship had everything—and nothing—to do with the governor of the state. On the one hand, party was all-important because candidates had to be Democrats to win. On the other, party had little to do with the decisions governors made.

With the emergence of partisan competition in Texas have come signs of party influence in the executive branch. Those signs have been especially evident in the hundreds of appointments Texas governors make to the boards and commissions that oversee many aspects of government in Texas. Since the late 1970s, Republican and Democratic governors alike regularly have appointed members of their own party to office.

Partisanship also has begun to have an effect on executive–legislative relationships in Texas. For example, Republican governor Bill Clements often found himself in conflict with the Democratic leadership of the legislature. The result was weeks and months of deadlock. Governor Bush developed a more congenial relationship with the Democratically-controlled legislature.

Partisanship and the Texas Legislature

Until recently partisanship played a small role in legislative politics in Texas. There were so few Republicans that partisan distinctions did not help either party. In recent years, however, certain critical votes have divided along partisan lines. In 1987, for example, the vote on a crucial tax increase pitted most of the Democrats (76.3 percent voting for) against most of the Republicans (87.2 percent voting against). During a special legislative session in the fall of 1992, a unified Republican minority in the state house of representatives made it impossible to achieve the two-thirds vote necessary to propose a constitutional amendment the Democratic leadership had introduced as part of its solution to the state's school finance crisis. Because partisan differences could not be resolved, the session adjourned with nothing accomplished. At critical moments, then, partisanship has had significant impact on legislative decisions.

Partisanship briefly played a role in the appointment of committee chairs in the Texas Senate. In the first session following the 1992 elections, Lieutenant Governor Bob Bullock departed from prior practice by appointing no Republican committee chairs. In the next session, however, Bullock retrenched. He decided that that kind of partisanship might encourage the Republicans to use their numbers to block the flow of legislation to the senate floor.

Partisanship and the Judiciary

Most judges in Texas—from justices of the peace to justices on the state supreme court—are elected in partisan elections. Until the 1980s, Democrats won all of those elections. But since then Republicans have been able to elect many candidates to local judicial positions. By the 1990s, in Dallas County and other urban counties, Republicans were dominating judicial elections, and Democrats were having a hard time recruiting candidates. Republican Thomas Phillips was elected chief justice of the Texas Supreme Court in 1990, and three of the associate justices were Republicans. After a highly publicized and bitterly fought campaign in 1992, Craig Enoch, a Republican, defeated liberal Democratic justice Oscar Mauzy. With the Republican party's success in local judicial elections and its victories on the Texas Supreme Court, partisanship clearly has come to the Texas judiciary. In the 1994 elections, the Republicans achieved a majority on the Supreme Court.

Party and the Electorate

One way of gauging the strength of the two parties in Texas today is to examine their relative support among the voters. **Party identification**—"a sense of attachment with one party or the other"—is one common measure of party support.[23] It has been used by the University of Michigan's Center for Political Studies in its studies of national elections and now is used by many other polling organizations as well. The Texas Poll (a statewide opinion poll conducted by the Office of Survey Research at the University of Texas) measures party identification by asking respondents, "Do you usually think of yourself as a Republican, a Democrat, an Independent, or what?" The pattern of responses to this question in successive polls reveals the trends in public identification with the political parties. According to Figure 3.2, which shows the level of support for each party at intervals from 1964 through 1998,

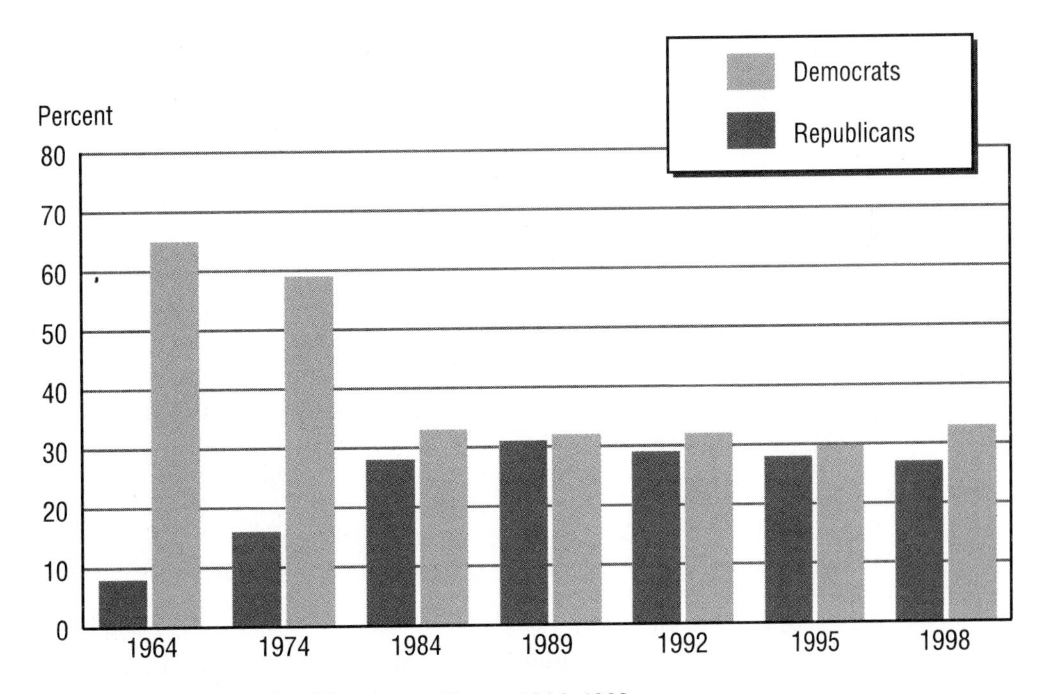

FIGURE 3.2 Party Identification in Texas, 1964–1998
Source: Data supplied by the Scripps Howard Texas Poll.

The Changing Face of Texas Politics

Angry White Males and Texas Political Parties

Democrat Ann Richards was widely regarded as one of the most popular of modern Texas governors, yet she lost her bid for reelection in 1994. Analysts, looking for an explanation for her defeat, soon turned their attention to a group they called "**angry white males.**" Exit interviews showed that 67 percent of white men gave their votes in the governor's race to the Republican candidate, George W. Bush; only 31 percent voted for Governor Richards. In the congressional elections that same year, 63 percent of men voted for Republican candidates; just 37 percent voted for Democratic candidates.[1] Polls indicate that the tendency for white males to support the Republican party and for women to support the Democratic party is not unique to Texas.[2]

Several factors are at work here. Republican promises of lower taxes and smaller government sound good to middle-class white men who are struggling to make economic ends meet. Many of these men also have come to resent the affirmative action programs initiated by Democrats to offer economic opportunities to minorities. That resentment has turned into votes for Republicans who promise to end "quotas, set-asides, and other preferential programs." White men also have come to resent welfare programs, government programs that give money to people who do not work. Bush capitalized on that feeling in his call for welfare reform in the 1994 campaign. Finally, the Republicans' get-tough-on-crime platform also appeals to white men. Bush's campaign promise to get tough on juvenile crime played to those sentiments. The upshot: many white men have become convinced that their political interests are best served by voting for the Republican party. And they did in 1994. The decline of the dominance of the white male is also evidenced in state officeholding. Four decades ago white male Democrats held 92 percent of statewide, congressional, and legislative offices. Today they hold less than 25 percent of the state's top elective posts.[3]

What is the significance of the angry-white-male vote in Texas? Today Texans are fairly equally divided among Democrats, Republi-

support for the Republican party went up significantly in the 1980s, reaching near-parity with the Democrats in 1989. By contrast the Democratic party, which had an impressive 65 percent of the electorate identifying with it in 1964, saw its support drop in the 1980s, when less than a third of the voters in Texas identified themselves with the party. This dramatic realignment of party support has ended the Democratic party's dominance in the Texas electorate.

It is also significant to note that many Texans no longer identify with either of the major political parties. In 1992 about 30 percent of the voters in the state were independents. That year, suggesting a dealignment in the Texas electorate, Democrats and Republicans each made up about 30 percent of the electorate too. About 10 percent refused to accept any label.[24] The trend in Texas toward more independents in the electorate parallels national trends.[25]

cans, and independents. This means that in any election, each party must reach beyond its own group of loyalists to garner support from independents or from voters who usually support the opposing party. Angry white males give the Republican party an advantage in the search for the votes needed to win a statewide election.

The Democratic party does have its own groups of loyal supporters—among them white women, African Americans, and Hispanics. But Democrats have had a hard time getting those groups to the polls on election day. Although white women have about the same tendency to vote as white males, the issues in recent elections have not been as likely to draw them to the polls. For example, Richards's belated attempt in 1994 to mobilize women voters by stressing her prochoice stand on abortion failed to rally women and actually may have alienated some Hispanic voters (who tend to be more conservative on the abortion issue). White males have an average to higher-than-average tendency to vote. With many campaign issues focused squarely on their concerns, they produced a decisive bloc of votes in 1994.

What is the challenge of the angry-white-male vote? Many analysts believe that the future of party competition in Texas rests on how the political parties respond to the gender gap among white voters. Can the Democratic party make it as the party of white women and minorities? Probably not in the near future . . . unless it can find a way to get those people to the polls on election day. Can the Republican party make it as the party of white men? Although that strategy might work in the short run, it may not be sound over the long run in Texas. Remember that demographic projections suggest that traditional minority groups will make up a larger share of the population in the future. Indeed, by the next century there may be no majority ethnic or racial group in Texas. A party of white men would be a declining force under those conditions. What may work to the advantage of the Republican party now, then, could be its undoing in years to come. Certainly the Democratic party has to find ways to woo white male voters in the near future; but it too must recognize the folly of letting short-term concerns weaken ties to ethnic and racial groups that have been loyal to the party in the past and may be even more important to the party in the future. ★

[1]David Jackson, "Male Call at the Polls," *Dallas Morning News*, December 28, 1994, 1A.

[2]"Poll of White Voters Shows Gender Gap," *Dallas Morning News*, November 27, 1994, 13A.

[3]Sam Attlesey, "Dwindling Dominance," *Dallas Morning News* (January 13, 1998), p. 1A.

The distribution of party identification appears to have stabilized and further change does not seem to be taking place. Most analysts argue that since the mid-1980s the Texas electorate has been divided roughly into thirds—one-third Democrats, one-third Republicans, and one-third independents.[26] While there is some fluctuation from poll to poll, this division into thirds now seems to be a reasonable way of thinking about the Texas electorate.

What kinds of people identify themselves as Republicans, Democrats, or independents? Table 3.7 shows that the Republican party does better among

- males.
- younger age groups.
- better educated.

Table 3.7 Demographic Characteristics of Texas Party Activists, 1998 (in percentages)

Characteristic	Republican	Democrat	Independent
Gender			
Male	29.1	28.9	27.2
Female	24.2	36.0	25.0
Age			
18–29	20.9	31.3	26.4
30–39	28.0	34.7	24.4
40–49	29.8	30.8	24.7
50–59	27.2	27.8	30.4
60–94	26.9	36.5	26.0
Education			
Some high school	16.1	35.5	26.9
High school grad	23.9	34.4	24.6
Some college	26.7	36.5	24.1
College grad	37.6	28.6	28.2
Graduate work	28.4	27.3	34.1
Race/Ethnicity			
Anglo	29.4	30.2	25.7
Black	3	72.1	17.6
Hispanic	10.8	41.4	25.0
Income			
Less than $10,000	14.3	31.0	28.6
$10,001–$20,000	18.3	38.9	27.8
$20,001–$30,000	19.1	34.3	27.5
$30,001–$40,000	28.7	36.4	24.0
$40,001–$50,000	29.9	34.5	27.6
$50,001–$60,000	23.3	41.1	17.8
$60,001 and above	46.7	22.3	23.9
Years in Texas			
10 or less	20.5	29.5	32.4
11–20	26.2	36.9	18.9
All life	25.5	36.9	24.6
Religion (top 4)			
Baptist	25.6	38.2	24.6
Catholic	16.7	37.0	24.8
Methodist	40.2	26.8	29.3
Other Protestant	42.2	26.5	19.6

Source: Data supplied by Scripps Howard Texas Poll. Data are from the February 1998 poll.

- whites.
- middle- to upper-income groups.
- those who have not lived in Texas all their lives.
- Protestants.

Democrats, on the other hand, do better among

- females.
- less well-educated.
- African Americans and Hispanics.
- low- and middle-income groups.
- those who have lived in the state longer.
- Roman Catholics and other religious groups.

Independents share many of the demographic characteristics associated with Republicans.

The ideological tendencies of party adherents are useful in identifying the sorts of policies the parties can reasonably support. If the parties behave

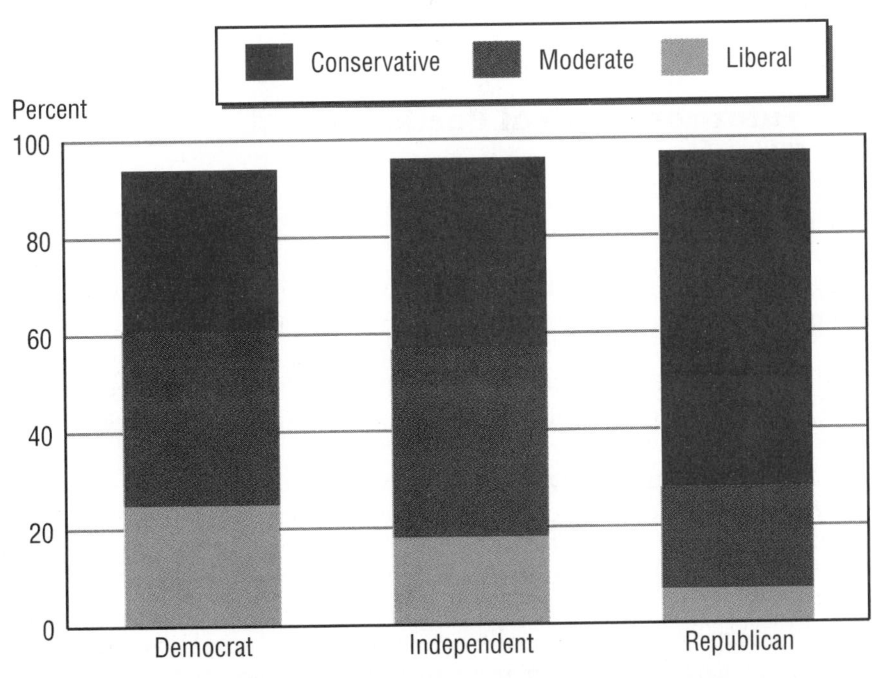

FIGURE 3.3 Texas Party Identification and Political Ideology, in 1987–1998

Source: Data provided by Scripps Howard Texas Poll. Pooled data from May 1997, August 1997, November 1997, and March 1998 polls. A total of 4,000 Texans were surveyed in these polls.

rationally, they must choose issue positions that appeal to potential voters. Figure 3.3 shows the ideological distribution of Texans by party identification. As might be expected, few respondents classified themselves as liberals, but Democrats and independents were more likely to classify themselves as liberals than were Republicans. Although the largest group of Democratic party identifiers classified themselves as moderates, some classified themselves as conservatives and some as liberals. The largest percentage of Republicans called themselves conservatives. A much smaller percentage identified themselves as moderates; and a very small percentage claimed to be liberals. The independents were evenly divided between moderates and conservatives, with a small proportion of liberals.

Given the distribution of its party identifiers, the Republican party must lean toward the conservative end of the spectrum on issues to reach the largest group of Republican voters. The Democratic party should aim its issue positions at the moderates to reach the largest group of party identifiers, but the party also must recognize that a significant portion of Democrats are liberals. And both parties must try to appeal to the independents, who are concentrated in the moderate category. For Democrats the best strategy would appear to be aiming for the moderate range, to appeal to their own identifiers and to independents. Republicans also must try to win moderate independents, but they have to cast their programs somewhat more conservatively than the Democrats to appeal to their own identifiers.

The Future of Political Parties at the Crossroads

Where are the political parties in Texas headed? It is hard to imagine a future for Texas that does not include a fairly vigorous two-party system. The Republican party can be expected to broaden and deepen its challenge to the Democrats. The Democratic party can be expected to respond to that challenge by defining its constituency more clearly and strengthening its organization. The result should be a political arena marked by robust political parties, not candidate-centered organizations or intraparty factionalism.

One change that is likely to influence party development in Texas is social diversity. Over the next few decades Texas is expected to become more ethnically diverse. Whites made up almost 61 percent of the state's population in 1990; by 2026 experts predict that only 47 percent of the population will be white.[27] Hispanics are expected to show the most growth. Because the Democratic party traditionally has done better among Hispanics than the Republican party has, the increase in the percentage of Hispanics in the population should provide fertile ground for Democrats in Texas.

Still, the Republican party should continue to expand. The party's base is in metropolitan areas, especially the suburbs—areas where most of the population growth in the state is expected. Past performance indicates that the Republicans' metropolitan base is strong enough to make the party competitive in statewide races when it is able to field good candidates who run good campaigns. Republicans also may be able to chip away at the Democratic base among whites in small towns. Although the white population on which the Republicans rely heavily will be a declining share of the electorate, there has traditionally been a higher turnout among whites than among other groups. And, of course, Republicans will continue to make appeals to Hispanics in hopes of broadening their electoral base. Overall the Republicans should be able to continue to put together a coalition of voters that will keep the party competitive in Texas politics.

It is also reasonable to expect that the party organizations will become stronger in Texas. As noted earlier, in the early 1980s the state Republican party already was rated moderately strong; and it has continued its efforts to strengthen its organization. In the same study the Democratic party was rated moderately weak, but the growing Republican challenge should prod the Democrats to strengthen their party's organization. The competition should leave both parties with stronger organizations.

What effect will a competitive two-party system have on the behavior of the government in Texas? Some argue that policy implications will be minimized as both parties try to represent the same part of the ideological spectrum.[28] The largest bloc of voters in Texas falls in the moderate to conservative part of the ideological spectrum. If the parties follow a vote-maximizing strategy, then, they naturally converge on the moderate-to-conservative center. The concentration of Texas voters in that range may limit the alternatives the Texas parties present. So party competition is not likely to produce major shifts in the policy choices made by the government in Texas.

Notes

1. Leon D. Epstein, *Political Parties in Western Democracies* (New York: Praeger, 1967), 9.

2. Angus Campbell et al., *The American Voter,* unabridged edition (New York: John Wiley & Sons, 1960), 534.

3. This section draws heavily on Mike Kingston, "A Concise History of Texas," in *Texas Almanac,* 1986–1987 (Dallas: A. H. Belo Corp., 1985), 167–224.

4. Chandler Davidson, *Race and Class in Texas Politics* (Princeton, NJ: Princeton University Press, 1990), 198.

5. John R. Knaggs, *Two-Party Texas: The John Tower Era, 1961–1984* (Austin: Eakin Press, 1986), 10–15.

6. James E. Anderson et al., *Texas Politics: An Introduction,* 5th ed. (New York: Harper & Row, 1989), 62.

7. Lori Stahl and Sam Attlesey, "GOP Christian Group Wielding Greater Clout," *Dallas Morning News,* May 22, 1994, 1A.

8. John F. Bibby et al., "Parties in State Politics," in *Politics in the American States,* 5th ed., Virginia Gray, Herbert Jacob, and Robert B. Albritton, eds. (New York: HarperCollins, 1990), 85–122.

9. Austin Ranney, "Parties in State Politics," in *Politics in the American States,* 2d ed., Herbert Jacob and Kenneth N. Vines, eds. (Boston: Little, Brown, 1971), 82–121. The classification table is on p. 87.

10. See Jewell and Olson, *American State Political Parties and Elections,* Revised edition (Homewood, Ill.: Dorsey Press, 1982), 107–110. The authors subdivide open primaries into "open primaries with party selection," in which a public choice between the parties must be made, and "completely open primaries," in which voters can choose a party primary at the time of the election without publicly disclosing their choice. Texas falls into the open-primaries-with-party-selection category in this scheme.

11. Frank J. Sorauf and Paul Allen Beck, *Party Politics in America,* 5th ed. (Glenview, IL: Scott, Foresman, 1988), 10–11.

12. Bibby et al., "Parties in State Politics," 94.

13. Stahl and Attlesey, "GOP Christian Group," in *Southern State Party Organizations and Activists,* Charles D. Hadley and Lewis Bowman, eds. (Westport, CT: Praeger, 1995), 78.

14. Texas Election Code, Sec. 191.007.

15. Frank B. Feigert and Nancy L. McWilliams "Texas: Yeller Dogs and Yuppies" in *Southern State Party Organizations and Activists,* Charles D. Hadley and Lewis Bowman, eds. (Westport, CT: Praeger, 1955), 78.

16. Bruce Nichols, "'Religious Right' Seizes Control of Harris County GOP," *Dallas Morning News,* December 9, 1992, 16A.

17. John F. Bibby, "State Party Organizations: Coping and Adapting to Candidate-Centered Politics and Nationalization," in *The Parties Respond: Changes in American Parties and Campaigns,* 3d ed., L. Sandy Maisel, ed. (Boulder: Westview Press, 1998), 23–49. The point made here is on p. 31.

18. Cotter et al., *Party Organizations,* 28–29.

19. Feigert and McWilliams, "Texas: Yeller Dogs and Yuppies."

20. The sample was drawn randomly from lists supplied by each party's state office. The questionnaire was administered by mail in 1991. The sample included 166 Democratic county chairs, 525 Democratic precinct chairs, 177 Republican county chairs, and 604 Republican precinct chairs. The data were supplied by Frank Feigert from the Texas data that were part of the Southern Grassroots Party Activists Project (Charles Hadley and Lewis Bowman, principal investigators).

21. See, for example, Herbert McClosky et al., "Issue Conflict and Consensus Among Party Leaders and Followers," *American Political Science Review* 54 (1960): 406–429; John Soule and James Clarke, "Amateurs and Professionals: A Study of Delegates to the 1968 Democratic National Convention," *American Political Science Review* 64 (1970): 888–899; Jeane Kirkpatrick, "Representation in the American National Conventions: The Case of 1972," *British Journal of Political Science* 5 (1975): 265–322; and Robert Montjoy et al., "Policy Preferences of Party Elites and Masses," *American Politics Quarterly* 8 (1980): 319–344.

22. Alan Abramowitz et al., "Party Activists in the United States: A Comparative Analysis," *International Political Science Review* 4 (1983): 13–19.

23. Angus Campbell et al., *The American Voter,* abridged edition (New York: John Wiley & Sons, 1964), 68.

24. *Texas Poll Report,* 9 (May 1992): 2; and 9 (August 1992): 12.
25. Warren Miller, "Party Identification and the Electorate of the 1990s," in *The Parties Respond,* 109–143. See especially p. 112.
26. *The Texas Poll Report,* 10 (July/August/September 1993), 2.
27. Texas Comptroller of Public Accounts, *The Changing Face of Texas: Texas Through the Year 2026* (Austin, 1992), 19.
28. Jeanie R. Stanley, "Party Realignment in Texas," in *Party Realignment and State Politics,* Maureen Moakley, ed. (Columbus: Ohio State University Press, 1992), 74–90. See especially the conclusions on p. 90.

4 Interest Groups in Texas Politics

Chapter Outline

In recent years, some of Texas' most powerful legislators have made trips to some pretty fancy resorts. One went to a resort in the Arizona desert that features an eighty-foot waterfall and restaurants that serve venison nachos and mesquite grilled ostrich fajitas. Another went to the Chateau Whister in the mountains of British Columbia, a renowned ski resort with golf courses designed by Jack Nicklaus and Arnold Palmer. What makes these trips noteworthy is that they didn't cost the legislators anything—the tab was picked up in each case by lobbyists tied to the powerful highway industry in Texas.[1]

The 1991 Texas ethics law outlawed the previously common practice of allowing interest groups to pay for the vacations of legislators. So, how did these legislators escape discipline for accepting these trips from lobbyists? The answer is that the legislators were performing a service for the lobbyist's interest group. They made speeches to the groups about their areas of legislative expertise. Thus, a loophole in the law allows legislators to enjoy the hospitality of lobbyists while spending several days socializing with group members.

During the 1997 legislative session, legislators dining at lobbyists' expense received dinner for two at the Café of the Four Seasons Hotel for a total cost of $176. Although this example may cite an extreme case, a number of legislators received dinners priced between $50 and $100 at such Austin establishments as the Shoreline Grill, Ruth's Chris Steak House, and Zoot. A lobbyist hosted a reception at the Four Seasons Hotel for members of the Hispanic Caucus to celebrate the groups' anniversary. The tab for the occasion ran to $23,000. Another lobbyist hosted a dinner party for twelve African-American senate and house members, with the cost of meals ranging between $40 and $110 each.[2]

What do these incidents reveal about Texas politics? The clearest revelation is that the tradition in Texas of close association between interest groups (also known as *pressure groups, special interests,* and *lobbies*) and the state's top-ranking politicians continues. Now the newer Hispanic and African-American legislators are being initiated into the politics of wining and dining. Lobbyists in Texas are powerful. In fact, in Texas, interest group representatives often are referred to collectively as *The Lobby*—with a capital *T* and a capital *L*.[3]

Any understanding of Texas politics would not be complete without a close look at the role that interest groups and their representatives play in state government. This chapter answers several questions about interest groups:

- What are interest groups?
- How do they go about influencing politics in Texas?
- Which interest groups are most influential in Texas?
- How powerful are interest groups in Texas compared with other participants in the political arena?

What Is an Interest Group?

An **interest group** is an organization of individuals who share a common interest and who work together to advance that interest.[4] Interest groups are not collections of people with some common attribute—red hair or an annual salary over $500,000. To form an interest group, people must share an interest and be willing to work together to further that interest. Blue-collar workers are not an interest group; but workers who belong to a labor union are an interest group. They share an interest in higher wages and better benefits and have organized to advance that interest.

The Recent Growth of Interest Groups

Researchers tell us that in the last twenty-five years, both the number of interest groups and the array of interests they represent have grown. In state capitals around the country, five types of interests usually are well organized and well represented: business, labor, education, farmers, and local government.[5] Sociocultural and single-issue groups—although an important influence on politics in state governments—tend to be less organized than the other types of groups.

Several reasons for the growth of interest groups in state politics have been suggested. First, as the economy has diversified, new groups have formed to represent new economic interests. Second, the increase in interest group activity parallels an increase in the activity of state governments. As the states have ventured into new policy areas and taken on new activities in traditional areas, groups have formed to respond to those initiatives. Third, some groups have formed in response to other new groups. As pro-choice groups formed to champion the right to abortion, pro-life groups formed to demand limits on the use of abortion. Fourth, the increased number of groups reflects the proliferation of groups representing traditional interests. For example, general business groups (one example is the Texas Association of Business) have been joined by groups that represent specific types of businesses (such as the Texas Bankers Association and the Texas Realtors Association). Finally, economic adversity in Texas and elsewhere have increased the number of groups actively defending existing state services and budgets.[6]

What Makes Interest Groups Powerful?

Interest groups have a lot of political power in the United States. In fact Americans have a long-standing fear of special interests dominating politics, leaving the general interests of the people ignored. What makes interest groups so powerful? Although several factors contribute to the power of interest groups, the key factor is organization. Organization makes it possible for groups to coordinate and mobilize their members. Organization makes it possible for groups to reward their supporters and to punish their opponents.

Organization also facilitates the process of gathering resources to promote the interests of a group. Money talks in politics, and some interest groups are able to speak loudly by using large amounts of money to influence politicians. These days, politicians need money—a lot of it—to run campaigns, and raising it in big chunks from interest groups is quicker and more efficient than raising it from hundreds of small individual contributors.

Interest Groups Versus Political Parties

Interest groups, like political parties, want to influence policymaking. That is an important similarity between the two types of organizations. Are there other similarities? Are there differences?

The relationship between interest groups and political parties has been the subject of considerable discussion in recent years. Some argue that as political parties have grown weaker, interest groups have taken over some of their functions. For example, one student of political parties insists that political campaigns have become candidate-centered enterprises that depend on interest groups to fund their advertising and public relations activities.[7] Others argue that although the activities of interest groups and political parties sometimes overlap, their roles are different.

Certainly the functions of interest groups and political parties overlap to some extent, but each has a distinct role to play in the political process. Interest groups want their members' concerns represented in the policymaking process. Political parties want to control the government, to influence policy on behalf of a broad electoral coalition.

How Interest Groups Influence Policy

Interest groups can choose many ways to assert their influence. The methods they do choose most often depend on the nature of the group, the money and membership available to support the group's efforts, and the ends the group is seeking (for example, support for a specific bill before the legislature or the reelection of a sympathetic incumbent).

Lobbying

Of all the techniques that interest groups use to advance their political interests, lobbying is one of the best known. **Lobbying** is an informal or formal attempt to influence the policy decisions of legislators or executive officials through direct contact.

The Texas legislative process brings legislators and lobbyists into frequent contact as the details of legislation are worked out.

Informal lobbying is about establishing relationships with politicians. When the legislature is in session, Austin is a whirlwind of social activity, much of it informal lobbying. In fact receptions have become so common that many lobbyists worry that they are losing their effectiveness. Dinner and drinks at the Petroleum Club or the Austin Club, golf at the Barton Creek Country Club, and hunting and fishing trips are standard fare. Lobbyist–legislator get-togethers in the past often resembled fraternity weekends but new regulations and a changing social climate have calmed things down somewhat in recent years. An ethics law passed in 1991 bans pleasure trips and limits the amount that lobbyists can spend on entertaining legislators to $500 per member each year and the gifts each member can receive to a total of $500 each year. Food and drink do not count under the limit.[8] Lobbyists are not happy about the new law. As one lobbyist from Texas complained, "If I can't take a guy hunting, it will be harder to get to know him."[9] The objective of informal lobbying is to establish relationships; lobbyists usually do not expect to make a hard sell to legislators while entertaining them. But the relationships are invaluable when the time does come to make a hard sell.

Opportunities for formal lobbying contacts abound in the political process. For example, interest groups regularly are invited to testify before legislative committees on pending policy decisions. They also can provide

Billy Clayton, former Speaker of the Texas House of Representatives, (shown in the center of this photo), is now a major contract lobbyist representing a number of clients before the Texas legislature.

written or oral testimony on how proposed regulations will affect their interests and should be modified. Proposed government regulations must be published in the *Texas Register* (a state publication in which policy changes and proposed changes in bureaucratic regulations are announced), and time must be allowed for interest groups to respond.

A **lobbyist** is "a person designated by an interest group to represent it to the government for the purpose of influencing public policy in that group's favor."[10] An interest group may be represented by one or more of several types of lobbyists.

Contract lobbyists make their services available to interest groups for a fee. Depending on their knowledge and experience, they usually have several clients. Although many contract lobbyists operate alone, lobbying firms and law firms that provide lobbying services are becoming common in Texas.[11]

Contract lobbyists usually have a background in state politics. Some are former legislative staffers; some are former legislators. Former speaker of the Texas house Billy Clayton is a prominent contract lobbyist in Austin. He listed twenty-nine clients in the information on file with the Texas Ethics Commission for 1997. When Gib Lewis left the speakership in 1992, he stayed on in Austin to work as a contract lobbyist. He listed thirty-seven clients in

1997.[12] Prominent politicians are valuable to interest groups on two counts: their knowledge of the legislative process and their vast network of friendships in the state capital.

Association lobbyists represent business, labor, professional, and trade associations. These in-house lobbyists work for the group they represent, and lobbying can be just one of their functions. For example, an officer of the Texas State Teachers Association may have both organizational and lobbying responsibilities.

Company lobbyists work for a business, and lobbying may be all or part of their job. The job descriptions of these lobbyists often refer to their work as "state government relations." Most company lobbyists whose principal activity is lobbying come from a background in politics. They are hired specifically for their political skills.[13]

Government lobbyists represent associations of local governments—cities, counties, or school boards, for example. They also can represent a particular city, county, or special district. For example, Billy Clayton listed the city of El Paso among his clients in 1992.[14] Government lobbyists come from varied backgrounds. Some start in local government and work their way into lobbying positions with associations. Others are hired as lobbyists by cities or associations because of their political skills.[15]

Cause lobbyists usually emerge out of the groups or causes with which they are associated. A cause lobbyist would represent a public interest group (such as Common Cause or the League of Women Voters), an environmental group (the Sierra Club or the Audubon Society), or a single-interest group (Texas Right to Life or the Abortion Rights League).[16]

Finally, **individual lobbyists** are motivated by the intensity of their own beliefs to try to influence public policy. For example, Mel and Norma Gabler, a husband and wife, regularly participated in the textbook selection process in Texas to protect schoolchildren from what they believe are bad influences in schoolbooks as long as the Texas Board of Education controlled textbook selection.

Electioneering

Because interest groups realize that their opportunities for influence are determined largely by who wins elections, they allocate resources to help elect supportive public officials through **electioneering.** Sometimes they actually recruit candidates, often by promising substantial campaign contributions. And even when they do not choose candidates, the promise of campaign contributions means that they influence who does get chosen. Because running for public office is so expensive today, group contributions are often the decisive factor in an individual's decision to launch a campaign.

Today many groups use a **political action committee** (**PAC**) to channel money into the political arena. PACs can be independent organizations, but often they are simply the legal device interest groups use to collect money from members for political ends. Business associations are usually the big-money players among PACs, and the largest contributions usually come from associations of doctors, trial lawyers, realtors, developers, teachers, and labor unions.[17] Texas law sets no limit on the amount of money a PAC can donate to a candidate for state office.[18]

PAC contributions tend to follow a pattern: incumbents usually get more money than challengers because incumbents are a known quantity. Legislative leaders—especially the speaker of the Texas house—get more money than rank-and-file lawmakers. Occasionally a PAC targets a specific race to try to unseat an "enemy." The Texas Civil Justice League (an association that represents business interests, the insurance industry, and defense lawyers) put money into Texas Senate races in an attempt to break the hold of the Texas Trial Lawyers Association on that body.[19] The strategy is not common, because it is expensive and risky if it should fail.

PACs in Texas give money to politicians for several reasons. According to one lobbyist, it is a "pay to play" system.[20] PACs that do not make contributions now will not have access to politicians later. In fact not making a contribution often seems more significant than making one. Most lobbyists believe that other things being equal, campaign contributions make the difference. Contributions, they claim, are a prudent investment.[21]

Money is not the only contribution interest groups make to candidates. Unless forbidden by law from doing so—as some corporations and labor unions are—interest groups can campaign for the candidate of their choice. Some groups, among them the Texas State Teachers Association and the Texas AFL-CIO, formally endorse candidates. Others simply encourage their members to work for certain candidates. Interest groups can help candidates find the corps of volunteers they need to run an effective campaign.

Grass Roots Mobilization

Interest groups with large memberships or with many sympathizers may try to influence public policymaking by **grass roots mobilization.** If they cannot persuade politicians directly, they may try to pressure them through their constituents. Groups alert their members and supporters to problems and urge them to contact legislators or other officeholders. Some advertise in the media or make direct mailings. Or they may pass the word through their own organizational structure and communications network. When lawmakers introduced legislation in 1991 to establish a state-run lottery, religious groups tried to mobilize their members against the lottery by emphasizing the evils of gambling. The Texas State Teachers Association uses its more than thirty field offices (linked by computer), a phone bank in its Austin office, newsletters, and legislative bulletins to alert its members to policies that could affect teachers and to encourage them to contact politicians.[22] The Texas Civil Justice League, a group that believes there are too many product liability suits

These nurses protest cutbacks by for-profit HMOs.

in the Texas courts, has forty phone bank operators in Austin. In one major drive the league called 35,000 supporters, sent them information and sample letters, and urged them to write to their legislators.[23]

Public Relations Techniques

Groups also use **public relations techniques** to improve the public's attitude toward them. For example, some corporations contribute to charities or to the arts to build goodwill. If the public feels good about a group, politicians have less trouble voting in favor of that group's interests.

Demonstrations and Protests

Interest groups that have limited financial resources are likely to turn to **demonstrations and protests** to influence policymaking. In the 1950s and 1960s, civil rights groups proved the effectiveness of these techniques. More recently, groups battling over the abortion issue have used them. When Operation Rescue attempted to block entry to clinics in Dallas, the National Abortion Rights Action League (NARAL) staged pro-choice demonstrations in response.

Demonstrations are effective only under certain conditions. First, there has to be widespread media coverage. Second, the group must have enough backing to assemble a large number of people for a march or rally. Media coverage must convey the impression that a large number of people support the cause. It is better to have no demonstration than to have news coverage of sparse crowds in a public square or empty seats at an indoor rally. Finally, the cause must be capable of generating a sympathetic response from a major segment of the population. When these conditions are met, demonstrations and protests can be effective means of overcoming limited financial resources.

Litigation

When other avenues of influence fail, an interest group may turn to the courts to advance its cause. **Litigation** is an expensive technique that often takes years to bear fruit, but it has become an increasingly common strategy for influencing public policy in recent years. The National Association for the Advancement of Colored People (NAACP) sued the state of Texas to force the legislature to provide fair representation to African Americans in its redistricting plans. Hispanics filed a suit for fair representation in state senate districts following the legislative redistricting in 1991. Representatives of poor school districts sued the state to get more money for their schools. In 1991, the Mexican-American Legal Defense and Education Fund sued the state to get more funds for higher education channeled into the Hispanic-dominated counties of South Texas.

Agency Capture

Another strategy interest groups use to influence public policies is "capturing" the agencies that control those policies. When sympathetic people control an agency, the agency is not likely to make policy that could harm a group's interests.

An interest group would attempt to control a public agency when the costs or benefits of that agency's decision making fall heavily on group members. For example, the Railroad Commission of Texas regulates oil and gas production in the state. Its actions benefit the oil and gas industry in the form of higher revenues. The oil and gas industry, then, has strong motivation to influence the commission. No group organizes to limit that influence because the cost of holding oil and gas prices up is not high enough per person to motivate consumers.

The members of the Railroad Commission are elected. This means that the best way for the oil and gas industry to protect its benefits is to bankroll the campaigns of sympathetic candidates. And it does. Candidates backed by the oil and gas groups often have the biggest campaign chests of all the candidates running for seats on the commission, giving those candidates a better-than-average chance of winning. The result is that the commission has continued to protect the industry's interests.

The Types of Groups in Texas Politics

Business and Professional Groups

Business groups. In Texas, as in other states, business groups have more registered lobbyists than does any other type of group.[24] These groups operate under many different guises, sometimes even in conflict with one another.

One powerful business group is the Texas Association of Business. Another is the Texas Research League. Many people do not realize that the league is an interest group. Certainly its name sounds like a research organization or think tank, an association the group reinforces by publishing position papers on the major issues facing the state. But in reality the Texas Research League is financed by and speaks for big business in Texas.

Several organizations represent the oil and gas industry, and surprisingly these groups are not always working toward the same ends. For example, the Texas Independent Producers and Royalty Owners Association, which represents small producers and royalty owners, sometimes is at odds with representatives of the big oil and gas producers, among them the Texas Mid-Continent Oil and Gas Association. But when a proposal is before the legislature that could impose extra costs or restrictions on the oil and gas industry, reducing profits, these groups coalesce quickly. Again, oil and gas groups focus much of their attention on the Texas Railroad Commission.

The chemical industry plays a significant role in the Texas economy. Its association, the Texas Chemical Council, has fought vigorously against stronger pollution controls in the state.

Retail associations are no less vigorous in pursuing their interests in the state capital. One group that is particularly well organized and well represented is the Texas Automobile Dealers Association. Its long-time lobbyist is former state representative Gene Fondren. The group works hard to fend off regulations that could make life difficult for car dealers. For example, the association was able to water down the provisions of a "lemon law," that might have forced dealers to make refunds to owners when new cars had more problems than dealers could rectify with normal warranty work. Other significant trade associations include the Texas Realtors Association, and the Texas Savings and Loan Association.

The Texas Good Roads and Transportation Association—also called the *highway lobby*—represents the private contractors who build and maintain state highways. (Texas does not hire its own crews.) The most important goal of this lobby is to maintain or expand the share of the Texas budget allocated to highway construction and maintenance. The lion's share of money available for highway construction comes from dedicated funds produced by taxes on motor vehicle fuels (principally gasoline). Historically the highway lobby has devoted much of its effort to defending this guaranteed source of funds from those who want to divert it to mass transit for cities or other uses. Because these funds must be supplemented by general revenue funds to round out the Texas Department of Transportation's budget, the highway lobby also is concerned about appropriations decisions made by the legislature. The highway lobby has its work cut out for it when the state is economically strapped and must find ways of trimming the budget. That is when the lobby has to fight to keep highway funds from being cut back in the general revenue budget. Because Texas is so large, the building of roads has wide support in the state, creating an environment that is usually fairly friendly toward the highway lobby.

Professional groups. Interest groups that represent various professions are also powerful players in Texas politics. The Texas Trial Lawyers Association is one group that is believed to be very powerful. It was alleged that until quite recently the Texas Senate was controlled by this organization.[25] Because trial lawyers make a large part of their living by filing personal injury suits on behalf of injured clients, any legislation that deals with personal injury, medical malpractice, product liability, and other civil liability matters (such as the tort reform legislation in the 1995 legislative session) attracts the interest of this group.

The Texas Medical Association is another powerful professional group. Its focus is on legislation that would affect malpractice suits or that would regulate medical costs and its PAC is usually a major campaign contributor.

A lobbying battle of the titans took place in 1989, when the legislature undertook a major overhaul of the state workers' compensation system. Business groups had demanded reform because premiums for workers' compensation insurance in Texas were among the highest in the nation (benefits were among the lowest). They were able to recruit support from the medical profession to limit the right of injured workers to seek compensation from personal injury suits, to limit them to workers' compensation benefits. The Texas Trial Lawyers Association opposed changes that would limit the rights of workers to file personal injury suits. The reform bill was enacted, but only because the governor and the legislature persisted through one regular session and two special sessions.

Teachers' Associations

Education is the number-one expense in Texas—as it is in many other states—which is why it often is at the center of policy disputes. Among the principal players in the politics of public education are the groups that represent teachers. Their objectives are to improve teachers' salaries and benefits and to advance the cause of public education in general. The Texas State Teachers Association has been very active in Texas politics in recent years. In fact observers rate the group among the most powerful in Texas today.[26] School reform legislation in the mid-1980s solidified the group.

Teachers were particularly outraged over the provision in the legislation that required teachers to pass basic literacy tests in order to keep their jobs. The thought of staking the future of a lengthy teaching career on the outcome of a single standardized test made teachers angry enough to turn the association against Governor Mark White when he ran for reelection in 1986. This defection of a group that had endorsed him in the previous election contributed to White's loss at the polls.

Labor Unions

Texas is a not particularly friendly territory for labor unions. The state's right-to-work law undermines union organization by making it illegal to require union membership as a condition of employment. Still, labor unions have managed to play a significant role in Texas politics from time to time. The strength of local affiliates of the AFL-CIO and other unions is concentrated in certain industries (transportation and communications, for example) and in certain locations (primarily, metropolitan areas). Union funds cannot be used directly in campaigns, but union PACs can make campaign contributions. Representatives of districts in which unions are powerful may depend on them for campaign contributions and support. In battles where union interests are at stake, unions are willing to call in their chips by telling politicians they must take the union position or lose future contributions. Although the number of legislators subject to this kind of pressure is small, it can be decisive on matters where just a few votes are needed to pass or defeat legislation. That was the situation in the 1970s, when the Texas legislature (acting as a constitutional convention) could not muster the votes necessary to propose a new constitution for the state (see Chapter 2). The source of the deadlock was a right-to-work provision in the proposed constitution. The unions warned any legislator who had received campaign contributions from organized labor not to vote for the constitution if they wanted contributions to continue in the future.

Sociocultural Groups

Racial and ethnic groups. Racial and ethnic groups in Texas, as elsewhere, are working actively for equality—for equal protection under the law, for a fair share of government benefits, and for economic opportunity. The NAACP continues to be an important advocate for African Americans, particularly in the areas of school desegregation and fair representation in the state legislature and on city councils. The group has relied heavily on litigation to achieve its goals.

In recent years Hispanic groups also have worked for a fair share of public benefits. Among the more active of these groups are the League of United Latin American Citizens and the Mexican-American Legal Defense and Education Fund (MALDEF). Equitable funding for local school districts has been a major concern of these groups. *Edgewood* v. *Kirby*, the case that forced

The fact that the Texas State Teachers Association has its headquarters in Austin helps the organization to be an effective player in Texas politics.

the state to restructure its school finance system, was filed in a predominantly Hispanic school district in San Antonio.[27] MALDEF also has tackled higher education. In response to a suit initiated by MALDEF, a local court ruled in 1992 that the state was not putting a fair share of resources into higher education in the predominantly Hispanic areas in the state. (For further discussion of this case see Chapter 13.)

Religious groups. Religious groups organize around issues that are perceived to involve public morality. In 1990, parimutuel betting at racetracks and a state lottery were major issues for these groups. Religious groups opposed the measures on the grounds that the state would be promoting gambling. Although these groups had defeated similar measures in the past, this time voters responded to the state's financial crisis and passed the bills.

Single-Issue Groups

Single-issue groups form to advocate for or defend against a single issue. For example, Mothers Against Drunk Driving (MADD) has lobbied legislators to crack down on drunk drivers. Abortion also draws out single-issue groups. The Texas Right to Life Organization is very active on the anti-abortion side. The Texas chapter of NARAL (National Abortion Rights Action League) has been active on the pro-choice side. Single-issue groups may not have the resources of larger groups, but they do have intensity and tenacity.

The Overall Power of Interest Groups in Texas

Scholars tell us that interest groups are more powerful in some states than in others. What factors affect the influence of interest groups at the state level? The literature indicates that a state tends to have powerful interest groups if its economy is not diversified, if its political parties are weak, and if its legislature is not professional.[28] An important recent study of interest group activity in the United States identifies seven factors that influence group power at the state level:[29]

- The nature of a state's policy domain
- Public attitudes
- The level of integration of the policy process
- The level of professionalization of the state government
- The level of socioeconomic development
- The extent and enforcement of public disclosure laws
- The level of campaign costs and sources of support

The *policy domain*—the set of policy questions with which a state is grappling—influences the types of groups that are likely to be active in a state. Texas is a case in point. Over time, as the public agenda has changed, different groups have moved into prominence. Education problems were very important in 1984 and again in 1990 and 1991, and education groups were key players during those periods. When property tax reform was being debated in 1997, business groups actively fought to prevent the tax burden from being shifted to them. (See the box on page 86.)

Public attitudes also affect both the power of groups in the state and the kinds of groups that are powerful. Where the general public stands on the liberal–conservative spectrum makes some groups acceptable and others unacceptable. Public concepts of the political culture also can affect groups by setting norms for participants in the policy process. The conservative, traditional nature of the people in Texas has made it difficult for groups that advocate for programs for the poor or for stronger regulation of the economy. On the other hand, probusiness groups—the Texas Chamber of Commerce is one example—have an easier time protecting their interests.

An *integrated policy process* limits the power of interest groups; a fragmented policy process multiplies opportunities for group influence. In an integrated policy process, political parties are strong, and responsibility is focused in the hands of the governor and appointed cabinet-level administrators. In a fragmented policy process, political parties are weak, and inde-

The Changing Face of Texas Politics

Governor Bush Gets Ambushed by The Lobby

Governor Bush's principal legislative proposal for the 1997 session of the legislature was for property tax reform. Bush was convinced that property taxes, especially school taxes, were growing too rapidly and were becoming a barrier to home ownership for some Texans. In addition, it was becoming apparent that too much of the burden for financing public schools was being placed on local property taxes, causing those taxes to soar and stretching the ability of some districts to raise enough money. And so, Bush announced that his main objective in the 1997 session of the legislature would be to lower property taxes and to lighten the burden of school finance on property taxes.

When the 1997 legislative session opened, it seemed that the odds should have been in favor of Bush's proposal. The facts were on his side. During the years from 1984 to 1995, the amount collected in local property taxes had almost doubled. School district property tax levies had grown by 124 percent.[1] It appeared that he had the people behind him—Bush's personal popularity was strong, with about 70 percent of the people saying they liked him. The legislative elections had gone his way, producing the first majority in the Texas Senate in modern times. The state's economy was doing well and the state treasury had a billion dollar surplus. So, the cards seemed stacked in Bush's favor.

But, by the end of the legislative session, Bush's proposal was in shambles, and he and the leaders were scrambling to deliver some small amount of property tax relief so that Bush would not appear to come away empty-handed. The house had passed a bill to the governor's liking, but the Senate had balked. So property tax reform ended with the governor and his supporters picking up the pieces where they could to cobble together even a modest property tax relief bill.

How had things gone so wrong when they had initially looked so good? Basically the an-

pendent boards and commissions and elected executive officials are common. The more independent decision points there are in the policymaking process, the greater the opportunity for group influence. Policymaking in Texas is fragmented, which means that opportunities for group influence abound. The weakness of Texas political parties was discussed in Chapter 3. (The fragmented nature of the executive branch is discussed in Chapters 7 and 8.)

Historically, the more *professional* the *state government,* the weaker the state's interest groups.[30] A professional government is one that adequately compensates elected officials and public employees, that hires employees on the basis of merit, and that provides staff support for the governor and legislators.[31] Although earlier studies found a strong relationship between the professionalism of government and the power of interest groups, an important recent work finds a weaker relationship.[32] Apparently other factors, such as swer is that Bush was whipped by The Lobby. The Lobby had mobilized when the legislature began trying to find ways to replace the revenue that would be lost if local property taxes were reduced. The simple reality was that property taxes couldn't be reduced much unless some other taxes were increased to provide support for the schools. Because the governor had ruled out a state income tax as a source of new revenue, some new business tax was the obvious place for the legislature to turn. When the legislature proposed new business taxes, business lobbies turned up the opposition.

One example of how a proposed tax could be struck by the lobby occurred when the legislature proposed reforming the state's major business tax (the corporate franchise tax) so that it would produce more revenue. Under the existing provisions of the law, the franchise tax applied only to businesses that were organized as corporations. The legislature proposed to broaden the tax by making it apply to business partnerships, as well as corporations. This immediately mobilized lawyers, accountants, doctors, and their interest groups to protest.

Another proposal that mobilized business groups against the effort was a proposal to shift the taxing of businesses to support the schools to the state level. Owners of business property sent their representatives to defeat the proposal. Thus, time and again legislators were faced with lobbyists insisting that someone other than their clients be taxed, if any new taxes were to be approved.

How was the business lobby able to override the interests of Texas homeowners in this battle? Part of the problem was the lack of any significant public outcry. Although Governor Bush had the facts right about increases in local property taxes, he was ahead of the public in demanding a change at this time. Senator Florence of Shapiro, from Plano, explained that "There wasn't that pounding on the door, 'Help me, help me, the sky is falling.'" Ultimately, even the governor was forced to admit that "the time just isn't right."[2] Thus, the lobby won because the public did not appear to be demanding property tax reform. A well-organized minority triumphed over a more apathetic majority once again—which is often the reason that interest group lobbying works as well as it does.★

[1] *Fiscal Size Up: 1998–99 Biennium* (Austin: Legislative Budget Board, 1997), pp. 2–10.

[2] Quoted in Clay Robison, "75th Legislature," *Houston Chronicle* (May 27, 1997), p. 13a.

the nature of the economy or the structure of the government, can override the effect of a professional government, creating strong pressure groups.

The government in Texas has been criticized over time for its lack of professionalism. Although a recent study rated the Texas legislature somewhat professionalized,[33] critics point to the low salary paid members (well below the national average) and the dominance of its presiding officers. In the executive branch, critics cite the many boards and commissions, elected department heads, and the tendency to disperse similar responsibilities among several agencies. All of these attributes make Texas susceptible to interest group activity. A weak legislature depends heavily on interest groups for information not available elsewhere. The many boards and commissions allow interest groups to focus their efforts on a small group of decision makers who often depend on local interests for campaign funds or for the information needed to run their agencies.

Socioeconomic development can affect the strength of interest groups by increasing the number of groups in a state and generating competition among them. Certainly states that depend on a single industry or on a small set of industries usually have powerful interest groups.[34] In a single-industry economy, groups that represent the key industry can argue realistically that what harms their interests harms the state's interests. Of course, the presence of many groups does not necessarily mean that groups are weaker. The overall influence of groups can remain quite strong in a developed, diversified economy.

The dominance of the oil and gas lobby in Texas is connected directly to the pivotal place the oil and gas industry holds in the state's economy. The collapse of oil prices in 1986 proved that when the oil industry does poorly, so does the rest of the state. Diversification of the economy in the years since has broadened the range of groups involved in Texas politics, reducing the dominance of the oil and gas industry. But the presence of more groups has not diminished the overall influence of social interests in the state.

Regulations imposed by the state, including public disclosure laws and lobbying laws, have an impact on interest groups in a state. Although not likely to change the overall power of groups, regulation and laws can force groups to change their tactics. The discussion of interest group regulation that begins on page 89 shows that Texas is not a state with strict regulations. Even in the face of demands for reform, interest groups for the most part have been able to carry out their activities with little interference.

Finally, *the level of campaign costs and the available sources of campaign funds* influence group power. If campaign costs are high and interest groups are the primary source of campaign funds, then groups are likely to be a powerful influence on the policy process. Texas has had some of the most expensive gubernatorial races in the country, and much of the money raised in those races was supplied by interest groups. Not surprisingly, politicians are more responsive to large donors than to other interests in state politics.

Looking at the factors that influence the strength of interest groups, how do scholars classify interest groups in Texas? A study published in 1983 listed Texas as one of twenty-two states with strong interest groups.[35] A study published in 1990 used three basic categories and two transitional categories to describe group power.[36] The basic categories were

- **dominant**—interest groups are an overwhelming and persistent force in policymaking.
- **complementary**—interest group power is balanced by the power of other significant actors on the political stage (political parties or the governor, for example).
- **subordinate**—interest group power consistently is subordinate to that of other players in the political arena.

The study identified nine states with dominant interest groups, eighteen states with complementary group power, and no states in which group power consistently is subordinate to other influences (Table 4.1). The transitional

Table 4.1 States Classified According to the Overall Strength of Interest Groups, 1990

States Where the Overall Strength of Interest Groups Is:

Dominant	Dominant/ Complementary	Complementary	Complementary/ Subordinate	Subordinate
Alabama	Arizona	Colorado	Connecticut	None
Alaska	Arkansas	Illinois	Delaware	
Florida	California	Indiana	Minnesota	
Louisiana	Georgia	Iowa	Rhode Island	
Mississippi	Hawaii	Kansas	Vermont	
New Mexico	Idaho	Maine		
South Carolina	Kentucky	Maryland		
Tennessee	Montana	Massachusetts		
West Virginia	Nebraska	Michigan		
	Nevada	Missouri		
	Ohio	New Jersey		
	Oklahoma	New Hampshire		
	Oregon	New York		
	Texas	North Carolina		
	Utah	North Dakota		
	Virginia	Pennsylvania		
	Washington	South Dakota		
	Wyoming	Wisconsin		

Source: Adapted from Clive S. Thomas and Ronald J. Hrebenar, "Interest Groups in the States," in *Politics in the American States: A Comparative Analysis*, Virginia Gray, Herbert Jacob, and Robert B. Albritton, eds. (New York: HarperCollins, 1990), 147.

categories were dominant/complementary and complementary/subordinate. States in these categories either alternate between two categories or are moving from one to the other. Texas was one of eighteen states in the dominant/complementary category, meaning that interest groups in the state are not completely dominant but are somewhat stronger than other forces.

Although the oil and gas industry no longer dominates the economy, other interests have become more powerful political actors. One team of researchers recently concluded that interest group politics in Texas could be summed up as "the triumph of many interests."[37] That is, Texas is now a state that has many powerful interest groups that play a very strong role compared to politicians and other institutions.

Regulating Interest Groups

Most states regulate the activities of interest groups within their boundaries. That regulation demands a fine balance between controlling special interests and allowing them access to the political process. On the one hand, there is the danger of organized special interests overpowering the political system, preventing it from following the will of the majority—a charge Texas has faced from time to time. There also is the danger of lobbyists undermining the independence and integrity of public officials with gifts and favors. On the other hand, organizing to protect a group's interests is a legitimate and effective form of political activity. In *NAACP* v. *Alabama* (1958), the U.S. Supreme Court recognized that the right of association is protected by the First Amendment to the U.S. Constitution.[38] This means that any effort to regulate or control interest groups still must allow those groups to engage in legitimate forms of participation.

How has Texas addressed the problems of balancing these conflicting interests? Historically, Texas has given lobbyists a fair amount of latitude. Regulation came only in the wake of successive scandals. In the early 1970s, the Texas government was rocked to the highest levels by the Sharpstown banking scandal. That scandal left many of the state's leading politicians tainted by association with the owner of Houston's Sharpstown Bank, Frank Sharp. Sharp had used bribes and sweetheart stock deals (Sharp sold stock in his insurance company at artificially low prices to politicians and arranged profitable sales to third parties) to encourage the passage of legislation that would allow his bank to escape the scrutiny of federal regulators. In the aftermath, the political careers of Governor Preston Smith and Lieutenant Governor Ben Barnes were ruined, and the speaker of the Texas House of Representatives, Gus Mutscher, was indicted and convicted on a bribery charge. The upshot was legislation, passed in 1973, that both defines and regulates lobbying.

According to the **Registration of Lobbyists Act,** *lobbying* is any direct contact with a person or agency in the executive branch, a legislator, a legislator-elect, or a candidate for the legislature. *Lobbyists* are those who spend or receive more than $200 per calendar quarter for direct communication to influence legislation; or those who lobby as a part of their regular employment. *Lobbyists* are required to file monthly reports when the legislature is in session and quarterly reports when the legislature is not in session. These reports must indicate where they got their money and what they spent it on. Lobbyists also must disclose what legislation they are interested in and whether they support or oppose it.[39] Although the legislation was a significant step forward in regulating lobbyists in Texas, it failed to authorize an agency to scrutinize the reports of lobbyists and to enforce the terms of the law. For the most part, the state has relied on the vigilance of the press to ferret out inaccurate reports and to embarrass violators into compliance.

In 1980 the speaker of the Texas house, Billy Clayton, was indicted on charges of bribery and conspiracy. In a much-publicized trial, Clayton was found not guilty. Still the legislature passed new laws tightening up limits on campaign contributions and increasing candidates' reporting requirements. But once again, lawmakers did not create an enforcement agency.

In 1990, Speaker Gib Lewis was indicted for accepting and failing to report a gift from a law firm that did business with the state. Lewis eventually pleaded *nolo contendere* (no contest) to the charges and chose not to seek reelection to the house. In 1991, the legislature passed an ethics bill and proposed a constitutional amendment creating an ethics commission. The voters approved the amendment in the next general election, and the **Texas Ethics Commission** began operations in January 1992. Although the new law tightened up restrictions on lobbyists giving and politicians accepting gifts, it still left loopholes. It did not require legislators to report the sources of their income, and it did not prohibit the use of campaign contributions for living expenses. It did provide civil and criminal penalties for failure to comply with the law. The appointees to the Texas Ethics Commission must come from a list supplied by the legislature, thus giving lawmakers some control over who regulates them.

The legislature has added to the powers and responsibilities of the Ethics Commission in recent sessions. In the 1995 session as a part of reforming judicial campaign finance, judicial candidates and officeholders for multi-county offices were required to file campaign reports with the Ethics Commission (Senate Bill 94). In the 1997 session, the legislature passed a voluntary Code of Fair Campaign Practices and made the Ethics Commission responsible for administering the code (House Bill 35). The legislature also tightened up some of the language in the election code dealing with registration of lobbyists and reporting of campaign finances (House Bill 3207). Some reporting requirements about the activities of lobbyists were transferred from the Secretary of State's Office to the Ethics Commission. Thus, the legislature has made incremental steps to broaden and strengthen the role of the commission.

The Future of Interest Groups in Texas

What change, if any, can be expected in interest group politics in Texas? In the aftermath of the oil and gas collapse in the mid-1980s, the Texas economy has become more diversified. Today the interests of the state are less dependent on the welfare of the oil and gas industry. In turn, the oil and gas industry is less able to identify the interests of the state with its own. Still Texas is not likely to turn its back on oil and gas. The petroleum industry is being transformed from the only interest that counts to one of several powerful interests.

The nature of the party system in Texas also is changing. As party competition grows, the parties may begin to play a larger role in the lives of public officials. There are some signs that this is happening, but party influence still is limited in the state.

Lawmakers in Texas have made some efforts to reduce their reliance on interest groups. By providing themselves with better staff and support services and by improving their expense allowances, lawmakers have taken steps in the right direction. But there still is more to do, starting with limitations on the amount of money PACs can contribute to a political campaign and on the uses that can be made of contributions.

In recent years, scandal has been the direct source of major reforms to regulate interest groups and politicians. The previous section cited three scandals and three reform efforts. But the power of interest groups was evident even in the midst of reform: special interests successfully limited enforcement mechanisms that might have made the legislation more effective.

Although interest groups probably will continue to be a powerful force in Texas in the future, the legal, institutional, and economic changes facing the state may help bring that power into balance with other forces. Today, however, interest groups are still among the most influential forces in Texas politics.

Notes

1. Mike Ward and Stuart Eskenazi, *Austin American-Statesman* (April 20, 1997), p. A1.
2. Stuart Eskenazi and Mike Ward, "Lobbyists Kept a Focus on the Legislators, Too," *Austin American-Statesman* (August 3, 1997), p. A10.
3. Richard West, "Inside The Lobby," in *Texas Monthly Political Reader,* 3d ed., David F. Prindle, ed. (Austin: Texas Monthly Press, 1985), 63–68.
4. David B. Truman, *The Governmental Process,* 2d ed. (New York: Alfred A. Knopf, 1971), 33.
5. L. Harmon Zeigler, "Interest Groups in the States," in *Politics in the American States: A Comparative Analysis,* 4th ed., Virginia Gray, Herbert Jacob, and Kenneth N. Vines, eds. (Boston: Little, Brown, 1983), 99.
6. Clive S. Thomas and Ronald J. Hrebenar, "Changes in the Numbers and Types of Interest Groups and Lobbies Active in the States," in *State Government: CQ's Guide to Current Issues and Activities: 1989–1990,* Thad L. Beyle, ed. (Washington, DC: Congressional Quarterly Press, 1989), 57–61.
7. William Crotty, *American Parties in Decline,* 2d ed. (Glenview, IL: Scott, Foresman, 1984), 73.
8. Alan Rosenthal, *The Third House: Lobbyists and Lobbying in the States* (Washington, DC: Congressional Quarterly Press, 1993), 95–102.
9. Quoted in Rosenthal, *Third House,* 103.
10. Thomas and Hrebenar, "Interest Groups in the States," 148.
11. Rosenthal, *Third House,* 25.
12. Texas Ethics Commission, "Registered Lobbyists, Their Employers and Clients of Employers." List provided on the web site of the Texas Ethics Commission. 1/14/98 (**http://www.ethics.state.tx.us**).
13. Rosenthal, *Third House,* 33 and 44.
14. Texas Ethics Commission, "Registered Lobbyists, Their Employers and Clients of Employers." List provided by the Texas Ethics Commission. November 23, 1992, 109.
15. Rosenthal, *Third House,* 34.
16. Rosenthal, *Third House,* 22–23.
17. Rosenthal, *Third House,* 134.
18. Candace Romig, "Placing Limits on Political Action Committees," in *State Government: CQ's Guide to Current Issues and Activities: 1985–1986,* Thad Beyle, ed. (Washington, DC: Congressional Quarterly Press, 1985), 55–60. See especially the chart on pp. 58–59.

19. Rosenthal, *Third House,* 142.
20. Quoted in Rosenthal, *Third House,* 139.
21. Rosenthal, *Third House,* 139–140.
22. Rosenthal, *Third House,* 159.
23. Rosenthal, *Third House,* 160.
24. Adapted from Keith E. Hamm and Charles W. Wiggins, "Texas: The Transformation from Personal to Informational Lobbying," in *Interest Group Politics in the Southern States,* Ronald J. Hrebenar and Clive S. Thomas, eds. (Tuscaloosa: University of Alabama Press, 1992), 160–161.
25. Rosenthal, *Third House,* 142.
26. Ronald J. Hrebenar, "Change, Transition, and Growth in Southern Interest Group Politics," in *Interest Group Politics in the Southern States,* Ronald J. Hrebenar and Clive S. Thomas, eds. (Tuscaloosa: University of Alabama Press, 1992), 321–352. See especially the chart on pp. 330–335.
27. *Edgewood* v. *Kirby* was the original name of the case in which the Edgewood School District sued William Kirby, the commissioner of education. The Texas Supreme Court case is cited as *William Kirby et al.* v. *Edgewood Independent School District et al.,* 777 S.W.3d 391 (1989).
28. Sarah McCally Morehouse, *State Politics, Parties and Policy* (New York: Holt, Rinehart & Winston, 1981), 101–140; and L. Harmon Zeigler, "Interest Groups in the States," in *Politics in the American States: A Comparative Analysis,* Virginia Gray, Herbert Jacob, and Kenneth N. Vines, eds. (Boston: Little, Brown, 1983), 97–129.
29. Thomas and Hrebenar, "Interest Groups in the States," 123–158.
30. Morehouse, *State Politics,* 132–133; and Zeigler, "Interest Groups in the States," 120–121.
31. John G. Grumm, "The Effects of Legislative Structure on Legislative Performance," in *State and Urban Politics,* Richard I. Hofferbert and Ira Sharkansky, eds. (Boston: Little, Brown, 1971), 307–322.
32. Thomas and Hrebenar, "Interest Groups in the States," 138.
33. Karl T. Kurtz, "The Changing State Legislatures (Lobbyists Beware)," in *Leveraging State Government Relations,* Wesley Pedersen, ed. (Washington, DC: Public Affairs Council, 1990), 23–32.
34. Morehouse, *State Politics;* and Zeigler, "Interest Groups in the States," 97–131.
35. Zeigler, "Interest Groups in the States," 97–131. See especially the table on p. 116.
36. Thomas and Hrebenar, "Interest Groups in the States," 123–158.
37. Hamm and Wiggins, "Texas," 174.
38. *NAACP* v. *Alabama ex rel. Patterson,* 357 U.S. 449 (1958).
39. Texas Government Code, Chap. 305. See especially Sec. 3–6.

5 Elections, Campaigns, and Voting in Texas

Chapter Outline

In 1992, when Lena Guerrero was campaigning for election to the powerful Texas Railroad Commission (to which she had been appointed by Governor Richards), all seemed to be going well until her Republican opponent exposed some errors in her official résumé. It seems Guerrero was neither an honors graduate of the University of Texas nor a member of Phi Beta Kappa. The media had a field day with Guerrero, her credibility was damaged, and her campaign stalled. She was forced to resign from the commission while she continued to campaign for election to that powerful board. In November, she lost to Barry Williamson.

In 1998, Barry Williamson was running for the office of Attorney General against former Supreme Court Justice Cornyn, when he was suddenly faced with the charge of inflating his résumé. Cornyn alleged that Williamson's claim that he had represented hundreds of clients and tried cases in federal and state courts in Texas was untrue. Cornyn's allegation was backed by an analysis of court records by the *Dallas Morning News.* Mr. Williamson claimed this his résumé was accurate, but the voters nominated Mr. Cornyn to run for attorney general.[1]

Obviously elections in Texas are not always "nice." Politicians in Texas, like politicians in other states, are willing to use negative campaigning when they think it is necessary. And bitter campaigns that are more about "slinging mud" than confronting the issues are common.

Of course the real importance of elections in Texas is derived from the functions they perform in a democratic society. Through the electoral process, citizens choose the people who run the government and hold those people accountable for what they do in office. So understanding elections and how citizens participate in them is helpful. This chapter answers several questions about elections and voting in Texas:

- How is the right to vote determined and regulated?
- What types of elections are held in Texas and how are they administered?
- How are political campaigns organized, carried out, and financed?
- What influences how the people in Texas vote?

Change in the Electoral Process

The forces of change in Texas elections have been both external and internal. It was the institutions of the national government—the federal courts and Congress—that forced an end to discriminatory policies about voting in Texas. And it was a national trend toward hiring political consultants that has altered the nature of campaigning for statewide office in Texas. One internal source of change—growing competition between the parties—saw the emphasis of campaigning shift from the primary elections to the general elections. Finally, the mass media have forced statewide candidates to alter the way they campaign. This chapter explores these changes and the ways they have reshaped electoral politics in Texas.

Suffrage: The Right to Vote

Participation in elections is regulated by national and state laws. The U.S. Constitution originally left the specifics of regulating **suffrage** to the states. That changed in 1870, with the ratification of the Fifteenth Amendment to the national constitution. The amendment prohibits the states and the national government from denying an individual the right to vote on the basis of race, color, or previous slave status. Although it does not address voting specifically, the equal protection clause of the Fourteenth Amendment also has had an impact on the types of regulations that states can impose on their citizens.

A History of Suffrage in Texas

The obstacles that Texas placed between its citizens and the right to vote were removed slowly over a fairly long period. Texas, like other southern states, used property qualifications, residence requirements, poll taxes, white primaries, and stringent registration criteria to limit suffrage. The removal of those obstacles was not voluntary; the state eliminated them when federal legislation or a federal court order required it to.

The constitution in Texas originally allowed a **property qualification** for voting—the requirement that an individual must own property (usually land) to vote. The requirement was used in this country as far back as the 1700s. Although states began eliminating the property restriction in the late nineteenth century, and most had eliminated it by the early twentieth century, many states (including Texas) continued to exclude non–property holders from local bond elections. Because bond elections authorized cities or counties to borrow money by selling bonds, debt that would be paid off by taxes on property, many thought it was reasonable to restrict participation in those elections to property owners. The practice continued until the U.S. Supreme Court found it unconstitutional in 1975.[2]

Many states also limited the right to vote with a **residence requirement** in the state for a stipulated period as a condition for voting. Under the Texas Constitution, individuals became eligible to vote only after they had lived in the state for at least a year and in their county of residence for at least six months. In 1972 the U.S. Supreme Court ruled that lengthy residence requirements were unconstitutional, and the restrictions were eliminated in Texas.[3] Now Texans can register to vote without a waiting period except for the thirty days before an election, when the books are closed so that final lists of voters can be prepared for the upcoming balloting.

In 1902 Texas adopted the **poll tax** as another obstacle to voting.[4] This tax, which had to be paid before an individual could register to vote, tended to exclude low-income people from voting: they simply could not afford to pay. Although the tax was not limited to racial minorities, it effectively excluded racial and ethnic minorities because many were poor. When the adoption of the Twenty-fourth Amendment to the U.S. Constitution in 1964 and a U.S. Supreme Court decision in 1966[5] made the poll tax unconstitutional, Texas removed it from its constitution.

The **white primary** was a restriction designed specifically to deprive African Americans of the opportunity to vote in the only meaningful elections in Texas—the Democratic party primaries—by stipulating that only whites could vote in primary elections. Remember that until the late 1970s, the Democratic primaries were the only elections in which real choices were made in Texas because the state had emerged from Reconstruction as a one-party system (see Chapter 3). In 1944, in *Smith* v. *Allwright,* the U.S. Supreme Court found the white primary to be unconstitutional, and Texas, like other southern states, was forced to give it up.[6]

Registration requirements also limited the right to vote in Texas. Research indicates that the more difficult it is to register in a state, the lower the percentage of eligible voters registered at election time.[7] Until the 1970s, Texas had a restrictive voter registration system that required potential voters to register far in advance of elections and to reregister annually. In 1971 a federal court found annual registration to be a violation of the Fourteenth Amendment's equal protection clause.[8]

The administration of Texas elections also must conform to the requirements of the U.S. **Voting Rights Act** Extension of 1975. That law was designed to protect the voting rights of minorities. It requires that ballots in Texas be printed in both English and Spanish to accommodate the state's Hispanic voters. In addition, the law requires the state and its political subdivisions to clear any proposed changes in electoral procedures with the U.S. attorney general's office or a federal court, to make sure that the changes would not discriminate against minority voters.

By the mid-1970s, universal adult suffrage had become the norm in Texas and in other southern states. Although some would argue that voting, particularly the registration process, could be made easier, the most serious obstacles have been removed.

Voter Registration Today

Today in Texas an individual is qualified to vote if he or she[9]

- is at least eighteen years of age.
- is a U.S. citizen.
- has not been determined mentally incompetent by a final judgment of a court.
- has not been convicted of a felony.
- is a resident of the state.

Before they can participate in elections, however, individuals must demonstrate that they meet these qualifications by registering to vote. The state requires registration to prevent those who are not eligible from voting and to prevent people from voting more than once. Those who complete the process are given a voter registration certificate as proof of their eligibility.

The **Texas Election Code,** a compilation of constitutional and statutory rules governing voting and elections, makes local county registrars responsible for registering voters. The county tax assessor–collector is the registrar of voters in most counties, but state law permits the transfer of those responsibilities to the county clerk or to a specially created office of county elections administration. Only a few of the larger counties, among them Dallas and Harris counties, actually have established an office of county elections administration. The state helps counties with the cost of voter registration. The amount paid annually to each county is based on the number of new registrations or renewal certificates it processes.

Registering to vote is now relatively easy in Texas. An individual may simply go to the appropriate county office and fill out an application, but registering in person is not required. An application can be mailed in, or a designated agent (a spouse, parent, or child, for example) can file an application.[10] The law also allows deputy volunteer registrars to register people at shopping malls or other public places.[11] As a result of the national Motor Voter law, one can also register when applying for or renewing a driver's license.

The registrar issues a voter registration certificate to all applicants who meet the requirements of the state law. The initial certificate is valid from the date of issue until January 1 of the following even-numbered year. At the end of that period, renewal certificates that are valid for two years are mailed to voters.[12]

A person's registration is canceled when he or she dies, has been declared mentally incompetent, has moved outside the county, has applied for registration in another county or state, or is on the list of those whose renewal certificates could not be delivered. Notice of cancellation must be sent to the registrant, except in the case of death. Procedures for reinstatement are in place if a cancellation was in error.[13]

Types of Elections

The state of Texas holds several different types of elections: primary elections, general elections, special elections, and referenda. Voters make different choices in each type of election.

Primary Elections

Primary elections are nominating elections. They were introduced in Texas in 1905 by the **Terrell Act,** a law that required most political parties to nominate candidates by primary. Texas held its first primary election in 1906. The Texas Election Code now requires any party whose candidate for governor polled at least 20 percent of the vote in the last gubernatorial election to nominate its candidates for county, state, and congressional offices by primary.

To get their names listed on the primary ballot, candidates file an application with either a filing fee or a petition. The amount of the filing fee depends on the level of the office. It ranges from $600 for commissioner of a county with less than 200,000 population, to $3,000 for governor and $4,000 for U.S. senator. The number of signatures required when a petition substitutes for the filing fee also varies with the level of the office. For a statewide office, 5,000 signatures are needed. For a district, county, or precinct office, the petition must have the lesser of 500 signatures or 2 percent of the total vote cast for all candidates in the most recent gubernatorial election.[14]

The **first primary,** which had previously been held in May, is now held the second Tuesday in March of even-numbered years, so that in presidential election years the Texas primary coincides with Super Tuesday. By moving the primary, legislators hoped that Texas and the other Super Tuesday states would have more influence on the choice of presidential candidates.

To win a party's nomination, a candidate must receive over 50 percent of the votes cast in the primary. If no candidate receives a majority in the first primary, the top two vote-getters compete in a **runoff primary.** Runoff primaries are held the second Tuesday in April.

General Elections

In **general elections,** voters choose the people who will hold public office. These elections are held the first Tuesday after the first Monday in November of the year in which the nominating primaries are held. A constitutional amendment in 1972 changed the schedule of general elections in Texas. Today elections for major state offices (governor, lieutenant governor, comptroller of public accounts, treasurer, attorney general, commissioner of agriculture, and commissioner of the General Land Office) are scheduled for nonpresidential election years. The legislators who drafted the amendment were afraid that if state elections were held the same year as presidential elections, the outcome of the state elections (especially the governor's race) would be influenced by the popularity of the presidential candidates—the **presidential coattail effect.** For example, a popular Republican presidential candidate might swing a state election to the Republican gubernatorial candidate.

In general elections, ballots list the names of those who have been nominated by one of the major political parties or who have filed a petition with the appropriate number of signatures. Third parties must file petitions with enough signatures to equal 1 percent of the total vote in the most recent gubernatorial election. To win an office in a general election, a candidate must receive more votes than any other candidate for the office—a plurality, not a majority.

Special Elections

Special elections are called by the governor to fill public offices that have been vacated by death or resignation. They differ from general elections in that no primary election (or other nominating process) precedes a special election. Candidates have their names placed on the ballot by filing the appropriate papers with the secretary of state and paying a filing fee. Candidates from both parties, as well as any independents who choose to run, compete in the same election. To win a special election, a candidate must receive a majority of the votes cast. If no candidate receives a majority in the first balloting, a runoff election is held between the top two vote-getters, regardless of their party affiliation. The winner of the runoff is elected to the office.

Referenda

The final type of election in Texas, the **referendum,** allows the voters themselves to decide policy questions. Voters simply cast yes or no votes on specific policy proposals. Referendum questions may be placed on the ballot during general elections. Local governments in Texas use referenda primarily to approve bond issues. The state government uses referenda only to ratify constitutional amendments. After the legislature proposes a constitutional amendment, it is submitted to the voters for ratification at the next general election. A majority of those participating in a referendum must vote in favor of an amendment to ratify it. Remember that the Texas Constitution is very detailed (see Chapter 2). Updating it by amendment, then, occurs frequently. In fact, several amendments are presented for ratification in most Texas general elections.

Administering Elections

Before an election can be held, ballots must be printed, people to work at the polls need to be recruited, and the voting equipment has to be set-up. The responsibility for conducting general elections, special elections, and referenda is delegated to county governments. Primaries, because they are used to nominate the parties' candidates, are conducted by party officials—although the county provides the voting equipment and the state pays the expenses of administering primaries.[15]

The **secretary of state,** the chief election officer for the state, oversees the conduct of elections by the local authorities. That office is responsible for the design and content of the ballots, the design of ballot boxes and voting booths, and standards for alternative voting systems (voting machines or punch card systems, for example). The secretary of state also is authorized to take whatever action is necessary to protect the voting rights of the citizens.

In 1997, Alberto Gonzales became the second Hispanic to be appointed as secretary of state by Governor Bush.

Texas counties carry the major burden of administering elections. The county commissioners subdivide the county into voting precincts, each with between 100 and 2,000 registered voters.[16] In March or April of odd-numbered years, the county commissioners must reexamine the precincts to be sure that they meet state standards and to adjust boundaries or create new precincts if necessary. The commissioners also choose the voting equipment: punch-ballot machines, pull-lever machines, or even paper ballots.

On election days the balloting in each precinct is supervised by election judges. The county commissioners appoint election judges for general elections from a list supplied by the county clerk. The county chair of each party chooses election judges for primary elections, with the approval of the county executive committee. In each precinct the election judge appoints at least two clerks to help administer the election.

The Texas Election Code specifies how ballots are laid out. For general elections, ballots are arranged in columns by party. The first column lists the offices for which elections are being held; the rest of the columns list each party's candidates for those offices. The order of the party columns is determined by the number of votes each party's candidate received statewide in the most recent gubernatorial election. The party whose gubernatorial candidate received the most votes is listed just to the right of the offices column; the other parties are added to the right in descending order of gubernatorial vote. General election ballots also must provide a procedure that can be used to vote a **straight ticket**—that is, to vote for all of a party's candidates for office. In nonpartisan elections or party primaries, ballots list the title of each office followed by a list of the candidates seeking that office. Ballots also must provide a way for voters to cast a write-in vote.

The way in which general election ballots in Texas are laid out helps some candidates and hinders others. The ballot encourages party loyalty by making straight-ticket voting easy (with a single mark on a paper ballot, a single punch on a punch card, or a single pull on a lever). The ballot also favors the party that tends to be most successful in gubernatorial elections by placing its candidates' names in the column next to the list of offices. Remember that these rules are written by legislators who are elected to office. The fact that they write rules to help their own parties should not be a surprise.

Although state law specifies the days on which elections in Texas should be held, in recent years lawmakers eliminated the requirement that all voters cast their ballots on a single day. In 1991 the legislature authorized a period of **early voting** before each election day. Before that law passed, only those who had a reason recognized by state law (being out of the county on election day, a disability, advanced age, religious restrictions, confinement in jail, or helping to administer the election) could vote early, by what was called *absentee voting.* Now early voting is available to everyone for whatever reason. Early voting is allowed from the twentieth day through the fourth day before a scheduled election. For a runoff election, early voting begins the tenth day before the election and continues through the fourth day.[17] Voters in Texas are becoming accustomed to the new procedure. In the 1992 presidential election, about 24 percent of the ballots cast were cast during the early voting period. In the 1994 election, almost 30 percent of the ballots for statewide offices were cast during early voting, and, in 1996, 32 percent chose this method.[18]

Campaigns

To get elected to public office, most candidates have to persuade people to vote for them. That is called **campaigning.** The nature of a political campaign is a function of the office. Campaigns for statewide office usually are more complex and costly than are campaigns for local office.

Campaigning for Statewide Office

Campaign organization. A run for statewide offices—governor, U.S. senator, or one of the cabinet-level offices in Texas—demands a well-organized campaign. In states with strong political parties, candidates can draw on the organizational resources of their party, supplementing those resources with their own. Where political parties are weak, candidates must rely on their own organizations. In Texas, candidates' personal organizations traditionally have dominated political campaigns. That is changing. With competition between the parties in races for state and local offices, the political parties have had to become more involved in campaigning. Old habits die hard, however. Most candidates still rely heavily on their own personal organizations and look to the party to play only a supporting role in the campaign.

Several steps are involved in campaigning. First, candidates must identify those citizens who will vote for them and where they are located. Second, campaign funds must be raised. Third, candidates must get their message out to the voters, especially those they have identified as likely supporters. Finally, those supporters have to be motivated to go to the polls and vote. Candidates rely on all kinds of people to carry out these tasks.

All campaign organizations rely on volunteers to put up signs, send out bulk mailings, knock on doors, and staff phone banks. Better-financed campaign organizations supplement volunteer workers with paid workers.

In recent years consultants have become a standard part of the campaign organizations of candidates for statewide offices in Texas. In fact a major statewide campaign might hire eight to ten **political consultants**[19] (see box on two leading Texas consultants).

One valuable expert is the public opinion pollster. Unlike Gallup, Harris, and Roper, these political pollsters conduct private polls and report the results only to the candidate who has hired them. Private polls are necessary for at least two reasons. First, candidates need more frequent measurements of public opinion than may be available from public polls. Second, and more important, candidates need information to help them formulate their campaign strategy. Political pollsters know the questions to ask, know which segments of the population are responding favorably to the candidate, and know which issue positions are producing positive or negative responses. In other words, pollsters help candidates identify their target constituency and the campaign issues that can help them win votes from that constituency.

Several organizations provide political-polling services to candidates in Texas. W. Lance Tarrance and Associates, a Houston-based organization, has worked with Republican candidates in Texas for many years. In 1978 the agency worked on Senator John Tower's reelection campaign and Bill Clements's successful gubernatorial campaign; in 1980 it worked on John Connally's presidential campaign.[20] Polling for Ann Richards's campaign in 1990 was done by Harrison Hickman, who was hired in 1988, just after Richards made a successful speech to the Democratic National Convention, to determine how Texans would respond to the idea of a woman governor.[21]

Media experts also are common in Texas campaign organizations. The first decision here is whether to use someone from the state or region or a national agency. Several national firms, among them Robert Goodman and Robert Squier, have played major roles in Texas campaigns. Robert Goodman, based in Maryland, shaped the media campaign for John Tower in 1978. Robert Squier, based in Washington, D.C., was Ann Richards's media consultant in 1990. On his advice, Richards saved most of her media money until the last three weeks before the primary and then the general election. Although this strategy allowed her opponents to build up big leads during the campaign, it delivered her message at a saturation level in the weeks just before the elections.[22] Late in the battle against the Republican nominee, Clayton Williams, Richards ran an attack ad that Squier had created. It showed a newspaper headline with the words "Lawsuits Allege Williams a Deadbeat." The ad did not show the last part of the headline: "Richards

Discloses." When Williams's people complained that the ad was misleading, Squier apologized. But Richards won the election.[23]

Another common political consultant in Texas is the direct mail specialist. These experts prepare mailing lists that target contributors and voters. Because the direct mail strategy assumes that mailings to thousands will produce responses from hundreds, mass mailings are essential. The strategy works in a state the size of Texas; it is much less effective in smaller states.

John Tower used direct mail successfully to raise funds for his campaign in 1978. Other candidates have also found it to be a good way of raising money. In the 1998 primary election to nominate a Republican candidate for attorney general, Barry Williamson used direct mail in the first primary to introduce negative material against his opponents (John Cornyn and Tom Pauken), and it helped him make it into the runoff primary. But, as noted at the beginning of this chapter, Williamson lost the nomination to Cornyn.[24]

Campaign tactics. Although every campaign is unique, Texas campaigns tend to use several of the same tactics. One tried-and-true tactic is **ideological labeling.** Texas is a conservative state, and candidates spend a lot of time trying to pin a conservative label on themselves and a liberal label on their opponents. As Texas moves into an era of two-party politics, Republicans increasingly are trying to preempt the conservative label for themselves and to pin the liberal label on the Democrats. And Democrats are spending a lot of time claiming to be moderate or conservative.

Negative campaigning is another tactic that has been evident in recent campaigns in Texas. This broad term encompasses a variety of activities, including personal attacks on opponents to undermine voters' confidence in them. By the end of the 1990 gubernatorial runoff campaign, even national newspapers—among them the *Washington Post* and the *New York Times*—were lamenting the level of negative campaigning in Texas.[25] The battle between Ann Richards and Clayton Williams in the general election that year was no kinder than the primary campaign. Williams raised the substance abuse question again, and Richards raised questions about his business practices. Although many Texans claim to dislike negative campaigning, the perception of candidates and their political consultants seems to be that it works, and so they use it. As the box in this chapter on political consultants makes clear, the 1994 campaign between Richards and Bush for the governorship was managed by two of the acknowledged experts on negative campaigning: George Shipley (for Richards) and Karl Rove (for Bush). Although the 1994 campaign turned less on personal attacks than the 1990 campaign, each side hammered away at undermining public confidence in their opponent. Bush succeeded in unseating one of the most popular governors in modern times.

The **political outsider tactic** is also common in Texas campaigns. Responding to the widespread perception in Texas that government and politicians are worthless or corrupt, candidates often point out with pride that they are not politicians. They claim that a business background is better than a political background because businesspeople know how to manage efficiently

The Changing Face of Texas Politics

Political Consultants: The Professionalization of Campaign Politics

Politics in Texas and other states is no longer a place for amateurs with good political instincts.[1] Today every major campaign is guided by consultants who are hired to perform a variety of campaign-related tasks, among them political polling, direct mailing, and creating media campaigns. In fact there are consultants for almost every political task. During the 1980s and 1990s, each political party has developed its own corps of advisers. Here the focus is on two of the major consultants: George Shipley, who works for the Democrats, and Karl Rove, who works for the Republicans.

George Shipley's client list sounds like a who's who of Democratic politics in Texas. He worked for Ann Richards in 1990 and 1994. In 1994 he also worked on Dan Morales's reelection campaign for attorney general and Richard Fisher's bid for the U.S. Senate. In addition former Dallas mayor Annette Strauss and former San Antonio mayor Henry Cisneros have used his services. He continued to work closely with Morales, consulting in 1997 and 1998 on the state's lawsuit against the tobacco companies. He continues to advise a number of other Democratic candidates.

Shipley is a native Texan; he grew up in the River Oaks section of Houston. His consulting firm is based in Austin, where he earned his Ph.D. in political science from the University of Texas. In addition to his consulting services, he teaches graduate students at UT's LBJ School of Public Affairs.

Although Shipley and his associates provide polling services and general advice on campaign strategy, he has become known for his skill in "opposition research"—digging up dirt on the opposition. In fact that skill has earned him the nickname "Dr. Dirt." In one of the most controversial moves of his career, Shipley started a rumor late in the 1990 gubernatorial campaign that Republican Clayton Williams was about to be indicted on a criminal charge. The story was not true, and Shipley has acknowledged that he knew it was not true at the time. But it was an effective campaign tactic. Shipley makes no apology for his hard-hitting tactics: "I personally believe that big-league politics in America today is a contact sport."[2] Shipley is so good at what he does that supposedly some candidates hire him so that he will not use his talents against them.[3]

Karl Rove is widely regarded as Shipley's counterpart on the Republican side. Like Shipley, Rove does more than dig for dirt. He is a direct mail specialist: he develops mailing lists that help candidates target their appeals for campaign contributions and their campaign literature to a receptive audience.

while politicians only know how to spend money on programs. This tactic worked for Governor Clements in his 1978 and 1986 races and almost worked for Clayton Williams in his 1990 race against Ann Richards. It was the central strategy of George Bush's campaign against Ann Richards in 1994. Bush stressed his business achievements and said in a television debate that he was proud of the fact that he had never held elective office. Despite Richards's

Rove's client list includes many of the leading Republican politicians in the state. He worked for Bill Clements, the first Republican to be elected governor since the Civil War. He helped Rick Perry unseat Jim Hightower in the commissioner of agriculture race in 1990. Many believe that Rove played a part in getting the FBI to launch an investigation into Hightower's office that resulted in the conviction of three of Hightower's aides. In 1994 Rove helped George W. Bush become the second Republican governor of Texas in the post–Civil War period. In addition he has worked for state supreme court justice Nathan Hecht, Railroad Commissioner Carole Rylander, and U.S. Senator Kay Bailey Hutchison. He has remained a close adviser to Bush throughout his governorship, and advised him on his re-election campaign in 1998.

Shipley is known for his flamboyance; Rove, for his attention to detail. Perry referred to Rove as a "genius with a gift for meticulous thought."[4] When Hutchison was indicted for destroying evidence that she had used her office for political purposes, Rove started a counterattack on the record-keeping practices of Governor Richards, whose office telephone records had been shredded. And it was Rove who uncovered inaccuracies in Railroad Commissioner Lena Guerrero's academic credentials during the 1992 election. Guerrero had claimed to be an honor graduate of the University of Texas. In fact she had not even completed her degree. She lost the election.

What effect have political consultants had on Texas politics? Certainly consultants have elevated the skill level in campaigns. Because they are professionals who do political battle from year to year, they have knowledge and experience that candidates are not likely to have. Consultants help candidates identify the issues that matter to voters and then help them hone a message that makes the best use of those issues.

But consultants also have helped "institutionalize" nasty campaigns. Before consultants, scandal could be used only if someone in a campaign organization knew about a problem or someone was motivated to supply damaging information to the organization. Now digging for dirt is an organized process, with political consultants offering a staff that can be put to work researching the opposition's record. They may add to the misinformation associated with a campaign, but they are good at knowing what is on the mind of the people and helping the candidates to get to those issues. To some, it would seem more pleasant to do without the dirt which they dig and encourage their candidates to dispense with mud-slinging campaigns. ★

[1]For a general discussion of political consultants, see Larry Sabato, *The Rise of Political Consultants* (New York: Basic Books, 1981).

[2]Quoted in Wayne Slater, "Digging Up Dirt," *Dallas Morning News,* July 25, 1994, 1A.

[3]Ibid.

[4]Ibid.

[5]Steve Blow, "Ann, George: Be Honest, Civil and Real, Please," *Dallas Morning News,* September 4, 1994, 37A.

efforts to discredit his business achievements, the outsider strategy held up for Bush.

In 1998, a new campaign tactic appeared among the Republican candidates. It might be called "hanging on to the governor's coattails." Because of Governor Bush's very strong standing in the polls, a number of Republican candidates tried to convey the message during the Republican primaries that he or she was the candidate favored by the governor. Although the governor endorsed no one, he could not avoid candidates clinging to his coattails.

Campaign finance. The costs of campaigning statewide for public office are high in Texas. The 1990 gubernatorial race set a record: the two candidates spent over $30 million.[26] The Bush and Richards campaigns spent a little less in 1994 on their quest for the governorship. By the time of the election, Richards had spent $14.5 million and Bush had spent $10.9 million.[27] Figure 5.1 compares the cost of campaigning for governor in the fifteen most populous states. That comparison for the most recent gubernatorial elections held before 1993 shows that Texas had the highest total expenditures and the second highest expenditures by the winner of the election. Figure 5.2 looks at the costs of campaigning from another perspective: what each vote costs. Texas had the highest cost per vote—$13.56—of the fifteen most populous states.

Why is campaigning so expensive in Texas? Size is partly to blame. Texas is the second largest state in population and the second largest state in geographic size. Candidates for statewide office, then, have a lot of people to reach and a lot of territory to cover.

Television is the vehicle most candidates use to reach those people and cover that territory, and it is a major campaign cost. Early in the 1990 race, Bob Squier advised Ann Richards's organization that television ads for the primary alone would cost between $700,000 and $800,000.[28] Clayton Williams spent just under $3 million on television in a single month, September 1990.[29]

Actually six counties (Harris, Dallas, Bexar, Tarrant, El Paso, and Travis) contain about half of the state's population, and a political advertisement in the three largest cities in Texas—Houston (Harris County), Dallas (Dallas County), and San Antonio (Bexar County)—reaches nearly 60 percent of the state's residents. But targeting the largest cities usually is not enough to win a statewide campaign. The size and diversity of the state force candidates to vary their techniques. One political consultant estimates that there are nineteen different media markets in Texas reaching people of all different cultures. This means that a candidate might have to advertise in Spanish in the Rio Grande Valley to supplement advertising in the largest cities.[30]

Political consultants also add to the expense of campaigns. Bob Squier's firm charges each client a $70,000 fee and then collects 15 percent of the cost of media time purchased for the campaign. In a hard-fought race, media purchases can run several millions of dollars, and Squier's fee might run as much as $1 million.[31] Because major campaigns use a number of consultants, the costs mount up.

Also to blame for the high cost of campaigning in Texas is the pattern of spending set in past campaigns. Because candidates in the past have been able to raise and spend such large amounts of money, future candidates are likely to think in comparable terms. This pattern will not be broken unless some sort of state regulation puts a stop to it.

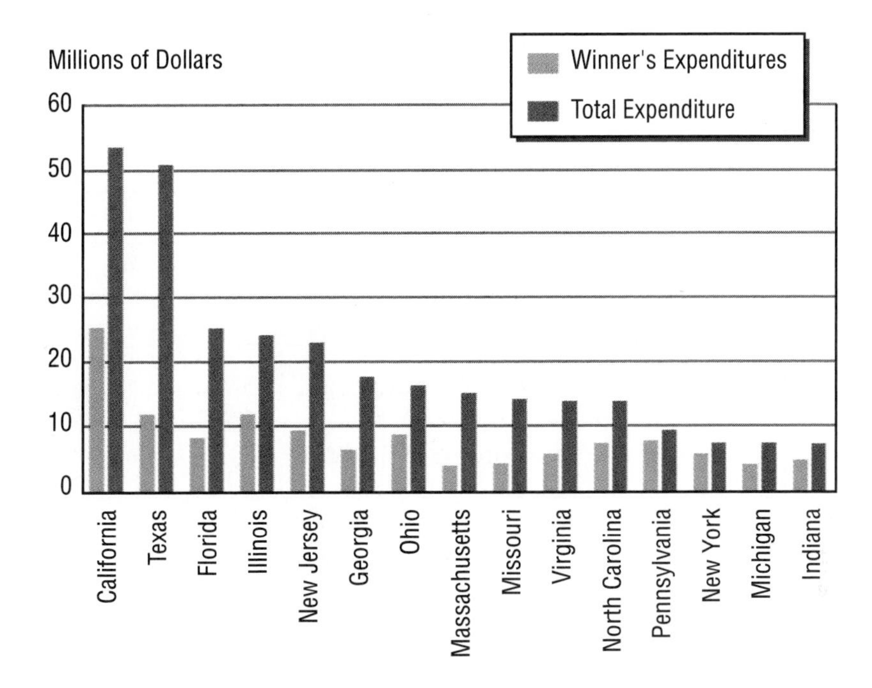

FIGURE 5.1 Costs of Campaigning for Governor in Most Recent Gubernatorial Election Before 1993, 15 Most Populous States
Source: Council of State Governments, Book of the States, *1994–95 (Lexington, KY: 1994), 39.*

Where do candidates get all this money? There are several sources of campaign funds. Some candidates support their own campaigns. Bill Clements provided much of the money for his races for governor (especially his first campaign, in 1978); and Clayton Williams did the same thing when he ran for governor in 1990. Congressman Jack Fields, a Republican candidate in 1993 for the U.S. Senate seat vacated by Lloyd Bentsen, promised to put up a million dollars of his own money to jump-start fundraising for the campaign.[32]

Because most candidates cannot afford to finance a campaign out of their own pockets, large individual contributors are another important source of campaign funds. Early in the 1990 governor's race, Ann Richards spent weeks going from law office to law office and from one corporate office to another in Houston, Dallas, San Antonio, El Paso, and other major cities, soliciting contributions for her campaign.[33]

PACs organized by interest groups or by private corporations are an increasingly important source of campaign funds. In fact, corporate PACs have been big players in Texas campaigns since the 1970s.[34] Ann Richards's 1990 campaign was boosted at its critical stages—early in the campaign and again at the beginning of the runoff campaign—by money from a prochoice feminist PAC called EMILY's List.[35] (*EMILY* is an acronym for "early money

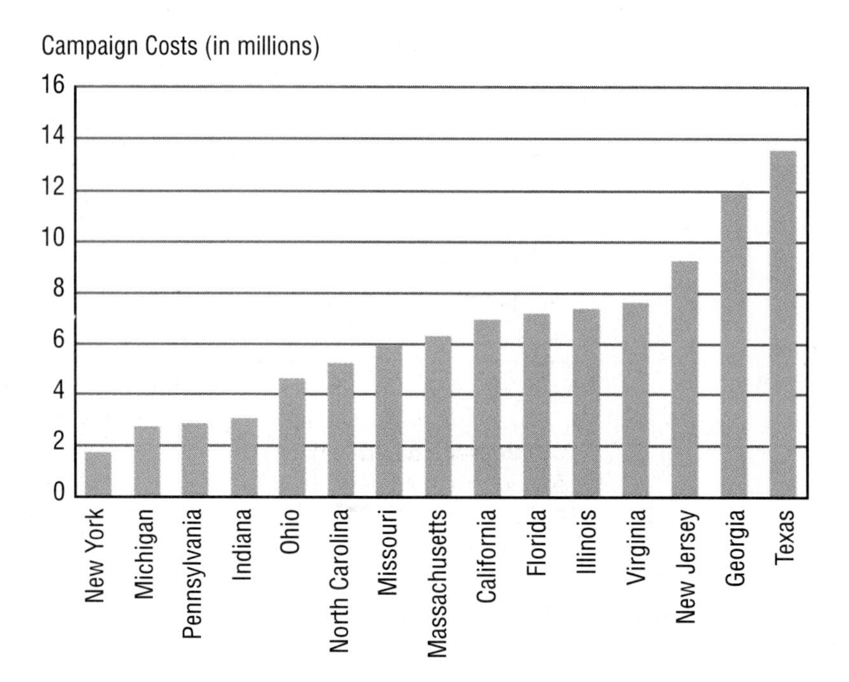

FIGURE 5.2 Cost Per Vote in Most Recent Gubernatorial Election Before 1993, Fifteen Most Populous States
Source: Council of State Governments, Book of the States, *1994–95 (Lexington, KY: 1994), 39.*

is like yeast"; it makes the "dough" rise.) Representative Pete Laney, who became speaker of the Texas house in 1992, received significant contributions from PACs. An investigation by the *Dallas Morning News* revealed that over a two-year period, 88 percent of the contributions to Laney's officeholder account (used to supplement state funds in defraying office expenses) came from PACs.[36] In light of the fact that Laney chaired the House State Affairs Committee, the legislative committee that considers utility regulations, it is noteworthy that PACs representing electric, gas, and telephone utility interests were big contributors.

Candidates also may receive funds from their national or state political party organization and from many small contributors. But the point here is that the high cost of running a statewide campaign puts a premium on big contributors, and candidates must focus much of their fundraising activities on those contributors.

Campaigning for Local or Legislative Office

The key tasks in a campaign for local or legislative office usually are registering people who are likely to vote for the candidate, identifying the people already registered who are most likely to vote for the candidate, and getting these two groups of people to the polls. Although most candidates and their campaign organization probably would prefer to focus on issues, the enormous job of getting elected and the almost inevitable lack of resources often force them to focus on turning out their own voters. The reality of local elections—low voter turnout—means that targeting and turning out a supportive constituency usually is the most effective strategy for winning.

Campaigns for local or legislative offices tend to involve simpler organizations than do campaigns for statewide office. Where statewide campaigns are likely to be run by paid consultants, local and legislative races are more likely to be managed by friends and volunteers. And in these races, because it usually cannot be targeted to the candidate's constituency, television is less important than printed campaign materials.

Direct contact is usually very important in local campaigns. Handing out printed literature door to door is common. Telephone campaigning also is important in these races. A group of friends working with targeted voting lists can get voters to the polls on election day.

Regulating Campaign Finance

The Texas Election Code sets restrictions both on candidates and officeholders who receive contributions and on those who make contributions (Table 5.1). Corporations and labor unions cannot make direct campaign contributions from their own funds. However, they can spend their organization's money on the costs associated with establishing or administering a PAC and soliciting political contributions. Spending corporate or union funds on nonpartisan voter registration drives and get-out-the-vote campaigns also is allowed.

Having noted these restrictions, it is equally important to note what is not restricted. There are no limits on the amount that a contributor can give to a candidate, the amount a candidate can accept (except for the limit on cash contributions), or the amount a candidate can spend. For the most part, then, campaign finance in Texas is wide open: individuals and groups can give whatever they can afford, and candidates can spend as much as they can raise.

Texas relies primarily on campaign reporting to restrain the use of money in politics (Table 5.2). The Texas Election Code requires that **campaign finance reports** be filed with the Texas Ethics Commission, the body responsible for overseeing the state's campaign finance laws. The Texas Ethics Commission can undertake enforcement actions on its own motion or in response to a sworn complaint. If violations are found, the commission can impose civil penalties; it also can refer matters for criminal prosecution.[37]

Presidential Elections in Texas

Because of its size, Texas is a powerful state in presidential politics. Its thirty-two votes in the electoral college make it significant in the strategic

Table 5.1 Campaign Finance Regulations in Texas

- Candidates and officeholders cannot accept cash contributions in excess of $100 during a reporting period.
- A statewide officeholder or a member of the legislature cannot receive contributions in the period beginning thirty days prior to a regular session of the legislature and ending with adjournment.
- A person who accepts contributions as a candidate or officeholder cannot convert the contributions to personal use. The personal-use exclusion does not apply to payments for rent, utilities, or other reasonable expenses incurred in maintaining a household in Travis County (in which the state capital is located) by members of the legislature who do not ordinarily live in Travis County.
- Candidates and officeholders cannot knowingly accept a contribution of more than $500 from an out-of-state political committee unless that committee is willing to provide a list of the names and addresses of all who contributed $100 or more during the preceding twelve months or a copy of its statement filed with the Federal Elections Commission (the national body that regulates campaign finances).
- Candidates and officeholders who make contributions from their personal funds cannot reimburse their personal funds with contributions in an amount that exceeds $500,000 for governor or $250,000 for other statewide office.
- Separate officeholder accounts now are prohibited. They once were common among legislators for supplementing their income and office expense accounts.

Source: Texas Election Code, Chap. 253.

planning of presidential candidates. And because the state has been competitive in recent years, neither of the national parties can concede it to the other party. In the twelve presidential elections from 1952 through 1996, the Democratic party carried the state four times, and the Republican party won the state eight times (Table 5.3).

That the parties believe Texas is a valuable state is clear. The Republican party has held its national convention in the state twice in recent years: in Dallas in 1984 when Ronald Reagan was renominated and in Houston in 1992 when George Bush was renominated. The number of visits to the state by presidential candidates also is evidence of the state's significance. Bill Clinton and Al Gore made one of their famous bus trips through the state in 1992. And both President Bush and Mrs. Bush made several appearances in the state that year too.

In hopes of increasing the state's impact in nominating presidential candidates, Texas changed the date of its party primaries to Super Tuesday, the second Tuesday in March in presidential election years. However, changing the primary date actually has had little impact on the presidential nominating process: the leading candidates usually have been identified before Super Tuesday. For example, in 1992 Bill Clinton already had established himself as the Democratic frontrunner by the time the Texas primary was held.

Table 5.2 Campaign Finance Reporting Regulations in Texas

Reports must include the following:

- The full name and address of each person who has contributed more than $50 and the date of the contribution
- The dates and terms of all loans that exceed $50, including the name of the institution making the loan and the name and address of each guarantor of the loan
- A list of all political expenditures that exceed $50, including the name and address of the vendor and the date and purpose of the expenditure
- A list of all expenditures from political contributions that were not political expenditures, including the name and address of the person to whom payment was made and its purpose
- The total amount of contributions under $50 accepted (or a specific list of them) and the total amount of political expenditures of $50 or less
- The total amount of all political contributions accepted and the total amount of all political expenditures made during the reporting period
- The name of each candidate or officeholder who benefits from a direct campaign expenditure made during the reporting period

Source: Texas Election Code, Chap. 254.

The behavior of Texas voters in presidential elections tends to follow national trends. The percentage of the vote won by each party in Texas closely approximates the percentage of the vote won by each party nationwide (see Table 5.3). In the most recent elections, the Republican party seemed to gain a slight advantage in the state.

Voting Behavior

Campaigns end on election day, when the votes are finally cast. Although people in Texas are as individualistic about their voting as they are about other things, some consistencies in their voting behavior have been noted. Studies of voting behavior point to two central decisions: the turnout decision and the choice of party. Voters must decide whether to vote and how political parties will affect their vote.

Voter Turnout

To better understand **voter turnout** in Texas, it is important to understand how the rate of voting there compares with that of other states. Figure 5.3 compares the turnout rate in Texas in the general election of 1994 (a non-presidential election year) with the rates in other large states. The percentage of eligible voters in Texas who voted in 1994 was lower than most of the large states, coming in twelfth out of fifteen. Fewer than 50 percent of the registered voters in Texas turned out that year.

How does Texas do in presidential years? Figure 5.4 compares the turnout in Texas in presidential election years between 1964 and 1996 with the

Table 5.3 Republican Party Success in Presidential Elections in Texas and the Nation, 1952–1996

Year	Party Carrying Texas	Republican Percent of Vote		Percent Difference Between Texas and U.S. Vote
		National	Texas	
1952	Republican	55.1	53.1	–2.0
1956	Republican	57.4	55.3	–2.1
1960	Democratic	49.5	48.5	–1.0
1964	Democratic	38.5	36.5	–2.0
1968	Democratic	43.4	39.9	–3.5
1972	Republican	60.7	66.2	+5.5
1976	Democratic	48.4	48.0	–0.4
1980	Republican	50.7	55.3	+4.6
1984	Republican	59.1	63.6	+4.5
1988	Republican	54.0	56.0	+2.0
1992	Republican	37.4	40.6	+3.2
1996	Republican	40.7	48.8	+8.1

Sources: Dennis S. Ippolito, "Texas," in *The 1984 Presidential Election in the South,* Robert P. Steed et al., eds. (New York: Praeger, 1986), 162; and *America Votes,* (Washington, DC: Elections Research Center, Congressional Quarterly Press, 1993), 463; *Statistical Abstract of the United States,* 1997 (Washington, DC: CTPO, 1997), p. 27.

national turnout. Although the turnout in Texas is higher in presidential elections than in nonpresidential elections, it lags behind the national average. The gap between the Texas figures and the national figures narrowed over the period, but only because turnout had been falling nationally. Turnout in Texas did not increase significantly at any time during the twenty years studied. A large proportion of Texans simply do not turn out to vote in either state or presidential elections.

Why is voter turnout so low in Texas? Several factors seem to be at work. One has to do with demographics: Texas has a low turnout rate because many of its citizens have low income and little education. According to a number of studies, as people's income and education level go up, so does the likelihood of their voting. Texas, like other southern states, ranks below the national average for both income and education. And because minority groups are overrepresented in the low-income and less-educated populations, they usually have lower turnout rates than do whites.[38]

A second factor that affects voter turnout in Texas is cultural. According to the literature, Texas blends individualistic and traditionalistic political cultures. Its people tend to believe that politics should be left either to the professionals (individualistic) or to the elite (traditionalistic).[39] Neither viewpoint encourages the general population to vote.

A third factor that affects turnout in Texas is the historical weight of the institutions that were designed to limit voting in the state. Remember that

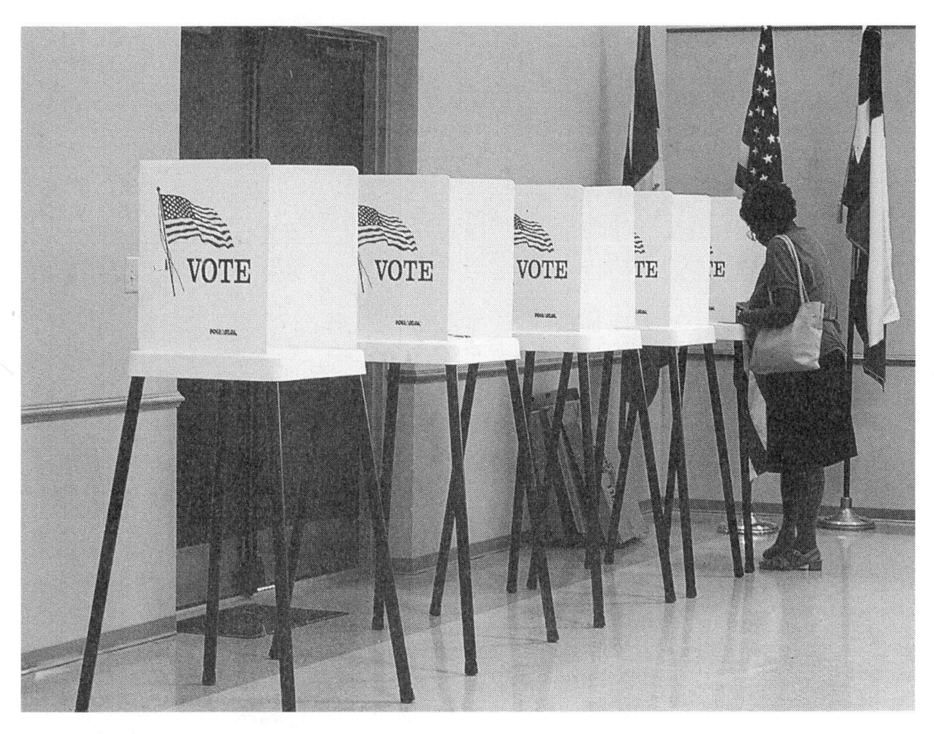

Low voter turnout has left some polling places almost deserted in recent years.

over the years, Texas used many devices to make it difficult to vote. Although those devices have been eliminated, their residual effects linger. Change takes time.

A final factor that contributes to low turnout in Texas is the practice of negative campaigning. By reinforcing the perception that no politicians are worthy of being elected, negative campaigning discourages voting. Voters often would rather stay home on election day than endorse the mean-spirited campaign of any candidate.

Partisan Choice

When voters go the polls, they have to make a partisan choice, they have to choose among the candidates of competing political parties. Not too many years ago, the only significant voting choices were made within the Democratic party primary. But as party competition has increased, **partisan choice** has become a more important factor in elections. This trend can be seen in Figure 5.5, which shows the percentage of the vote polled by Democratic and Republican candidates for governor in the elections between 1950 and 1998. In 1950 the Republican candidate received just 10 percent of the vote; the Democratic candidate received 90 percent. Throughout the 1950s and 1960s,

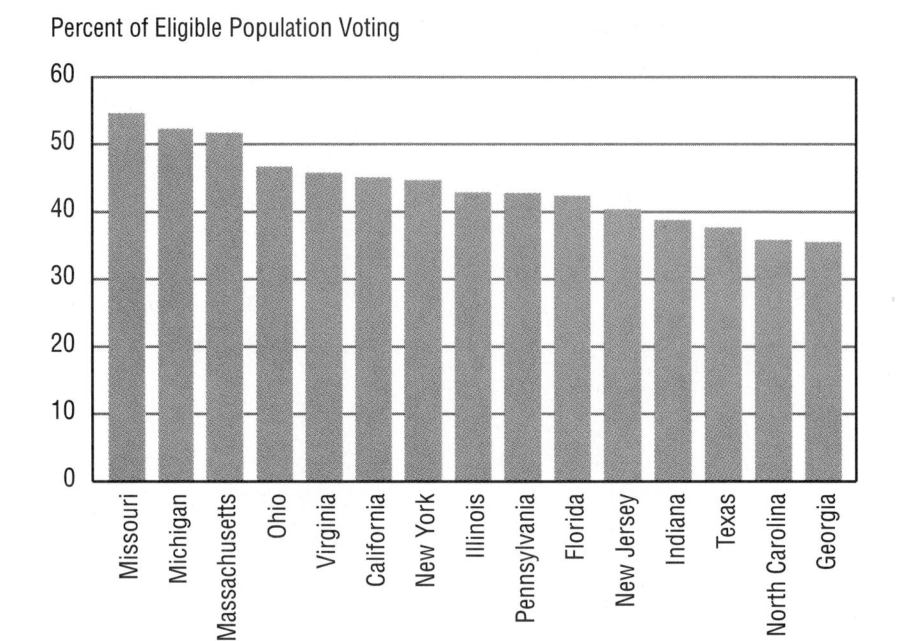

FIGURE 5.3 Turnout in 1994, Texas and Fifteen Largest States
Source: Statistical Abstract of the United States, *1996. (Washington, DC: U.S. Government Printing Office, 1996), p. 287.*

only one election, in 1962, was even close. Gubernatorial elections began to get more competitive in the 1970s, and the Republicans finally won an election in 1978. Since then, gubernatorial elections have continued to be close. Choice between the parties has become a serious matter in Texas today—at least for major statewide offices.

From the thousands of individual decisions voters make on election day emerge general patterns that tell us who is likely to vote for the candidates of each political party and where they come from.

Types of voters. Each party has a base of voters that can be depended on from election to election, almost without regard to candidates or issues, to provide it with 35 to 40 percent of the vote. A victory, then, means attracting voters who are not committed to a party.

The Democratic base is composed of older voters, blue-collar workers, prochoice women, "**yellow dog Democrats**" (people who would vote for a Democrat even if he or she were a yellow dog), African Americans, and Hispanics. The Republican base is made up of the Religious Right, white-collar conservatives, and wealthy Texans. Middle-class urban and suburban voters are **swing voters,** the voters both parties need to court if they want to win elections.[40]

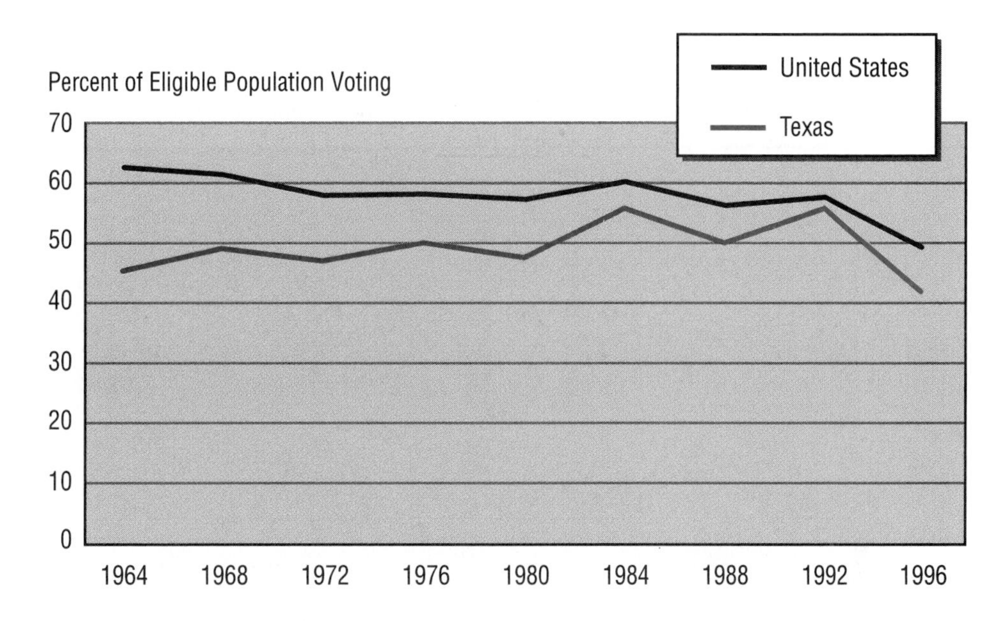

FIGURE 5.4 Voter Turnout in Presidential Elections, Texas and the United States, 1964–1996
Source: Statistical Abstract of the United States, *1980, 1988, 1989, 1993, and 1997.*

Because Democrats have an advantage in rural Texas (Republican strength is almost entirely urban based), one strategy for the Democratic party is to solidify its base in the rural areas and to try to split the urban areas with the Republicans.[41] On the other hand, if the Republican party does well in the cities and suburbs, its candidates can win without strong support elsewhere. One study of the 1994 gubernatorial race demonstrated that Bush's margin in four mostly Anglo suburban counties offset Ann Richards's lead in twenty-three mostly Hispanic counties along the Rio Grande.[42]

Geography. There are eight regions in Texas that vary by topography, economy, ethnicity, and a number of other factors (Figure 5.6). It is not surprising, then, that they also vary in partisan choice.

Working from east to west, *East Texas* is most clearly southern. This rural, pine-wooded region has a higher percentage of African Americans than other parts of Texas. In political terms, it traditionally has been the home of the yellow dog Democrats. Although Democratic candidates generally do well in this region and often depend on it to offset Republican strength elsewhere in the state, the area does have some pockets of Republican strength, among them the cities of Tyler and Longview. Governor Bush did well in this area in 1994.

The *Golden Triangle* sits between East Texas and the Gulf Coast. It is named after the three cities that give the region its style—Beaumont, Orange,

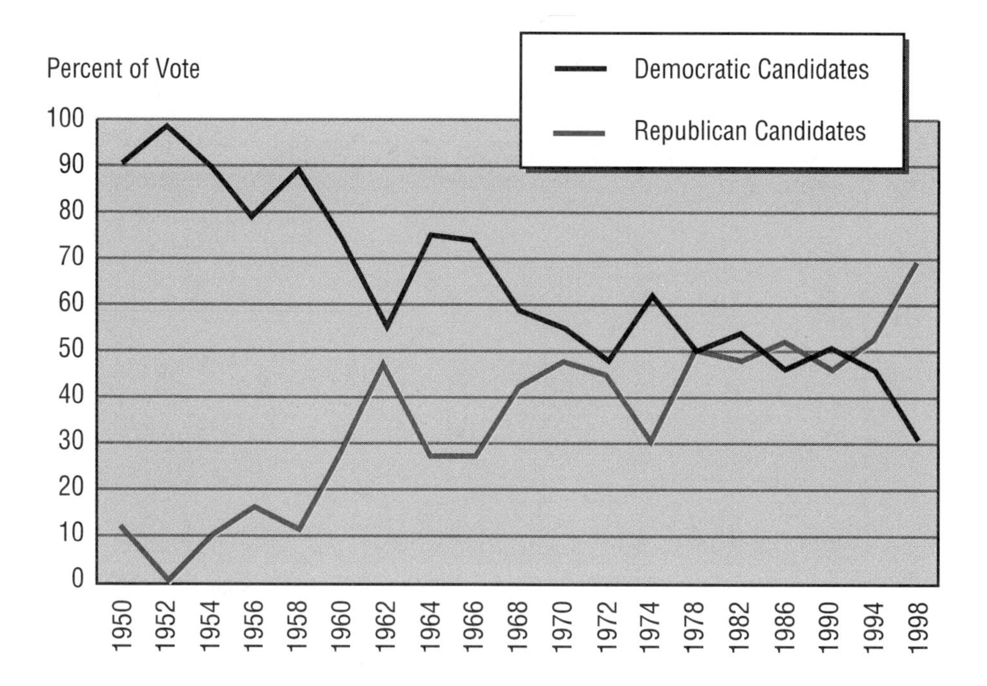

FIGURE 5.5 Gubernatorial Vote in the General Elections in Texas, 1950–1998
Source: Richard Scammon and Alice V. McGillivray, eds., America Votes 19 *(Washington, DC: Congressional Quarterly Press, 1991), 416;* Houston Chronicle, *November 10, 1994, p. 1A;* Dallas Morning News, *November 5, 1998, p. 29A.*

and Port Arthur. The Golden Triangle is one of the most industrialized areas in the state, but its dependence on the oil and gas industry has led to hard times in recent years. Because of its blue-collar industrial tone, this region is a Democratic stronghold and often is written off by Republican strategists.

The *Metroplex,* located in the north central part of the state, is strongly Republican. Dallas and Fort Worth give this area its defining characteristic—it is highly urbanized. The affluent city neighborhoods and the suburbs vote heavily Republican. The inner cities provide what Democratic strength can be found in the area.

Central Texas stretches south from the Metroplex to the Gulf Coast. Austin and Waco, its major cities, are a contrast in political styles. Austin, with its universities and many state government offices, has a tendency to support Democratic candidates—even some of the more liberal of them. Waco is a conservative city that leans toward the Republican party. The region as a whole is strategically important in statewide contests because it can go in either direction, depending on the candidates.

Harris County, on the Gulf Coast, is dominated by Houston. As a whole, it is less Republican than the Metroplex, but the suburbs surrounding Houston are just as loyal to the Republican party as those surrounding Dallas and Fort Worth. The inner-city precincts of Houston are pockets of Democratic

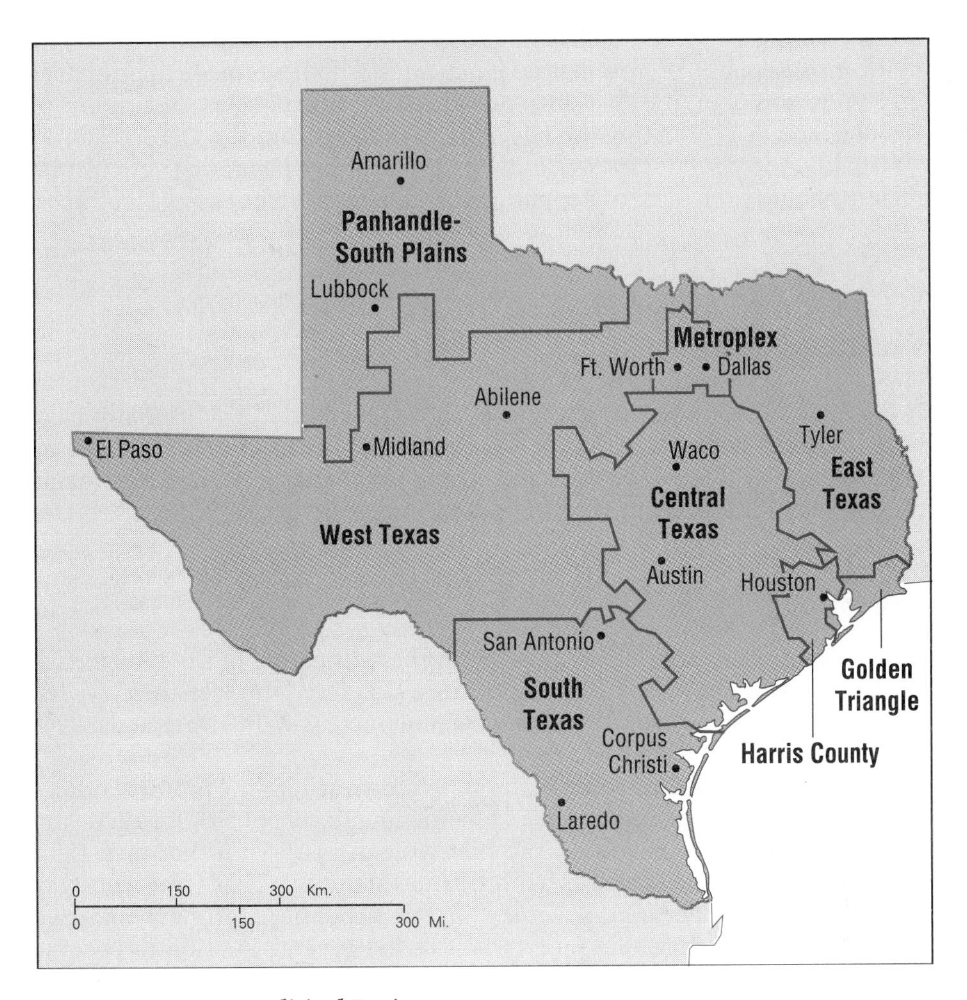

FIGURE 5.6 Texas Political Regions
Source: Adapted from Dallas Morning News, *January 7, 1990, 9J.*

strength. There are enough votes available to both parties to make it strategically worthwhile to focus some effort on this county.

West Texas is a large area geographically. Its voters have a strong tendency to vote Republican, except in El Paso. Although El Paso is geographically part of this region, it has more in common with its neighbors in Mexico and New Mexico than with other cities in the region. West Texas has one of the oldest Republican strongholds in the state: the German counties. Located north of San Antonio and west of Austin, these counties were settled in the 1800s by antislavery Germans who opposed the proslavery Democratic leaders of the state.

South Texas is one of the poorest regions in the state. Its principal cities are San Antonio, Corpus Christi, and Laredo. With its high concentration of Hispanics, South Texas is a source of many votes for Democratic candidates.

Still Republican strategists have not written off the Hispanic vote here. The number of Republican presidential candidates who have made appearances in San Antonio in the last few presidential campaigns is testimony to Republican hopes of taking the Hispanic vote away from the Democrats.

Finally, the *Panhandle–South Plains* is a sparsely populated agricultural region that has been loyal to Republican candidates in all but a few local races.

Women and Minorities in Texas Politics Today

It is important to note the progress of those groups that traditionally have been outsiders in Texas politics, observers in a political game dominated by white males. Women and racial and ethnic minorities have had to struggle for political influence, but they have made progress.

Women

Women gained full suffrage in Texas with the ratification of the Nineteenth Amendment to the U.S. Constitution in 1920. Over the last thirty years, women in Texas, as elsewhere, have become increasingly aware and active politically.

That women can hold some of the state's highest-ranking political offices is proof of the growing importance of women in Texas politics. In 1990 Ann Richards was elected governor, the first woman to serve in her own right (Miriam Ferguson had served as her husband's stand-in). That same year, Kay Bailey Hutchison defeated a woman in the Republican primary and two women (one Democrat, one Libertarian) in the general election to become state treasurer. In 1992, Rose Spector became the first woman elected to the Texas Supreme Court (others had served as appointees). In 1997, women held thirty-three of the 181 seats in the Texas legislature. And women now serve in many city and county offices.

African Americans

Winning the right to vote was a long arduous struggle for African Americans in Texas. With the most serious obstacles to suffrage out of the way, how has this group fared in Texas politics? The 1992 race for the Place 5 seat on the Texas Court of Criminal Appeals is one indicator. That race between Democrat Morris Overstreet and Republican Louis Sturns was the first statewide race between African-American candidates in the state's history.[43] Fourteen seats in the Texas House of Representatives and two in the Texas Senate are now held by African Americans, as are many seats in county, city, and school district governments.

Senator Royce West of Dallas has become a powerful influence in the Texas Legislature.

African Americans today support the Democratic party, as they have since the 1930s. This group is one of the most loyal components of the Democratic base in Texas. About 88 percent of the African-American vote in Texas went to Bill Clinton in 1996. In five of the most urban counties (Bexar, Dallas, Harris, Tarrant, and Travis), one study estimates that 97 percent of African Americans voted for Clinton.[44]

Hispanics

The Hispanic vote is an increasingly powerful force in Texas politics. Hispanics are now assuming leadership positions in the state government. One victory for this group was the election in 1990 of Dan Morales as the state's attorney general—the first statewide nonjudicial elective office held by a Hispanic. Raul Gonzales serves on the Texas Supreme Court, surviving a bitter primary battle in his reelection bid in 1994. There are now thirty-five Hispanic members of the Texas legislature.

Although courted fervently by the Republican party, Hispanics have been loyal to the Democratic party. In 1990, Ann Richards won 78 percent of the Hispanic vote, and in 1994 she received 76 percent of the Hispanic vote.[45] Bill Clinton also garnered 76 percent of the Hispanic vote in 1996.[46] As this group becomes a larger percentage of the state's population, it may well be the key to future development of political parties in Texas. In fact, the support of Mexican Americans in Texas already is avidly sought by Democratic candidates.[47] In December 1997, former Governor Bill Clements wrote an open letter to the Republican party arguing that "the victories of the past will be nothing more than a flash in the pan unless Republicans reach out to Hispanics."[48]

The 1998 Election and the Future of Elections and Voting in Texas

After the 1998 election, most observers of Texas politics were speculating about the future of Texas parties and elections. The Republicans had won all statewide offices and Governor Bush was reelected by a landslide of 69 percent. Only two of the statewide races were close; Rick Perry (who won the lieutenant governorship) and Carol Rylander (who won the comptroller's race) each received barely 50 percent of the vote. The only state-level goal the Republican party failed to achieve in 1998 was to capture a majority in both houses of the legislature. They retained a narrow majority in the state senate, but failed to get a majority in the house.

For some, the 1998 election raised questions about the future of the party system in Texas. Was this victory a prelude to a period of Republican dominance? Can the Democrats continue to compete in Texas? While the Republican sweep was dramatic, it was built on a specific set of circumstances including the personal popularity of one governor, the positive feelings generated by a healthy economy, and the Republican party's careful effort to expand its constituency. By campaigning in Hispanic areas and speaking Spanish in some speeches, Bush won 40 percent of the Hispanic votes—a record level for a Republican candidate. The governor's coattails clearly helped the Republican party to victory in some of the close races.

A low turnout of only 32 percent of the state's registered voters also contributed to the Republican victory. Since the Democratic party depends heavily on groups that have had lower than average voter turnout (especially low-income and minority voters), low turnout is almost never good news for Democrats—it means they are not getting their voters to the polls.

It seems premature to assume that the Democratic party can no longer compete in Texas. The Republican party has proved itself as a contender, but the future competitiveness of each party will depend on the candidates and the issues—as it always has.

The low voter turnout in this election was disappointing to those who value vigorous democratic participation, but it could have been a sign of voter satisfaction. Polls showed Governor Bush's overwhelming lead over his opponent throughout the campaign, indicating that voters were pleased with the way things were going. Many voters may have stayed home because they were satisfied and were confident that their candidate was going to win anyway. Thus, low turnout was not necessarily a sign that anything was wrong with the system—elections can still be doing their job even if participation is low.

Notes

1. Christy Hoppe, "Attorney General Candidate Williamson Maintains His Résumé is Accurate," *Dallas Morning News* (April 4, 1998), 22A.
2. *Hill* v. *Stone,* 421 U.S. 289 (1975).
3. *Dunn* v. *Blumstein,* 405 U.S. 330 (1972).
4. Chandler Davidson, *Race and Class in Texas Politics* (Princeton: Princeton University Press, 1990), 21.
5. *Harper* v. *Virginia Board of Elections,* 383 U.S. 663 (1966).
6. *Smith* v. *Allwright,* 321 U.S. 649 (1944).
7. Steven J. Rosenstone and Raymond E. Wolfinger, "The Effect of Registration Laws on Voter Turnout," *American Political Science Review* 72 (1978): 22–45.
8. The law was first found unconstitutional in federal district court in *Beare* v. *Smith,* 321 F.Supp. 1100 (1971). The decision was upheld in the federal court of appeals in *Beare* v. *Briscoe* 498 F.2d 244 (1974, CA5 Tex.).
9. *Vernon's Texas Code Annotated,* Sec. 11.02. Convicted felons must have received a certificate of discharge by the Board of Pardons and Paroles, completed a period of probation, or been pardoned or otherwise released from the disability to vote resulting from the conviction.
10. *Vernon's Texas Code Annotated,* Secs. 13.121 and 13.003.
11. *Vernon's Texas Code Annotated,* Sec. 13.031.
12. *Vernon's Texas Code Annotated,* Sec. 14.001.
13. *Vernon's Texas Code Annotated,* Secs. 16.031, 16.032, 16.036, and 16.037.
14. *Vernon's Texas Code Annotated,* Secs. 172.024–172.025.
15. *Vernon's Texas Code Annotated,* Sec. 173.001.
16. *Vernon's Texas Code Annotated,* Secs. 42.006 and 43.001.
17. *Vernon's Texas Code Annotated,* Sec. 85.001.
18. Texas Secretary of State, "1992 General Election: Unofficial Election Tabulation," November 5, 1992, 22; "Election Night Reports," November 7, 1994. (Unpublished reports from the Texas Secretary of State.)
19. James P. Sterba, "Democracy Inc.: Politicians at All Levels Seek Expert Advice, Fueling an Industry: Even Minor-League Races Can Involve Consultants," *Wall Street Journal,* September 1, 1992, 1A.
20. Larry Sabato, *The Rise of Political Consultants* (New York: Basic Books, 1981), app. A.
21. Morris, *Storming the Statehouse,* 31.
22. Morris, *Storming the Statehouse,* 122–123.
23. James M. Perry, "Politics and Policy—Campaign '92: Bob Squier, Doyen of the Big Media Consultants, Savors a Banner Year of Campaigning," *Wall Street Journal,* June 2, 1992, 16A.
24. R. G. Ratcliffe, "Cornyn is EOP's Nominee for Attorney General," *Houston Chronicle,* April 15, 1998, p. A1.
25. Morris, *Storming the Statehouse,* 100.
26. Council of State Governments, *Book of the States, 1990–91,* (Lexington, KY: 1990). p. 52; and Morris, *Storming the Statehouse,* 163.

27. George Kuempel, "Richards, Bush Spend $25 Million in Campaign," *Dallas Morning News,* November 6, 1994, 39Q.

28. Morris, *Storming the Statehouse,* 54.

29. Morris, *Storming the Statehouse,* 163.

30. "State's Sheer Size Makes Deep Pockets a Campaign Must," *Dallas Morning News,* January 7, 1990, 9J.

31. Perry, "Politics and Policy," 16A.

32. *Texas Weekly,* February 1, 1993, p. 3.

33. Morris, *Storming the Statehouse,* 50.

34. Davidson, *Race and Class,* 146–149.

35. Morris, *Storming the Statehouse,* 46 and 98.

36. Wayne Slater, "Lobbyists, PACs Give Heavily to Likely New Texas Speaker," *Dallas Morning News,* January 12, 1993, 1A and 10A.

37. Texas Ethics Commission, *Agency Strategic Plan for the 1992–1998 Period* (Austin, 1992), 3–6.

38. See, for example, Angus Campbell et al., *The American Voter* (Chicago: University of Chicago Press, 1960); Sidney Verba and Norman Nie, *Participation in America* (New York: Harper & Row, 1972); and M. Margaret Conway, *Political Participation in the United States,* 2d ed. (Washington, DC: CQ Press, 1991).

39. Daniel J. Elazar, *American Federalism: A View from the States,* 3d ed. (New York: Harper & Row, 1984). See Chap. 5.

40. "'Yubba' Bloc May Hold Key to Lone Star Presidential Vote," *Dallas Morning News,* September 7, 1992, 16A.

41. "'Yubba' Block," 16A.

42. R. G. Ratcliffe, "Grand Old Takeover," *Houston Chronicle* (January 11, 1998), p. 1A.

43. *Texas Almanac, 1992–93,* (Dallas, TX: A. H. Belo Corp., 1992), 423.

44. Frank, B. Feigert and John R. Todd, "Texas: Suppose They Have an Election and Nobody Came," in *The 1996 Presidential Election in the South,* Laurence W. Moreland and Robert Steed, eds. (Westport, CT: Praeger, 1997), pp. 57–107, see especially p. 206.

45. James M. Perry, "Politics & Policy: Hispanic Voters Turn Their Backs on GOP Offerings," *Wall Street Journal,* October 27, 1992, 18A.

46. Feigert and Todd, p. 205.

47. Sam Attlesey, "How to Take Texas: Experts Say Democrats Must Note State's Diversity," *Dallas Morning News,* February 24, 1992, 10A.

48. Ratcliffe, "Grand Old Takeover," p. 1A.

6 THE TEXAS LEGISLATURE

CHAPTER OUTLINE

The Politics of the Legislative Process

Timing
Presiding Officers of the Texas House and Senate
The Committees
Lobbyists
The Governor
Political Parties
The Courts

Legislative Support Services

Legislative Council
Legislative Reference Library
Legislative Budget Board
House and Senate Research Organizations
Staff

Change in the Texas Legislature

In 1997, the Texas legislature worked its way through some fairly tough issues, including the governor's property tax relief proposal. Thus, they might reasonably have finished the session with some sense of satisfaction in their work. But, when the public was asked their opinion of the legislature's work in May of that year, only 44 percent thought the legislature was doing a "good" or "excellent" job; 48 percent thought the legislature had been doing a "fair" or "poor" job.[1]

The Speaker of the House of Representatives, Pete Laney, characterized the results as "a tribute to the hard work of the women and men of the Legislature." How could the speaker be so proud of a poll indicating that almost a majority of Texans disapproved of the job the legislature was doing? The answer lies in the law of comparative judgment. That is, how one evaluates something is relative to what one is comparing it. In the case of the Texas legislature, a 48 percent disapproval rating appears positive when one is aware that in 1992, just before Laney became speaker of the house, 69 percent of Texans thought the legislature was doing a "fair" or "poor" job. Thus, the speaker and the Texas Legislature could rightfully be proud of the institution's improved standing in the eyes of Texans.

This incident in the history of the Texas legislature emphasizes that change, and even improvement, have been part of the story of the modern Texas legislature. This chapter will survey the legislative branch of Texas government in order to describe how it has changed and to determine where improvement still needs to take place. In the process, it answers several key questions:

- How is the Texas legislature organized?
- What essential functions does the legislature carry out?
- How does a bill become a law?
- What are the major influences on the legislative process?
- How has the legislature changed, and what are the prospects for change in the future?

Change Trends and the Texas Legislature

In a review of contemporary state legislatures, one noted scholar emphasized that legislatures have become more professional and that they are dealing with more profound problems than ever before. Ironically, though, as their capabilities have improved, legislatures have confronted rising expectations of the people and an increasingly critical press. In this threatening environment, state legislatures have a hard time earning public respect.[2]

In the survey that follows, it is clear that the Texas legislature is undergoing some of the changes common to all state legislatures but lags behind in others. It also is clear that the Texas legislature is caught in the conflict that faces other state legislatures.

An Overview of the Texas Legislature

The first step in understanding the Texas legislature is to get a basic overview of its structure. This section focuses on the basic elements of that structure; later sections examine how the system operates.

Bicameralism

Like all state legislatures except Nebraska's, the Texas legislature is *bicameral*—that is, it has two chambers, and each chamber has different members, rules, and procedures. The lower chamber, the Texas House of Representatives, has 150 members elected for two-year terms. The upper chamber, the Texas Senate, has 31 members elected for staggered four-year terms. To guarantee some continuity in membership from session to session, half the senate is up for reelection every two years. The only exception comes in the first election following a census and the redrawing of districts, when all state senate seats are up for election at once. When the next legislative session begins, staggered terms are restored: the members draw lots to determine whether they will serve two- or four-year terms.[3]

Sessions

Unlike most state legislatures, the Texas legislature meets in **biennial sessions**—that is, they meet just once every two years. Regular sessions convene on the second Tuesday in January of odd-numbered years. The Texas Constitution limits those sessions to a maximum of 140 days.

Special sessions, which only the governor can call, were once fairly common, but have not been called in recent years. Governor Clements set a record for calling special sessions—eleven in two terms in office.[4] The Seventy-first Legislature set a record by meeting 152 days in special sessions.[5] Clements called two special sessions in 1989 to deal with workers' compensation reform and four in 1990 to deal with school finance reform. Governor Richards called the Seventy-second Legislature into two special sessions during 1991 (to deal with the budget crisis), and two special sessions in 1992 (one to deal with legislative redistricting and one to deal with school finance).[6] The legislature has not met in special session since 1992.

Membership in the Texas Legislature

Formal qualifications for membership in the Texas legislature are quite simple. State representatives must hold American citizenship and must be at least twenty-one years old, a resident of the state for two years, and a resident of the legislative district for one year.[7] State senators must hold American citizenship, and must be at least twenty-six years old, a resi-

The House of Representatives chamber includes laptop computers on each desk to help members keep up on pending bills.

dent of the state for five years, and a resident of the senatorial district for one year.[8]

Informal qualifications for membership in the Texas legislature can be inferred by examining the people who usually get elected. From Table 6.1 it is apparent that white male Democrats still have the best chance of getting elected, but the pattern has been changing. As late as 1971 there were only

Table 6.1 Composition of the Texas Legislature

	1991	1993	1995	1997
	72nd Legislature	73rd Legislature	74th Legislature	75th Legislature
Democrats	115	110	106	96
Republicans	66	71	75	85
Male	158	152	148	147
Female	23	29	33	33
African Americans	15	16	16	16
Hispanics	24	31	33	35
Anglos	142	134	132	130

Source: Adapted from *Dallas Morning News,* January 13, 1993, 8A, January 10, 1995, 1A; *Houston Chronicle,* January 12, 1997, p. 1.

The Senate chambers seem less crowded than the House floor because there are only thirty-one senators.

two women, three African Americans, and eleven Hispanics in the state legislature. By 1997 there were thirty-three women, sixteen African Americans, and thirty-five Hispanics. Although the legislative profile is beginning to reflect the state's demographic profile, it still falls short of representing major groups in the proportion they make up of the population. For example, in 1997 African Americans made up about 12 percent of the state's population; that year they made up about 9 percent of the state legislature, and Hispanics (who make up 25 percent of the state's population) hold 19 percent of the legislative seats. Since women make up over 50 percent of the state's population and hold only 18 percent of the legislative seats, they are more seriously underrepresented than African Americans or Hispanics.

It is also worth noting that the Democrats no longer dominate the legislature. By 1997 the Republicans had captured 45 percent of the seats in the house and 55 percent of the seats in the senate. It may not be long before the typical Texas legislator is no longer a Democrat.

Compensation

The salary for lawmakers is set by the Texas Constitution at $600 a month ($7,200 a year) plus a daily expense payment called a *per diem.* Legislators receive per diems when the legislature is in session and may receive compen-

Growth in minority membership had led to minority caucuses that help minority members focus their efforts.

sation when the legislature is not in session if they are conducting legislative business. Members also are reimbursed for travel expenses at the same rate per mile as other state employees.[9] The 1991 constitutional amendment that created the Texas Ethics Commission gave it the authority to set the amount of the per diem (currently $95 a day) and to recommend salary increases for members of the legislature and the presiding officers.[10] Recommendations are subject to voter approval. The commission has not chosen to recommend a salary increase for the legislature or legislative leaders. Over the years, Texas voters have been reluctant to grant legislative pay raises. The last time the electorate approved a pay increase was in 1975, when legislators' monthly pay was raised from $400 to $600. Constitutional amendments in 1984 and 1989 that would have raised legislators' pay were defeated soundly.[11] In comparison to other states, particularly large and heavily populated states, legislative pay in Texas is embarrassingly low. In 1990 the average annual salary for state legislators nationwide was about $16,500; and New York paid its state legislators $57,500.

Legislative Districts

To elect the legislature's 150 representatives and 31 senators, the state must be divided into electoral districts (Figures 6.1 and 6.2). The way district lines are drawn can affect the party, the race, even the gender of the people who

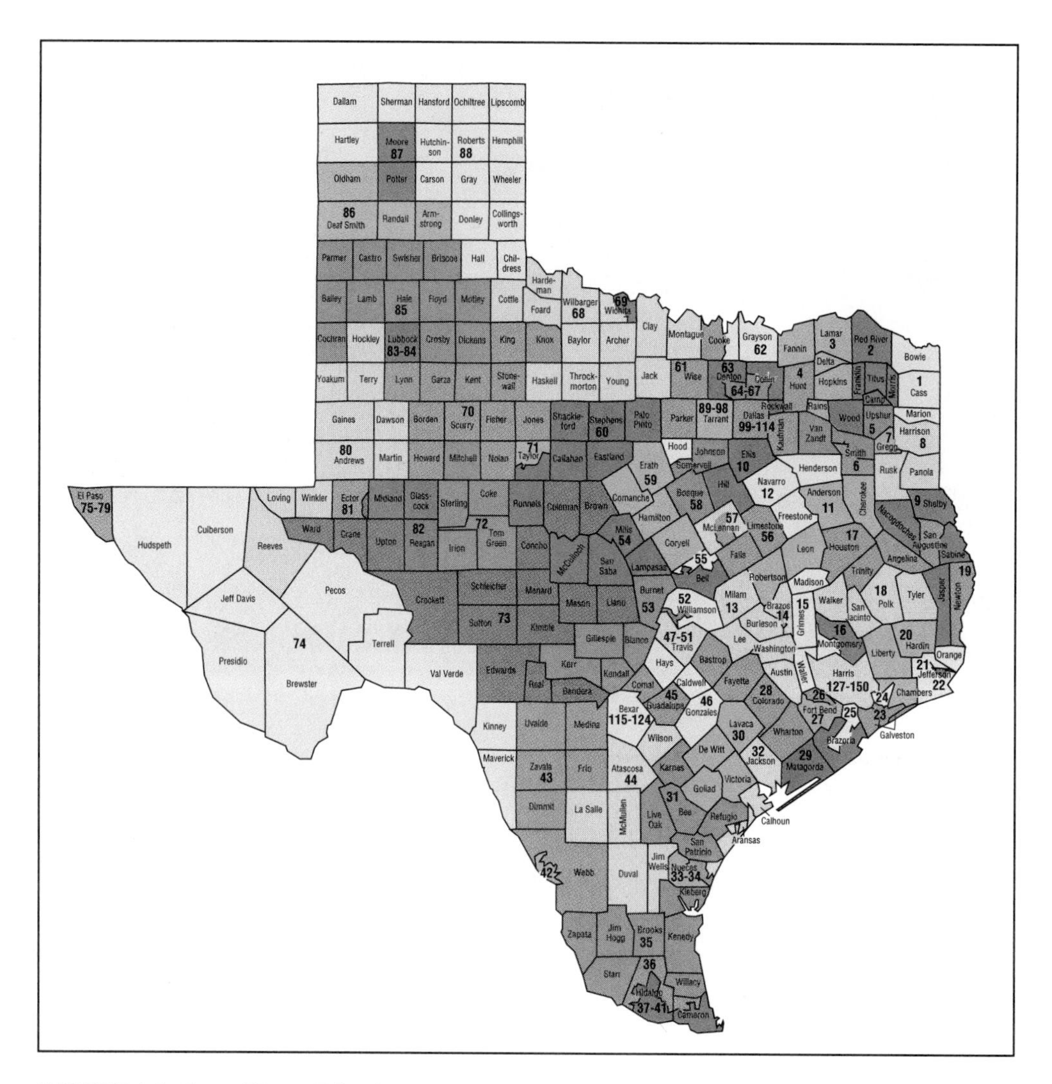

FIGURE 6.1 State House Districts
Source: Guide to the Texas Legislature *(Austin: Reference Guides, 1994), Exhibit B.*

get elected. It is no wonder, then, that battles over district lines are so hotly contested.

After each national census, district lines must be redrawn to reflect population shifts over the ten years since the previous census. For many years, Texas and many other states made only token efforts at redrawing district lines. In the years after World War II, the population of the United States rapidly shifted from rural to urban areas. The failure to recognize that change by reapportioning legislative seats created serious problems of rural over-representation and urban underrepresentation. The situation came to a head

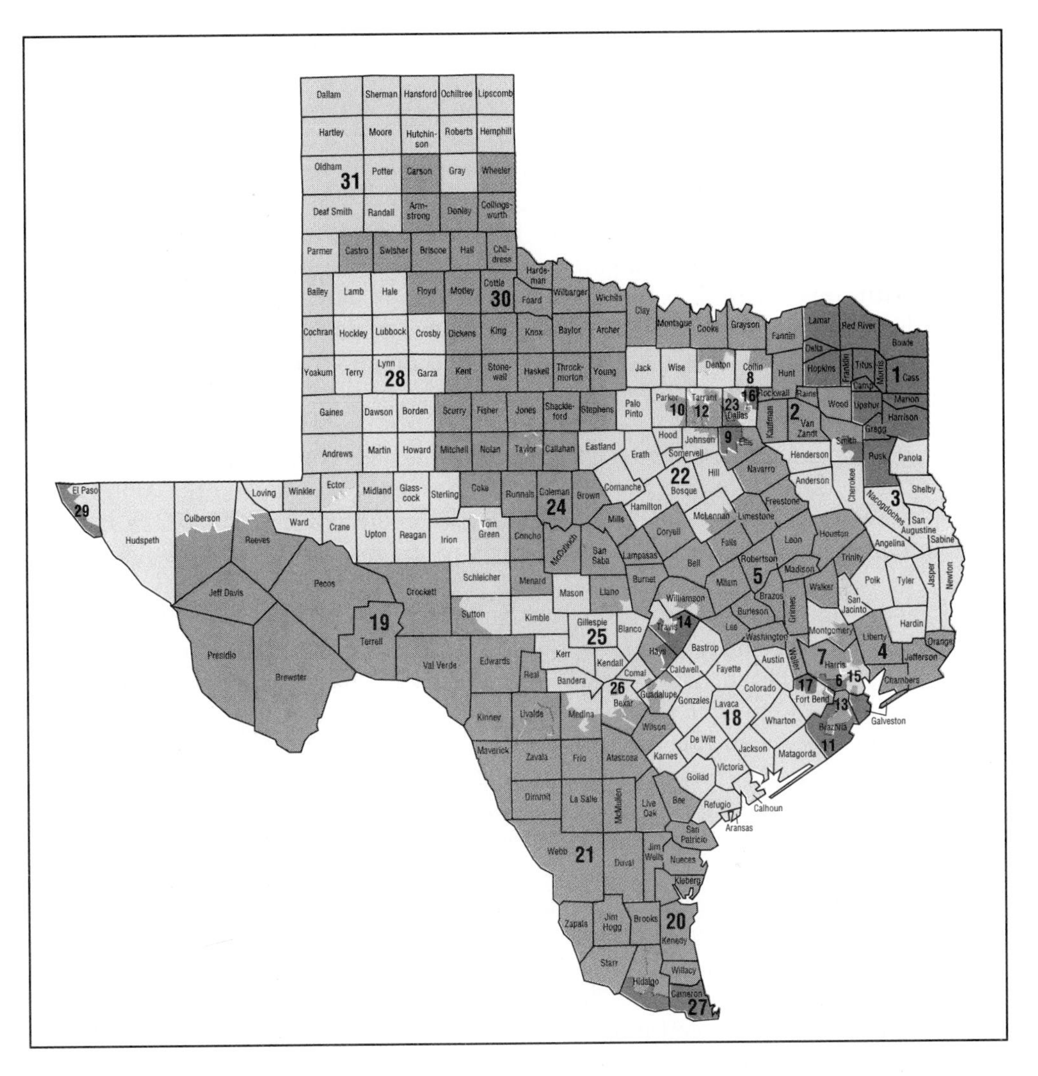

FIGURE 6.2 State Senate Districts

Source: Guide to the Texas Legislature *(Austin: Reference Guides, 1994), Exhibit A.*

in the 1960s, when underrepresented groups sought relief in the federal courts. In 1962 the U.S. Supreme Court reversed an earlier precedent, ruling in *Baker* v. *Carr* that under- and overrepresentation were a violation of the equality principles of the national constitution and were subject to judicial correction.[12] Two years later the court followed up by saying that districts should (as nearly as is practicable) contain the same number of people and that representation in both chambers of state legislatures should be based on population.[13] To enforce these rulings, the federal courts were prepared to order new districts into effect if legislatures were unable or unwilling to draw new district lines themselves. If a state does not redraw district lines fairly after a census, a federal judge will.

In the Texas legislature each chamber is responsible for redrawing its own electoral district lines. The process is very much a political one, in which partisan groups attempt to retain their power by drawing district lines that favor them.

Because district lines affect the outcome of elections, the process of redrawing those lines can stalemate. A 1948 amendment to the Texas Constitution created the **Legislative Redistricting Board** to perform the task if the legislature is unable to agree on district lines during the first session following a census. The board is made up of the lieutenant governor, the speaker of the Texas house, the attorney general, the comptroller of public accounts, and the commissioner of the General Land Office.

Beyond judicial efforts to enforce numerical equality among voting districts, the national government also has tried to prevent the states from drawing districts that discriminate against the voting rights of minorities. Minorities have turned to the courts to prevent their underrepresentation in state legislatures. The NAACP and other groups often have challenged redistricting plans in Texas, so court involvement in redistricting there has become fairly common. One successful challenge ended the use of multimember districts, which tend to make it hard to elect minority representatives; another led to the creation of more districts with a minority majority. According to the Voting Rights Act Extension of 1975, any changes in electoral districts in Texas must be cleared by the U.S. Department of Justice to prevent discrimination against minorities. Control over Texas legislative districts, then, is not solely the province of the state legislature.

In the most recent redistricting effort the courts once again played a role. This time Republicans were challenging the new districts, ostensibly to protect the interests of minority voters. The Republicans prevailed in the courts: the 1992 senate elections were held using a set of districts drawn up by a federal judge. In 1993 a federal appeals court sided with the Democrats, and subsequent senate elections have used the districts drawn by the senate.[14]

The Legislative Task

Lawmaking

The legislature's first and foremost responsibility is to make law. Texas laws often are the product of a complex system of political relationships. Ideas for bills and resolutions come from legislators themselves, their constituents, the governor, or lobbyists, or in response to a crisis in the state. But only members of the house and senate can introduce a law directly into the legislative process. To become law, a bill or resolution must pass both chambers of the legislature with at least a majority vote and then must be approved (actively or passively) by the governor. A law made by the Texas legislature is called a **statute.**

Budgeting

One of the legislature's primary responsibilities each session is to enact a budget. The powers to tax and to appropriate money are assigned to the legislature by Article VIII of the state constitution. The legislature must allocate available financial resources among the various programs and agencies of the state. Remember that the Texas Constitution prohibits the legislature from appropriating more money than is estimated to be available over a budget period (see Chapter 2). This means that the legislature must either keep expenditures within available revenues or be prepared to enact the tax increases necessary to balance the budget.[15]

Dealing with Constitutional Change

The Texas legislature is authorized to propose amendments to the state constitution through the adoption of joint resolutions. The adoption of a joint resolution requires a two-thirds vote of both chambers. As noted in Chapter 5, changes to the Texas Constitution do not become final until the voters ratify them through a referendum. Although the number of amendments proposed each year fluctuates, almost every legislative session produces proposed constitutional amendments.

Overseeing Administrative Agencies

Administrative oversight is the responsibility of the Texas legislature to supervise agencies in the executive branch. The legislature performs this function by

- creating, reorganizing, or dissolving administrative agencies in the normal course of the legislative process.
- appropriating funds for administrative agencies.
- auditing the expenditures of administrative agencies.
- applying sunset legislation.
- accepting or rejecting executive appointments to agencies and departments.

The legislature has the power to create agencies and to abolish those agencies it has created. Agencies created by the Texas Constitution can be abolished only by constitutional amendment. But often the legislature can transfer functions from one agency to another or reorganize agencies.

Of course the primary source of legislative control over executive agencies is its control of the purse strings. Through appropriations bills, the legislature decides how much money each agency can spend over a budget period.

Agencies that lose legislative support also are likely to lose funding in the next budget.

The legislature audits the expenditures of state agencies through the office of the state auditor. The Legislative Audit Committee appoints the state auditor (subject to senate confirmation), who oversees a staff of auditors.[16] The auditor's office conducts

- financial audits (to check the accuracy of accounting and record keeping).
- compliance audits (to ensure that the agency is complying with state laws, rules, and regulations, and to determine whether appropriated funds were spent in the manner intended).
- economy and efficiency audits (to evaluate the use and management of state resources).
- effectiveness audits (to determine whether the agency's goals are being reached and whether programs are duplicating other agencies' programs).

This agency helps the legislature determine the honesty and the effectiveness with which agencies are using the state's resources.

Probably the most important new tool available to legislators to control the executive branch is **sunset legislation.** According to these laws, after a specified date agencies or programs are terminated automatically unless the legislature takes the necessary steps to reauthorize them. Sunset legislation ensures that the work of executive agencies and departments is reviewed periodically. Without that scheduled review, agencies and programs might continue to exist well beyond their useful life.

Finally, the senate must confirm gubernatorial appointments to various agencies. The confirmation hearings give legislators an opportunity to see to it that qualified managers supervise executive agencies.

Disciplining Corrupt Officials

The **impeachment process** is the principal legislative device for dealing with corrupt officials in other branches of the government. The process begins with the Texas House of Representatives formulating impeachment charges against a public official. The senate then tries the official. The constitution empowers the senate to try the governor, the lieutenant governor, the attorney general, the treasurer, the commissioner of the general land office, the comptroller of public accounts, and the judges of the Texas Supreme Court, the courts of appeals, and the district courts. To remove a state official from office, two-thirds of the senators present must vote in favor of conviction. An official who has been convicted cannot hold public office. Texas, like other states, rarely uses impeachment. It was last used in the state in 1976, when District Judge O. P. Carrillo of Duval County was impeached and removed from office.

The legislature also has the power to remove certain judicial officers by **legislative address** for willful neglect of duty, incompetence, habitual drunkenness, or oppression in office.[17] This procedure can be applied to justices of the Texas Supreme Court, the courts of appeals, and the district courts. The constitution stipulates that the governor must remove a judge on the address of two-thirds of each chamber of the legislature. This procedure is used even less often than impeachment.

Representing Constituents

Legislators represent constituencies. This means that they are expected to make decisions that reflect the views of a majority of their constituents. For example, in 1993, when the legislature was working on school finance reform, legislators from wealthier school districts tried to protect their districts from a law that would transfer wealth to other districts. Those who represented poorer districts felt an equally strong obligation to get as much funding as possible for their schools.

Legislators also are expected to "look out" for their districts, to protect resources already available to their districts, and to promote projects that will generate jobs and income in their districts. For example, legislators who represent districts with state universities are expected to defend the budgets for those institutions from appropriations cuts. Finally, representation requires legislators to get the local bills passed that increase the powers granted to cities and counties in their districts.

Steps in the Legislative Process

Legislators can introduce two basic types of actions: bills and resolutions. **Bills** make changes in existing statutes or propose new laws. Resolutions express the legislature's opinion on some matter or call on another authority to take action.[18] Legislation—except for revenue measures, which must originate in the house—can originate in either chamber.

There are several stages through which a bill must pass before it can become a law (Figure 6.3). This means that there are several stages at which a bill can be defeated. Of course someone who opposes a piece of legislation must succeed at only one of those stages to stop a bill; a proponent must win at each stage. For major pieces of legislation, each chamber may develop its own bill, and the two chambers may work on a policy simultaneously.

Introduction and First Reading

Members of the legislature introduce bills or resolutions by filing copies with the chief clerk. Filing before a session begins is common and can occur as early as the first Monday after the general election. After a bill is introduced, it gets a perfunctory first reading. The title is read, and a statement of its subject matter is made. Then the bill is given a number, and the presiding officer assigns it to a committee.

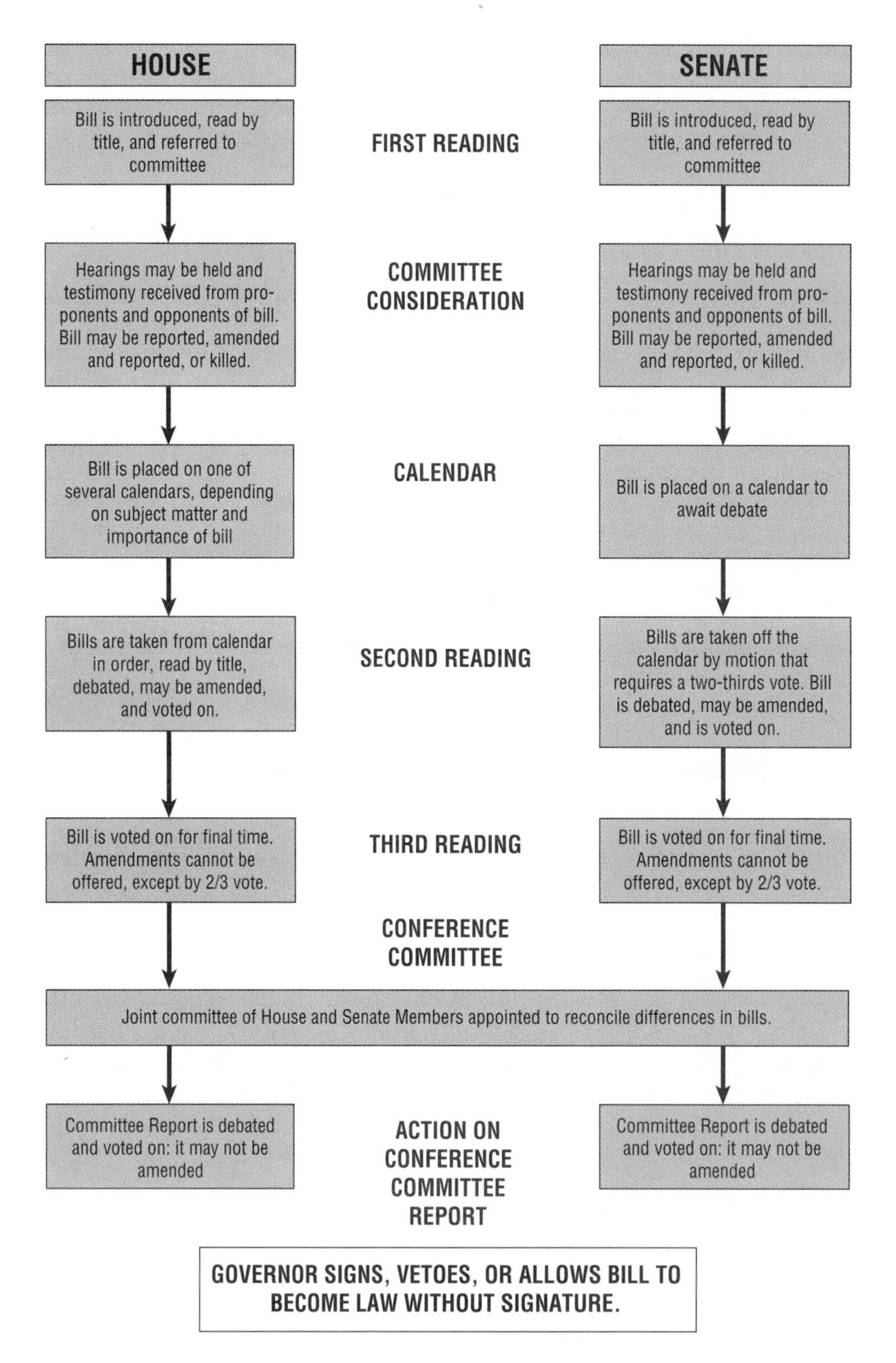

FIGURE 6.3 How a Bill Becomes a Law

Committee Consideration

At the committee stage, the chair of the committee receiving the bill determines whether or not it will get serious attention. More bills are defeated by lack of attention in committees than for other reasons. If hearings are scheduled, lobbyists and other interested individuals can testify in support of or opposition to the bill. Committees can rewrite a bill, alter various portions of it, or simply change bits and pieces here and there. The final content of a bill depends in large part on what the committee does to it. If the committee approves a bill, it is reported with a favorable recommendation.

Calendar

After a committee reports a bill, it is placed on a **calendar** to wait its turn for floor consideration. Making it to the calendar stage is a major milestone in the legislative process. Around two-thirds of the bills introduced die before reaching a calendar.[19]

Both chambers of the Texas legislature manage the flow of legislative business by dividing legislation between two types of calendars: one for uncontested bills (local and consent calendars) and another set for major bills. Bills coming from local and consent calendars are disposed of fairly quickly. Most floor consideration time is given to bills coming from the other calendars.[20]

Second Reading: Floor Consideration

Procedures for moving a bill from a calendar to floor consideration differ in the two chambers. House rules require that bills be taken up on the floor as they appear on the calendars, unless the rules are suspended or a member attaches a preference number to a bill. A preference number gives a bill special status and allows it to be considered early.

The senate normally does not follow its calendar for major bills. A motion to take a bill off the calendar out of order is the usual parliamentary procedure for bringing up a bill for floor consideration in the senate. The rules require that senators intending to ask that a bill be taken off the calendar file a notice of intent the day before. The secretary of the senate publishes an intent calendar at the end of each legislative day. A motion to take a bill off the calendar for floor consideration requires a two-thirds vote of the members present.[21] The departure from calendar order reflects the informality of the senate, the smaller chamber. At the same time, the procedure allows any eleven senators (or fewer if all members are not present) to stop a bill from coming to the floor.

When a bill comes up for floor consideration, it receives a second reading: the bill's title is read aloud. Debate and amendments are in order at the second reading. In the house, each legislator is limited to ten minutes to speak for or against a bill, unless a vote is taken to suspend the rules and allow the members more time. Sponsors and members who worked on the bill in committee often get more time than other legislators. Senate rules allow filibusters during debate. A **filibuster** occurs when a senator or a group of senators gain control of the floor and attempt to talk a bill to death or delay the operations of the chamber. The filibuster is most effective at the end of a legislative session, when time is running out. A filibuster in the Texas Senate is not as powerful a weapon as it is in the U.S. Senate. Stopping a filibuster in Texas requires only a simple majority vote; in the national senate, a three-fifths vote is required.

Third Reading: Final Consideration

If approved by a majority vote at the second reading, a bill is engrossed (a final check for accuracy is made) and prepared for a third reading, which normally must wait until the next legislative day. Adding amendments at the time of the third reading requires a two-thirds vote. If passed by a simple majority vote at the third reading, the bill is sent to the other chamber for consideration.

Conference Committee and Action on the Committee Report

If a bill is passed by both chambers but with different provisions, it is sent to a **conference committee** appointed by the presiding officers (the speaker and the lieutenant governor). If the committee agrees on a compromise, its version of the bill goes back to each chamber for debate and a vote. Each chamber must accept or reject the conference bill without amendment. To pass, a majority must vote for it. If the conference committee bill passes, a final copy of the bill is prepared. The presiding officers sign the bill and then send it to the governor.

Action by the Governor

When the governor receives a bill, he or she has three choices: (1) sign the bill, (2) allow it to become law after ten days, excluding Sundays, without a signature, or (3) **veto** the bill within ten days. After a session has adjourned, the governor has twenty days, including Sundays, to veto bills. Unlike the president of the United States, the governor of Texas does not have a *pocket veto* (the right to allow a bill to die by taking no action if the bill is received when the legislature is not in session). Bills that are not vetoed by the governor automatically become law with or without a signature.

In the case of appropriations bills only, the governor also has the power to veto line items. Legislators have learned to play games with the budget to protect specific programs from the governor's **line-item veto.** For example, they may combine an item they want to protect with another item that the governor cannot afford to or does not want to veto.

The legislature can override a veto by a two-thirds vote of the members present in the house or by a two-thirds vote of the membership of the senate. But because most bills pass in the last two weeks of a legislative session, the governor's veto usually holds. And a postadjournment veto writes the bill's final chapter. Those bills passed by the legislature that survive the governor's veto become law. All bills except appropriations and emergency matters go into effect ninety days after the session adjourns.

The Politics of the Legislative Process

Getting a bill through the Texas legislature is a political process—a give and take to garner the votes necessary for passage. All bills introduced do not have an equal chance of passing; in fact the overwhelming majority of bills are defeated. It is a strategic combination of people and forces that keeps a bill alive.

Timing

One factor that influences a bill's likelihood of passing is the timing of its consideration. Timing is particularly important in legislative bodies with short working sessions, like the Texas legislature. One study suggested that the 140-day regular session could be divided into three stages: agenda building, initial agenda clearing, and accelerated agenda clearing (Figure 6.4).[22]

The **agenda-building stage** occupies the first 60 days of the session. According to the constitution, the first 30 days should be taken up with introducing bills and resolutions, acting on emergency appropriations, confirming appointments made by the governor during the recess, and acting on any matters that the governor designates an emergency. The next 30 days should be devoted to committee hearings and gubernatorial "emergencies." Because of the restrictions on passing bills during the first 60 days of the session, the legislature spends that time building its agenda.

The second stage—**initial agenda clearing**—extends from the 61st through the 126th day. In this stage, restrictions on enacting bills are lifted, but limits on the introduction of new bills apply. In this stage, then, the legislature begins to clear its agenda by acting on bills.

Accelerated agenda clearing, the final stage of the legislative session, lasts from the 127th day through the end of the session. About 80 percent of the bills passed are acted on during the final two weeks of the session. In 1991, the house acted on more than half of the bills passed during the last three days of the session.[23] The press of legislation seems overwhelming, but the workload is moderated by the fact that about half of each day's work during this stage is taken up by minor bills from the local or consent calendars.[24]

The end-of-session logjam concerned the Texas house enough that it adopted new rules in 1993 to alleviate some of the pressure. Those rules

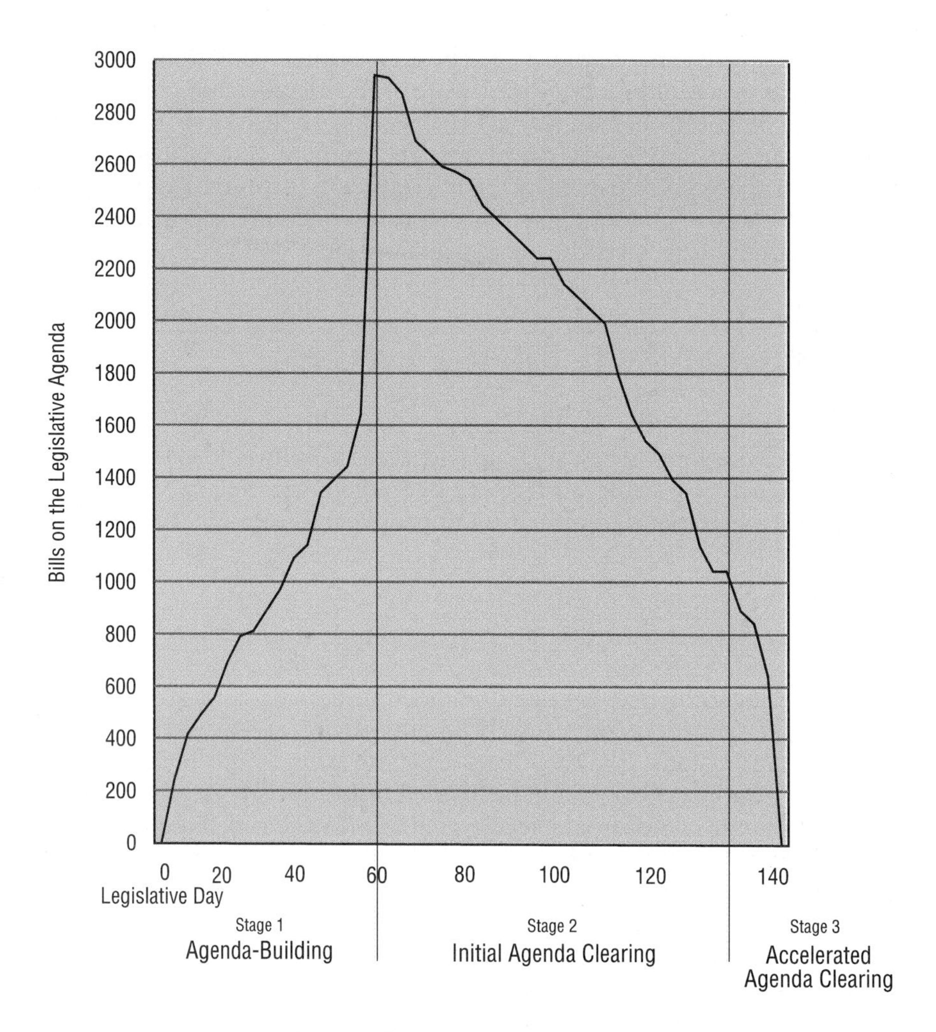

FIGURE 6.4 Stages in the Legislative Session
Source: Adapted from Harvey J. Tucker, "Legislative Workload Congestion in Texas," Journal of Politics, 49 *(May 1987): 569.*

stipulate that no major house bills can be considered during the final seventeen days of a session and that no bills from the senate can be taken up during the last five days. As always, the house can suspend its rules by a four-fifths vote.[25]

Choosing the right time to introduce a bill is a strategic decision in getting a bill passed. Research indicates that bills that make it through committee to a calendar usually are introduced later than bills that do not reach a calendar. Filing bills later improves their chance of passing for a couple of reasons. First, these bills are likely to be drafted more carefully. Second, introducing a bill later gives the sponsor more time to build a coalition of supporters. A bill brought up before a coalition has been solidified and necessary compromises have been worked out can die a quick death. Major bills tend to be introduced earlier; minor bills, later.[26] Experienced legislators learn the best times to try to pass or kill a bill.

Presiding Officers of the Texas House and Senate

All observers of Texas politics agree that the presiding officers—the **speaker of the house** and the **lieutenant governor**—are key players in the legislative process. Their support for a bill dramatically increases its chances of passing; and their opposition almost certainly dooms it to failure. Understanding the role they play, then, is crucial to understanding the Texas legislative process.

The speaker is elected by the members of the house at the beginning of each session. When an incumbent speaker is not seeking reelection, campaigning for the office starts at least a year in advance. Candidates for the speakership ask house members to sign pledge cards indicating their intention to vote for them. The capital press usually knows who has lined up a majority of pledges long before the session begins and a speaker formally is elected. In November 1992, two months before the beginning of the legislative session, Pete Laney was able to announce that he had enough pledges to win the speakership for the 1993 session.[27]

The lieutenant governor, the presiding officer of the senate, is elected by the people of the state to a four-year term. Although it is tempting to compare the lieutenant governor and the vice president of the United States—both preside over an upper legislative chamber by constitutional provision—there are more differences than similarities between the two officers. The vice president is a figurehead in the U.S. Senate; the Texas lieutenant governor is a powerful legislative leader.

The presiding officers have many tools of influence. They have substantial control over **committee assignments,** and they designate committee chairs. Because committees make crucial legislative decisions, determining their membership is perhaps the most important power in the Texas legislature. By appointing members to committees, the presiding officers can increase or decrease the likelihood of certain kinds of legislation passing.

In the house, support for the speaker's positions on issues and early help in the speaker's campaign for the office influence the allocation of good committee assignments. For example, early on Libby Linebarger and Mark Stiles both supported Pete Laney's candidacy for speaker. Linebarger was named chair of the Public Education Committee and Stiles got the powerful Calendars Committee chair. By contrast Wilhelmina Delco, who was late in coming to Laney's support, lost her position as chair of the Higher Education Committee and was demoted to chairing the General Investigating Committee.[28]

Because committee assignments are so important, the rank-and-file members of the house periodically have tried to limit the speaker's control over committee membership and the chairs. In the early 1970s, the members of the Texas house managed to carry out several reforms, including a

Pete Laney became speaker of the house of representatives in 1993 and promised more democratic procedures in that chamber.

limited seniority rule, a reduction in the number of committees, and a restructuring of committees. The seniority rule provides that half the committee assignments be made by a combination of member preferences and seniority and that the other half be made by the speaker. Because committee chairs, subcommittee chairs, and positions on the Appropriations Committee are not among the positions decided by member preference and seniority, preference and seniority determine less than half the committee assignments.

The lieutenant governor exercises an even greater degree of control over senate committee appointments than the speaker does over house committee appointments. The only restriction on the lieutenant governor is that three members of each committee with ten or fewer members and four members of each committee with more than ten members must have served on the committee during the last session.

The leaders also can influence legislative outcomes through their bill referral power, which allows them to determine the standing committee that will receive a bill for examination. Remember that the committee's treatment of a bill usually determines the bill's chance of passing. Within certain bounds, the leaders are able to refer bills that they favor to committees that will receive them warmly and to refer less-favored bills to other committees.

The procedure for taking bills up for activity on the senate floor is another source of influence for the lieutenant governor. The senate regularly takes bills from the calendar out of order. Before a senator can suggest considering a bill out of order, the lieutenant governor must recognize the senator. This floor procedure gives the lieutenant governor greater control over the scheduling of legislation in the senate than the speaker enjoys in the house.

In recent years, the retirement of leaders who had held their positions for several years brought new people and perspectives to these positions. In 1990, Bill Hobby retired from politics; he had held the office of lieutenant governor longer than any other individual. His successor and former comptroller, Bob Bullock, played a central role in the legislative process as well, but tended to direct more than mediate. Bullock's retirement in 1998 opened the door to further changes in the senate.

After his election in 1998, Lieutenant Governor Rick Perry reassured observers that he would preserve the spirit of bipartisanship in the senate by appointing some Democrats to committee chairmanships and by keeping his door open to all senators.

At the end of the 72d session, Gib Lewis stepped down as speaker of the house of representatives. Pete Laney, from the Panhandle town of Hale Center, was elected speaker for the 73d session in 1993. Laney was a reform candidate: he pledged to make the house more responsive to the membership. And he has changed the house in several important ways. He forced the Calendars Committee to operate openly and by majority rule in making its decisions. He pushed through new rules limiting the last-minute crush of legislation. He reduced the number of committees and juggled committee assignments and chairs. Lobbyists quickly learned that having the speaker on their side was not enough to protect their interests; individual members also had to be lobbied. Laney has refrained from steering the legislative process with the heavy hand that had been characteristic of his predecessors. He chooses to let bills stand or fall on their own and not to rule out bills that he does not think should pass. Some legislators complain that the institution is out of control. Others applaud the speaker's efforts to open participation to all members.[29]

The Committees

In the Texas legislature, as in almost all legislative bodies, committees largely determine the success or failure of legislation. One study found that 55 percent of the bills submitted die in committee.[30] The committees play a major role filtering out bills, preventing them from going further in the legislative process.

The Texas legislature, like other state legislatures, depends on standing committees to carry out much of its work. Committees exist because of the volume and complexity of legislation. It would be impossible for individual

THE CHANGING FACE OF TEXAS POLITICS

Partisan Change and the Texas Senate: Can the Delicate Balance Be Maintained?

Partisan change has caught up with the Texas Senate. What was an overwhelmingly Democratic body a few years ago, has seen a steadily increasing number of Republican members. By 1997, there were seventeen Republican state senators and fourteen Democrats.

With this partisan division of the senate, the body's operating rules make it increasingly difficult to avoid deadlock. Because bills normally come to the floor of the senate on a motion to suspend the rules and take up a bill, putting a bill on the floor requires a two-thirds vote. This means that if more than a third of the senators vote against suspending the rules, a bill cannot be taken up for floor consideration. In numerical terms, that gives any eleven members of the thirty-one-member senate the power to prevent the senate from considering a bill. Democrats still have more than enough votes to block any measure they oppose.

How does the Texas Senate keep working? Managing the delicate balance that keeps the senate functioning has traditionally fallen to its presiding officer. Former Lieutenant Governor Bob Bullock pursued a strategy of bipartisanship, putting important legislation and important committee assignments into the hands of senators from both parties. By playing down partisan differences, the lieutenant governor forged a delicate working relationship in the senate.

Where diplomacy did not work, Bullock used the senate rules. To place a bill on the floor of the senate, a senator must be recognized by the

legislators to read all the bills placed before them in a session, much less understand them and respond rationally to them. Moreover, the house and senate are too large for detailed discussion of legislation.

Standing committees are the workhorses of the legislative process. They undertake the hard work of evaluating the quality of proposed legislation and putting that legislation into a form that can be passed into law. Committees are work groups of reasonable size, each of which specializes in a specific subject matter. As a consequence, members of standing committees develop some expertise in the area of jurisdiction of their committee. The same standing committees usually exist from one legislative session to the next. Presently there are thirty-six standing committees in the house and twelve in the senate (Table 6.2).

One of the trends seen today in many state legislatures is the increasing independence of standing committees.[31] That is, in many states standing committees have become autonomous decision centers. This is not yet the case in Texas. The presiding officers of the Texas legislature still have enough lieutenant governor. Bullock used that power to decide what could and could not be brought up. He was also capable of managing by intimidation. He was well known for his tendency to "chew out" those he thought were getting in the way of achieving the significant objectives he had set for the senate.

The future operation of the Texas Senate ultimately rests on how the issue of partisanship is resolved in that body. Leaders of both parties have traditionally concluded that an open partisan war would only cripple the senate, making it impossible to get anything done. But will that bipartisan spirit hold up now that the Republicans have succeeded in winning a majority of the seats in the senate? That Bob Bullock managed to avoid any challenge to his authority in the 1997 session of the legislature rested on his tradition of even-handedness in dealing with both parties and the recognition that he was a politician who knew how to reward friends and punish enemies. But, Bullock's retirement may reopen the question of the lieutenant governor's role in the senate. Will senators of both parties be willing to trust a new lieutenant governor in the same way that they trusted Bob Bullock? The senators serving in the legislature in 1999 will have to answer that question.

If the Texas Senate is faced with confrontational partisanship, it will have no choice but to change the way it operates. The current system for calling bills to the floor cannot work with partisanship in full bloom. It is a recipe for deadlock. Confrontational partisanship almost certainly would require a reworking of the senate's basic procedures.

That partisanship also might bring an attack on the lieutenant governor's power. The power granted that office under current senate rules is enormous—particularly in light of the fact that the senate leader is not elected by the senators. So an effort to reduce the power of the lieutenant governor might be one consequence of the full flowering of partisanship in the Texas Senate. ★

control over who the chairs and members are to mold committees to suit them.

Currently the most important committees in the House are Appropriations, House State Affairs, Ways and Means, and Calendars. The first three are important because most key pieces of legislation are referred to them. Of these committees, House State Affairs may be the most pivotal. It is filled with loyal supporters of the speaker and receives some of the most important and most difficult pieces of legislation in every session.[32] The Calendars Committee is important because of the role it plays in determining if and when bills come to the floor for consideration.

In 1993 new legislative rules trimmed the power of the house Calendars Committee. They put an end to a practice called *tagging* that allowed individual members of the Calendars Committee to block floor consideration of a bill simply by stating their objection to it either in a committee meeting or in private communications with other committee members. Under the new rules, the committee must decide about placing bills on a calendar in a

Table 6.2 Roster of Standing Committees in the Texas Legislature, 1997

Texas House Committees	Chair	Chair's Party
Agriculture and Livestock	Pete Patterson	Democrat
Appropriations	Robert Junell	Democrat
Business and Industry	Kim Brimer	Republican
Calendars	Mark Stiles	Democrat
Civil Practices	Patricia Gray	Democrat
Corrections	Allen Hightower	Democrat
County Affairs	Ron E. Lewis	Democrat
Criminal Jurisprudence	Allen Place	Democrat
Economic Development	Rene Oliveira	Democrat
Elections	Debra Danburg	Democrat
Energy Resources	Steve Holzheauser	Republican
Environmental Regulation	Warren Chisum	Democrat
Financial Institutions	Ken Marchant	Republican
General Investigating	Pete Gallego	Democrat
Higher Education	Irma Rangel	Democrat
House Administration	Tony Goolsby	Republican
Human Services	Harvey Hilderbran	Republican
Insurance	John T. Smithee	Republican
Judicial Affairs	Senfronia Thompson	Democrat
Juvenile Justice and Family Issues	Toby Goodman	Republican
Land and Resource Management	Fred Bossee	Democrat
Licensing and Administrative Procedures	Ron Wilson	Democrat
Local and Consent Calendars	Ciro Rodriguez	Democrat
Natural Resources	David Counts	Democrat
Pensions and Investments	Barry Telford	Democrat
Public Education	Paul Sadler	Democrat
Public Health	Hugo Berlanga	Democrat
Public Safety	Keith Oakley	Democrat
Redistricting	Delwin Jones	Republican
Rules and Resolutions	Al Edwards	Democrat
State Affairs	Steven Wolens	Democrat
State Recreational Resources	Edmund Kuempel	Republican
State, Federal and International Relations	Bob Hunter	Republican
Transportation	Clyde Alexander	Democrat
Urban Affairs	Fred Hill	Republican
Ways and Means	Tom Craddick	Republican

public meeting and by majority vote. Furthermore, if the Calendars Committee does not act on a bill within thirty days of receiving it, the bill's author can make a motion on the floor to put it on a calendar. If that motion receives a majority vote, the bill is placed on a calendar for consideration.[33]

In the senate, the Finance, State Affairs, Jurisprudence, and Education committees are the most influential committees, in large part because the

Table 6.2 *Cont.*

Texas Senate Committees	Chair	Chair's Party
Administration	Chris Harris	Republican
Criminal Justice	John Whitmire	Democrat
Economic Development	David Sibley	Republican
Education	Teel Bivins	Republican
Finance	Bill Ratliff	Republican
General Investigating	Mike Moncrief	Democrat
Health and Human Services	Judith Zaffirini	Democrat
Intergovernmental Relations	Eddie Lucio	Democrat
International Relations, Trade & Technology	Carlos Truan	Democrat
Jurisprudence	Rodney Ellis	Democrat
Natural Resources	J. E. Brown	Republican
Nominations	Frank Madla	Democrat
State Affairs	Kenneth Armbrister	Democrat

Source: Harvey J. Tucker and Gary M. Halter, eds., *Texas Legislative Almanac 1997* (College Station: Texas A&M University Press, 1997).

most important pieces of legislation usually are referred to them. Because of their central role in the legislative process, positions on these committees are sought with some degree of fervor.

Conference committees are also crucial to the legislative process. Remember that both chambers of the legislature must agree on one version of a bill before it can be passed. Conference committees work out the differences between house and senate versions of a bill. Again, the presiding officers choose conference committee members, usually from the members of the standing committee in each chamber that originally worked on the bill. Chairs of the standing committees normally are included. Conference committees are ad hoc committees appointed to work on a single piece of legislation. When a conference committee completes the work of reconciling the two different versions of a bill, it dissolves.

Conference committees are critical to most major pieces of legislation. If the conference committee cannot work out a compromise, the bill fails. If the conference committee does work out a compromise, the two chambers must accept that version of the bill or the bill cannot pass.

The last type of committee is the **interim committee,** which has the authority to meet between sessions. These committees allow legislators to conduct studies and formulate proposals between sessions, away from the daily grind of a legislative session.

Lobbyists

As Chapter 4 explains, interest groups in Texas traditionally have played a critical role in the legislative process, from the election of legislators through the passage of key pieces of legislation. In the 1997 session, for example, business interests fought to protect themselves from additional taxation as the legislature wrestled with the property tax relief issue. They were successful in their efforts.

The Governor

Texas governors have several tools available with which to influence the legislative process. At the beginning of each regular session, the governor presents a legislative agenda and a budget proposal. The governor also can designate certain items as emergency matters, allowing the legislature to deal with them during the agenda-building stage, when the constitution otherwise restricts legislators to filing bills and holding committee hearings. During special legislative sessions, the governor alone sets the agenda. The governor's most potent weapon for guiding the legislative process is the threat of a veto. If the governor makes it known that particular bills are going to be vetoed, the legislature quickly realizes that pursuing those bills is a waste of precious time.

Political Parties

For most of the state's history, political parties played a minor role in the legislative process. Democrats dominated the legislature to such an extent that there was no need for partisan structures in the legislative body. As Figure 6.5 shows, the Republicans held only token membership in both chambers during the 1960s and 1970s. By the 1980s, Republicans had become a significant minority party. By 1997, they held 17 (55 percent) of the 31 seats in the senate and 68 (45 percent) of the 150 seats in the house. The growth of the Republican party in Texas parallels a similar trend in other southern states, among them Florida, Georgia, the Carolinas, and Virginia.[34]

With both parties significantly represented in the legislature, both parties have created **caucuses** to plan their legislative strategy. The party caucuses allow each party to plan a group strategy for handling major legislative issues. For example, the Republicans and Democrats could each decide how they wanted to handle the governor's tax reform proposal in the 1997 session. The House Democratic Caucus formed in 1981.[35] Republicans initially resisted forming a caucus. They were afraid that the Democratic leadership would retaliate by excluding them from committee chairs. But in 1989 the House Republican Caucus was formed. Party caucuses also function in the Texas Senate.

How has this changing partisan distribution altered legislative strategy? Democratic legislative leaders have had to decide if they should continue to appoint Republicans as committee chairs. After excluding Republicans during the 72d session, in 1991, Lieutenant Governor Bullock reversed his position and appointed Republicans as committee chairs in subsequent sessions. Gib Lewis and Pete Laney appointed Republicans as chairs, albeit to fewer top positions.[36] Texas legislative officers apparently have decided

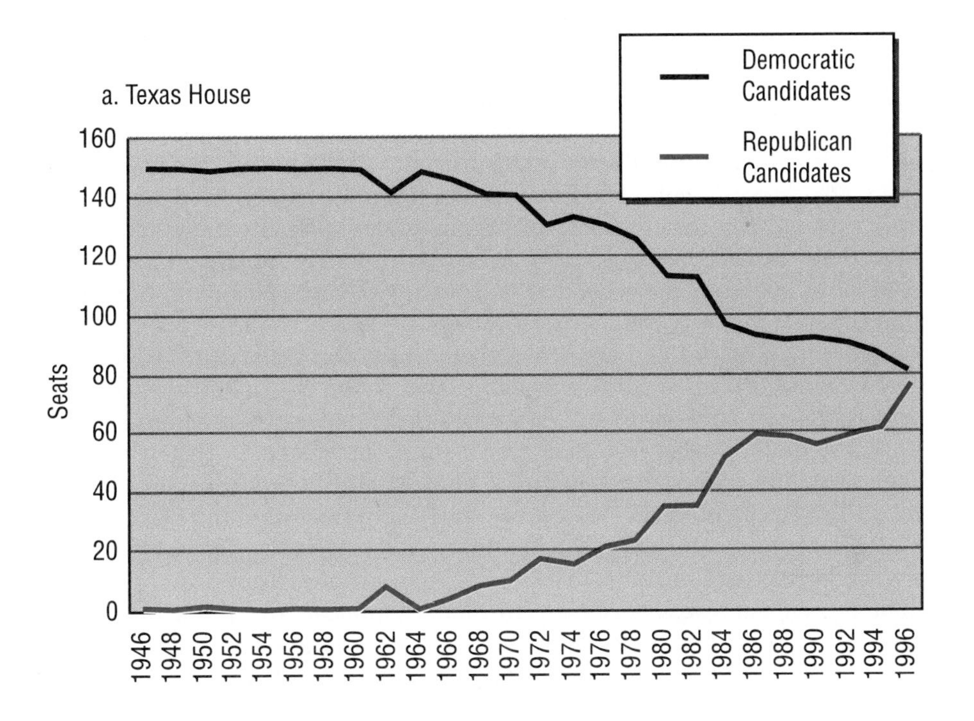

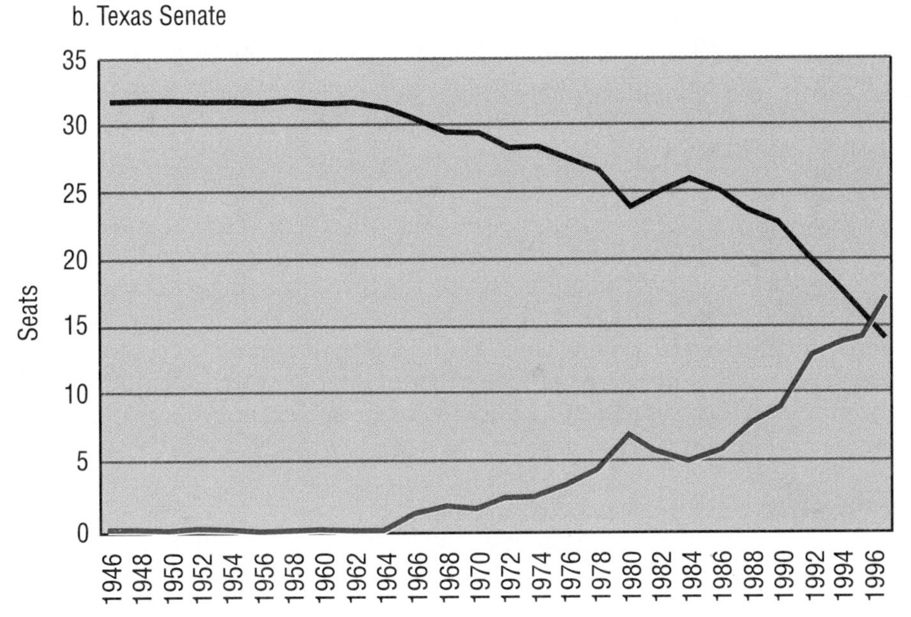

FIGURE 6.5 Distribution of Seats in the Texas Legislature by Party, 1960–1996

Source: U.S. Census Bureau, Statistical Abstract, *1993;* Dallas Morning News, *January 13, 1993, p. 8A, November 10, 1994, 42A; Harvey J. Tucker and Gary M. Halter,* Texas Legislative Almanac 1997 *(College Station: Texas A&M University Press, 1997), p. 6.*

that drawing Republicans into the leadership is more productive than drawing partisan lines. Certainly if Republicans were excluded from committee chairs they could choose to obstruct the legislative process, making it difficult, if not impossible, to pass major pieces of legislation. As a Democrat, Lieutenant Governor Bullock's relationship to the Republican party became especially delicate when the Republicans became the majority party in the 1997 session. To alienate the Republicans under such circumstances would have been to risk losing some powers of his office because most of the lieutenant governor's powers derive from the senate rules, which could be changed by a majority vote.

With increased Republican membership in the legislature, some wondered if Republicans would form a bloc that voted consistently against the Democrats. An analysis of roll call votes in the Texas House found that by 1989, the Republicans were a cohesive group, increasingly distinct from the Democrats. Moreover, the Republican bloc was differentiating itself ideologically from the Democrats—as a conservative alternative to the Democrats.[37] By 1993, Republicans had reached a level of strength that made bloc voting a winning strategy in some cases. That year, senate Republicans had more than the eleven votes necessary to block a motion to take a bill off the calendar early, and house Republicans had enough votes to block the passage of constitutional amendments. During the 1993 session, house Republicans delayed action on a proposed constitutional amendment dealing with school finance reform. Speaker Laney eventually was able to break the Republican bloc and muster the necessary one hundred votes, but not without considerable bargaining. So, although a consistent pattern of straight-party voting has not emerged in the Texas legislature, straight-party voting has become more frequent since the 1980s.

The Courts

The courts often have had an impact on the legislature in recent years. They have forced issues ranging from prison overcrowding to school finance reform onto the legislative agenda and sometimes even have set deadlines for legislative action. In 1998, a group of school districts were attempting to get the courts to intervene in the school finance issue again.[38]

Legislative Support Services

As their workload has increased, state legislatures began to create agencies and to establish support services to help them carry out their responsibilities.

Legislative Council

The **Legislative Council** was created in 1949 and began providing support services for the legislature in 1950. The lieutenant governor, the speaker of the house, the chair of the Senate Administration Committee, the chair of the House Administration Committee, nine members of the house (appointed by the speaker), and four senators (appointed by the lieutenant governor) make up the council. The council appoints a director to oversee the agency's staff.

Background research on upcoming legislation is one of the Legislative Council's principal contributions to the lawmaking process. The Council employs a staff to research the problems that are expected to be discussed in upcoming legislative sessions. The Legislative Council also drafts bills for legislators. Drafting legislation is a complicated task that most legislators have neither the time nor the ability to carry out. Lawmakers bring ideas for legislation to staff members who convert them into bills that will accomplish what the legislators had in mind. The council also runs an orientation session for new members.

Finally, the Legislative Council is a source of the following information services:

- On-line text processing for drafts, bills, resolutions, and House and Senate journals
- Computerized system to track bill status and legislative committee activity
- Automated procedures for budget analysis and appropriations bill processing

By automating many routine legislative tasks, the council allows legislators to track bills and resolutions through the legislative process.

Legislative Reference Library

The **Legislative Reference Library** (established in 1909) maintains a collection of state documents and other reference materials to help legislators or the Legislative Council staff research the policy issues confronting them. The library also participates in the legislature's bill status system and operates a statewide phone service for information when the legislature is in session. This allows people who are interested in a bill to be sure that they appear at committee hearings or that they are prepared for floor consideration.

Legislative Budget Board

The **Legislative Budget Board,** created in 1949, helps the legislature meet its budget responsibilities. Texas and California were among the first states to create legislative budget agencies.[39] The lieutenant governor, the speaker of the house, and four members of the house and senate (including the chairs of the House Appropriations Committee, the House Ways and Means Committee, the Senate Finance Committee, and the Senate State Affairs Committee)

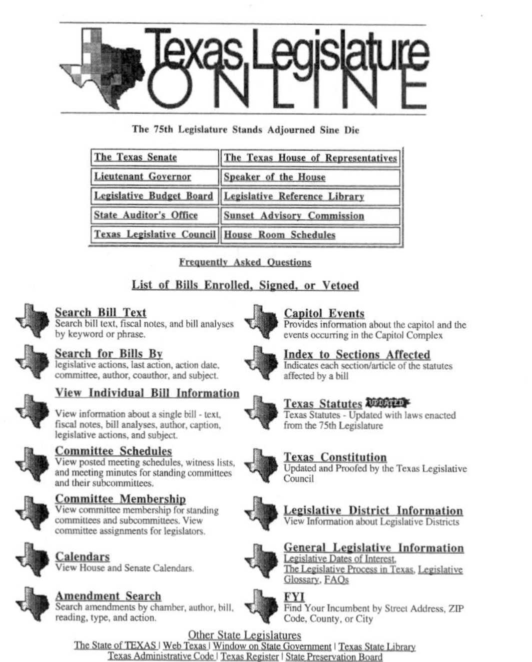

Online information about the legislature and its actions make it easy for legislators—and citizens—to keep informed.
(Source: http://www.capitol.state.tx.us.)

make up the board. They hire a full-time director who oversees the work of the agency's staff.

The board performs three important services:

- Preparing a budget proposal for the legislature's consideration
- Providing staff support to the Appropriations committees during legislative sessions
- Evaluating state agencies

This agency generally is considered to be one of the most important influences on budget decisions made by the Texas legislature.

House and Senate Research Organizations

Each chamber of the legislature now has its own research and information organization. The House Research Organization publishes background reports on issues of legislative interest and a daily floor report when the legislature is in session that includes analyses of the major bills scheduled for floor consideration each day. The Senate Research Center does background research and analyzes every stage bills pass through in the senate. The center also publishes a summary of significant legislation at the end of each session.[40]

Staff

Staff is one of the most important support systems that modern legislators have. Most state legislators worked alone, without office or staff, at the end of World War II. Since then, as states have expanded their activities, the need for legislative support has grown.

Two kinds of staff work with legislators: personal staff and committee staff. *Personal staff* help individual legislators carry out their personal responsibilities. They research issues, gather political intelligence, write speeches, and do whatever else needs to be done to help their bosses do their jobs. They serve as the extra set of eyes, ears, arms, and legs that legislators need to get the job done. Individual legislators choose their own staff members.

Committee staff are assigned to the standing committees, not to individual members. They do research and provide other support services to help the committees carry out the job of evaluating the bills that are assigned to them. Committee staffers are chosen by the committee chair.

By 1996, Texas was ranked fourth among the states in the size of its legislative staff. New York, Pennsylvania, and California ranked above it.[41]

Change in the Texas Legislature

Two types of changes have affected the Texas legislature: institutional change and political change. Over time, structural reforms have improved the capabilities of the institution. And in more recent years, political change—most notably real party competition—has challenged the traditional ways of working in the Texas legislature.

In 1971 the Citizens Conference on State Legislatures published a study that called on the states to modernize their legislatures.[42] Almost thirty years later, the Texas legislature has made some strides toward reforming itself:

- Court rulings governing electoral districts have made the Texas legislature more representative. The overrepresentation of rural areas has disappeared, and previously excluded groups—women, African Americans, and Hispanics—have gained representation.
- Support services have been improved and expanded.
- Rules governing members and lobbyists have limited the influence of special interests in the legislative process.
- Rules and procedures in the house have expanded the participation of individual members and reduced the speaker's dominance in the legislative process.
- Sunset laws have led to the systematic review of administrative agencies.

Despite these changes, significant institutional limitations remain. The most noteworthy of these is the schedule of regular sessions. In about three-quarters of the states in this country legislatures meet annually. Why, then, does Texas persist with biennial sessions? Two factors seem to be at work here. First, Texans are fond of the citizen-legislator concept, the idea that legislative service should be part-time. Defenders of the current system talk disparagingly about a system that would turn Texas legislators into full-time politicians. The second factor is the generous use of special sessions to supplement regular sessions. Although this device allows the legislature to handle the state's business, it does so by surrendering substantial control of the legislative agenda to the governor. Annual sessions would put the legislature on a more equal footing with the governor.

Another significant constraint on the legislature is the low level of compensation paid to members. A salary of $7,200 a year, even supplemented with expenses, may well limit the opportunity to serve in the legislature of those who are not financially well off. The failure to compensate legislators adequately also may have contributed to a system of gifts and financial arrangements by which lobbyists threaten the integrity of lawmakers.

The Texas legislature also has been influenced by political change. The most significant is party diversity in the legislature. There are now enough Republicans in both chambers of the legislature for the party to become a force in the legislative process. So far Republicans have tended to accept the principle that going along is necessary to getting ahead in the Texas legislature. They realize that constant opposition to the Democratic leadership would cost them access to key committees. Republicans would like to be the majority party in both houses. As Republicans hold a larger share of seats in the legislature, they may find it in their interest to differentiate themselves from the Democrats more clearly.

The Texas legislature is constrained by institutional structures that make it difficult for it to function as an equal partner in the Texas government. At the same time, legislators are being bombarded by social, economic, and political changes that are forcing them to be ever more ingenious to keep up. The final steps toward modernizing the legislature ultimately depend on winning the confidence of the people of Texas, so that they support the professionalization of the legislature and are willing to trust that body with the power to make laws. Until that time—and it may be quite a long time—the Texas legislature is going to have to continue to make do with the powers and institutions granted it by a constitution more intent on limiting power than expanding it.

Notes

1. Steve Scheibal, "Lawmakers Reach a Hilltop in Valley of Public Disregard," *Austin American-Statesman* (May 10, 1997), p. B1.
2. Alan Rosenthal, *The Decline of Representative Democracy* (Washington, DC: CQ Press, 1998), p. 2.
3. Texas Constitution, Art. III, Sec. 3.
4. Donnis Baggett, "It's Politics as Usual," *Dallas Morning News*, January 3, 1993, 40A.
5. House Research Organization, *Wrap-up of the 1990 Special Sessions on Public Education* (Austin, 1990), 52.
6. House Research Organization, *Summary of 1991 Special Session Legisla-*

tion (Austin, 1991); and *Journal of the House of Representatives of the Second, Third, and Fourth Called Texas Legislative Sessions of the 72nd Legislature of Texas, VII.* (Austin, 1992).

7. Texas Constitution, Art. III, Sec. 7.
8. Texas Constitution, Art. III, Sec. 6.
9. Texas Constitution, Art. III, Sec. 24.
10. Texas Constitution, Art. III, Sec. 24a.
11. House Research Organization, *1991 Constitutional Amendments* (Austin, 1991), 41.
12. *Baker* v. *Carr,* 369 U.S. 186 (1962).
13. *Reynolds* v. *Sims,* 84 S.Ct. 1362 (1964) (equal districts); and *Wesberry* v. *Sanders,* 84 S.Ct. 526 (1964) (representation based on population).
14. Sam Attlesey, "U.S. Judicial Panel Upholds Democrats' Remap of Senate," *Dallas Morning News,* April 6, 1993, 1A.
15. Texas Constitution, Art. III, Sec. 49–a.
16. The committee consists of the lieutenant governor; the speaker of the house; and the chairs of the Finance, State Affairs, Appropriations, and Ways and Means committees.
17. Texas Constitution, Art. XV, Sec. 8.
18. Texas Legislative Council, *Guide,* 17.
19. Harvey J. Tucker, "Legislative Calendars and Workload Management in Texas," *Journal of Politics* 51 (August 1989): 631–646. The point made here is on p. 634.
20. Tucker, "Legislative Calendars," 633–634.
21. Texas Legislative Council, *Guide,* 5.
22. Harvey J. Tucker, "Legislative Workload Congestion in Texas," *Journal of Politics* 49 (May 1987): 565–578. The point made here is on p. 570.
23. Carolyn Barta, "Texas House Cleans Up Its Act," *Dallas Morning News,* February 1, 1993, 21A.
24. Tucker, "Legislative Workload," 574–575.
25. George Kuempel, "New House Rules Aim to Diffuse Power, Curtail 11th-Hour Rush of Bills," *Dallas Morning News,* January 23, 1993, 42A.
26. Tucker, "Legislative Calendars," 635–636.
27. George Kuempel and Anne Marie Kilday, "Laney Says He Has Votes to Win State Speaker Job," *Dallas Morning News,* November 11, 1992, 1A.
28. Wayne Slater, "The Powers That Be," *Dallas Morning News,* January 10, 1993, 21A.
29. Sylvia Moreno, "Laney Brushes Up House Image," *Dallas Morning News,* June 6, 1993, 49A and 56A.
30. Tucker, "Legislative Workload," 569.
31. Alan Rosenthal, "Legislative Institution," in *The State of the States,* 2d ed. Carl E. Van Horn, ed. (Washington, DC: CQ Press, 1993), 115–148.
32. Gregory S. Thielemann, "Minority Legislators and Institutional Influence," *Social Science Journal* 29 (1992): 411–421. The point made here is on p. 413.
33. George Kuempel, "New House Rules," 42A.
34. Patterson, "State Legislators," 161–200. The point made here is on p. 183.
35. Robert Harmel and Keith Hamm, "Development of a Party Role in a No-Party Legislature," *Western Political Quarterly* 39 (March 1986): 79–92.
36. Keith E. Hamm and Robert Harmel, "Legislative Party Development and the Speaker System," *Journal of Politics* 55 (November 1993): 1140–1151. The point made here is on p. 1149.
37. Hamm and Harmel, "Legislative Party Development," 1143.

38. Terence Stutz, "Schools' Fund Fight Reignited," *Dallas Morning News* (May 8, 1998), p. 1A.

39. Rich Jones, "The Role of Staff in State Legislatures," *Journal of State Government,* 61 (November/December 1988), 188.

40. Texas Legislative Council, *Guide to Legislative Information* (Austin, 1992), 15.

41. National Council of State Legislatures, "Size of State Legislative Staff: 1979, 1988, 1996," (at web site **http://www.ncsl.org**).

42. John Burns, *The Sometime Governments* (New York: Bantam Books, 1971).

7

TEXAS GOVERNORSHIP

CHAPTER OUTLINE

In Texas, May 1998 produced a rather bizarre turn of events—even for Texas government. The newspapers announced that the attorney general was suing the governor! How had such an unusual situation come to pass? The battle between the governor and the attorney general began over the state's suit against the tobacco companies. Texas, like many other states, had sued the tobacco companies to recover damages resulting from the costs to the state of treating diseases related to cigarette smoking. Early in 1998, the attorney general had announced that the state had negotiated a settlement that would commit the cigarette companies to paying more than $15 billion to the state.[1] The fly in the ointment, from the governor's point of view, was that the agreement called for the state to pay $2.2 billion to private lawyers who had worked on the case in the state's behalf. Attorney General Morales defended the payment to the lawyers because they had worked for the state on a contingency basis and, therefore, had risked a considerable investment of their time. In February, the governor and seven state legislators filed suit to try to block the deal and reduce the payment to the lawyers.[2] Finally, in May, the attorney general filed suit against the governor and the legislators to prevent them from interfering with the settlement that had been previously worked out. In addition, the attorney general had asked a U.S. district judge to assess $25 million in penalties against Bush and the legislators.[3]

Although this battle is interesting in itself, it also reveals some defining characteristics about the executive branch of Texas government and the role of the governor in it. One might assume that the governor is the attorney general's boss; however, this case shows that it is not so in Texas. As an independently elected official, the attorney general's job depends on keeping voters happy—not on keeping the governor happy. The case also clearly illustrates that the governor has a limited ability to give direction to some executive officials, because the governor does not hire them and has little or no authority to remove them. The Texas governmental system makes the office of chief executive a real challenge for Texas governors.

Clearly executive power in Texas is fragmented. To understand the governor's role in state politics, then, includes a grasp of the limitations on gubernatorial power. This chapter answers several questions about the structure of the governor's office and the behavior of its occupants:

- What are the formal powers granted to the Texas governor, and how do they compare with the powers of other state governors?
- What factors in addition to the formal authority of the office influence a governor's ability to lead?
- How has the governor's office in Texas changed over the years?

Change and the Governorship: An Introduction

Although governorships in the United States historically have been weak, the office has been changing in recent years. One book captures the essence of those changes in its title, *Goodbye to Good-Time Charlie.*[4] An office once occupied by political hacks and buffoons today is expected to be a source of the leadership that is necessary to help states solve their problems. As expectations for the office have grown, many states have endowed the occupants of the office with the authority to function as chief executive officers.[5]

Two of the same forces that have led other states to increase their governor's authority are present in Texas: growing public expectations that the state will deal with significant policy problems and the willingness of the national government to cede policy leadership in many areas. But the restructuring of the Texas governorship has not kept pace with changes in other states. This chapter identifies what changes have been made in the governor's office and analyzes why those changes have not been as far-reaching as changes in other states.

The Office of Governor

Article IV of the Texas Constitution establishes an executive department and declares that the governor shall be the chief executive officer. Governors are paid a salary set by the legislature ($115,345 a year in 1998), live in the state-owned governor's mansion, and have access to a state-owned airplane and a helicopter. Governors also are reimbursed for their travel expenses.

The constitution provides that the governor be elected by the people. Candidates for governor usually are nominated by a political party and then compete in a general election. Gubernatorial elections are held in nonpresidential election years to eliminate the influence of popular presidential candidates. Gubernatorial candidates have to face the electorate without the benefit (or burden) of presidential coattails.

Texas governors now serve four-year terms. A constitutional amendment, approved in 1972, changed the term from two to four years. The election of 1974 was the first in which candidates ran for a four-year term. Texas governors can run for reelection. In the twenty years since the four-year term went into effect, no governor had won two successive terms of service, until George Bush broke the one-term string in 1998.

Texas governors can be removed from office by **impeachment.** The process is outlined in Article XV of the state's constitution. The house adopts the articles of impeachment, which set forth the charges against the governor; then the senate tries the governor on those charges. Only one governor, James E. "Pa" Ferguson, has been removed from office by impeachment and conviction. In the aftermath of a bitter battle with various political leaders over control of the University of Texas, Ferguson was impeached in 1917 for the misapplication of state funds. In an effort to avoid being barred from future office by impeachment, Ferguson tendered his resignation the day before the senate voted. That did not, however, prevent the senate from convicting him and barring him from future officeholding.

Qualifications for Office

According to the Texas constitution, a gubernatorial candidate must be at least thirty years old, a U.S. citizen, and a resident of the state for five years. Once elected, a governor cannot hold any other office, public or private.[6] The constitution stipulates the formal qualifications for governor; the informal qualifications can be inferred by examining the people who have been elected governor in recent years. Most were men, white, and politically conservative; and most either have had a lot of money themselves or could raise large amounts of money.

Only two Texas governors have been women. The first, Miriam "Ma" Ferguson, was elected in 1924 and again in 1932. The second, Ann Richards, a former state treasurer, was elected in 1990. The only other woman to come close in a gubernatorial election in the state was Frances Farenthold. She made it to the Democratic runoff primary in 1972.

All the governors to date have been anglos. La Raza Unida did nominate a Hispanic candidate in 1972 and 1974 but was not able to gain widespread support for him. No African American has been a viable candidate for the governor's office.

Political conservatism is still a basic requirement for winning the governorship in Texas. The kiss of death in Texas politics is being tagged a liberal.

Finally, in recent years successful candidates for governor have needed access to large amounts of money for campaign expenses. The cost of running for governor in Texas is high (see Chapter 5). Before the 1990 election, Clayton Williams, the Republican candidate, spent approximately $20 million; Ann Richards, the Democratic candidate, spent about $12 million. Some candidates have spent large amounts of their own money. This was the case with Governor Clements (especially in 1978) and with Williams.

Some unwritten characteristics that once seemed essential for winning no longer seem necessary. For example, it is no longer necessary to belong to the Democratic party to win the governorship of Texas. From the end of the Civil War until 1978, all of the governors of Texas were Democrats. Clements's successful races in 1978 and 1986, Clayton Williams's close race with Ann Richards in 1990, and George W. Bush's victories in 1994 and 1998 suggest that the governorship is no longer a position for which only Democrats need apply.

Experience in state office also has become less important in Texas gubernatorial politics. Recent Republican candidates have done well campaigning as nonpoliticians, arguing that their business experience actually gives them the best skills for managing the state. Clements used this approach in three races (especially his 1978 race), Williams used it in 1990, and Bush used it successfully in 1994. Most Democratic candidates have had experience in state office. But political experience is an asset that can turn into a liability if a candidate can be made to appear responsible for the state's problems in the past. That happened to Ann Richards in 1994.

The Responsibilities of the Office

The Texas Constitution assigns several responsibilities to the governor.[7] The first is to ensure that the laws of the state are executed faithfully. Second, the governor is commander in chief of the state militia; he or she has the power to call on the militia to enforce the laws of the state when necessary. Third, only the governor—not the legislature itself—has the power to call the legislature into special session. Fourth, the constitution gives the governor the power to grant pardons for state criminal charges on the recommendation of the Board of Pardons and Paroles. Finally, the governor can approve or veto bills passed by the legislature. The ability of governors to discharge the responsibilities of the office effectively depends on several other powers.

Appointment and removal powers. Traditionally the Texas governor's ability to choose the people who head state agencies or to remove those whose service is unsatisfactory has been limited. Of constitutionally created executives, the governor appoints only the secretary of state. The treasurer, the comptroller, the attorney general, the commissioner of agriculture, and the commissioner of the General Land Office all are elected by the people. Many state agencies are supervised by boards or commissions (see Chapter 8). Within a four-year term, a governor appoints (subject to senate confirmation) about four thousand people to those boards and commissions.[8] But because board members usually serve for fixed staggered terms, it is almost impossible to appoint a majority during a single gubernatorial term.

The Texas Constitution and statutes traditionally have limited the power of governors to appoint department heads. In recent years, however, Texas governors have gained the right to make appointments to several important agencies:

- Governor Clements won the right to name the commissioner of education, who heads the agency that oversees the state's primary and secondary schools. That power was strengthened in 1995, when the elected Board of Education's power to nominate candidates for the office was eliminated.[9]

- The Texas Insurance Board, with which both Governors Clements and Richards struggled, has been abolished. Today a single commissioner, appointed by the governor for a two-year term, directs the Texas Department of Insurance.[10]

- The Health and Human Services Commission, which was created in 1993 to coordinate the services provided by several agencies, is headed by a commissioner who is appointed by the governor to a two-year term.[11]
- The governor appoints the director of the Department of Housing and Community Affairs, who serves at the pleasure of the governor.[12]

Although the governor may not be able to appoint a majority of a board, he or she can exert influence over certain important agencies by designating the chair of the agency's supervisory board or commission. For example, the governor can name the chair and vice chair of the Texas Higher Education Coordinating Board, which supervises the state's colleges and universities.[13] The three full-time commissioners who oversee the Texas Natural Resource Conservation Commission serve staggered six-year terms. The governor can designate one of them as chair.[14] The governor also designates the chair of the Texas Board of Criminal Justice, which supervises the Department of Criminal Justice, the agency that runs the state's prisons.[15]

The governor's power to remove officials is more limited than the power to appoint them. With the consent of the senate, governors can remove their own appointees but cannot remove the appointees of other governors. Thus governors are held responsible for the operation of agencies even when they are unable to choose the people who manage those agencies.

Different studies have compared the powers of governors in all states. One classified the removal power of each state governor into one of five categories, ranging from "broad" to "very restricted." Only twenty-two states granted their governors "broad" to "moderately broad" removal powers; the rest gave their governors "restricted" or "very restricted" removal powers. The Texas governorship fell into the "restricted" category—the most populated category. The people who conducted the study found that states that grant more-generous removal powers are likely to have revised their constitutions or reorganized their executive branch of government recently.[16] Texas has done neither.

Why does Texas restrict the governor's powers to appoint and remove officials? **Jacksonian Democracy,** a movement during the second quarter of the nineteenth century, popularized the idea that political executives could best be held accountable through elections. Many states expanded their list of elected executives from the governor and lieutenant governor to cabinet-level offices. In the last quarter of the nineteenth century, widespread corruption and the abuse of authority further undermined governors' appointment and removal powers. During that period, the states adopted constitutional provisions limiting those powers. In Texas the administration of Governor E. J. Davis (see Chapter 2) convinced many that excessive gubernatorial power was dangerous, that governors could not be trusted to discharge the appointment power fairly. The product of that thinking was a constitution that made the election of many top political executives mandatory and that insulated agencies from gubernatorial meddling by giving boards the authority to supervise them.

Budget power. Forty-seven states assign primary budget authority to the governor. In these states, governors use the budget to set priorities for the state and have the power to implement those priorities. Only three states—Mississippi, South Carolina, and Texas—force their governor to share budget authority with others.[17]

An important step in the budget process is drafting a proposal that suggests priorities for allocating the state's resources over the budget period. In Texas the Governor's Office of Budget and Planning prepares the governor's budget proposal; at the same time, the Legislative Budget Board prepares its own proposal. Although the staffs of the two agencies have cooperated in recent years, most observers think that the Legislative Budget Board has more influence on the form the budget eventually takes (see Chapter 11).

Divided control—when one party controls the governorship and the other controls the legislature—further diminishes the governor's role in the budget proposal stage. When Bill Clements was governor, the leaders of the Democratic-controlled legislature were not inclined to take the budget proposals of a Republican governor seriously. This reinforced the legislature's tendency to follow the counsel of its own staff and to ignore the governor's proposed budget. Governor Bush has deferred to the legislature on budgetary matters.

The governor of Texas does have three tools with which to set budget limits for the legislature. The threat of a veto—making it clear that the inclusion of new taxes or appropriations for a particular program will elicit a veto—is a potent weapon. Governor Clements set the limits for three special sessions by insisting that he would veto any school reform bill that required a tax increase. Subsequent governors have also made "no new taxes" a budgetary assumption.

The second tool is the **line-item veto,** which allows a governor to veto specific items in an appropriations bill. It removes the take-the-bill-as-a-whole-or-lose-everything dilemma from appropriations bills. Instead, specific expenditures that the governor believes excessive, unnecessary, or politically unwise can be deleted.

The third tool is the **budget execution power,** the power to supervise the way executive agencies handle their budgets. The legislature has authorized the governor to issue budget execution orders, subject to the approval of or modification by the Legislative Budget Board. (The Legislative Budget Board also can issue budget execution orders that are subject to the governor's approval.) A budget execution order can transfer appropriations from one state agency to another, use agency appropriations for another purpose, or change the timing of agency appropriations.[18] This power gives governors the flexibility to adapt a budget to changes that take place after the budget has been enacted.

Legislative powers. A governor's power to influence the legislature may be the key to exerting real influence in a state. What kinds of legislative powers do governors commonly have?

Addressing the legislature, as Governor Bush does here, can be an effective tool in the hands of a skillful governor.

- The **message power**—the right to address the legislature and suggest policies
- The **special session power**—the right to call the legislature into special session
- The **veto power**

Each of these legislative powers is significant alone. Collectively they give the governor substantial influence over the policymaking process. All of these powers are available to the governor of Texas.

The governor's message power comes from the Texas Constitution's requirement that the governor provide information on the state of the state at the beginning of each legislative session and at the end of his or her term. The message power gives the governor an opportunity to set an agenda at the beginning of each legislative session.

The constitution also grants the governor the exclusive power to convene special sessions of the legislature. In addition, in any special session the governor has the right to limit the topics the legislature can consider.

Finally, veto is a powerful means of setting limits for legislative work. By threatening to veto a bill, a governor defines acceptable policy options. Because a vote of two-thirds of those present is required in each legislative chamber, overriding a gubernatorial veto is difficult under any circumstances, and lawmakers do not have an opportunity to override vetoes made after the

Contemporary Texas governors are expected to promote international trade and investment. Here, Governor Bush accepts a pair of cowboy boots from a Japanese company doing business in Texas.

legislative session has ended. (Remember that most important bills are acted on at the end of a legislative session.)

Intergovernmental powers. The Texas Constitution (Article IV, Section 10), says that the governor shall handle all "intercourse and business of the State with other states and with the United States." Given the complex system of federal grants-in-aid and the shared federal–state responsibility for administering many significant programs, the governor's relationship with the national government can be critical to the state's well-being. When a site for a national government project is being decided, the governor is expected to be a salesperson for the state.

To facilitate lobbying at the federal level, Texas and many other states keep an office in the nation's capital. The director of this office works under the governor's supervision to protect the state's interests on legislative matters and to help lobby for projects that would benefit the state.

The governor also is responsible for relationships with other states. For example, Texas and other states along the Mexico–United States border have talked about the problems of illegal immigration from Mexico. When the state is ready to negotiate any interstate compact (a treatylike agreement) with other states, the governor is responsible for the negotiations.

Although neither the U.S. nor the Texas Constitution mentions this responsibility, recent governors have worked with leaders of foreign governments to open markets for the state's goods, to promote tourism in the state, and to encourage foreign investment in the state.[19] An example: Texas has long kept an office in Mexico to handle the variety of trade problems that arise because of a shared border.

The Governor's Staff

To meet the responsibilities of the office, the governor relies on a network of assistants and staff agencies (Table 7.1). Most of the staff helps the governor carry out his or her official responsibilities. This group includes several personal assistants, a chief of staff, a scheduling office, and an appointments office. A communications director helps with media relations. A budget staff helps prepare the governor's budget proposal and recommends budget execution strategies. A legislative liaison staff works with the legislature on the governor's behalf. The Criminal Justice Division administers funds for criminal justice planning.

Other staff groups were transferred to the governor's office because the legislature did not have another place to put them. For example, the film and music promotion offices, which had been in the Department of Commerce, were transferred to the governor's office by the legislature.

The Lieutenant Governor

The Texas Constitution describes the lieutenant governor as an executive officer (Article IV, Section 1), but in most ways that description is misleading. The executive powers of the lieutenant governor are quite limited. The constitution essentially describes this officer as the one who serves "in case of the death, resignation, removal from office, inability or refusal of the Governor to serve, or his impeachment or absence from the State."[20] Under most circumstances, this means that the lieutenant governor will be asked to discharge the governor's responsibilities when he or she is out of the state. Thus, as an executive official, the lieutenant governor is a standby or a stand-in—not a very strong platform for executive leadership.

In fact, the lieutenant governor is not the passive standby or stand-in that focusing on executive powers might suggest. The real power of the lieutenant governor is based on the constitutionally designated role of the office as president of the senate. As the presiding officer of the senate, lieutenant governors have shared a prominent role in state policy making, and they, along with governors and speakers of the House of Representatives, are usually thought of as the most influential leaders of the state. But, the power of lieutenant governors in the senate is not inevitable. As the vice president of the United States and the lieutenant governors of many other states would attest, that title can be simply an honorary designation. However, as Chapter 6 pointed out, the Texas lieutenant governor is granted an extraordinary amount of power by the rules of the senate. Those rules make what could be just an honorary leadership position into a position of true

Table 7.1 Office of the Governor

Executive Office	Provides oversight and direct support for the governor's activities.
Administration	Provides direct support for the governor's staff including: accounting, internal budget, human resources, computer services, operations, and mail room.
Appointments	Recommends individuals for appointments to boards, commissions, and advisory committees.
Budget and Planning	Provides fiscal information and analysis relating to the state's fiscal policies.
State Grants Team	Monitors federal, state, and private funding information resources and alerts state agencies, non-profit organizations, units of local government, and other entities to funding operations.
Communications	Responsible for all news media inquiries, news releases, and public information, speech writing, correspondence, citizens assistance office.
General Counsel	Provides legal advice on matters involving the state.
Legislative Office	Advises the governor on legislative matters and assists in developing and passing the governor's legislative initiatives.
Policy Office	Provides information and analysis on state policy matters and works closely with the state's constituents.
Governor's Mansion	The historic residence of the governor and his family.
Governor's Commission for Women	Provides information and referral to the general public on issues regarding women and volunteerism.
Criminal Justice Division	Administers and allocates state and federal grants for criminal justice planning.

Table 7.1 *Cont.*

Criminal Justice Division
Administers and allocates state and federal grants for criminal justice planning.
Governor's Committee on People with Disabilities
Advises on policies and programs relevant to people with disabilities.
Film/Music/Multimedia Offices
Assists the various elements of the entertainment industry in finding Texas locations, talents, and services.
Division of Emergency Management
Advises the governor on emergency developments and disasters of the state and issuance of emergency proclamations.
Texas Council on Work Force and Economic Competitiveness
Advises the governor and the legislature on strategic direction for and evaluation of the state's workforce development system.

Source: Governor's web site (**http://www.governor.state.tx.us**).

power. The lieutenant governor will continue to be powerful in the senate so long as the senate wants it that way—those powers are not constitutionally guaranteed.

It should also be noted that the office of governor and lieutenant governor are not united on the ballot in Texas as they are in some other states. Some states require the two officers to run together as a team. There has been no such constitutional requirement or tradition in Texas. Statewide elective officers campaign independently and measure their success by their ability to please their own electorates—not by the nature of their relationship with the governor.

The Governorship and Leadership

The office of the governor has specific responsibilities, but the key to being a good governor depends on the ability to use the office to lead the state. **Leadership** is using available resources to get others to cooperate in solving problems. Certainly leadership depends in part on the authority to command others, but governors also must rely on other resources to secure cooperation. Understanding the governorship, then, involves knowing when the Texas governor is likely to muster the formal and informal resources necessary to be an effective leader.

The likelihood of a governor's exerting leadership at a particular time depends on institutional, personal, political, and external factors. **Institu-**

tional factors either grant authority (facilitating leadership) or withhold authority (limiting leadership). **Personal factors** are the individual characteristics of governors—personality or an effective media style, for example—that make it easier or more difficult to be an effective leader. **Political factors**—examples are the comparative strength of the political parties and the nature of public opinion—can increase leadership opportunities or limit them. Economic conditions and other **external factors** over which the governor may have little control make leadership more or less difficult. Whether leadership is effectively exerted at a particular time depends on a complex mixture of these forces.

Institutional Factors

The National Governors' Association has concluded that "the framework in which a Governor performs his or her job can be an important factor in a successful governorship."[21] But in Texas, almost all Texas governors have complained that the office does not provide power that is equal to its responsibilities.

To assess institutional factors as they affect Texas governors, ratings comparing the institutional powers of the Texas governorships to other state governorships can be helpful. The commonly used rating system for the governor's institutionalized powers includes tenure potential, appointment power, removal power, budgetary power, veto power, legislative power to change the budget, and governor/legislature partisan agreement. Each component of gubernatorial power was rated from 1 to 5 and the component scores were averaged for each governorship (Table 7.2). Although thirty states got scores of 3.5, or 4, the Texas governorship was rated 3.0 along with sixteen other states. Comparing ratings for 1965 with those for 1994 shows that Texas and thirty-seven other states had experienced little change in the institutional strength of the office.[22]

An examination of the component ratings reveals more clearly the ways in which the Texas governorship is weak. The Texas governorship is above average on tenure potential and veto powers but below average on appointment power, removal powers, and budget powers. The governor is also weak compared with the legislature on budget matters.[23] As a result, Texas governors usually must rely heavily on factors other than institutional power to be strong leaders.

Personal Factors

The personal characteristics of governors influence their ability to lead. Governors who lack strong institutional powers can compensate by relying on personal skills.[24]

Personality often influences a governor's leadership potential. Some governors have a charismatic personality that attracts loyal support. John Connally was an example in the 1960s. Ann Richards and George Bush are

Table 7.2 Ratings of Institutional Powers of Governors, by State, Summer 1994

5.0 (strong)	4.5	4.0	3.5	3.0	2.5	2.0	1.0 (weak)
		Hawaii	Alaska	Alabama	North Carolina		
		Iowa	Arizona	California	South Carolina		
		Maryland	Arkansas	Colorado	Vermont		
		New Jersey	Connecticut	Florida			
		New York	Delaware	Georgia			
		Ohio	Illinois	Idaho			
		Pennsylvania	Kansas	Indiana			
		Tennessee	Kentucky	Maine			
		West Virginia	Louisiana	Massachusetts			
			Michigan	Mississippi			
			Minnesota	Nevada			
			Missouri	New Hampshire			
			Montana	Oklahoma			
			Nebraska	Texas			
			New Mexico	Virginia			
			North Dakota	Washington			
			Oregon	Wyoming			
			Rhode Island				
			South Dakota				
			Utah				
Average score: 3.4			Wisconsin				

Source: Thad Beyle, "Governors: The Middlemen and Women in Our Political System," in *Politics in the American States*, 6th ed., Virginia Gray and Herbert Jacob, eds. (Washington, DC: CQ Press, 1996), p. 237.

contemporary examples. Although much public support is performance based and must be earned by solving public problems, these governors indicate that some popularity is simply personality-based. Bush, for example, was popular even before he had a chance to perform. His early polls in 1995 showed a high level of personal approval before he had much of a record of public achievement.

Vision is another personal factor that can affect gubernatorial leadership. *Vision* is a sense of what a state can do and how it can do it. Governor Mark White, for example, had a vision of a better educational system that was the driving force of his administration. Governor Bush communicated a clear agenda in his 1994 campaign and was successful in getting legislative action on most of it. In 1997, Governor Bush's proposals for providing property tax relief were less successful, reminding us that visions are not always realized. This kind of dream both motivates governors and becomes a rallying point for their supporters. Governors with vision are more likely to exert leadership than those without, but they also must have the skills to sell their dreams to the voters.[25]

Political Factors

Several political factors influence gubernatorial leadership. One is the size of the governor's electoral majority. A governor who wins by a landslide is more likely to be influential than one who wins by a narrow margin.

Support from members of the governor's party in the legislature also can affect a governor's leadership opportunities. When a majority of the members of the legislative body belong to the same party as the governor, the likelihood of their cooperating with the governor increases. Even when the governor is from one party and the majority of the legislators are from another, partisan loyalty can play a role in a governor's ability to lead. For example, in 1990 Governor Clements called on Republican legislators to support his veto of the school reform legislation. As party competition grows, governors probably will rely more on partisan appeals to rally support behind them.

Public opinion also influences gubernatorial power, because the governor can use public support as a leverage when bargaining with legislators or bureaucrats. A governor with strong backing from the public usually is more influential than one who has weak public support—nobody wants to cross a very popular governor. Figure 7.1 shows the highest approval rating for recent governors. Governor White's popularity waned during his term of office

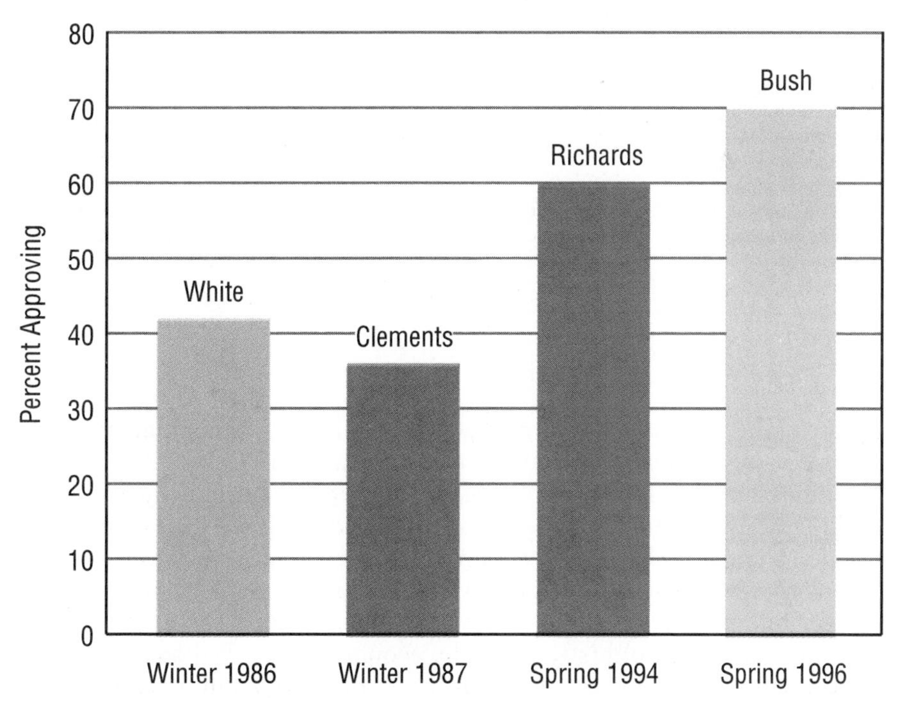

FIGURE 7.1 Highest Job Approval Ratings Achieved by Recent Governors in the Texas Poll

Source: Data provided by Scripps Howard Texas Poll.

THE CHANGING FACE OF TEXAS POLITICS

What Will Popularity Do for a Governor? The George Bush Story

One of the notable features of George Bush's tenure as governor is the high level of popularity that he has experienced. When Bush started his term in 1995, he had about 49 percent popular approval of his work. A year later he had 70 percent popular approval of the job he was doing as governor! And, his approval ratings have stayed in the upper 60 percent since. While Anne Richards was governor, the press had proclaimed her to be the most popular governor in modern times, but Bush clearly succeeded her in that category. Richards's highest approval rating was 60 percent, and that point was reached just before she entered into the campaign against Bush in 1994. How important is this kind of popularity to a governor's career? To understand the role of popularity in gubernatorial politics, it will be helpful to take a look at what popularity has gotten for Bush, and what it has not been able to deliver.

At first, it appeared that popularity might also be the ticket to legislative success for Bush. At the end of his first legislative session in 1995, the press proclaimed Bush a legislative success because most of his campaign promises had been enacted by the legislature.[1] Although Bush's strategy of endorsing proposals the legislature already favored accounted for part of his success, being a popular governor certainly did not hurt. But, when Bush was emboldened to take on the issue of property tax reform at the next legislative session in 1997, he was considerably less successful. In February 1997, Bush's chances looked good. The Texas Poll indicated that 69 percent of the people approved of his performance as governor, and nearly two-thirds said they backed the governor's plan.[2] But, as was noted in Chapter 4 on interest groups, the business lobby defeated the governor's plan and forced him to settle for a much watered-down version. Nevertheless, at the end of the session Bush's popularity was still high, and few of the citizens blamed him for the failure of the property tax proposal.[3]

because of the educational reforms he pushed. That loss of popularity reduced his ability to lead and contributed to his defeat in 1986 by Bill Clements. Governor Clements started his second term with low ratings—near the level at which Mark White left office. Soon after taking office, Clements's popularity fell sharply as the state's economy faltered and as it became known that the governor, while serving on the SMU Board of Regents, had been involved in the university's football recruiting scandals. Clements's public support grew toward the end of his term as the economy improved and memory of the scandal waned. Governors Richards and Bush took public approval to a new level. Richards's personality and her talent for avoiding the personal blame for difficult choices helped her retain this high level of support. As Figure 7.2 reveals, she still had high approval ratings before losing the election

Thus, the lesson of the 1997 session was that even great popularity does not guarantee that a governor can get his legislation passed.

One of the more bizarre things that his popularity got for Governor Bush was an endorsement by the opposing party's top-ranking officeholder. Early in the 1998 campaign, Lieutenant Governor Bob Bullock (a Democrat) announced that he thought Governor Bush was unbeatable and suggested that the Democrats might as well not even run anyone against him. Bullock went on to endorse the Governor![4] Admittedly, this happened under unusual circumstances: Bullock was retiring from office and could risk alienating his own party. This was an event not likely to become a common occurrence in Texas politics.

As the campaign progressed into 1998, Bush found that his popularity brought him a number of friends among other candidates. Fellow Republicans seeking other state offices rushed to associate themselves with the governor, in hopes that some of his good fortune would rub off on their campaigns. Clinging to the governor's coattails became a new style of campaigning.

Finally, one of the things that Bush's popularity got him was a place on the list of potential Republican presidential contenders for the election in 2000. As a highly popular governor and the son of a former president, Bush became a credible contender for the presidency. In fact, his campaign strategies for re-election to the governorship in 1998 involved reassuring people that he was truly interested in the governorship, and that it was not just a steppingstone to the presidency.

George Bush's experience as governor illustrates the point that popularity can help the governor achieve his or her goals. He began his campaign for re-election so far ahead in the polls that some, including the lieutenant governor who came from the opposition party, thought that campaigning against him was futile. But, Bush's experience also makes the point that popularity does not guarantee success, as Bush failed to get most of what he wanted in property tax reform in 1997. Thus, popularity certainly helps a governor, but it does not solve every problem. ★

[1]Jane Ely, "Gov. Bush Gets Good Marks All Around," *Houston Chronicle,* May 17, 1995, 28A.

[2]Wayne Slater, "Texans Back Tax Plan, Poll Finds," *Dallas Morning News,* February 23, 1997, p. 45A.

[3]Clay Robison, "Texans Still Back Bush, Poll Finds," *Houston Chronicle,* August 30, 1997, p. A37.

[4]Sam Attlesey, Wayne Slater, "Bush Virtually Unbeatable for Re-election, Bullock Says," *Dallas Morning News,* July 26, 1997, p. 1A.

in 1994. Governor Bush started at a low approval rating, but climbed to a record setting level by 1996. He retained the approval of almost two-thirds of the people through 1997.

External Factors

External factors also affect a governor's opportunities for leadership. In the 1970s, high oil prices allowed the state to finish its fiscal years with surpluses in the treasury. This meant that governors could initiate new programs without raising taxes. In the mid-1980s, when oil prices plummeted and the state was in an economic slump, it was difficult for the governor to be an

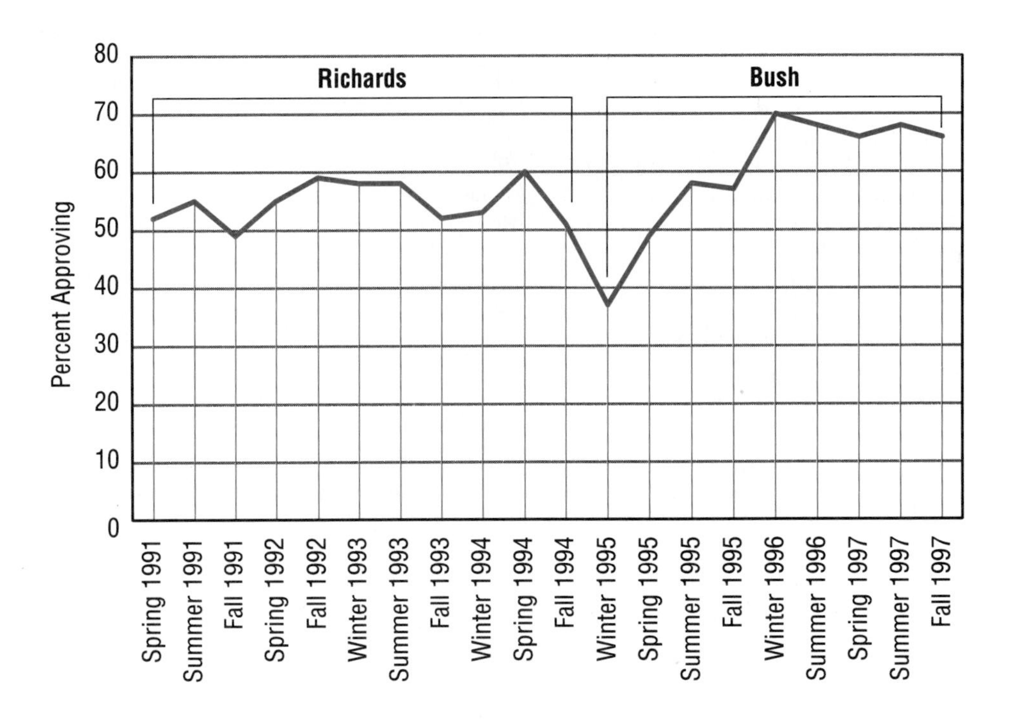

FIGURE 7.2 Approval Ratings for Governors Richards and Bush, 1991–1997
Source: Data provided by Scripps Howard Texas Poll.

effective leader. All of the state's resources, all of its leader's energy, had to be focused on solving the economic crisis.

Decisions by other government authorities also can influence a governor's leadership opportunities. Several Texas governors have been affected by court rulings that forced prison conditions, funding for public education, and the election of state judges onto the public agenda. In his second term, as the number of court orders accumulated, Governor Clements protested that "these judges are going to have to get in line."

 Governors and the Governorship

Table 7.3 lists all the Texas governors. Several of these men and women are noteworthy for the ways they shaped the office.

James Stephen Hogg—When he took office in 1891, Hogg brought to an end a line of Democratic governors who had been Confederate soldiers. Hogg was an advocate of regulation against entrenched business interests. He pushed for better regulation of the railroads and persuaded the legislature to set up the Texas Railroad Commission. Hogg continued to press for the regulation of business through his second term in office.

Governor Ann Richards, the state's second woman governor, was quite popular and noted for her forceful speaking.

James E. and Miriam Ferguson—"Pa" Ferguson was elected governor in 1914 and reelected two years later. "Ma" Ferguson was elected in 1924 and again in 1932 after her husband was removed from office by impeachment and conviction, which barred him from further officeholding. Between them the Fergusons were major players in Texas politics for twenty years. Together they made the governor a champion of the little people and a guardian against bigotry. In James Ferguson's first term, he led the legislature to pass legislation limiting tenants' rents and increasing aid to rural schools. He and his wife opposed Prohibition. Miriam Ferguson defeated the first Klan-backed candidate for governor in 1924.

W. Lee O'Daniel—O'Daniel brought showmanship to the governor's office. Elected in 1938, during the Great Depression, "Pappy" O'Daniel was a colorful figure. He was known as a flour salesman and the leader of a radio show with country appeal. In his campaigns there was more country and western music than substance. The same could be said of his administration.

Allan Shivers—In 1949 Shivers succeeded Governor Beauford H. Jester, the only Texas governor to die in office. Shivers ushered in the contemporary period of the Texas governorship. He saw the governor as a force for modernization. Although Shivers was a conservative, state spending more than doubled during his three full terms in office, and the state's budget first topped the $1 billion mark. The Texas economy was industrializing and Shivers helped expand the scope of government to respond to that change.

Table 7.3 The Governors of Texas, 1846–1998

Governor	Term
J. Pickney Henderson	February 19, 1846–December 21, 1847
George T. Wood	December 21, 1847–December 21, 1849
P. Hansbrough Bell	December 21, 1849–November 23, 1853
J. W. Henderson	November 23, 1853–December 21, 1853
Elisha M. Pease	December 21, 1853–December 21, 1857
Hardin R. Runnels	December 21, 1857–December 21, 1859
Sam Houston	December 21, 1859–March 16, 1861
Edward Clark	March 16, 1861–November 7, 1861
Francis R. Lubbock	November 7, 1861–November 5, 1863
Pendleton Murrah	November 6, 1863–June 17, 1865
Andrew J. Hamilton	June 17, 1865–August 9, 1866
James W. Throckmorton	August 9, 1866–August 8, 1867
Elisha M. Pease	August 8, 1867–September 30, 1869
E. J. Davis	January 8, 1870–January 15, 1874
Richard Coke	January 15, 1874–December 1, 1876*
Richard B. Hubbard	December 1, 1876–January 21, 1879
Oran M. Roberts	January 21, 1879–January 16, 1883
John Ireland	January 16, 1883–January 18, 1887
Lawrence Sullivan Ross	January 18, 1887–January 20, 1891
James Stephen Hogg	January 20, 1891–January 15, 1895
Charles A. Culberson	January 15, 1895–January 17, 1899
Joseph D. Sayers	January 17, 1899–January 20, 1903
S. W. T. Lanham	January 20, 1903–January 15, 1907

*Resigned to enter the U.S. Senate.
†Impeached and removed from office in 1917.
‡Died in office.

John Connally—Elected in 1962, Connally made the governor a champion of education. He aggressively pushed the legislature to increase funding for education at all levels. And he built on the expansion and improvement of services started by Shivers.

William E. Clements—Clements will be remembered for pioneering the Republican-businessman-outsider role in the Texas governorship. He proved that a Republican who was not an Austin insider could get elected by making a virtue of not being a politician. In effect Clements opened a new door to the Texas governorship.

Ann Richards—When Ann Richards won the governor's office in 1990 after a bitter campaign, she faced what observers called "the bleakest political prospects of all the nation's new governors."[26] Texas was in the middle of some very difficult problems: a financial crisis, a prison crisis, and an education crisis. In the face of numerous obstacles, Richards emerged as the most popular governor in a decade. She combined an appealing personality, a good sense of humor, and a gift for oratory that helped her maintain her

Governor	Term
Thomas Mitchell Campbell	January 15, 1907–January 17, 1911
Oscar Branch Colquitt	January 17, 1911–January 19, 1915
James E. Ferguson	January 19, 1915–August 25, 1917[†]
William Pettus Hobby	August 25, 1917–January 18, 1921
Pat Morris Neff	January 18, 1921–January 20, 1925
Miriam A. Ferguson	January 20, 1925–January 17, 1927
Dan Moody	January 17, 1927–January 20, 1931
Ross S. Sterling	January 20, 1931–January 17, 1933
Miriam A. Ferguson	January 17, 1933–January 15, 1935
James V. Allred	January 15, 1935–January 17, 1939
W. Lee O'Daniel	January 17, 1939–August 4, 1941*
Coke R. Stevenson	August 4, 1941–January 21, 1947
Beauford H. Jester	January 21, 1947–July 11, 1949[‡]
Allan Shivers	July 11, 1949–January 15, 1957[§]
Price Daniel	January 15, 1957–January 15, 1963
John Connally	January 15, 1963–January 21, 1969
Preston Smith	January 21, 1969–January 16, 1973
Dolph Briscoe	January 17, 1973–January 16, 1979**
William P. Clements	January 16, 1979–January 18, 1983
Mark White	January 18, 1983–January 20, 1987
William P. Clements	January 20, 1987–January 15, 1991
Ann W. Richards	January 15, 1991–January 17, 1995
George W. Bush	January 17, 1995–

[§]As lieutenant governor, Shivers succeeded Jester in 1949; he was elected in his own right in 1950.

**Effective in 1975, the term of office was increased to four years.

Source: Derived from *Texas Almanac, 1994–95* (Dallas: A. H. Belo, 1994), 519.

popularity under adverse conditions. But even with great personal popularity, Richards lost the 1994 election. Her failure to communicate a clear agenda for a second term contributed to that loss.

Gubernatorial Leadership: Present and Future

Over the years since 1874, the Texas governorship has changed considerably. The governor, once a caretaker, now holds a major leadership role. Governors today are expected to head up a large bureaucracy and to address whatever problems confront the state. But growing expectations for gubernatorial leadership are offset by the longstanding distrust of executive power that has been part of the state's political culture at least since the end of Reconstruction.

Given the increased demands on the office, individual governors probably will continue to press for more power whenever they can, like Governors Clements and Richards did for the right to appoint department heads. But these kinds of changes have depended on an environment of crisis or corruption to open the door to greater gubernatorial power. Changes, then, have been incremental. Even the fiscal crisis of the 1980s did not force the state to rethink the governor's role in any comprehensive way.

The future of the Texas governorship is likely to be shaped by partisan considerations. If divided control of the governorship and the legislature becomes a recurring fact, the governor's power is unlikely to increase. Leaders of the party that controls the legislature are not going to want to give more power to a partisan enemy in the governor's mansion. A period of sustained Democratic leadership might create a political climate in which the governorship could be strengthened. But if the Republican party succeeds in controlling both the executive and legislative branches in the state, its conservative ideology could prevent a strengthening of the governor's powers.

Notes

1. Richard A. Oppel, Jr. and Mark Curriden, "$15.3 Billion Tobacco Deal Reached," *Dallas Morning News,* January 17, 1998, p. 1A.
2. Richard A. Oppel, Jr. and Mark Curriden, "Bush Challenges Fees in Tobacco Settlement," *Dallas Morning News,* February 6, 1998, p. 1A.
3. Clay Robison, "Morales Lights New Fire in Tobacco Feud," *Houston Chronicle,* May 28, 1998, p. A17.
4. Larry Sabato, *Goodbye to Good-Time Charlie,* 2d ed. (Washington, DC: CQ Press, 1983).
5. Thad L. Beyle, "Being Governor," in *The State of the States,* 2d ed., Carl E. Van Horn, ed. (Washington, DC: Congressional Quarterly Press, 1993), 79–113.
6. Texas Constitution, Art. IV.
7. See Texas Constitution, Art. IV.
8. Legislative Budget Board, *Fiscal Size Up: 1992–93 Biennium* (Austin, 1991), 9–7.
9. Texas Education Code, Sec. 11.51.
10. Texas Insurance Code, Sec. 1.09.
11. Texas Revised Civil Statutes, Art. 4413, Sec. 5.
12. Texas Government Code, Sec. 2306.036.
13. Texas Education Code, Sec. 61.023.
14. See Texas Water Code, Secs. 5.052, 5.057, and 5.058.
15. Texas Government Code, Sec. 492.005.
16. Thad Beyle and Scott Mouw, "Governors: The Power of Removal," *Policy Studies Journal* 17 (Summer 1989): 819.
17. Sabato, *Goodbye,* 83.
18. Legislative Budget Board, *Fiscal Size Up: 1992–93, 9-7.*
19. John Kincaid, "The American Governor in International Affairs," *Publius* 14 (Fall 1984): 95–114. See also Martin Tolchin and Susan Tolchin, "The States' Global Hustlers," in *State and Local Government,* 4th ed. (Guilford, CT: Dushkin Publishing Group, 1989), 185–193.

20. Texas Constitution, Art. IV, Section 16.

21. National Governors' Association, Office of State Services, *The Institutionalized Powers of the Governorship, 1965–1985* (Washington, DC, 1987).

22. Thad Beyle, "Being Governor," in *The State of the States,* 3d ed., Carl E. Van Horn, ed. (Washington, DC: CQ Press, 1996), pp. 77–107. The point made here is on p. 87.

23. Thad Beyle, "The Powers of Governors," in *State Government: CQ's Guide to Current Issues and Activities, 1990–91,* Thad Beyle, ed. (Washington, DC: CQ Press, 1990), 124–125.

24. Regina Brough, "Strategies for Leaders Who Do Not Have a Lot of Power," *Journal of State Government,* July/August 1987, 157–161.

25. Dan Durning, "Change Masters for the States," *Journal of State Government,* July/August 1987, 145–149.

26. Richard Murray and Gregory R. Weiher, "Texas: Ann Richards, Taking on the Challenge," in *Governors and Hard Times,* Thad Beyle, ed. (Washington, DC: Congressional Quarterly Press, 1992), 179–188. The quoted phrase is on p. 179.

8 Texas Bureaucracy

Chapter Outline

Every year the welfare of thousands of Texas children depends on the quality of the work done by the Texas Department of Protective and Regulatory Services (DPRS). Among other things, this agency is responsible for investigating family situations that might put children at risk and for removing and caring for those who are determined to be at risk. Thus, children who may be abused or neglected by their families depend on this agency to provide them with the protection and relief that they need.

Protective and Regulatory Services has a difficult and often overwhelming responsibility. In 1997, the agency received over 100,000 reports of child abuse or neglect. A caseworker must investigate these reports and determine the degree of risk to the child. If the child is found to be in immediate risk of harm, the agency can remove the child from the home and place him or her in a foster home or alternative care arrangement. In 1997, the agency had about 12,000 children in such arrangements. Once a child is placed in foster care, the agency must monitor the family situation and determine whether the risk has been removed so that the child can be safely returned home, or whether the more serious step should be taken to terminate parental rights so that the child can be put up for adoption. Seven out of ten cases result in the child's return home or placement with relatives. Nevertheless, in recent years the average stay in foster care has lasted twenty-two months and might involve as many as three different placements for the child.[1]

In 1996, the Department of Protective and Regulatory Services was reviewed as part of the Texas system of periodic review of all state agencies. The Sunset Review Advisory Commission that studied the agency criticized it for keeping children in foster care much too long. They argued that lengthy foster care was costly to the state and risked emotional harm to the children. In response to that report, the Texas legislature passed new legislation in 1997 that provided additional grounds for terminating parental rights and making children eligible for adoption and by setting a twelve-month deadline for DPRS to seek termination of parental rights or return the child to the parents.[2]

This story about DPRS suggests several things about the Texas bureaucracy. First, the story reminds us that bureaucracy is not just about paper pushing and pointless routines. Government agencies are created to provide services, and DPRS as well as other Texas agencies deal with real human problems as they struggle to provide good service.

Second, this story reminds us that government agencies are not free to spend taxpayer dollars without accountability. Agencies are held accountable for the dollars they spend by the Texas legislature and agencies such as the Sunset Advisory Commission that help the legislature carry out its work.

Finally, this story reminds us that government agencies often face formidable challenges. Agencies are often held in low public regard because people think they are not able to accomplish much, but these agencies often deal with complex and difficult problems for which there are no simple solutions. Problems persist because they are difficult and intractable—not simply because agencies are inept or uncaring.

Because of the essential services these agencies provide, it is necessary to have a knowledge of the work for which the agencies comprising the government bureaucracy are responsible. With the goal of describing bureaucratic structures and the work of government agencies, this chapter answers several questions:

- What is the bureaucracy and why is it so important?
- How is the Texas bureaucracy organized?
- Is the Texas bureaucracy doing its job effectively?
- What are the prospects for the bureaucracy doing its job better?

What Is the Bureaucracy?

People use the term **bureaucracy** in different ways. Sociologists use it to refer to a large organization characterized by the division of labor, a hierarchy, and professionalism. Political analysts use the term to distinguish between agencies that are part of the executive branch of government and those that are part of the legislative or judicial branches. Here the term refers to all executive agencies with responsibility for operating state programs or enforcing state regulations.

The executive agencies that make up the bureaucracy are the state's service-delivery system. They bring people and resources together to produce public schools, public higher education, highways, public safety, public health programs, and many other critical services. The quality of the services citizens receive from the state depends on the quality of the bureaucracy that delivers those services. The best-designed programs do not work if the bureaucracy does a poor job of running them.

State Bureaucracies and Change

A recent assessment of the condition of state bureaucracies focused on accountability.[3] Accountability has become increasingly important as the costs of the services state agencies provide have outpaced the level of resources available to them.

There is widespread agreement that agencies must be responsible for what they do and how they use the state's resources. There is less agreement about how and to whom agencies should be held accountable. As a result, state bureaucracies sometimes are caught in the middle as governors, legislators, courts, interest groups, and voters all try to hold them accountable.

Change in Texas seems to be consistent with these national trends. The **Texas Performance Review** has become a continuing call for streamlining the state's administration and using resources more efficiently as it issues a new report at the beginning of each legislative session. It is also true that Texas has not settled on a single approach to bureaucratic accountability. In the following survey of the bureaucracy, it should become clear that Texas continues to struggle with ways to get the most services for the least money

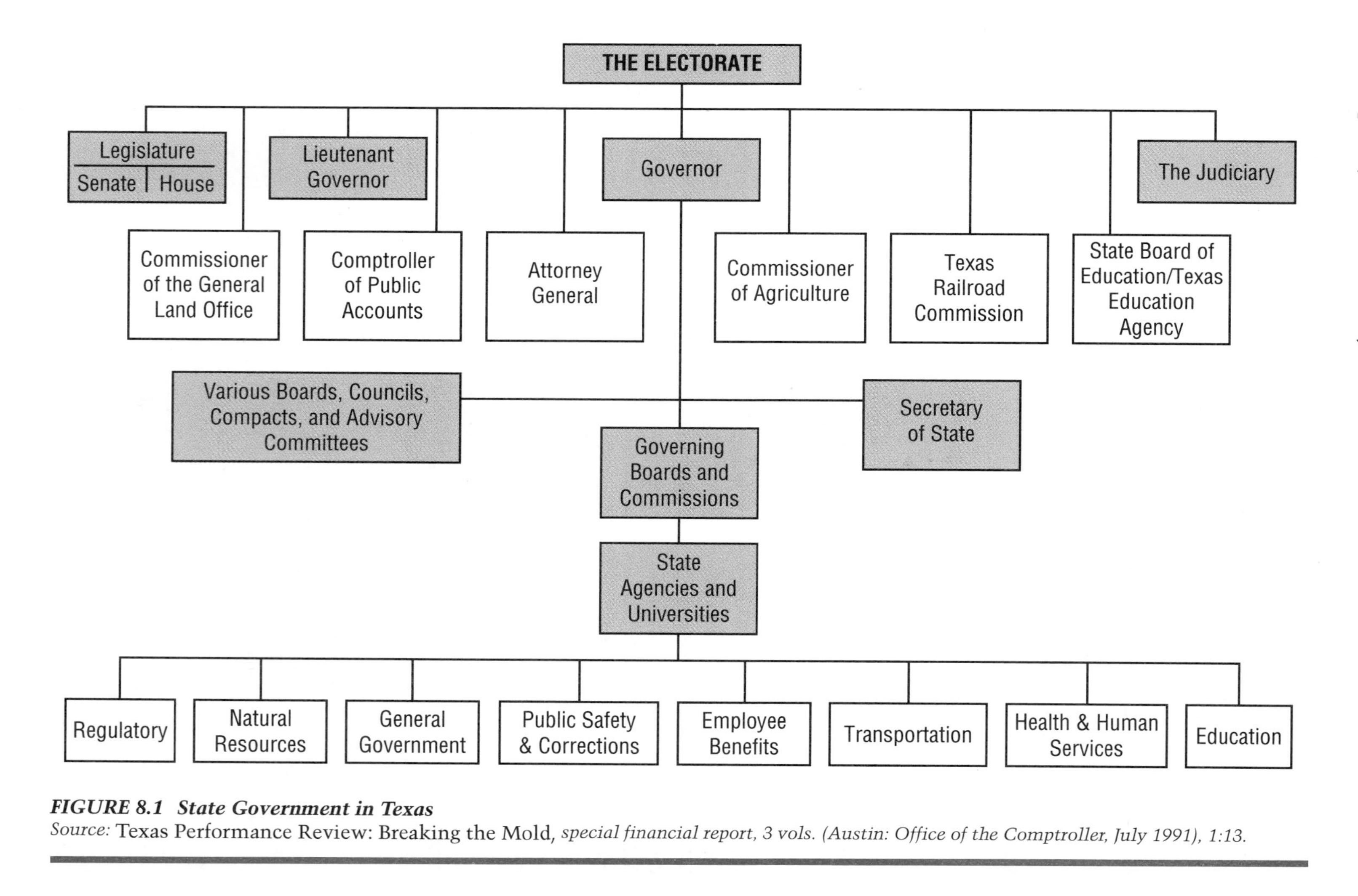

FIGURE 8.1 State Government in Texas
Source: Texas Performance Review: Breaking the Mold, *special financial report, 3 vols. (Austin: Office of the Comptroller, July 1991), 1:13.*

and with ways to ensure that the bureaucracy serves its customers—the citizens of the state—effectively.

Figuring Out the Texas Bureaucracy

The Texas bureaucracy is a very complex organization. Figure 8.1, a diagram of its basic structure, disguises much of the organizational complexity by grouping agencies together under headings like "Education," "General Government," and "Natural Resources." Table 8.1 and the overview here add detail to the picture: a description of the programs the Texas bureaucracy provides and a sense of the complexity that exists in many areas.

Education Agencies

The discussion here begins with education, the largest item in the state budget. Education was allocated about 44 percent of all state appropriations for the 1998–1999 biennium.[4] The state's educational services fall into two categories: elementary and secondary education and higher education. The Texas Education Agency manages the schools; the Texas Higher Education Coordinating Board manages the colleges and universities.

The *Texas Education Agency (TEA)* sets curriculum standards for the schools, administers teacher certification programs, and authorizes the textbooks that local schools use. The TEA also administers the Foundation School Program, which distributes the state's financial support to local school districts.

The fifteen members of the TEA's governing board, the State Board of Education, are elected for four-year terms. Board members' terms are arranged so that the terms of eight members expire in odd-number years and the terms of seven expire in even-numbered years. The chief executive officer, the commissioner of education, is appointed by the governor to a four-year term. The commissioner's term expires at the same time as the governor's.

The TEA has been at the center of controversy in recent years. In 1984, Governor Mark White appointed a commission headed by H. Ross Perot to recommend educational reforms. The work of the Perot Commission (as it came to be called) led the state to adopt major reforms in school curriculum, teacher certification, and the role of extracurricular activities in schools. In the 1990s, equalizing financial support for local school systems has been a major concern. The legislature has made several attempts to reform the system, and in 1993 it finally passed a plan that the Texas Supreme Court approved.

In 1995, the legislature undertook another revision of Texas education. (For additional discussion, see Chapter 13.) The basic structural elements were retained: the board of education, commissioner of education, and the Texas Education Agency. But, both the governor and legislative leaders had promised to trim the power of TEA and to leave more educational decisions

Table 8.1 Texas Administrative Agencies Grouped by Function, 1998

Education	Health and Human Services	Business and Economic Development	Public Safety and Criminal Justice
Higher Education Coordinating Board • thirty-five General academic teaching institutions • three lower division centers • fifty community/junior college districts • one technical college • seven state medical schools • three dental schools • Allied health and nursing units **Texas Education Agency**	**Children's Trust Fund of Texas Council** **Health and Human Services Commission** • Commission for the Blind • Commission for the Deaf and Hearing Impaired • Commission on Alcohol and Drug Abuse • Department of Health • Department of Human Services • Department of Mental Health and Mental Retardation • Department of Protective and Regulatory Services • Department on Aging • Interagency Council on Early Childhood Intervention • Texas Rehabilitation Commission • Texas Youth Commission **Texas Cancer Council**	**Department of Housing and Urban Affairs** **Lottery Commission** **Texas Aerospace Commission** **Texas Department of Economic Development** **Texas Department of Transportation** **Texas Workforce Commission**	**Adjutant General's Department** **Alcoholic Beverage Commission** **Board of Private Investigators and Private Security Agencies** **Commission on Fire Protection** **Commission on Jail Standards** **Commission on Law Enforcement, Officer Standards, and Education** **Council on Sex Offender Treatment** **Criminal Justice Policy Council** **Department of Criminal Justice** **Department of Public Safety** **Juvenile Probation Commission** **National Guard Armory Board** **Polygraph Examiners Board** **Texas Youth Commission**

Table 8.1 Cont.

General Government	Natural Resources	Regulatory Agencies
Commission on Human Rights	Animal Health Commission	Credit Union Department
Commission on the Arts	Department of Agriculture	Department of Insurance
Comptroller of Public Accounts	General Land Office and Veterans' Land Board	Department of Licensing and Regulation
Department of Information Resources	Low-Level Radioactive Waste Disposal Authority	Finance Commission of Texas • Department of Banking • Office of Consumer Credit Commissioner • Savings and Loan Department
General Services Commission	Natural Resource Conservation Commission	Office of Public Insurance Counsel
Incentive and Productivity Commission	Parks and Wildlife Department	Office of Administrative Hearings
Office of State-Federal Relations	Railroad Commission of Texas	Office of Public Utility Counsel
Office of the Attorney General	River Compact Commissioners	Public Utility Commission
Office of the Governor	Soil and Water Conservation Board	Racing Commission
Secretary of State	Water Development Board	Real Estate Commission
State Preservation Board		State Securities Board
Texas Bond Review Board		Various boards to regulate individual professions
Texas Ethics Commission		Workers' Compensation Commission
Texas Public Finance Authority		
Veterans Commission		

Source: Adapted from Legislative Budget Bureau, *Fiscal Size Up, 1998–1999* (Austin: Legislative Budget Board, 1998).

to local school districts. SB 1, the education reform bill of 1995, specifies that "an educational function not specifically delegated to the agency or board under this code is reserved to and shall be performed by school districts or open-enrollment charter schools."[5]

Higher education in Texas is the responsibility of the *Texas Higher Education Coordinating Board.* The fifteen members of that board are appointed by the governor for six-year terms. The board itself appoints the commissioner of higher education, who supervises the agency's staff. The board coordinates the state's many institutions of higher education (see Table 8.1). One of its primary tasks is to prevent duplication of effort among the state's institutions of higher education. The agency also shapes the formulas that determine the amount of money each institution of higher education gets from the state. The board's management efforts sometimes are thwarted by the legislative intervention.

Health and Human Services Agencies

The second largest functional area in the Texas administration is health and human services. This area was allocated about 30 percent of the state's appropriations for the 1998–1999 biennium.[6] The administrative organization in health and human services is a good deal more fragmented than it is in most other areas (see Table 8.1). In 1991, the *Texas Performance Review* found fourteen primary service-delivery agencies and at least twenty-five other agencies that were involved in some aspect of delivering services.[7]

In response to the *Texas Performance Review*'s recommendations, the legislature created the *Health and Human Services Commission* to oversee and coordinate the efforts of several agencies (Table 8.1).[8] The legislation also created the position of commissioner of health and human services. The first commissioner took office in June 1992. Although this change does not consolidate the various agencies into one department, the commission reviews agency-proposed rules, settles interagency disputes, and prepares a consolidated budget. It also developed and is responsible for updating a strategic plan for providing health and human services in Texas.

The legislature also ordered structural reorganization. The Department of Protective and Regulatory Services was created and made responsible for adult-protective services, child-protective services, child-care licensing, and a variety of other child- and youth-related services. In addition, various services were moved among departments so that related services are housed in the same agency.[9]

The *Department of Health* has the largest budget of the health and human services agencies. The Texas Board of Health, with six members appointed for six-year terms, oversees the department and appoints the commissioner of health, the agency's chief executive. One of the agency's largest responsibilities is managing Medicaid services. Medicaid is a national program that provides medical services to the poor. About 60 percent of the agency's funding comes from the national government. The Special Supplemental

Food Program for Women, Infants, and Children (WIC) is another large federal program administered by the agency. Other services focus on community and rural health, family health, disease prevention, special health problems, and consumer and environmental health.

The *Texas Department of Human Services,* the second largest of the health and human services agencies, manages the state's public welfare system. Most of its services are targeted at people with income significantly below the federal poverty line. The department oversees welfare payments, food stamp distribution, family support services (for example, day care or employment services), and nursing care and community services for the elderly and disabled. Most of the services are provided by joint federal–state programs that the state administers.

The governor appoints the six-member *Texas Board of Human Services,* which oversees the Department of Human Services. The members serve six-year terms. The board appoints the department head, the commissioner of human services.

The third major agency in the health and human services area is the *Department of Mental Health and Mental Retardation* (*MHMR*). This agency is supervised by the Texas Board of Mental Health and Mental Retardation. The nine members of the board also are appointed for six-year terms. The department has two divisions: mental health services and mental retardation services. The mental health division operates state mental health facilities for inpatient care and community mental health services for outpatient care. The mental retardation division operates thirteen state schools that provide inpatient services for people who are retarded. In 1992 a state task force designated two schools to be closed.

Recent developments in MHMR have been shaped by the court case of *Lelsz* v. *Kavanagh.* This 1983 case has brought about improvements in mental retardation services.[10] Plaintiffs demanded more community-based services and a higher level of care for people who are mentally retarded.[11] The state reached settlements in this and an earlier 1981 case that increased funding in this service area. Still, agency officials insist that available funds do not allow them to meet all legitimate needs.

Business and Economic Development

Business and economic development programs consume the third largest share of the state's financial resources. For the 1998–1999 budget, these programs were allocated almost 12 percent of the state's total appropriations.[12] Over 70 percent of the money allocated to this area went to the Department of Transportation. In the 1991 session, the legislature approved the merger of all transportation-related agencies—including the State Department of Highways and Public Transportation, the Department of Aviation, the Motor Vehicle Commission, and the Texas Turnpike Authority—into the *Texas Department of Transportation.* The merger was completed in 1997, when the Texas Turnpike Authority joined the department.

THE CHANGING FACE OF TEXAS POLITICS

Texas Performance Review: A Voice for Improving Government Performance

When the legislature assembled in 1991 for its regular session, available revenue fell far short of the estimated cost of funding the state's existing programs, much less supporting the cost of new or expanded programs. Lawmakers, realizing that cutting expenditures was essential, authorized the *Texas Performance Review*, a thorough audit of the state government to find places to save money and improve efficiency. The task was assigned to the office of the Comptroller of Public Accounts. It has become a continuing responsibility: the office now is expected to issue a report to each regular session of the legislature suggesting ways that government operations can be improved. The most recent report, *Disturbing the Peace*, suggested hundreds of changes in the state government.[1] The performance audits have been so well received that the comptroller's office has been asked to make policy recommendations on a variety of state issues, including welfare reform.

What have performance reviews contributed to the dialogue about the Texas bureaucracy? The first report of the *Texas Performance Review* highlighted the organizational problems in Texas government and suggested that those problems were contributing to the inefficiency

Other major agencies included in this area are the Texas Department of Economic Development, the Texas Workforce Commission, the Department of Housing and Community Affairs, and the Lottery Commission. Of these, the Texas Workforce Commission had the largest budget for the 1998–1999 biennium.

The transportation department's principal mission is building and maintaining state highways. About 50 percent of the agency's funding goes into highway construction.[13] The other responsibilities of the department—helping cities with mass transportation systems, promoting aeronautics, and developing a statewide system of airports—consume small percentages of the agency's budget. The Texas Transportation Commission, a three-person board whose members are appointed by the governor, governs the Texas Department of Transportation. The commission appoints the department's executive director.

In 1995, the Texas Employment Commission was renamed the **Texas Workforce Commission.** In addition to its traditional responsibility to administer the unemployment compensation program, the agency was charged with developing an integrated workforce development system by consolidating the state's diverse job-training and employment-related educa-

and ineffectiveness of many state programs. A 1991 recommendation that was implemented in 1995 is the Lone Star Card, an electronic benefits transfer system that replaces food stamps. The card eliminates the cost of printing coupons and prevents the fraudulent use of food stamps. In response to a 1993 suggestion, the legislature created the Council on Competitive Government, which uses competitive bidding to determine what the state pays for sorting mail, printing, operating its data center, and long-distance telephone service.

In 1995, the principal recommendation focused on workforce training. Recognizing that a well-trained workforce is key to the state's economic development, the report called for consolidating programs that presently are scattered among bureaucratic agencies and focusing training on jobs that really exist. This recommendation led to the creation of the Texas Workforce Commission. The performance review also suggested expanding the use of the Lone Star Card to handle other benefits—such as Medicaid and unemployment compensation—electronically. One commonsense recommendation was that the state's official mileage chart (used to reimburse state employees for travel) be distributed electronically by the comptroller's office, a simple change that would save the state more than $70,000 in printing costs over three years.

The incremental effect of the performance review's constant focus on efficiency, effectiveness, and responsiveness has brought incremental improvement, as *Gaining Ground* (its 1994 report) acknowledges. But, as the report also concedes, much more remains to be done. ★

[1]Texas Comptroller of Public Accounts, *Disturbing the Peace* (Austin, 1996).

[2]Texas Comptroller of Public Accounts, *Gaining Ground* (Austin, 1995).

tional programs under the agency's jurisdiction.[14] This change implemented one of the recommendations from the 1995 report of the *Texas Performance Review.*

The *Texas Department of Economic Development* is primarily responsible for economic development in the state and for improving the economic climate. It was established in 1998 from what had been the Department of Commerce. Since the reorganization, the director of the department is supervised by a nine-member board appointed by the governor. The board appoints the executive director.

Public Safety and Criminal Justice

The next most important area in terms of budget is public safety and corrections. About 8 percent of the state's budget goes into this area.[15] Table 8.1 shows that several agencies operate here, but two—the Department of Public Safety and the Department of Criminal Justice—are most significant.

The *Department of Public Safety* was established in 1935 and was reauthorized by the legislature in 1993, when it came up for sunset review.

Because of the state's size and urban growth, highway construction (the responsibility of the Texas Department of Transportation) is an important state responsibility.

It is governed by the three-member Public Safety Commission, which appoints the director. The agency's responsibilities fall into three categories: traffic law enforcement, criminal law enforcement, and emergency management. The traffic law division supervises traffic on the state's highways and administers the laws that regulate drivers and vehicles in the state. The department's criminal law enforcement responsibilities involve working closely with city and county law enforcement officials. The best-known law enforcement agency in Texas—the Texas Rangers—now functions as a division of the Department of Public Safety. The emergency management division works with local authorities responding to disasters or potential disaster situations, including floods, hazardous-materials spills, tornadoes, and hurricanes.

The *Department of Criminal Justice* was created in 1990 from the merger of the Texas Adult Probation Commission, the Texas Board of Pardons and Paroles, and the Texas Department of Corrections. The department is governed by the Texas Board of Criminal Justice, whose nine members are appointed by the governor for six-year terms.

The Department of Criminal Justice manages fifty-nine prison units, thirteen transfer facilities, and other correctional units.[16] A federal court's decision in *Ruiz* v. *Estelle* (1982), directed the state to increase prison capacity, a task that has been a central responsibility of the agency over the last decade.[17]

General Government Agencies

General government agencies consume just over 2 percent of the state's budget.[18] These agencies do not deliver services; they provide administrative support. The list of general government agencies is a long one (see Table 8.1). The discussion here focuses on the most important departments.

The *Office of the Attorney General* is the state's legal department: it represents the state in civil and criminal matters. The attorney general's advisory opinions about the Texas Constitution serve as official interpretations unless they are overruled by the state's court system.

The *Texas comptroller of public accounts* is the state's chief accounting officer, tax collector, and revenue forecaster. The vigor with which the comptroller's office collects taxes is critical to the state's economy. Because the Texas Constitution prohibits the legislature from appropriating more money than the comptroller says will be available, the comptroller's forecasts set binding limits on the budget process. In recent years the office was assigned responsibility for the *Texas Performance Review.* In 1992 the comptroller's office launched the Texas lottery, an important source of new revenue. In 1993 the state created the Texas Lottery Commission and transferred supervision of the lottery to it.

The *Office of the Secretary of State* oversees state elections and maintains official election records (see Chapter 5). It also files and publishes the bills passed in each legislative session. The office is responsible for publishing the *Texas Register,* the official publication for administrative rules, proclamations, and regulations. This office was created by the constitution and its head is appointed by the governor.

The *Treasury Department,* which had previously been a major agency in this category, was abolished by a constitutional amendment that transferred most of its responsibilities to the Comptroller of Public Accounts.

The *Texas Ethics Commission* was formed in 1992, the year after voters approved an authorizing constitutional amendment. The commission is made up of eight members, four appointed by the governor, two appointed by the lieutenant governor, and two appointed by the speaker of the Texas house. No more than four members can be affiliated with the same political party.

The commission's tasks include administering and enforcing the laws that regulate political funds and campaigns, enforcing standards of conduct for state officers and employees, enforcing lobbying regulations, receiving the financial reports of candidates and lobbyists, and issuing advisory opinions on state ethics regulations. Many tasks assigned to the commission previously were carried out by the secretary of state's office.

Natural Resources Agencies

This group of agencies consumes about 2 percent of the state's budget.[19] As Table 8.1 shows, the responsibility for protecting the state's natural resources is divided among several agencies. The discussion here focuses on the most important of those agencies.

The *Texas Natural Resource Conservation Commission* is the newest agency in this group. The legislature created the commission in 1991 in response to the *Texas Performance Review*'s call to consolidate programs that protect the natural environment.[20] When it began operations in 1993, the agency absorbed the Texas Water Commission, the Air Control Board, the Well Drillers Board, and the Texas Board of Irrigation. In addition, the solid-waste, sewage, and wastewater treatment program and the radioactive waste disposal program were transferred to the new agency from the health department. The agency is supervised by a three-member commission appointed by the governor. The commissioners appoint the agency's executive director.

The *Department of Agriculture* has two important functions that are not always compatible. On the one hand, it is responsible for promoting Texas agriculture and opening new markets for the state's products. On the other hand, it is responsible for regulating Texas agriculture to protect public health and safety. The conflict between these two functions was apparent in the 1989 session of the Texas legislature. Commissioner of Agriculture Jim Hightower, the head of the department, had angered agricultural interests by rigorously enforcing state pesticide regulations. Some farmers believed that the enforcement effort had cost them profits. The controversy led to talk of dissolving the department under the state's sunset law provisions. A compromise was reached: the department was reauthorized, but the power of the commissioner was limited. A board was created to share the decision-making authority on pesticide regulations with the commissioner. The commissioner of agriculture is elected by the people of Texas to a four-year term. The fact that the governor was a Republican and the commissioner was a Democrat intensified the pesticide controversy. The Republicans wanted to embarrass a prominent Democrat who might have ambitions to become governor. The Democrats wanted to promote a possible candidate and embarrass the Republican governor. When efforts to resolve policy issues are complicated by the interests of political parties, a unified approach to management becomes almost impossible.

The *General Land Office and Veterans' Land Board* is the custodian of public lands. It is supervised by the commissioner of the general land office, who is elected to a four-year term. The land office administers more than 20 million acres of public lands, including the offshore shelf.[21] The agency manages the revenue opportunities that arise from these public lands by negotiating oil and gas leases and grazing leases allowed on them. It is also responsible for protecting the environmental quality of public lands and waters. The need to generate revenue from public lands is not always compatible with the responsibility to protect environmental quality on those lands. Historically, the office has given more weight to generating revenue than to protecting the environment. The office also administers the Veterans' Land Program, which makes low-interest loans for the purchase of land to Texas veterans.

As commissioner of insurance, Elton Boomer oversees the regulation of insurance in Texas.

The mission of the *Texas Parks and Wildlife Department* is to manage and conserve the natural and cultural resources of Texas."[22] The nine members of its governing board are appointed to six-year terms by the governor. The board chooses the agency's executive director. To accomplish its mission, the agency is organized into four main divisions: fisheries and wildlife, law enforcement, public lands, and resource protection. The resource protection division, whose purpose is related most directly to protecting natural resources, was created by the legislature in 1985. Under guidelines set forth by the legislature, this division is responsible for protecting fish and wildlife and can act to recover damages for fish or wildlife taken or killed illegally.[23]

Finally, three members of the *Railroad Commission of Texas,* (commonly called the Texas Railroad Commission) are elected for six-year terms. Created in 1891 to regulate railroads, the commission was assigned a critical new authority in the 1920s and 1930s—the power to regulate oil and gas production in the state. That power soon became its most important responsibility. By controlling oil and gas production, the commission maintains oil and gas prices (and the profits of oil and gas producers). When prices fall, the commission orders producers to pump less oil and gas; when prices go up, production quotas go up too. Certainly private owners have benefited from this regulatory practice, but the state also has benefited. Thousands of jobs and much of the state's revenues are directly or indirectly derived from the oil and gas industry. That is why the general attitude has been that what is good for the oil and gas industry is good for Texas.

Regulatory Agencies

This group of agencies is responsible for regulating various businesses in the state. There are many agencies in this group (see Table 8.1), but less than 1 percent of the state's budget goes to these agencies. The discussion here focuses on the two whose decisions affect the most people in the state.

The *Texas Department of Insurance* is responsible for regulating the rates charged by insurance companies and for overseeing the financial soundness of those companies. In its short life, the department has undergone major reorganization. The legislature created the department in 1991, absorbing the State Board of Insurance. The department then consisted of a three-person board, a commissioner appointed by the board, and the agency's staff. In 1993 the legislature reorganized the agency, abolishing the board and turning its responsibilities over to the commissioner, who is appointed by the governor for a two-year term.

The other regulatory agency with wide impact is the *Public Utility Commission.* This agency regulates the rates charged by privately-owned electric power companies; its power to regulate local telephone service rates was reduced in 1995. The commission's three members are appointed by the governor for six-year terms. The executive director, who is appointed by the board, supervises the agency's staff. In an era of deregulation, the commission's first goal is to encourage competition.

Two agencies—the Office of Public Insurance Counsel and the Office of Public Utility Counsel—have particular relevance for the regulatory agencies discussed here. Each of those offices is headed by a gubernatorial appointee who represents the public interest in the agency. This type of organization is designed to offset the power of the companies that appear before the commissions pressing for higher rates.

How Does the Texas Bureaucracy Measure Up?

Now that the structure of the Texas bureaucracy has been described, it is time to assess its organization. Four questions are raised in this section:

- Is the bureaucracy too large?
- Is the bureaucracy well organized?
- Is the bureaucracy held accountable?
- What do the people think of the bureaucracy?

These are questions that all public bureaucracies must answer.

Is the Bureaucracy Too Large?

One charge commonly leveled against modern bureaucracies is that they always grow larger, consuming more and more of limited resources and making efficient management difficult. Is the Texas bureaucracy too large?

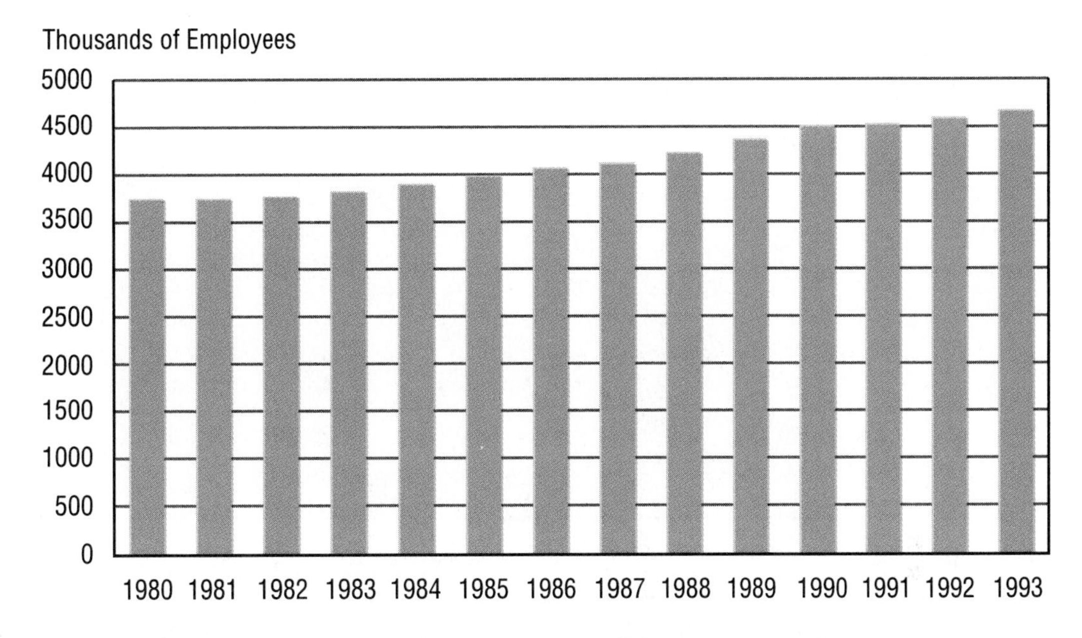

FIGURE 8.2 Growth in Total Employment Among All States, 1980–1993
Source: U.S. Department of Commerce, Bureau of the Census, Statistical Abstract, *Washington, DC: Government Printing Office, 1993, Table 499, and 1996.*

One sign that a bureaucracy is growing is an increase in the number of people it employs. This kind of growth has been common in state bureaucracies. State government employment grew steadily across the state between 1980 and 1993 (see Figure 8.2).

In Texas, employment grew at an annual rate of 4 percent between 1988 and 1993, which was faster than the national average.[24] The *Texas Performance Review* listed three reasons for this: First, Texas had to expand certain state services because the courts ordered it to. For example, a federal court ruling that ordered Texas to reduce overcrowding in state prisons forced the state to build new facilities and to hire people to run them. Employment in corrections rose at an annual rate of 18 percent between 1980 and 1989. New services mandated by the national government also have contributed to higher-than-average growth in Texas state employment. As the senior partner in several programs funded jointly by the national and state governments, the federal government sets rules that the states must follow in administering programs. In one case, for example, a federal change in Medicaid eligibility rules required Texas to expand its services and hire more people. Finally, some additional hiring simply reflects expansion necessitated by growth in the state's population.[25]

It is clear that the Texas bureaucracy has grown, but is it too large? Answering this question is not easy. The problem is finding an objective basis for what is a subjective judgment. One way to approach the question is to compare Texas with similar states. The bars in Figure 8.3 show state employ-

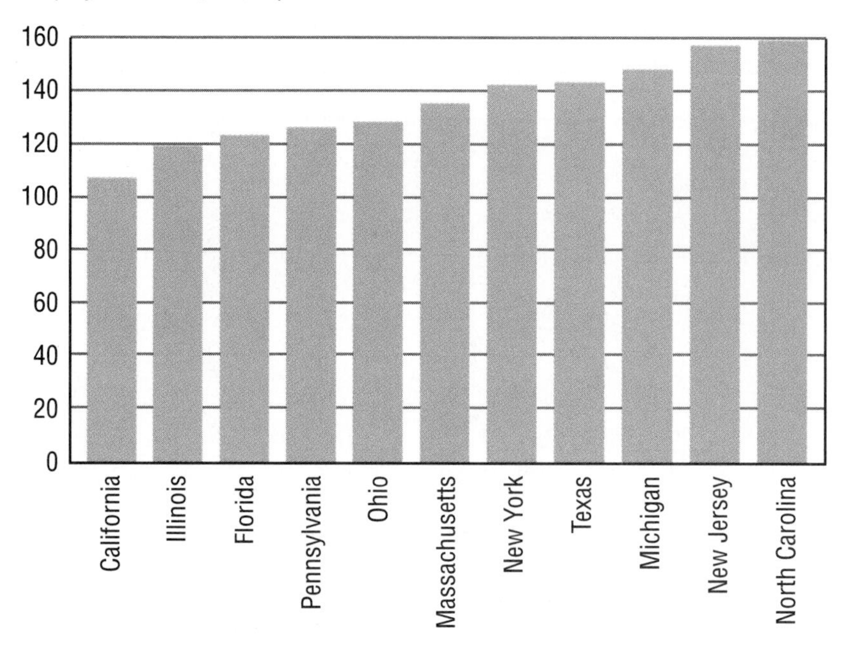

FIGURE 8.3 Number of State Employees Per 10,000 Population, Largest States, 1995

Source: Legislative Budget Board, Fiscal Size Up: 1998–98 *(Austin, 1997), 3-14.*

ment figures for Texas and the ten other largest states in the country in 1995. State employment must be related to state population to figure out whether the number of people Texas employs is too large for its size. Texas falls right in the middle of this group. Compared with the bureaucracies of other large states, then, the Texas bureaucracy does not seem bloated. In fact the 1991 *Texas Performance Review* concluded that "the state work force is relatively lean given the size of the population it serves."[26] In 1995 Texas ranked fortieth among the states on the number of employees per 10,000 population.[27]

Although it recognized that the Texas bureaucracy was not overly large when compared to other states, the 1995 *Texas Performance Review* expressed concern over the possibility of continued growth at the rate of 4 percent per year. Consequently, this study recommended capping Texas public employment at 1994 levels.[28] Although the legislature did not mandate that ceiling, it did set employment targets for all state agencies when it passed the budget bill in 1995.[29]

Although it can be established that the Texas bureaucracy is not exceptionally large when compared with other states, this fact alone cannot be taken as a definitive answer to the question, "Is the bureaucracy too large." As noted at the beginning of this discussion, assessing appropriate size is a complex question. A secondary question is whether each agency is too large—or too small—for its assigned responsibilities. If agencies find themselves overstaffed for the job at hand, they usually will eliminate jobs as the legislature reduces appropriations; on the other hand, growing demand or need for a service may lead to agency expansion. In recent years there has been much talk about "right-sizing" agencies so that they make the most efficient use of their resources, but it is not always obvious what the right size is. Nevertheless, bureaucratic size is probably best reduced to the agency level and assessed on a case-by-case basis. The legislature and its staff agencies bear the responsibility for making those assessments.

Is the Bureaucracy Held Accountable?

As noted earlier, accountability has become a central issue as state bureaucracies face a demand for services that is growing much faster than their resources. How are public agencies held accountable?

Electoral accountability is one mechanism for holding state agencies accountable. In Texas the attorney general, the comptroller, the treasurer, the commissioner of the General Land Office, the commissioner of agriculture, and the members of the Texas Railroad Commission are elected directly by the people.

For this approach to work, voters must understand what these officials do and how to evaluate their performance, and then must vote based on that evaluation. Do voters behave that way? The evidence suggests no. Most Texans know very little about the work public agencies do or how to evaluate their performance. Only when one of these elected officials is caught in a scandal or controversy that the media can publicize is the public likely to be aware of them. And when they do vote for these officials—participation in these elections usually is lower than it is in a governor's race—there is a strong tendency to return the incumbents to office. Texans seem to assume that everything is all right in these agencies unless the media tell them otherwise.

Direct elections make unrealistic assumptions about voters' ability to evaluate the performance of agency heads; they also create a problem with long ballots. The more positions on the ballot, the fewer informed choices voters can make. And the fewer informed choices voters can make, the fewer elections they participate in. As a result, elected officials often are chosen by a small percentage of those who vote.

Although several important administrative positions in Texas are elective, far more agency heads answer to appointed boards that supervise their performance. These officials head up some of the largest service-delivery agencies in the state, among them the Department of Health, the Department of Human Services, and the Texas Department of Transportation.

The governor also has limited power to hold agency heads accountable. Article IV of the state constitution requires administrative officials to make semiannual reports to the governor on how they are handling the funds allocated to their agencies. The same article authorizes the governor to gather additional information if necessary. But these powers usually do not give the governor enough leverage to deal with state agencies. As explained in Chapter 7, the inability to control the choice of most agency heads or to remove from office those who might have mismanaged their agencies severely limits the governor's supervisory powers. Remember that recent governors have tried to increase their power to appoint and to remove key officials whenever possible. But the number of department heads who can be appointed or removed by the governor still is small.

The legislature holds the bureaucracy accountable through its budget authority. That is, the legislature can require agencies to justify their programs and expenditures. Moreover, legislative review of agency work has been formalized by the sunset laws, which require the legislature to reauthorize programs periodically.

Recognizing that taxpayers are concerned about getting their money's worth from government agencies, the Texas legislature has moved toward incorporating **performance measures** into the budgeting process. For each agency, the Legislative Budget Board has developed a set of performance measures to use in assessing that agency's performance. Although developing performance measures can be more difficult for some agencies than for others, in all cases the performance measures are designed to help the legislature determine whether an agency is meeting its goals and whether it is effective. For example, performance measures for higher education emphasize such goals as graduating students in a reasonable time, recruiting a racially and ethnically diverse student body, retaining students who have enrolled, and graduating a reasonable proportion of those who enroll. The legislature has not yet moved very far in this direction, but its leaders hope that they may soon be able to take agency performance into consideration when deciding how much money to allocate to an agency. Currently, the Legislative Budget Board publishes an annual performance assessment for all agencies, in which it summarizes both the percent of performance targets that have been met by an agency and the comparison between targets set and agency performance.[30]

The Texas Sunset Act was passed in 1977. The act created the Sunset Advisory Commission, made up of four senators and a public member appointed by the lieutenant governor and four house members and a public member appointed by the speaker. From its inception to 1997, the commission reviewed 267 agencies. Of those agencies, two were abolished, eight were combined with other agencies, and two were separated from each other. In the 1997 session, the legislature acted upon **sunset reviews** by abolishing two more agencies and transferring their functions to other agencies. Nineteen agencies were renewed.[31]

Legislative oversight is not as effective as it might be in Texas. Because legislative sessions are short, time constrains legislators' ability to review bureaucratic operations. Even sunset reviews have become routine, with little serious consideration given to eliminating agencies. As one study points out, most of the abolished agencies were of little consequence, such as the Pink Bollworm Commission, the Stonewall Jackson Memorial Board, and the Texas Historical Resources Development Council.[32] In the 1993 session of the legislature, a proposal was offered that would have abolished the Sunset Advisory Commission and turned its work over to legislative committees. Opponents of the measure argued that the proposal would limit the effectiveness of the sunset law. Ultimately the proposal failed.

The courts also play a role in holding agencies accountable by insisting that they meet constitutional and statutory requirements. As noted, the Texas Department of Criminal Justice had to reduce prison overcrowding in response to a court order and the Texas Department of Mental Health and Mental Retardation had to change the way it provided services.

Obviously a variety of mechanisms—elections, appointed boards, the governor, the legislature, the courts—are in place to hold Texas agencies accountable for what they do and how they do it. Texas is not alone in using multiple, and possibly conflicting, mechanisms of accountability. In fact most states do.[33] As discussed above, most observers would question the effectiveness of these accountability mechanisms, especially the electoral mechanisms.

Is the Bureaucracy Well Organized?

A well-organized bureaucracy groups agencies together by function, to coordinate their work and to avoid duplication of effort. Using this **functional organization** criterion, is the Texas bureaucracy well organized? The 1991 *Texas Performance Review* found several independent agencies doing closely related work. Fourteen agencies were providing health and human services, seven agencies were collecting state taxes, and ninety-eight separate institutions were providing public education.[34] In recent sessions the legislature has taken steps to rectify some of the problem. The Texas Natural Resource Conservation Commission merged a number of environmental agencies. The Department of Protective and Regulatory Services consolidated a number of protective services for children and adults. Still, many of the corrective actions recommended in the Texas Performance Review have not been carried out.

What Do the People Think About the Bureaucracy?

The last, but perhaps most important question to ask when trying to determine whether the Texas bureaucracy measures up is: "What do the people think?" Because bureaucratic agencies use taxpayer dollars to provide services to the people, the most powerful judges of the bureaucracy are the people themselves. What really matters is whether they believe that the government agencies do a good job and whether they do them fairly.

In 1996, the Texas Poll asked a sample of Texans what they thought of the job being done by Texas government agencies. Table 8.2 summarizes some of

Table 8.2 Public Attitudes Toward Texas Government Agencies, 1996

Texas state government agencies . . .	Percent Agreeing
serve the public well.	52
respond effectively to any citizen regardless of sex, ethnicity, or income.	48
are known for the high quality of their customer service.	41
produce high quality work with few errors.	29

Source: Data from Texas Poll as reported in Denise Gamino, "Most Texans Upbeat About State Government," *Austin American-Statesman*, September 30, 1996, p. B1.

their responses. The first response to note is that a majority of the respondents agreed with the statement that "Texas state government agencies serve the public well." Despite the fact that ridiculing government agencies is a national pastime, most Texans actually thought agencies did what they were supposed to do—serve the people—and that they did it well.

It is also noteworthy that almost a majority of the people (48 percent) thought that the bureaucracy responded effectively to all citizens, without regard to gender, ethnicity, or income. Clearly many believed that government agencies delivered services fairly—an important consideration in a diverse state like Texas.

Attitudes about the quality of work done by Texas agencies are mixed. Two-fifths of the respondents thought that Texas agencies were known for high quality service, but only 29 percent thought they were known for high quality work. This suggests that people believed that government employees sincerely tried to provide good customer service. They were less certain that the quality of the work was always high.

The poll data reviewed here suggest that Texans tend to believe that government agencies do measure up. They serve the public well, emphasize customer service, and deliver service in a nondiscriminatory fashion. Thus, Texans may join in the national pastime of bashing the bureaucracy, but experience appears to lead most to conclude that government agencies are hard-working, service-oriented organizations.

Prospects for Change

Although the 1996 poll shows that most Texans are reasonably satisfied with the bureaucracy's performance, the fact that a significant minority were unsatisfied suggests that there is still room for improvement. In fact, in many cases the bureaucratic structure in Texas does not conform to the standards of good organization. Why hasn't the system been reorganized? What are the prospects for change?

Several factors make changing the system difficult. First, because the structure of some agencies is spelled out in the constitution, that structure can be changed only by constitutional amendment—a process that requires both legislative action and ratification by the voters. Second, a basic distrust of a strong chief executive makes reorganization difficult. That is, the legislature is always reluctant to increase the power of the governor. That reluctance is even stronger when the governor belongs to one political party and a majority of the legislature belongs to another—as has been the case three times since 1978.

Despite the forces that make reorganization difficult, there has been some pressure for change in recent years. The courts have required individual agencies to change the way they do things; but they have not ordered bureaucratic consolidation or reorganization throughout the administration. Moreover, it is not likely that court-ordered reforms would produce a general reorganization. Cases brought to the courts involving the bureaucracy usually deal with the equitable provision of a single service. These cases logically do not lead to demands for a total overhaul of the state's administrative structure.

Another pressure for administrative change is the *Texas Performance Review.* In its effort to reduce the cost of providing state services, the report has recommended reorganization in several service areas: health and human services, transportation, public safety and corrections, general government, natural resources, and regulatory. Although lawmakers were responsive to many of the review's recommendations, they did not enact all of them.

At least two forces have worked against a thorough overhaul of the bureaucracy. First, the legislature has faced too many other pressing issues. Undertaking a major reorganization of the state bureaucracy has been more than the legislature could handle in its short regular sessions. Second, large-scale reorganization is a threat to interest groups, which vigorously lobby against changes that might undermine their members' benefits. It is not surprising, then, that legislators sometimes sidestep difficult battles over reorganization.

A final pressure for bureaucratic reform is the governor. Recent governors have been especially interested in reforms that would increase their ability to control the bureaucracy, and they have had some success. Governor Bush got the legislation to grant the governor the power to name the Commissioner of Education, and the legislation made the Commissioner's term commensurate with the governor's. Governor Richards got lawmakers to give her the right to appoint the commissioner of insurance. These reforms strengthened the chain of command in the bureaucracy.

Future political conditions also affect the likelihood of bureaucratic reform. Reorganization is not likely to occur when opposing parties control the governorship and the legislature. The suspicion that marks party relationships is far more likely to lead to inaction than to a willingness to increase the influence of officeholders who belong to the opposition party.

Bureaucratic reform will be achieved only when political leaders in the legislative and executive branches see a political advantage in it. The ongoing shortage of revenue could lead to a bureaucratic overhaul. Certainly before they can ask the citizens of Texas to pay more taxes, the state's leaders will have to convince the public that they are making efficient use of available funds. Bureaucratic reorganization makes sense in that context. On the other hand, a surge in the state's economy probably would put this issue on the back burner.

Notes

1. "Children in the Void," *Fiscal Notes* (December, 1997), p. 6.
2. Ibid.
3. William T. Gormley, Jr., "Accountability Battles in State Administration," in *The State of the States,* 2d ed., Carl E. Van Horn, ed. (Washington, DC: Congressional Quarterly Press, 1993), 171–191.
4. Legislative Budget Board, *Fiscal Size Up: 1998–99* (Austin: Legislative Budget Board, 1997), p. 1-2.
5. SB1, An Act Pertaining to the Education System, passed by the 74th session of the Texas legislature, 1995, Title 2, Subtitle B, Section 7.003.
6. Legislative Budget Board, *Fiscal Size Up: 1998–99,* p. 1-2.
7. *Breaking the Mold,* vol. 1, 43.
8. Legislative Budget Board, *Fiscal Size Up: 1992–93,* 5-2.
9. Legislative Budget Board, *Fiscal Size Up: 1994–95 Biennium* (Austin, 1994), 5-3.
10. *Lelsz* v. *Kavanagh,* 710 F.2d 1040 (1983).
11. Legislative Budget Board, *Fiscal Size Up: 1998–99,* 5-27.
12. Legislative Budget Board, *Fiscal Size Up: 1998–99,* p. 1-2.
13. Legislative Budget Board, *Fiscal Size Up: 1998–99,* 10-7.
14. HB1863, An Act Relating to Eligibility for and the Provision of Services and Programs for Needy People, passed by 74th Legislature, 1995, Section 301.001.
15. Legislative Budget Board, *Fiscal Size Up: 1998–99,* p. 1-2.
16. Legislative Budget Board, *Fiscal Size Up: 1998–99,* 8-6.
17. *Ruiz* v. *Estelle,* 666 F.2d 854, (1982).
18. Legislative Budget Board, *Fiscal Size Up: 1998–99,* p. 1-2.
19. Ibid.
20. "State Environmental Agency Due to Be Operating in 1993," *Fiscal Notes,* August 1991, 7.
21. *Breaking the Mold,* 1:16.
22. Legislative Budget Board, *Fiscal Size Up: 1998–99,* 9-13.
23. Legislative Budget Board, *Fiscal Size Up: 1992–93,* 10-11–10-12.
24. Comptroller of Public Accounts, *Gaining Ground,* 2: (Austin, 1994), 319.
25. *Breaking the Mold,* 1:19.
26. *Breaking the Mold,* 1:19.
27. Legislative Budget Board, *Fiscal Size Up: 1998–99,* p. 3-13.
28. Comptroller of Public Accounts, *Gaining Ground,* 2: (Austin, 1994), 319.

29. See Article IX, Section 153 of HB1, Appropriations Bill for 1996–1997 Fiscal Year, 74th Texas Legislature, 1995.

30. Legislative Budget Board, "Fiscal Year 1997 Performance Assessment," available at the agency's web site (**http://www.lbb.state.tx.us**).

31. Legislative Budget Board, *Fiscal Size Up: 1998–99,* 12-3.

32. Charles Mahtesian, "Why the Sun Rarely Sets on State Bureaucracy," in *State Government: CQ's Guide to Current Issues and Activities, 1993–94,* Thad L. Beyle, ed. (Washington, DC: CQ Press, 1993), 147–150. The point made here is on p. 149.

33. See Gormley, "Accountability Battles," 172ff.

34. *Breaking the Mold,* 1:17.

9 TEXAS JUDICIARY

CHAPTER OUTLINE

The 1992 race between Oscar Mauzy and Craig Enoch for a seat on the Texas Supreme Court seemed to signal the end of an era. Justice Mauzy, a Democrat, had long worked to expand the rights of consumers and workers. His opponent, Craig Enoch, a Republican appeals court judge, was more conservative: he argued that judges should apply the law, not write it.

Because of its significance, large amounts of money flowed into this race. Each side raised more than $1 million. Mauzy's money came mostly from plaintiffs' lawyers; Enoch's came from business trade groups, insurers, and defense lawyers. This pattern of contributions was not atypical. One study found that of the $3.2 million that had been contributed to supreme court candidates in Texas by June 1992, about 80 percent of it came from lawyers, doctors, PACs, and business interests.[1]

The campaign rhetoric was pointed. Justice Mauzy's ads emphasized his opponent's ties to the insurance industry. Judge Enoch's ads talked about Mauzy's willingness to accept campaign contributions from trial lawyers. Enoch's campaign made frequent mention of the fact that Mauzy had been featured in a "60 Minutes" segment entitled "Is Justice for Sale in Texas?"[2]

With Mauzy's defeat in 1992, the days of dominance of the Texas Supreme Court by politicians who were obligated to the Texas Trial Lawyers Association were over. Maybe justice was no longer for sale in Texas. Or was it? Was justice no longer for sale, or had the buyer simply changed? By 1998, a nonprofit organization called Texans for Public Justice issued a report arguing that contemporary Supreme Court justices were funding their election campaigns through contributions from corporations and large law firms. The report pointed out that the justices they studied had taken 40 percent of their campaign donations from interests with cases pending before the Supreme Court.[3] Thus, the charge was the same as it had been: that justices were taking contributions from donors with cases pending before them, and that the justices decisions were thereby influenced. The charge was the same, only the identity of the donors had changed. One could easily be reminded of the old saying, "The more things change, the more they stay the same."

This narrative illustrates several things about the Texas courts. First, it shows the deep ideological division over the appropriate role of the courts. Second, it shows that the Texas courts are deeply enmeshed in the partisan battle to control the state. Finally, this case makes clear that the courts handle important issues that affect the lives and property of significant interests in the state, and that those interests will use politics to protect themselves.

The courts play a critical role in Texas government. This chapter describes the courts and that role. The text here addresses several questions:

- How are Texas courts organized, and what do the various courts do?
- How are judges selected, and what are the consequences of the selection process?
- What forces for change affect the courts, and what are the prospects for change?

In 1992, Rose Spector (on the far right) became the first woman to be elected to the Texas Supreme Court.

Change and the Courts: An Introduction

How have state courts changed in recent decades? One scholar argued that as the courts entered the 1950s and 1960s, they began to make more liberal decisions, especially in the areas of tort law (involving suits for damages) and civil liberties.[4] In other words, state supreme courts have shown an increasing tendency to sympathize with plaintiffs in personal injury cases and to defend the rights of individuals in civil liberties matters. At the root of that tendency have been changing public attitudes and the vigorous activity of organized groups. In addition, federal courts have deflected certain issues down to the state courts for settlement. For example, that a significant number of state courts still are dealing today with school finance is the product of an unsuccessful effort to take that issue to the federal courts (see Chapter 13).

The Texas courts share in many of these national trends. A liberal leaning in tort cases has fueled controversy in the state. And the Texas courts have been working on school finance since the 1980s. Landmark civil liberties decisions are less common in the state's judicial system. Overall, though, Texas courts have been faced with the kind of change that is going on nationally.

The Structure of the Texas Courts

The Texas court system is complex, and understanding the structure of the courts and their jurisdictions can be difficult. An examination of that structure, then, should begin with the nature of court jurisdictions.

Types of Jurisdictions

A court's **jurisdiction** is its authority to make judgments in a given area. The jurisdiction of Texas courts is based on territory, subject matter, and hierarchical position.

Territorial jurisdiction. Most Texas courts serve a specific territory in the state, i.e., their **territorial jurisdiction.** Municipal courts serve specific cities; justice of the peace courts serve designated precincts within a county; county courts serve the county in which they are located; district courts serve a specific district; intermediate courts of appeals serve specific regions within the state. Only the courts of last resort—the state supreme court and the court of criminal appeals—have the entire state as their jurisdiction.

Subject-matter jurisdiction. The jurisdiction of Texas courts also is based on the types of disputes the courts handle, i.e., their **subject-matter jurisdiction.** The broadest classification distinguishes between criminal jurisdiction and civil jurisdiction. Within these categories, some courts specialize still further. For example, some courts deal only with matters that involve young people; others are limited to probate matters (settling estates).

Criminal cases are actions brought by the government against individuals charged with violating criminal laws. Criminal laws define crimes against the public order and the punishments for those crimes. Punishments vary from fines, to imprisonment, to execution, depending on the severity of the crime.

Civil cases are disputes between private individuals or groups over contracts, marriages, divorces, or injuries that one party has caused another. The "punishment" in civil suits is not a jail term; it usually involves financial compensation for the injured party.

Hierarchical jurisdiction. Courts are arranged in a hierarchy that reflects the seriousness of the issues they deal with and the role they play in applying the law. In the criminal courts, serious crimes are called **felonies,** and less serious crimes are called **misdemeanors.** Felonies are punishable by one year or longer in prison; jail sentences in misdemeanor cases are less than a year. In civil cases, the seriousness of the issue depends on the value of the property contested or the amount of the settlement sought. Courts that handle more-serious cases are higher in the court hierarchy than those that handle less-serious cases.

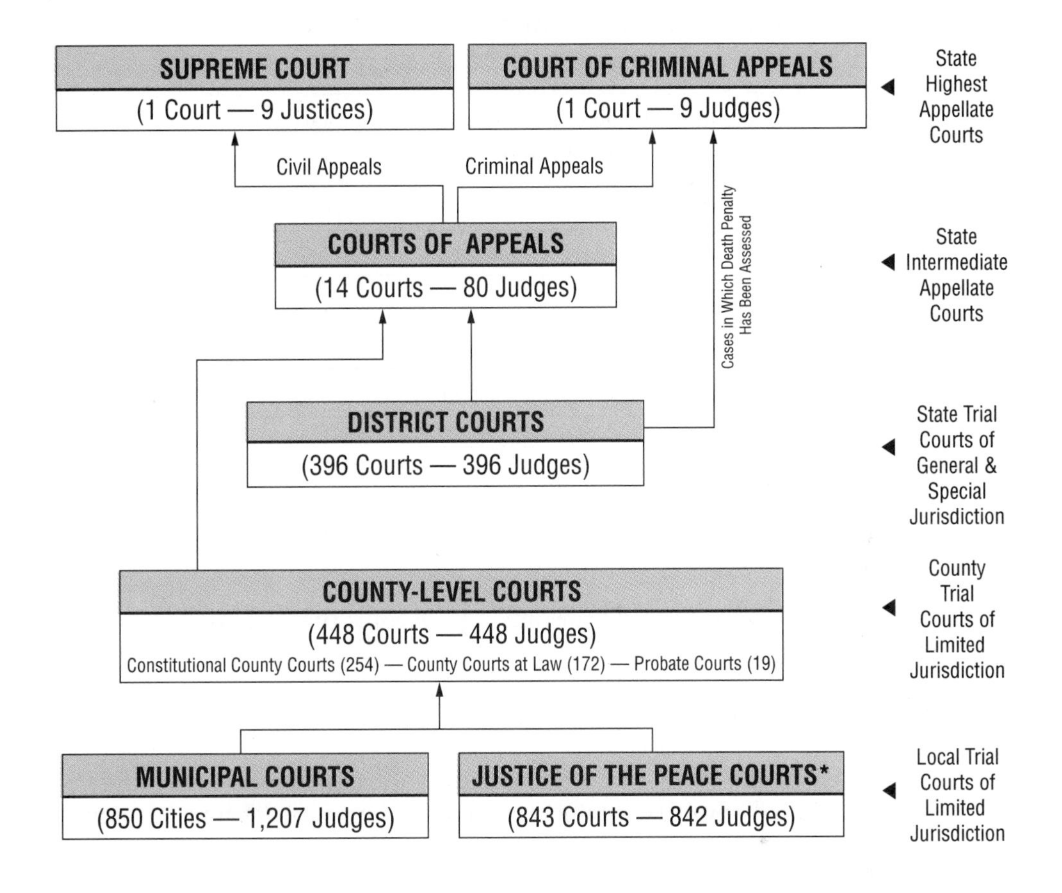

FIGURE 9.1 The Court System in Texas, 1997
**Most municipal courts and all justice of the peace courts are not courts of record. Appeals from these courts are by trial* de novo *(a new trial is held) to the county courts or, in some instances, to the district courts. Appeals from municipal courts that are courts of record are taken on the record to the county courts. Source: Office of Court Administration, Austin.*

Another hierarchical distinction in Texas and in other legal systems is made between courts of original jurisdiction and appeals courts. Courts of **original jurisdiction** are the trial courts that first hear a case. Municipal courts, justice of the peace courts, county courts, and district courts are all trial courts in Texas (Figure 9.1). Courts with **appellate jurisdiction** hear cases on appeal from lower courts. They review the procedures used in a trial and the fairness of the verdict rendered. The courts of appeals, the Texas Supreme Court, and the Texas Court of Criminal Appeals are appellate courts.

Sometimes the jurisdiction of courts at different hierarchical levels in the system overlap. The law can give a court **exclusive jurisdiction** over a type of case, or it can give **concurrent jurisdiction** to two or more courts. A court's

Table 9.1 Municipal Courts at a Glance

Jurisdiction
• Exclusive original jurisdiction over cases involving violations of city ordinances • Concurrent jurisdiction with justice of the peace courts in misdemeanor cases involving fines of $500 or less • No civil jurisdiction
Judges' Qualifications
Set by individual cities
Term of Office
Set by individual cities; two-year terms are common
Salary
Set by individual cities

jurisdiction is exclusive if it is the only type of court that has jurisdiction over a type of case.

Trial Courts

Trial courts are courts of original jurisdiction, the courts where cases are first heard. Texas has several types of trial courts, their jurisdictions varying by territory and subject matter.

Municipal courts. At the lowest level of the Texas court system lie the municipal courts. The state legislature created these courts by statute. In 1996 there were 844 of them (some large cities have more than one municipal court). Individual city governments set the qualifications for judges and their salaries, which vary considerably from one city to another. A single judge usually presides in each municipal court. Some municipal court judges are elected; others are appointed by the local city council. Judges usually are appointed to two-year terms and serve at the will of the city council. Most municipal court judges work part-time, holding court only for a few hours each day.

Municipal courts enforce city ordinances and deal with misdemeanor cases that involve violations of state law (Table 9.1). Besides handling the cases within their jurisdiction, municipal court judges also serve as magistrates: they hold preliminary hearings, issue search and arrest warrants, conduct inquests, and set bail for people who have been arrested. These functions allow judges of higher courts to devote more time to the disposition of cases.

As Figure 9.2 shows, most municipal court cases involve traffic offenses. Of the nontraffic cases, 81 percent involve infractions of state laws, and only

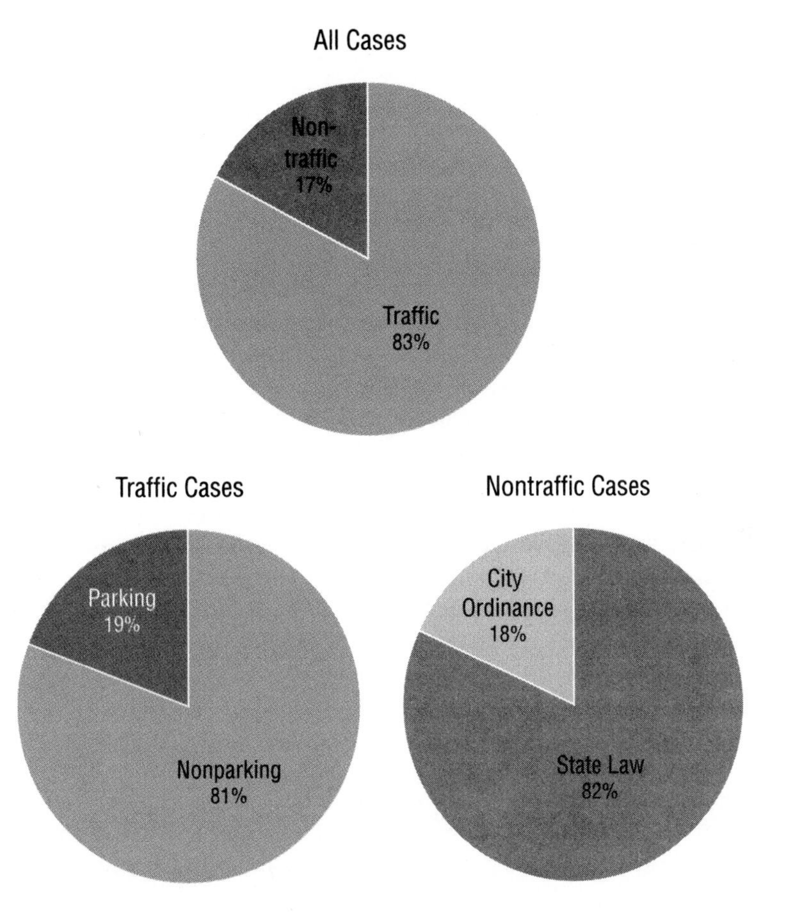

FIGURE 9.2 Types of Cases Handled by Texas Municipal Courts, 1996
Note: More than 1,100 Texas cities have the authority to operate municipal courts, and the total number of active courts varies from year to year. Source: Texas Judicial Council, Texas Judicial System Annual Report *(Austin: Office of Court Administration, 1997), 408.*

19 percent pertain to city ordinances. Only about 15 percent of traffic cases go to trial, and less than 1 percent of those are tried before juries.[5] Most defendants plead guilty. And because attorneys' fees often would outweigh potential penalties, few retain lawyers.

Most municipal courts are not **courts of record**: no transcript of the proceedings is kept. Consequently cases appealed from them to higher courts must be accorded a **trial *de novo***—all evidence and testimony are presented again in the court of appeals. Defendants who understand the process can use it to their advantage. They may appeal traffic offenses to a higher court, hoping that caseloads in the higher court will prevent their case from being heard or that their case will be dismissed because the police officer who issued the original traffic citation cannot appear. In 1987 the legislature authorized all cities to upgrade their municipal courts to courts of record, but the expense kept most cities from doing so.[6]

Justice of the peace courts. Justice of the peace courts share the bottom rung of the judicial ladder with the municipal courts. The constitution of the Republic of Texas established the position of justice of the peace in 1836, and it has been retained in each of the state's subsequent constitutions. The current constitution requires each county to create from one to eight judicial precincts (or districts); one or two justices are elected in each precinct.[7] In 1996, 839 justice of the peace courts were in operation.

Justices of the peace are elected in partisan elections. There are no statutory or constitutional qualifications for the office. Only about 5 percent of these judges are lawyers.[8] Because county commissioners set the salaries for justices of the peace, salaries vary from county to county.

Justice of the peace courts have original jurisdiction over some misdemeanors and civil jurisdiction over small claims (Table 9.2). These courts also exercise concurrent jurisdiction with county courts in some civil matters. And like municipal court judges, justices of the peace act as magistrates for higher-level courts.

As Figure 9.3 shows, about 89 percent of the cases heard by justices of the peace are criminal cases, and about 11 percent are civil cases. Of the criminal cases, 73 percent have to do with traffic violations. Of the civil matters, 27 percent are small claims suits and 45 percent are forcible entry and detainer suits. In 1997 most criminal cases were handled without a trial; most civil suits were decided by trial.[9] Trials are informal and often are conducted without attorneys. Here, too, no official transcript of proceedings is kept. Appeals from justice of the peace courts must be tried *de novo.*

Table 9.2 Justice of the Peace Courts at a Glance

Jurisdiction

- Original jurisdiction over misdemeanors punishable by fines under $500
- Exclusive jurisdiction over civil matters where the amount in controversy is $200 or less
- Concurrent jurisdiction with county courts in civil matters involving amounts between $200 and $5,000 that have not been designated specifically for a higher court

Judges' Qualifications

No professional qualifications

Term of Office

Elected in partisan elections for a four-year term

Salary

Set by county commissioners

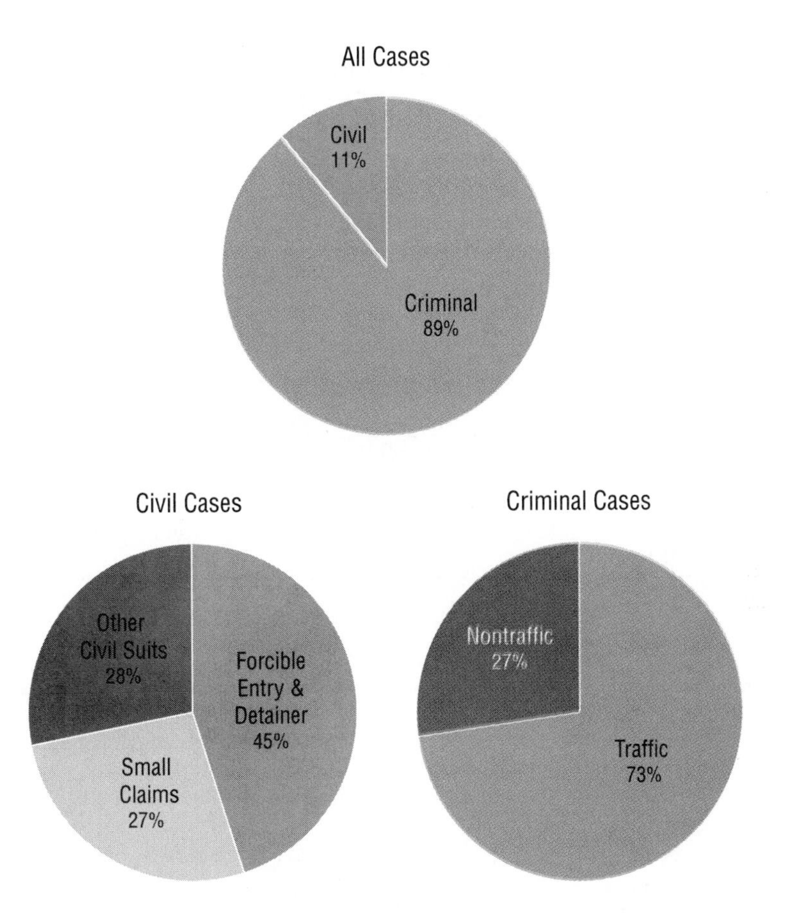

FIGURE 9.3 Types of Cases Handled by the Texas Justice of the Peace Courts, 1997

Source: Texas Judicial Council, Texas Judicial System Annual Report *(Austin: Office of Court Administration, 1997), 382.*

Beyond their judicial responsibilities, justices of the peace serve as coroners in counties that do not have a medical examiner. This means that in many Texas counties, a justice of the peace is responsible for determining the cause of death in accidental or unattended deaths, yet no law stipulates how this responsibility should be discharged by someone who is not a medical doctor. Justices of the peace commonly rely on private pathologists to perform autopsies on a fee-for-service basis, but they are not required to do that by the law.

County courts. The county courts are the next level up in the hierarchy of Texas courts. There are two types of county courts: *constitutional county courts* and *statutory county courts* (county courts at law). The Texas Constitution mandates a constitutional county court for each of the 254 counties

Table 9.3 Constitutional County Courts at a Glance

Jurisdiction

- Concurrent civil jurisdiction with justice of the peace courts where the matter at issue has a value greater than $200 but less than $5,000
- General jurisdiction in uncontested probate matters
- Jurisdiction over matters that involve juveniles
- Exclusive original jurisdiction over misdemeanors where the fine allowed exceeds $500 or where a jail sentence can be imposed
- Appellate jurisdiction over cases appealed from the municipal courts or the justice of the peace courts

Judges' Qualifications

Must be informed in the laws of the state

Term of Office

Elected in partisan elections for a four-year term

Salary

Set by county commissioners

in the state. County courts at law are statutory courts; they are created by legislative statute.

Judges of constitutional county courts must be "informed" in the law of the state, but they are not required to have a law degree or a license to practice law.[10] County judges are chosen in partisan elections for four-year terms. Because the salaries of the judges are set by the county commissioners, they vary substantially from county to county.

A 1985 constitutional amendment abolished all parts of the constitution that described the jurisdiction of the county courts, leaving the jurisdiction of these courts to be defined by legislative statute (Table 9.3). In civil matters, the county courts share jurisdiction with the justice of the peace courts in small claims suits. These courts also have general jurisdiction over probate matters and cases involving juveniles. They handle some misdemeanor criminal cases, and they hear cases appealed from the municipal courts and the justice of the peace courts. All county courts are courts of record.

Each county court judge also serves as the presiding officer for the county commissioners' court, the governing body of the county government. In the more populated counties, the work with the commissioners' court may take up most of a county court judge's time. In those counties, the state legislature has created statutory county courts and other specialized county-level courts (including courts with principal jurisdiction over domestic relations and juveniles) to take over some or all of the load from the constitutional county courts. By 1997, the legislature had created 191 statutory courts (courts of law and probate courts) in seventy-two counties.

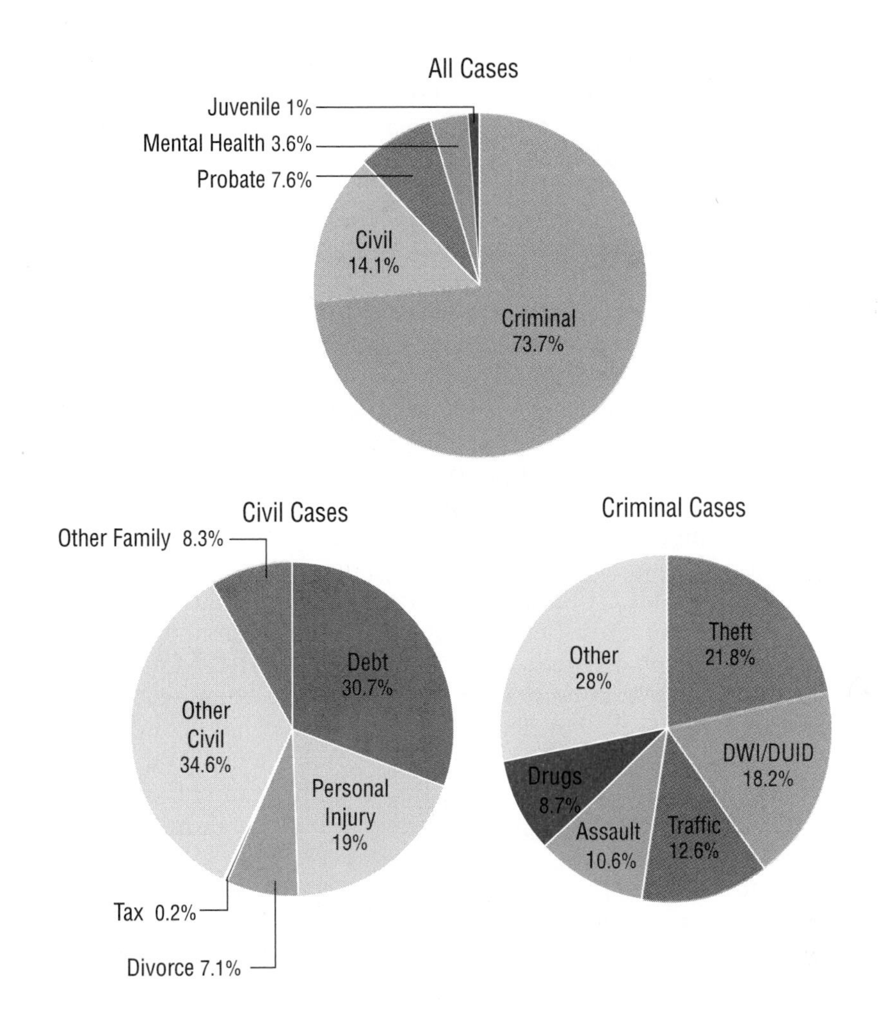

FIGURE 9.4 Types of Cases Handled by the Texas County-Level Courts, 1997
Note: Includes cases appealed from lower courts. Source: Texas Judicial Council, Texas Judicial System Annual Report *(Austin: Office of Court Administration, 1997), 302.*

The jurisdiction of county courts at law varies from county to county and from court to court, depending on the statute under which they were created. Judges of these courts must be trained in the law. Like constitutional county court judges, they are elected in partisan elections for four-year terms. Their salaries are set by the county government and vary from county to county.

Over 72 percent of the caseload of the county courts involves criminal matters (Figure 9.4). The remaining cases are divided between civil and more specialized matters. The largest single category of criminal matter reported in 1997 involved theft (21.8 percent), followed by driving while intoxicated or driving under the influence of drugs (18.2 percent).

District courts. At the next level of the judicial hierarchy are the district courts, the trial courts for the most serious cases. In 1997 there were 395 district courts in Texas, each serving a geographic district determined by the legislative statute that created it. District courts in rural areas may cover several counties; in urban areas, where the population density warrants it, several district courts (with one judge each) may handle the work in one district. New district courts are created by the state legislature in almost every session.

District court judges in Texas are chosen in partisan elections for four-year terms. Because of the serious matters that come before them, district court judges must meet higher qualifications than lower-court judges (Table 9.4). The state pays district judges, but their salaries may be supplemented by the county government. A district court judge's salary must be at least $2,000 less than a Texas Supreme Court justice's salary.

District courts have "exclusive, appellate, and original jurisdiction of all actions, proceedings and remedies, except in cases where exclusive, appellate, or original jurisdiction may be conferred . . . on some other court, tribunal, or administrative body."[11] Since this constitutional provision gives the district courts jurisdiction in all matters except those delegated to other courts, the jurisdiction of any district court depends on the jurisdiction of the other courts in its area. District courts have original jurisdiction over major civil and criminal cases (Table 9.5). The district courts may have concurrent civil jurisdiction with county courts at law concerning some civil matters. In metropolitan areas, courts often specialize in civil, criminal, or family law matters. Courts that exercise only criminal jurisdiction commonly are called *criminal district courts.*

Civil cases make up the bulk of the district courts' work, accounting for about 65 percent of all new cases filed in 1997 (Figure 9.5). Over half the civil cases were divorce and family matters. Drug offenses made up the largest

Table 9.4 County Courts At Law at a Glance

Jurisdiction
Varies depending on the statute creating the court. May be limited to criminal or civil matters or to matters dealing with juveniles or probate.
Judges' Qualifications
Must be trained in the law
Term of Office
Elected in partisan elections for a four-year term
Salary
Set by county commissioners

Table 9.5 District Courts at a Glance

Jurisdiction

- Original criminal jurisdiction over all felonies and over misdemeanor cases involving official misconduct
- Civil jurisdiction over divorces and controversies involving land titles and liens and in all matters where the contested value is over $200
- Concurrent civil jurisdiction with county courts at law concerning some civil matters
- Exclusive civil jurisdiction in cases where the disputed value is over $100,000

Judges' Qualifications

- U.S. citizenship
- Residence in the district for two years
- Licensed to practice law in Texas
- Four years' experience as an attorney or a judge

Term of Office

Elected in partisan elections for a four-year term

Salary

Base salary from state $98,100; can be supplemented by the county

proportion of criminal matters; burglary and thefts were second and third in share of caseload.

Appellate Courts

At the highest levels of the Texas judiciary are the appellate courts. Their responsibility is to review the work of the trial courts to determine whether an error was made that justifies overturning a lower court's decision.

Courts of appeals. The courts of appeals are the first level of courts with appellate jurisdiction (Table 9.6). The Texas Constitution authorizes the legislature to divide the state into districts and to establish a court of appeals in each district.[12] There are now fourteen courts of appeals. Two—the first and fourteenth—serve the same territory in the Houston area (Figure 9.6).

Each court of appeals has a chief justice and at least two associate justices. The number of associate justices allocated to a court is set by the legislature and varies between two and twelve. Courts of appeals justices are chosen from their district in partisan elections for six-year terms. The terms are staggered so that one-third of the justices face reelection every two years.

Each court of appeals has jurisdiction over both civil and criminal matters appealed from the trial courts in its district. Until 1981 these courts had only

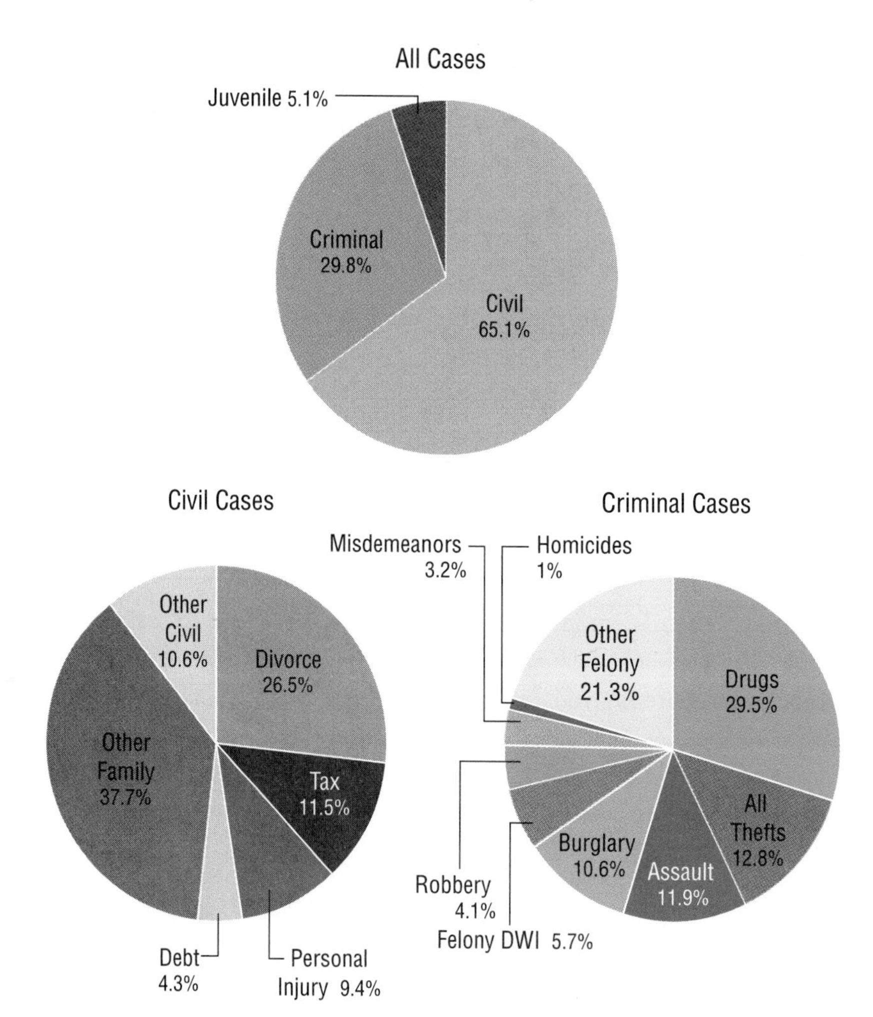

FIGURE 9.5 Types of Cases Handled by the Texas District Courts, 1997
Source: Texas Judicial Council, Texas Judicial System Annual Report *(Austin: Office of Court Administration, 1997), 178.*

civil jurisdiction; an amendment to the constitution passed that year expanded their jurisdiction to include criminal matters. These courts of appeals have final civil jurisdiction in cases involving divorce, slander, and contested local elections; other civil cases can be appealed to the Texas Supreme Court. Courts of appeals are bypassed in death penalty cases, which are appealed directly to the Texas Court of Criminal Appeals.

Appellate courts perform quite differently from trial courts. In reviewing the work of lower courts, the appellate courts rely on the written record of the trial along with the written and oral arguments of the appellate lawyers. Decisions are made by the justices, not by juries. If an appellate court finds a

Table 9.6 Courts of Appeals at a Glance

Jurisdiction
• Jurisdiction over both civil and criminal matters appealed from the trial courts in its district • Final civil jurisdiction in cases involving divorce, slander, and contested elections for local offices
Judges' Qualifications
• U.S. citizenship • At least thirty-five years old • Licensed to practice law in Texas • Ten years' experience as an attorney or a judge (or some combination of the two)
Term of Office
Elected in partisan elections for staggered six-year terms
Salary
• Chief Justice $104,050; counties may add supplement • Associate Justice $103,550; counties may add supplement

reversible error in a case, it can return the case to the trial court for retrial or dismissal.

The workload of the courts of appeals has grown steadily (Figure 9.7). The number of new cases added each year went from almost 8,000 cases in 1988 to about 11,000 cases in 1997. The workload of individual courts of appeals varies considerably. The two courts in Houston and the Dallas court shoulder the heaviest burden: about 27 percent of all new cases filed in a court of appeals in 1996 were filed in one of the courts located in Houston; and another 20 percent were filed in the Fifth Court of Appeals in Dallas. The Fifth Court of Appeals had the highest average number of new cases filed per justice (162) during 1996; the Sixth Court of Appeals in Eastland had just 69 cases filed per justice.[13]

The work of the courts of appeals is divided between criminal and civil cases. In 1997 criminal matters made up 68 percent of the cases.[14] The courts of appeals reversed the decision of the trial court in about 10.6 percent of the cases disposed of during 1997.[15]

The Texas court of criminal appeals. At the highest level of the Texas judicial hierarchy are the courts of last resort. Most states have just one court of last resort. Texas has two: the Texas Court of Criminal Appeals and the Texas Supreme Court.[16] The Texas Court of Criminal Appeals was created by the constitution of 1876. Originally called the Court of Appeals, it had both civil and criminal appellate jurisdiction. In 1891 the judiciary article of

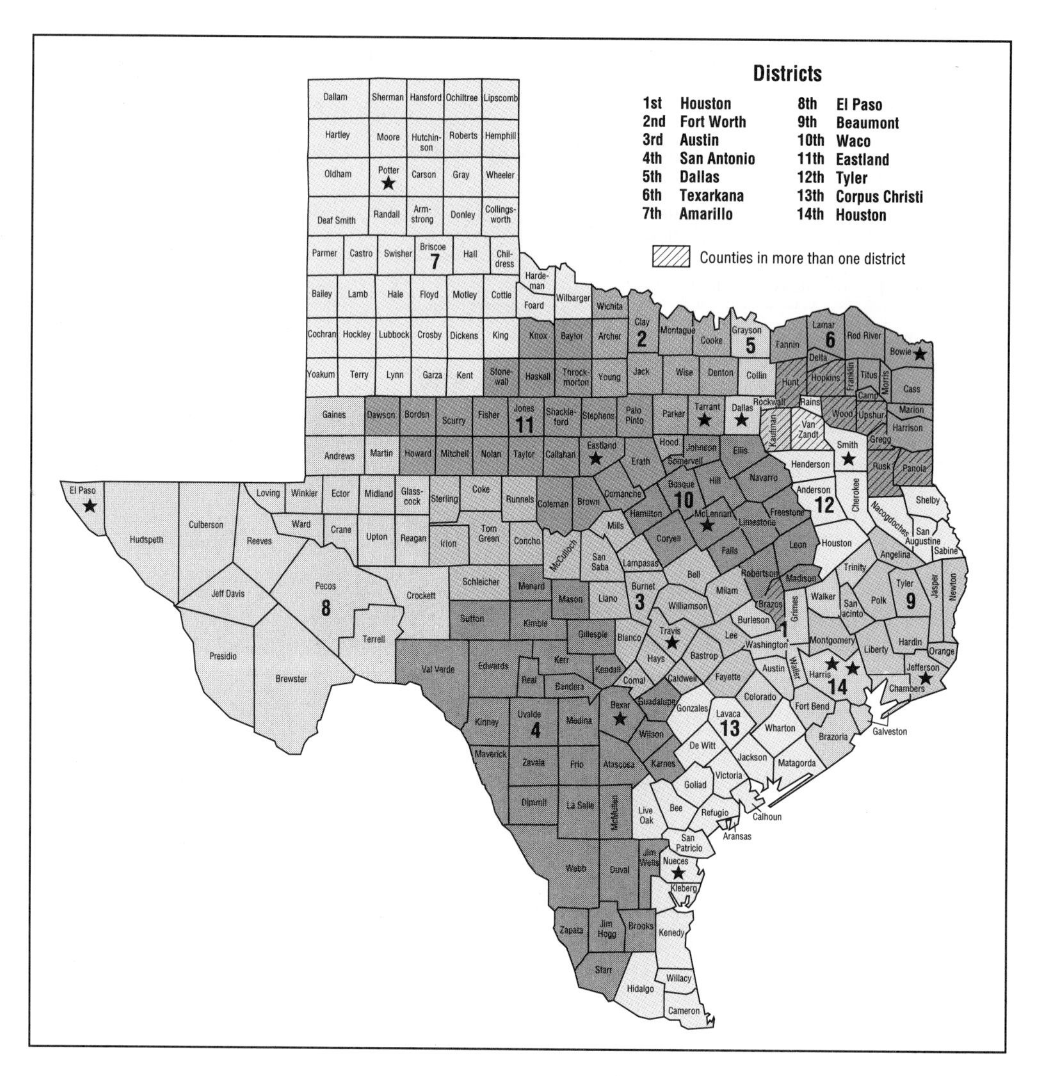

FIGURE 9.6 Courts of Appeals Districts, 1993
Source: Texas Judicial Council, Texas Judicial System Annual Report *(Austin: Office of Court Administration, 1993), 163.*

the constitution was amended, and the court's appellate jurisdiction was limited to criminal matters.

Today the Texas Court of Criminal Appeals is made up of a presiding justice and eight associate justices, all elected for six-year terms in a statewide partisan election. To speed up the processing of cases, the constitution authorizes the court to hear cases in three-judge panels. When hearing death penalty cases, all nine justices sit together.

The members of the Court of Criminal Appeals. Standing: Sue Holland, Sharon Keller, Tom Price, Paul Womack. Seated: Lawrence E. Meyers, Charles F. Baird, Michael J. McCormick (presiding judge), Morris L. Overstreet, Steve Mansfield.

The Court of Criminal Appeals has final appellate jurisdiction in all criminal matters (Table 9.7). Before a 1981 constitutional amendment gave the intermediate courts of appeals criminal jurisdiction, the Texas Court of Criminal Appeals received all criminal appeals from district and county trial courts in the state. Now the court receives appeals from the intermediate courts of appeals. Only death penalty cases go directly from the district courts to the court of criminal appeals. The court also has authority to issue rules of evidence and appellate procedures for criminal cases. As Figure 9.8 shows, the caseload for the Court of Criminal Appeals has dropped off in the 1990s. Although appeal to this court is direct in death penalty cases, the court exercises discretion in deciding which other appeals to hear. The court appears to have left more decisions to the courts of appeals in the 1990s.

The Texas Supreme Court. The Texas Supreme Court is the other court at the highest level of the Texas judiciary. The court has been included in every constitution since the days when Texas was a republic. Its current structure was created by constitutional amendment in 1945.

Table 9.7 Texas Court of Criminal Appeals at a Glance

Jurisdiction

- Final appellate jurisdiction in all criminal matters
- Receives appeals directly from the district courts in death penalty cases

Judges' Qualifications

- U.S. citizenship
- At least thirty-five years old
- Licensed to practice law in Texas
- Ten years' experience as an attorney or a judge (or some combination of the two)

Term of Office

Elected in statewide partisan elections for six-year terms

Salary

Set by legislature. In 1997, associate justices received $109,000; the presiding judge received $110,000.

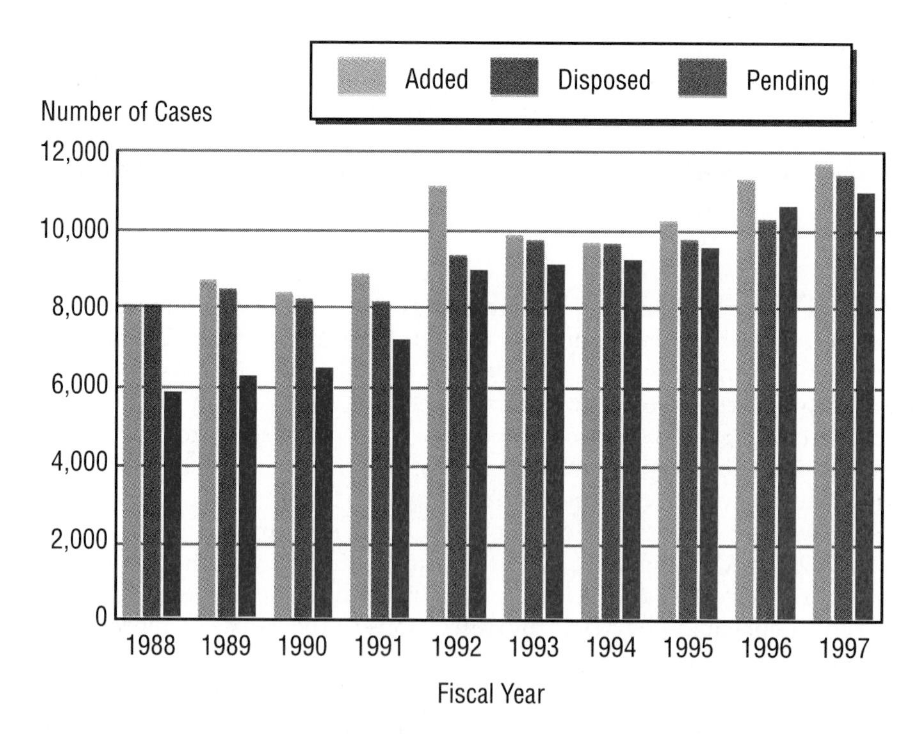

FIGURE 9.7 Texas Courts of Appeals Caseload Trends, 1988–1997

Source: Texas Judicial Council, Texas Judicial System Annual Report *(Austin: Office of Court Administration, 1997), p. 114.*

The members of the Texas Supreme Court. Standing: Priscilla R. Owen, Craig Enoch, Rose Spector, James A. Baker, Deborah G. Hankinson. Seated: Greg Abbott, Raul A. Gonzales, Thomas R. Phillips (chief justice), Nathan L. Hecht.

The Texas Supreme Court has nine members—one chief justice and eight associate justices—all elected for six-year terms. The justices serve staggered terms to provide continuity on the court (Table 9.8).

The state supreme court has final appellate jurisdiction over most civil and juvenile cases. It also has authority to prescribe rules of civil procedure, rules of administration for the Texas judicial system, rules of procedure for the Commission on Judicial Conduct (concerned with disciplining or removing judges), and rules for the operation of the Court Reporters' Certification Board (sets standards for court reporters). The Texas Supreme Court also has responsibility for several administrative matters. It has authority to approve Texas law schools; to supervise operations of the state bar and the rules for admission, discipline, supervision, and disbarment of lawyers; and to transfer cases from one appellate court to another.

The Texas Supreme Court receives cases on writs of error (petitions to review the judgment of a Court of Appeals), and regular cases (regular appeals and actions originating before the Supreme Court). As Figure 9.9 shows, the court took on an increasingly heavy caseload of both types of cases through 1993. Caseloads have fallen since then, prehaps reflecting the presence of a more conservative Republican majority on the court.

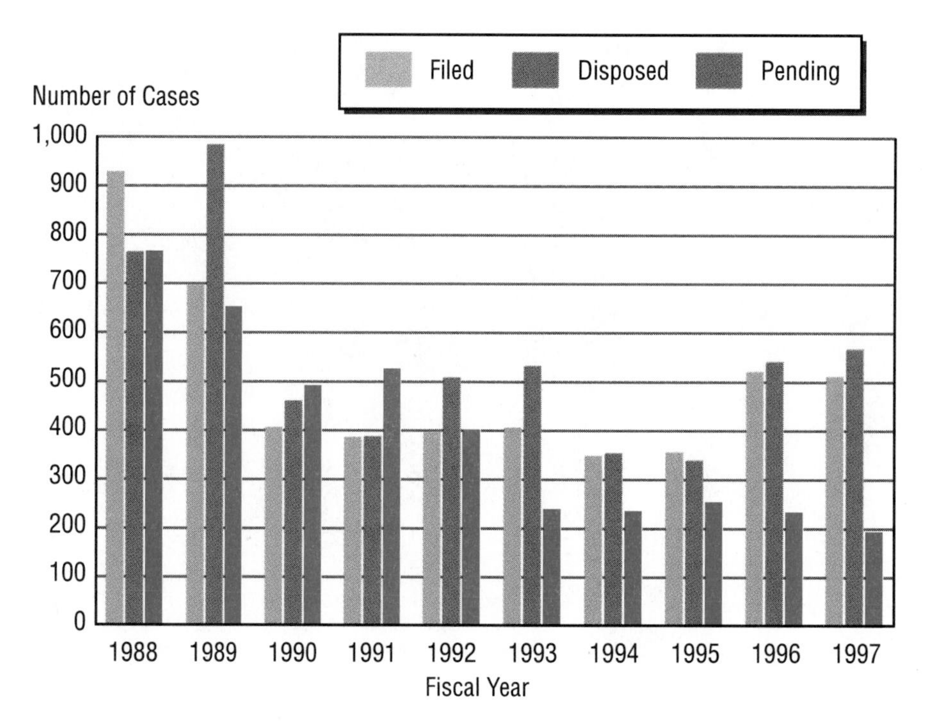

FIGURE 9.8 Texas Court of Criminal Appeals Caseload Trends, 1988–1997
Source: Texas Judicial Council, Texas Judicial System Annual Report *(Austin: Office of Court Administration, 1997), 93.*

Structural Reform of the Courts

The 1993 report of the Citizens' Commission on the Texas Judicial System concluded that "Texas has no uniform judicial framework to guarantee the just, prompt and efficient disposition of a litigant's complaint."[17] An earlier study had concluded that it was difficult to call the Texas judiciary a system at all.[18] These studies and their conclusions have called attention to the need for a structural overhaul of the Texas judiciary. In fact, the Texas judicial structure has been the subject of several reform efforts over the last twenty years, but the structure of the Texas judiciary has undergone only minor piecemeal change.

The failure of successive proposals for structural reforms is a testimony to the strength of organized stakeholders. That is, structural reforms have typically failed because those groups who thought they had something to lose were vigorous opponents and overwhelmed other less intense groups who supported reform. Judges, such as justices of the peace and county judges, saw their job security threatened by a reform that might abolish their courts. Republican legislators were suspicious that reform efforts would reduce the

Table 9.8 Texas Supreme Court at a Glance

Jurisdiction
Final appellate jurisdiction over most civil and juvenile cases
Judges' Qualifications
• U.S. citizenship • At least thirty-five years old • Licensed to practice law in Texas • At least ten years' experience as an attorney or a judge (or some combination of both)
Term of Office
Elected in statewide partisan elections for six-year staggered terms
Salary
Set by the Texas legislature. In 1997, associate justices received $109,000; the chief justice received $110,000.

number of judgeships won by Republicans. Particularly when reform requires a constitutional amendment, organized and intense minorities hold the upper hand. They do not need to have a majority of the vote—they only need to prevent the opposition from getting two-thirds of the votes. Thus, until discontent with the court system becomes more widespread and more intense in other groups, structural reform of the Texas courts has a low probability of success.

How Judges Are Chosen in Texas

One of the most controversial aspects of the Texas judicial system is its use of elections to choose judges. There are several judicial selection methods, including legislative appointment, gubernatorial appointment, and a number of merit selection plans.[19] All Texas judges, except the municipal court judges, are elected in partisan elections. Although the constitution stipulates that most Texas judges be elected, it also allows the governor to fill vacancies until the next election.[20] It is not uncommon, then, for individuals to reach the judicial bench by gubernatorial appointment and then to have the advantage of running as an incumbent in their first race for a judgeship.

The controversy over judicial elections focuses on different issues depending on the level of court considered. At the trial-court level, at-large elections are held throughout the county or district. Minority groups argue that this system prevents them from electing a fair share of the state's trial-court judges because they are outnumbered in all districts. Many state leaders agreed. For

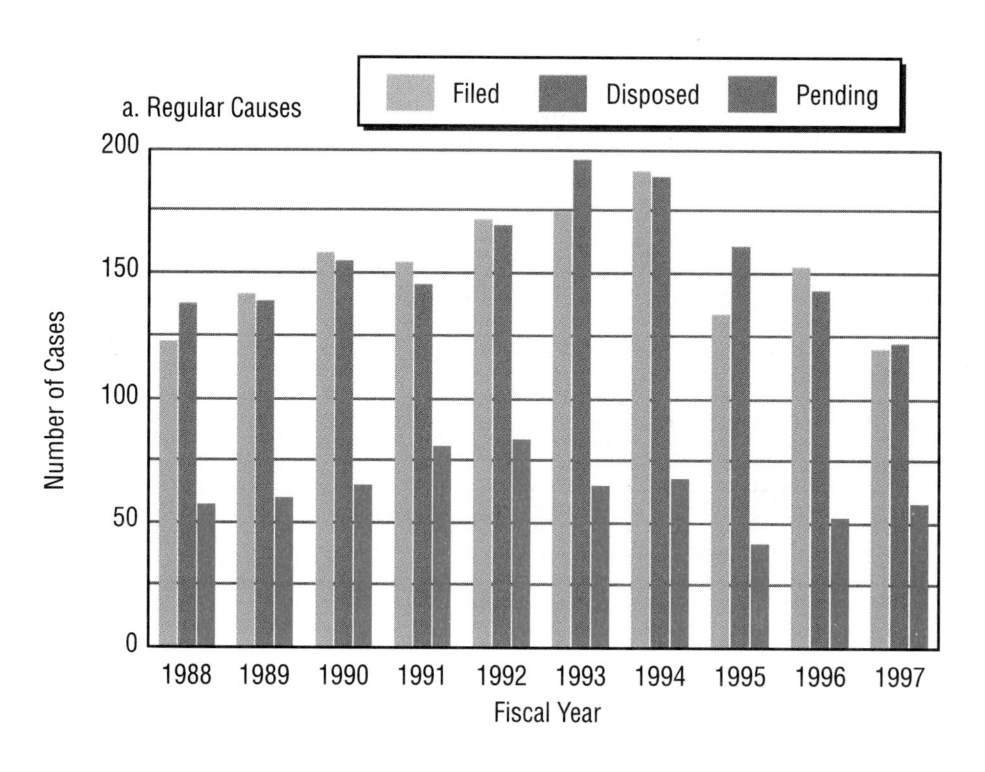

a. Regular Causes
Filed
Disposed
Pending
200
150
100
50
0
Number of Cases
1988
1989
1990
1991
1992
1993
1994
1995
1996
1997
Fiscal Year

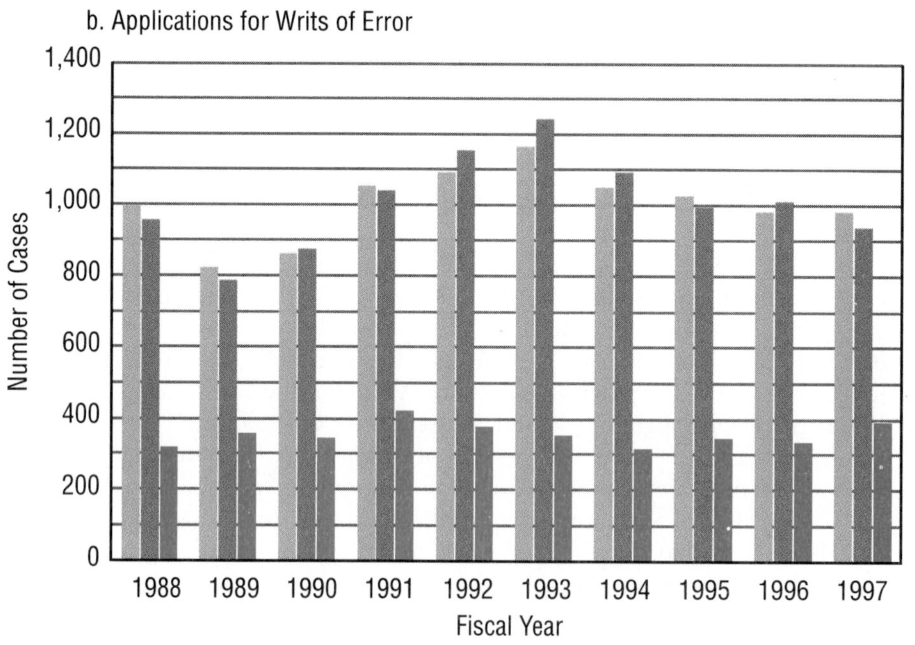

b. Applications for Writs of Error
1,400
1,200
1,000
800
600
400
200
0
Number of Cases
1988
1989
1990
1991
1992
1993
1994
1995
1996
1997
Fiscal Year

example, in 1993 Thomas Phillips, the chief justice of the Texas Supreme Court, pointed out that in Dallas County, 37 percent of the people were African Americans or Hispanics but that less than 14 percent of the judges were from either group. In Harris County, African Americans and Hispanics make up 42 percent of the population but only 9 percent of the judges.[21] Attorney General Dan Morales agreed with Chief Justice Phillips on the need for new judicial election procedures, disagreeing only on the details of a new system.[22]

The controversy over electing trial-court judges was taken to the federal courts by the League of United Latin American Citizens and other minority-group plaintiffs, who argued that the system violates the Voting Rights Act Extension of 1975. A series of conflicting decisions resulted. On January 2, 1990, Federal Judge Lucius Bunton ruled in favor of the plaintiffs and decreed that judges in the nine largest Texas counties should be elected from districts, not the county. The Fifth U.S. Circuit Court of Appeals ruled on January 11, 1990, that the task of creating a single-member district system should be left to the legislature.[23] In January 1993, a three-judge panel from the Fifth U.S. Circuit Court of Appeals decided that the judicial election system in Dallas, Bexar, Ector, Harris, Jefferson, Lubbock, Midland, and Tarrant counties was unconstitutional and ordered the legislature to produce a new plan within 180 days. By this time most of the state's political leaders—including Governor Richards, Attorney General Morales, and Lieutenant Governor Bullock—had concluded that the state should stop appealing the case and negotiate a settlement.[24] But in August 1993, the court reversed itself and ruled that the judicial elections did not violate the Voting Rights Act.[25] What had looked like a victory for the minority groups was a defeat, and the state made no changes in the selection of district judges in 1993.

Elections to appellate courts, especially to the Texas Supreme Court, have become a battleground for groups with opposing philosophies on the appropriate role of the courts. On one side, the Texas Trial Lawyers' Association—a group whose members sue businesses, doctors, and insurance companies—

FIGURE 9.9 Texas Supreme Court Caseload Trends, 1988–1997
a. Regular Causes are regular appeals or original actions pending before the court. Normally, they reach this status when a Writ of Error is granted in the cause. Petitions for Original Mandamus and Habeas Corpus, which are not disposed of upon initial review, and in which the petition is granted, may also become regular causes.
b. An Application for Writ of Error is a request filed by one of the parties, requesting the Supreme Court to review the judgment of a Court of Appeals. If four or more of the nine justices concur, the writ is granted and the cause is scheduled for argument before the court. Source: Texas Judicial Council, Texas Judicial System Annual Report *(Austin: Office of Court Administration, 1997), p. 78.*

The Changing Face of Texas Politics

Do Judges Make the Law?

One of the continuing debates challenging courts and the judges who decide cases is whether the judges should "simply interpret the law" without inserting their own opinions into the case or whether they must necessarily inject their opinions into a case in order to make a decision. In Texas, this debate has often been a partisan one with Republicans charging that Democrats are the ones who like to go beyond the law while they pledge to simply interpret the law. Others argue that the attitudes of judges will inevitably enter into their decisions, and that elections simply decide whose opinions will prevail.

This issue was reopened in a recent Texas Supreme Court case concerned with whether parental consent should be required for a public health agency to dispense birth control pills. The foundation for the controversy was provided by the Texas legislature when it slipped a rider into the state's 1997 appropriation bill that prohibited using state money to dispense prescription drugs to minors. A rider is substantive matter that is inserted into an appropriations bill, and riders are certainly nothing new to Texas legislative practice. This rider—Rider 14—was inserted into the section making appropriations for the Texas Department of Public Health. Its author, Republican Senator Steve Ogden, justified his action by saying, "I think Texans would be amazed to know that 12-, 13- and 14-year-olds can now receive free prescription drugs without their parents' knowledge."[1]

Planned Parenthood brought suit in state court arguing that the rider was in conflict with national policy and also violated the state constitution. The Planned Parenthood organization argued that their agency would be injured if funds were cut off for distributing birth control pills to minors.

When the case was heard in district court, Judge Scott McCown was presiding—a Democratic judge who had previously ruled on school finance cases. Judge McCown found the rider to be unconstitutional. He ruled that the rider violated the state's constitutional ban on amending or repealing general state law through the budget bill.[2]

The state appealed Judge McCown's ruling to the Texas Supreme Court. In June 1998, the

has backed judicial candidates who are receptive to civil suits and the claims for damages they make. On the other side, groups led by the Texas Civil Justice League that believe that Texas courts have become a litigator's heaven, back more conservative candidates.

As the 1995 legislative session neared, once more it seemed possible that the legislature would address the problem of judicial elections. Lieutenant Governor Bob Bullock had appointed a group to study the issue, and they offered a reform proposal to the legislature. Their plan, which came to be called the "Bullock plan" during the session, called for the governor to appoint judges to appellate courts with **retention elections** to be held periodically thereafter. For district-level courts, the plan called for nonpartisan elections to fill vacancies and periodic retention elections for incumbents. In

Supreme Court overturned the lower court ruling and allowed the rider to stand.[3] In the majority opinion, the court argued that the case had not sufficiently "ripened" for the court to be able to decide the substance of the case. The court noted that "ripeness asks whether the facts have developed sufficiently that an injury has occurred or is likely to occur, rather than being contingent or remote." They noted that no injury to Planned Parenthood had occurred at the time of the hearing. In fact, the Department of Health had found a way around the rider by shifting funds so that no *state* funds were used to provide birth control pills to minors.

What does this case reveal about how the courts go about making their decisions? It is not possible to get inside the heads of judges, but it seems likely that personal and partisan considerations entered into the decisions of the respective judges. Is it not possible that Judge McCown, a Democrat, was looking for a way to prevent the state from imposing a requirement that would be unpopular with Democratic voters? Of course, it is entirely possible that Judge McCown found no conflict between his personal views and what he may have considered politically expedient. Does it not seem equally possible that the Republican majority on the Texas Supreme Court was looking for a way to uphold the legislature's decision and to uphold a position popular with Republican voters in the state? In fact, the Supreme Court cleverly found a way of permitting the rider to stand without having to deal with the substantive issues involved. Essentially it invoked a procedural device by asking whether the plaintiff had actually suffered any damages in the case.

Thus, this case reminds us that arguments about "injecting opinions into cases" or "sticking to the law" are mostly a smokescreen. Most experts on the courts believe that the opinions of judges inevitably play a part in deciding cases. The real issue is whose opinions will be deciding the cases. This case reminds us that a more realistic way of making choices among competing judges is not to assume that one candidate will inject his or her views into the case and another will not. The more realistic assumption is that judges' opinions matter, and voters should vote for judges whose views are compatible with their own. ★

[1]Quoted in Terrence Stutz, "Suit Challenges Birth-Control Access Law," *Dallas Morning News,* August 24, 1997, p. 47A.

[2]Suzanne, Gamboa, "Birth Control Consent Law Struck Down," *Austin American-Statesman,* August 30, 1997, p. A1.

[3]*Texas Department of Health* v. *Planned Parenthood of Houston and Southeast Texas, Inc.,* 1998 Tex. Lexis 104.

the largest counties, district-level judges would have been chosen from county commissioners' districts—instead of their current countywide election. The Bullock plan never made it to the floor of the house of representatives because of opposition from Hispanic and Republican legislators. Hispanics thought the system unlikely to help elect Hispanic judges; Republicans feared that it would help elect Democratic judges. Thus, the hundred votes necessary to propose a constitutional amendment could not be found, and the proposal failed. The legislature did, however, order the Texas Supreme Court to study judicial selection and racial diversity in the courts—along with some other issues. To support this charge, the legislature appropriated $100,000 to carry out the study, which was to be presented to the legislature in 1997.[26]

The only reform of judicial elections that could be accomplished in 1995 was to put limits on campaign contributions (SB 94). The campaign finance bill set mandatory fund-raising restrictions on judicial candidates and voluntary campaign spending caps in county, district, appellate, and statewide judicial elections. The law limits individual contributions to $5,000 for the high courts (e.g., Supreme Court). Aggregated contributions from members of the same law firm (including firm PACs) are limited to $30,000 for high court races and six times the individual limit for other courts. Although PAC contributions are not limited, candidates cannot accept more than $300,000 in PAC funds or political party contributions. The voluntary limits on campaign expenditures are $2 million for the Supreme Court and the Court of Criminal Appeals, $350,000 to $500,000 for appeals courts, and $100,000 to $350,000 for district courts.[27]

The reform of the judicial selection process failed once again in the 1997 session of the legislature. The Commission of Judicial Efficiency, which had been formed by the Texas Supreme Court in response to a mandate from the 1995 legislature, was unable to agree on one plan to recommend to the legislature. When it met in December 1996, the commissions votes were evenly divided between two plans. Half the group favored an appoint-elect-retain plan, which would have allowed the governor to appoint judges to fill vacancies, subject to senatorial confirmation. After confirmation, each judge would have been required to face an open, contested, nonpartisan election. After this initial election, the judge would have been required to stand in periodic yes or no retention elections. The alternative plan would have separated procedures used for appellate courts from those used for the lower courts. The lower court judges would have been selected initially by nonpartisan elections and followed by retention elections.[28] The higher level courts would have followed the plan outlined above. When the legislature tried to address this issue, the house passed a watered-down bill and the senate failed to pass a bill.

Although reform of judicial selection failed, most of the other recommendations of the Commission on Judicial Efficiency were passed by the legislature. The most notable was a substantial raise for judges, who had not been granted a raise since 1991. Senate Bill 1417 set up statutory guidelines for courts to monitor the demographics of law clerks and staff attorneys and to develop plans for recruiting minorities. The legislature appropriated $3.5 million for computers and software to modernize the work of the courts. Thus, the legislature made some efforts to modernize the courts and to attract good judges, even while dodging the central issue.[29]

The problems of reforming judicial elections in Texas stem from both the complexity of the issue and the number of competing agendas that come into play. For some, judicial reform is primarily about making the Texas judiciary more representative. This point of view is common among minority leaders. For others, judicial reform is mostly about removing the potential for conflict of interest from judicial elections. This is the primary concern of those who would like to take the appellate courts out of the arena of electoral politics. The complexity of the issue has made it difficult to pull together a block of votes that will stay together long enough to get a reform measure passed. What strengthens the bill for those who want a more representative judiciary may be exactly the thing that loses votes among those who simply want to regulate campaign finance.

Partisanship also seems to affect people's responses to judicial reform. The current system tends to favor Republican candidates in large metropolitan areas like Houston and Dallas. Republicans believe that a more representative judiciary means more Democratic seats—a goal they cannot embrace. For many Democrats, giving the governor the power to appoint appellate judges seems to favor the Republicans who control the governorship. In the end the complexity of the issue and the partisan concerns attached to the issue made it impossible to pull together the votes needed to address the issue. An approach that would unify the diverse interests in reform and overcome their partisan differences did not emerge.

The Discipline and Removal of Judges

Judges in Texas are expected to behave appropriately for the serious responsibility with which they have been entrusted. In fact the state has a code of judicial conduct. The Commission on Judicial Conduct is responsible for receiving and reviewing complaints against judges. It has jurisdiction over all of the state's judges. The commission is made up of eleven members: five appointed by the Texas Supreme Court, two appointed by the state bar association, and four appointed by the governor. They serve six-year terms and are compensated only for expenses associated with serving on the commission. If the commission concludes that a judge is guilty of willful or persistent misconduct, it can issue a private reprimand, publicly censure the judge, or recommend to the supreme court that the judge be removed from office. Decisions of the commission are subject to review by a special court of review. Judges also can be removed from office by the legislature through impeachment proceedings or judicial address (see Chapter 6).

Support Systems and Judicial Administration

Several agencies help the courts get their job done. The *Office of Court Administration*, created in 1977, collects information about the court system and provides support services to the trial and appellate courts and judicial agencies.

The *Texas Judicial Council* studies the Texas judicial system.[30] The council, established by the legislature in 1929, includes the chief justice of the Texas Supreme Court and the presiding judge of the Texas Court of Criminal Appeals (or their designees from their respective courts), two justices from the courts of appeals (chosen by the governor), two presiding judges from the administrative judicial regions (chosen by the governor), the chairs and immediate past chairs of the Judicial Affairs Committee and the Jurisprudence Committee, seven licensed attorneys (chosen by the governor), and two nonlawyer citizens chosen by the governor (one of whom must be a journalist). Each year the council files a report with the governor and the supreme court filled with information about the workings of the courts and recommendations for change. The Office of Court Administration gathers information and acts as support staff for the council.

The task of managing caseloads falls to nine administrative judicial regions and to the Texas Supreme Court. In each administrative judicial region, the governor designates a district judge (active or retired) to be presiding judge. The Office of Court Administration provides a monthly caseload report to help each presiding judge administer the workload. The supreme court equalizes dockets among the courts of appeals using caseload information collected by the Office of Court Administration.

Juries in Texas Courts

Juries play a significant role in Texas trial courts. Two types of juries are used: grand juries and petit juries.

Grand Juries

The Texas Bill of Rights prohibits felony charges in the absence of a grand jury indictment.[31] Grand juries do not decide guilt or innocence; their task is to decide whether there is sufficient evidence to charge someone with a crime. An **indictment,** or **true bill,** is the formal statement of charges brought by a grand jury. When a grand jury does not find sufficient evidence to indict, a **no bill** is returned.

Grand juries are selected by district judges. The judge first appoints a jury commission consisting of three to five prominent citizens from different parts of a county. Each commission draws up a list of approximately twenty prospective jurors. From this list, the district judge selects twelve grand jurors and designates one of them as foreman. Grand juries usually serve from three to six months, but their terms can be extended for special investigations.

Grand juries have been criticized for several reasons. The most common is that their decisions largely rubber-stamp the prosecutor's recommendations. Because most grand jurors are not trained in the law, they tend to depend on the prosecutor, who decides what evidence they hear and makes recommendations to indict. Grand juries also are criticized because:

- their proceedings are secret;
- those under investigation by a grand jury do not have the right to appear before the grand jury in their own defense;

- those under investigation by a grand jury do not have the right to be represented by counsel;
- those under investigation by a grand jury do not have the right to confront witnesses and cross-examine them.

Because they are provided for in the Texas Constitution, grand juries probably will continue to be used despite these criticisms.

Petit Juries

Petit juries play an important role in trial courts. In criminal proceedings, they judge the guilt or innocence of the accused and sentence those found guilty. In civil suits, they must decide whether the defendant is liable for damages because of some injury to the plaintiff and set the dollar amount of awards. A unanimous verdict is required in criminal cases; in civil suits, ten jurors must agree.

The twelve members of a petit jury are selected from a list of those eligible for service. The nature of the list determines whether juries are likely to be representative. People who are not on the list cannot be called for jury duty. Until recently Texas relied primarily on voter registration lists, lists that tend to underrepresent lower-income groups and minority groups. To avoid that bias in the jury selection process, the Texas legislature decided in 1991 that the pool of eligible jurors should include those holding a valid driver's license or a Department of Public Safety identification card, as well as all registered voters.[32] When trials are scheduled, the courts randomly select a pool of potential jurors from the juror list. The lawyers for each side then select a jury from that pool.

In 1996, the Texas Supreme Court appointed a seventy-seven-member task force on juries to consider ways of strengthening the jury process and restoring public confidence in juries. That group completed its report in September 1997—too late to be considered by the legislature that year. One of its principal recommendations was that pay for jurors increase from $6 per day to $40 per day, to encourage participation. It also recommended that the legislature consider a variety of procedural changes that might improve the work of juries.[33]

Crime, the Courts, and the Prisons

A significant part of the work courts do is deterring crime by dispensing punishment to those convicted of criminal wrongdoing. The punishment aspect of the courts' work is linked to the work of the state prison system. The punishments dispensed by the courts work only if the prison system administers them as intended.

In Texas the relationship between courts and prisons has been strained in recent years because of a crisis in prison space. As more people were sentenced to prison, the Texas prisons became severely overcrowded. Those conditions

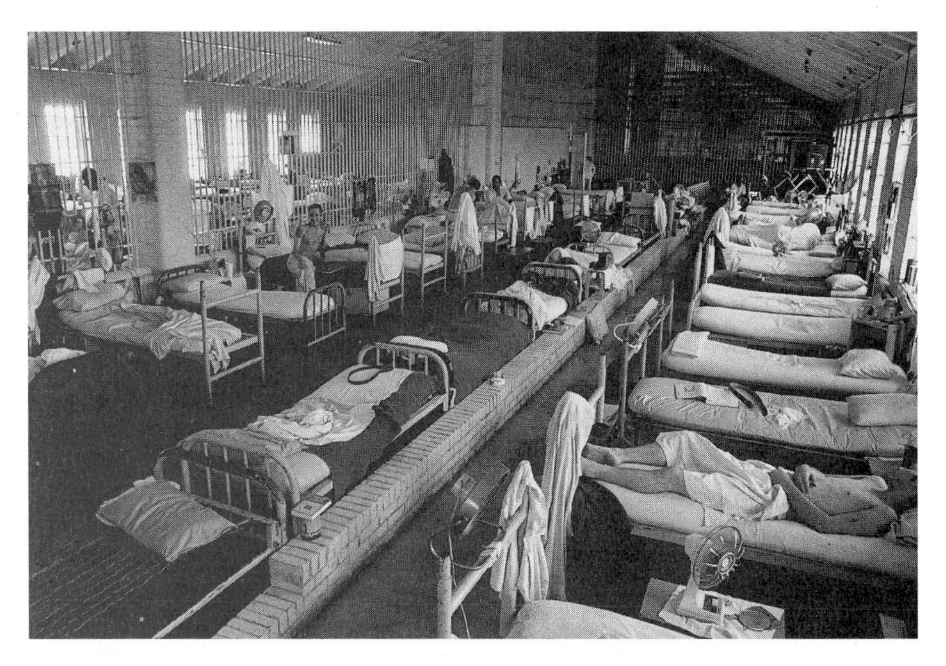

Overcrowded prisons make it difficult to insist that long sentences be completed; sentencing rigor must be balanced against available space.

led inmate David Ruiz to send a handwritten complaint to a federal court in 1972. His case, ***Ruiz v. Estelle,*** came to trial in 1978; it was the longest trial on the issue of prisoners' civil rights in the nation's history.[34] Eventually Federal Judge William Wayne Justice ruled that the overcrowding violated the national constitution's guarantee against cruel and unusual punishment. In 1981 the state entered a consent decree, agreeing to operate the prison system at no more than 95 percent of capacity. In addition the state agreed to group inmates by security classification, to eliminate the use of inmates as guards and supervisors, to increase guard-to-inmate ratios, and to minimize the use of force. The decree also required the state to provide adequate medical and psychiatric care for inmates.

Meeting the court's demand to stop prison overcrowding forced the state to take some unusual steps. During the early days of the crisis, the prison system literally closed its doors, refusing to accept prisoners transferred from county jails. Then the prison system began a revolving-door policy, each day releasing the same number of prisoners that it took in. Early paroles were used routinely to reduce the prison population. Local jails began to fill with prisoners waiting to be transferred to state prisons. Some of the largest counties, among them Harris County, sued to force the state to pay the costs of housing state prisoners. The Texas Supreme Court ruled in favor of the counties and ordered the state to compensate them. The state began making payments in 1992. Appropriations for this purpose for the 1994–1995 biennium totaled $205 million.[35]

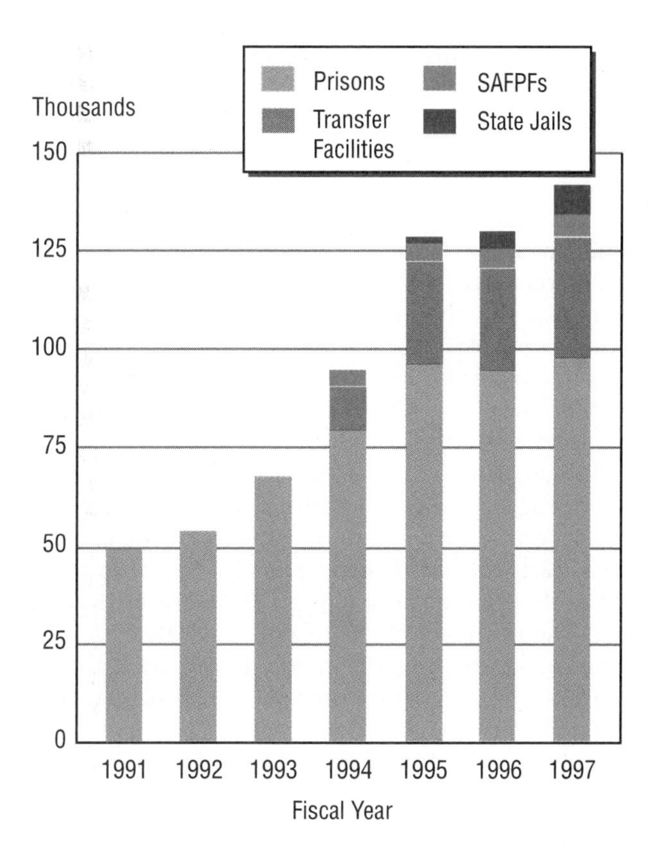

FIGURE 9.10 Texas Correctional Populations, Fiscal Years 1991–1997*
**As of August of each year.*
Source: Legislative Budget Board, Fiscal Size Up 1998–99 *(Austin: Legislative Budget Board, 1998), p. 8–6.*

To address the need for more prison space, the state dramatically increased appropriations for prison operations and construction. In fiscal year 1980 the legislature appropriated $154 million for those purposes; by 1990, total appropriations had reached $961 million. In addition, the voters approved bond issues of $1 billion in 1991 and again in 1993 to fund prison construction.[36]

The *Ruiz* case was settled, and the state's prisons were released from judicial supervision in 1993, but prison space has continued to be a critical problem for the state. Between 1991 and 1997, the prison population in Texas more than doubled. By August 1997, there were almost 140,000 people incarcerated in Texas prisons (Figure 9.10), and that population was projected to rise at an exponential rate through the end of the century.[37] Texas has the highest ratio of prisoners to population (659 inmates for ever 100,000 population in 1996) of all the states.[38]

The 73d session of the legislature (meeting in 1993) passed additional measures to address the prison problem. To reduce the backlog of prisoners in county jails, the legislature appropriated $125 million to construct transfer facilities, to hold prisoners for up to a year while they are awaiting transfer to regular prison units. In addition, $428 million was appropriated to build state jails to house nonviolent offenders. Finally, the legislature revised the state's penal code to reduce sentencing for some nonviolent crimes (at the same time eliminating parole for these crimes) and to ensure that violent offenders would spend more time behind bars.[39]

How did the crisis in prison space affect the performance of the criminal justice system? Initially the crisis dramatically reduced the time spent in prison by all but the most violent prisoners. So the public demand that the state's judges get tougher on criminals was undermined by the shortage of prison space. Moreover, strict parole policies had prolonged the backlog of prisoners in county jails waiting to transfer to state prisons.[40] By 1994 the pendulum had swung back in the direction of longer sentences and less easy parole. Governor Richards pointed with pride to achievements in the area of crime. The Texas crime rate had dropped 9.7 percent in 1992 and then 8.8 percent in 1993. Early releases from prison also had been reduced from 150 a day when she took office to 60 a day in 1993. But critics pointed out that juvenile crimes had risen sharply in recent years. By 1998, Texas was facing problems caused by an ongoing prison population, with almost 2,000 prisoners over sixty years old. The cost for such prisoners was estimated to be $14.50 per day, compared to $5.20 for younger inmates. The state was forced to consider early release for elderly inmates.[41]

Reform in the Role of the Courts

The role of the courts continued to be controversial, and in 1995 the legislature passed a series of **tort reform** bills to change the way the courts can be used in Texas. A series of bills were passed changing several aspects of court operations. SB 31 discourages frivolous lawsuits by allowing costs to be assessed against the loser. A bill (SB 32) passed preventing lawyers from shopping among courts to find a favorable court. Another law (SB 25) limits the amount of punitive damages that can be awarded a plaintiff in a civil suit. Still another law (HB 668) amends the state's Deceptive Trade Practices Act to cover only matters valued at $500,000 or less.[42] Thus, the backlash against the litigious society that swept the country in 1994 and 1995 and was included in the national Republican House members' Contract with America, had its effect in Texas in 1995. Thus, while some argued that the Texas courts had been freed from a tilt towards the plaintiff, others argued that big business had emerged victorious in these reforms.[43]

Conclusion: Change and the Texas Courts

Several forces have worked to change the Texas courts. Interest groups representing plaintiffs and defendants in civil suits have tried hard to shape the role of the courts through the electoral process. Two-party competition in Texas has helped channel many of these conflicts into the public arena because the two parties represent opposing sides in this argument. Public opinion has been aroused by political leaders who charge that Texas courts are too proactive, that they encourage litigation. Minority groups have looked for ways to make the courts more responsive to them by altering the way judges are elected. Individual political leaders have led crusades to reform the structure of the court system.

How have all these forces influenced the courts? How have the courts changed? The forces waging the battle to end the proplaintiff bias in Texas courts have won some battles. The Republicans captured a majority of seats on the supreme court; they also persuaded the legislature to pass two pieces of legislation that narrowed the courts' jurisdiction and redefined the rules in product liability cases.[44]

The champions of structural reform of the courts lost yet another battle. The legislature refused to carry out the recommendations of the latest commission. Minority groups lost their battle to alter the electoral system in a way that would make it possible for them to elect more trial-court judges. No change was made in the process for choosing the state's highest-ranking judges. No consensus has emerged on the kind of system that should replace elections. As a result, no change in the process seems near. Lawmakers' refusal to act was strong testimony to the power of those who occupy positions in the judicial structure that might be threatened by reform. Overall the Texas court system is a living testament to the resistance of institutions to change. Without a clearer consensus about the direction of change, the status quo will remain just that for the immediate future.

Notes

1. Christi Harlan, "Texas Supreme Court Race Pits Lawyers Against Business Interests," *Wall Street Journal,* November 2, 1992, 4B.
2. Harlan, "Texas Supreme Court Race," 4B.
3. Bruce Nichols, "Study Faults Justices for Business Ties," *Dallas Morning News,* February 24, 1998, p. 1A.
4. Lawrence Baum, "Making Judicial Policies in the Political Arena," in *The State of the States,* 2d ed., Carl E. Van Horn, ed. (Washington, DC: Congressional Quarterly Press, 1993), 149–170.
5. Texas Judicial Council, *Texas Judicial System Annual Report* (Austin: Office of Court Administration, 1997), 410.
6. *Vernon's Texas Code Annotated,* Government Code, Title 2, Subtitle A, Chapter 30, Sec. 481ff.
7. Texas Constitution, Art. V, Sec. 18.
8. *Texas Judicial Council, Annual Report,* 1997, 35.
9. *Texas Judicial Council, Annual Report,* 384.
10. Texas Constitution, Art. V, Sec. 15.
11. Texas Constitution, Art. V, Sec. 8.
12. Texas Constitution, Art. V, Sec. 6.
13. *Texas Judicial Council, Annual Report,* 114.

14. *Texas Judicial Council, Annual Report,* 113.
15. *Texas Judicial Council, Annual Report,* 115.
16. Oklahoma is the only other state that has two courts of last resort.
17. Citizens' Commission on the Texas Judicial System, *Report and Recommendations* (West Publishing Co., 1993), 3.
18. Texas Research League, *Texas Courts: Report 1, the Texas Judiciary: A Structural Functional Overview* (1990), xvii.
19. Herbert Jacob, "Courts: The Least Visible Branch," in *Politics in the American States: A Comparative Analysis,* 5th ed., Virginia Gray, Herbert Jacob, and Robert B. Albritton, eds. (New York: HarperCollins, 1990), 252–286. See especially pp. 266–267.
20. Texas Constitution, Art. IV, Sec. 12.
21. Tom Phillips, "Texas Needs New Method to Choose Judges," *Dallas Morning News,* March 28, 1993, 5J.
22. Dan Morales, "But Don't Establish Retention Elections," *Dallas Morning News,* March 28, 1993, 5J.
23. "Judicial Changes in Texas Blocked by U.S. on Appeal," *Wall Street Journal,* January 12, 1990, 2B.
24. Christy Hoppe and Terry Box, "Appeals Court Rejects System for Electing District Judges," *Dallas Morning News,* January 28, 1993, 21A and 26A.
25. *League of United Latin American Citizens* v. *Clements,* 999 F.2d 831 (5th Cir., 1993).
26. Janet Elliott and Robert Elder, Jr., "Judges' Money, Not Elections Changed," *Texas Lawyer* (June 5, 1995), 4.
27. Ibid.
28. Kate Thomas, "Overhaul for Texas Vote," *National Law Journal* (December 30, 1996/January 6, 1997), p. A14.
29. Susan Borreson, "75th Legislature in Review; The Judiciary: Pay Hike Soars While Selective Reform Flops," *Texas Lawyer,* June 9, 1997, p. 21.
30. *Vernon's Texas Civil Statutes,* Art. 2328a.
31. Texas Constitution, Art. I, Sec. 10.
32. *Vernon's Annotated Texas Statutes,* Sec. 62.001.
33. Mark Curriden, "State Panel Seeks Pay Raise for Jurors," *Dallas Morning News,* September 15, 1997, p. 1A.
34. *Ruiz* v. *Estelle,* 666 F.2d 854 (1982).
35. Legislative Budget Board, *Fiscal Size Up: 1994–95 Biennium* (Austin, 1994), 8–9.
36. Texas Comptroller of Public Accounts, *Fiscal Notes,* April 1992, 5–6.
37. Texas Comptroller of Public Accounts, *Forces of Change,* 2 vols. (Austin, 1994), 2:349.
38. Legislative Budget Board, *Fiscal Size Up: 1998–99,* 3-18.
39. Legislative Budget Board, *Fiscal Size Up: 1994–95,* 8-8–8-9.
40. Clay Robison, "Campaign '94: Ann Richards; Prison Expansion, Parole Crackdown Mark Initiatives on Crime," *Houston Chronicle,* May 1, 1994, 27A.
41. "State Considers Early Release for Elderly Inmates," *Dallas Morning News,* May 18, 1998, p. 20A.
42. Walt Borges, "Tort Reform Becomes a Package Deal," *Texas Lawyer,* (May 8, 1995), 11.
43. Charles B. Camp and Richard A. Oppel, Jr., "Big Business is a Big Winner in Legislative Session," *Dallas Morning News,* May 30, 1995, 1D.
44. "Consumer Group Seeks Vetoes: Richards Plans to Sign Legislation Limiting Businesses' Liability," *Dallas Morning News,* February 27, 1993, 18B.

10 Local Government in Texas

CHAPTER OUTLINE

Recent developments in the Dallas metropolitan area illustrate some of the tensions and troubles of contemporary urban life in Texas. The cities of Dallas and Plano reveal some of the modern day problems of governance in metropolitan Texas.

In 1998, Dallas submitted two major projects to its voters for a decision. The first proposed building a new sports complex for its professional basketball and hockey teams. The second proposed a bold development along the Trinity River that promised to provide flood control to residents of South Dallas, ease traffic problems through the southern part of the city, and turn the Trinity River valley in Dallas into a beautiful recreation area. Both these proposals barely squeaked by when the votes were counted. The sports arena proposal was approved by a margin of just 1,700 votes.[1] The Trinity River project also passed by a slim majority with only 2,357 more votes for the project than against it.[2]

How did projects like these fail to get more enthusiastic support from the voters? Lack of effort to persuade the voters can be set aside quickly as a possible explanation. In both these cases, the vote came after a well-planned, well-financed, and carefully orchestrated effort by some of the city's best known political and business leaders to persuade the voters to support the projects. It was also the case that a well-organized and financed opposition campaigned against each of these initiatives. Thus, lack of persuasive effort cannot account for such weak support by the voters.

These votes indicate a deeply divided city, with serious disagreement among various factions about the best use of the city's resources. Racial and ethnic tensions came into play as various groups asked what the projects would do for them. In Dallas, one of the major political fault lines runs between North Dallas, which tends to be an Anglo middle-class area, and South Dallas, which tends to be a lower-income area with a preponderance of African-American residents. Each of these areas of the city worry that costs will be unfairly allocated to them, while benefits are allocated to the other part of town. Because growth in Dallas has been oriented toward the northern side of town, South Dallas has often felt neglected when the city decided where to spend its money.

Another aspect of the problem in Dallas can be traced to the nature of its political structures. Dallas is a city that has drunk deeply from the well of political ideas associated with the reform movement (which will be explained more fully in this chapter). The reform model downplays the role of political leadership and has traditionally tried to convert urban problems into management problems to be handled by professional managers (for example, city managers). In addition, Dallas, like other cities, has had its political landscape reshaped by federal court decisions requiring electoral systems that emphasize representation of the major racial and ethnic groups in the city (more about this later). Although the increased representation is laudable, the new electoral system also increases the amount of conflict in the system.

The result of these trends is to produce a fragmented political system that led *Governing* magazine to include Dallas among a set of cities that it called nearly ungovernable. In fact, the article questioned whether anyone could seriously be considered to be "in charge" in cities like Dallas.[3] As the article suggests, struggling to decide major issues that will shape the city's future development has become common, not just in Dallas, but in many major cities in Texas and around the country.

The typical view is that while cities are struggling, suburbs are flourishing. Suburbs are not without problems, but their problems are often different than the problems in central cities. A look at Plano, a suburb of Dallas, will shed some light on that view.

Plano is widely regarded as a contemporary success story.[4] This suburb of Dallas grew from fewer than 20,000 people in the early 1970s to more than 150,000 people by 1993—all the while preserving a comfortable middle-class lifestyle there. Legacy Park, a large business park initially home to Electronic Data Systems (then H. Ross Perot's company), helped the city attract businesses and jobs. Legacy Park became headquarters for Frito-Lay, J. C. Penney, and other corporations. An early city plan gave the city a good start and saved the cost of redoing work by requiring the construction of quality housing and a durable infrastructure of streets, sewers, and water mains. Fundamental to the plan was a system of multilane thoroughfares that move traffic through the city and subdivide it into a series of square-mile neighborhoods, each with a park and a school.

Although most describe Plano's growth in positive terms, some talk about the city's growth as urban sprawl. For all its middle-class amenities, they argue, Plano has a fairly typical suburban design: single-family homes, strip shopping centers, and shopping malls. Because building codes encourage the construction of relatively expensive homes, lower-income workers have difficulty finding homes in the city. The city's teachers, police, and firefighters for the most part cannot afford to live where they work. And the city's dense development has contributed to two problems: the pollution caused by automobile exhaust fumes and the difficulty of planning an effective mass transit system. In recent years the community has been jolted by new stories revealing drug use and drug overdoses among its youth.

Clearly Texas cities face a variety of problems. Young cities, like Plano, have to deal with rapid population growth and development. Mature cities face environmental problems, racial and ethnic tensions, and land-use battles. Texas cities constantly are being challenged to adjust to new conditions. Some of those conditions are internal; others are external—the product of state and national mandates. Moreover, in recent years Texas cities have been forced to solve a growing number of problems with increasingly limited resources.

This chapter examines the factors that influence the ability of cities to respond to change and manage their problems. Knowledge of how Texas cities have developed and how local governments manage the provision of services is crucial to appreciating government in Texas. This chapter answers several questions about local governments:

- What is the relationship between local governments and the state of Texas?

- What are the major types of local governments in Texas, and what do they do?
- What are the major problems facing local governments in Texas?
- What is the future likely to bring to local government in Texas?

Change and Local Government: An Introduction

The real challenge in local government today is meeting rising demands with limited resources. Grants and other types of financial help from the national government were reduced in the 1980s, shifting burdens to local taxes. Some local-government agencies are being challenged to show that they can produce services as efficiently and as cheaply as providers in the private sector. Local governments are challenged to provide more services and higher quality services without much help from the state or the national government.

Local Government and the State

In Texas (and in the South and Southwest generally) there are three principal types of local government: counties, cities, and special districts. **County governments** are created by the states to perform tasks at the local level that the state needs to have done. **City governments** are created principally as instruments of local self-government, to serve the interests of a local group of people and to give them the legal powers necessary to meet their needs. **Special-district governments** are created to perform specific tasks that are not appropriate for county or city governments. They usually provide a single type of service or a small, closely related set of services. School districts, hospital districts, flood control districts, and transportation districts are all single-function governments.

All local governments are legally creatures of the state, having only those powers delegated to them by the state. According to **Dillon's Rule,** the legal principle that traditionally is used to define local-government powers, local governments have those powers expressly delegated to them, those necessarily or fairly implied, and those essential to carrying out their objectives.[5] Local governments, then, can exercise those powers granted them in the constitution or by statute—and no others.

County Government

Organization

County government in Texas is a loosely related set of offices and authorities created by the state constitution and state laws. Each office is charged with carrying out a specific responsibility within the county (Figure 10.1), and,

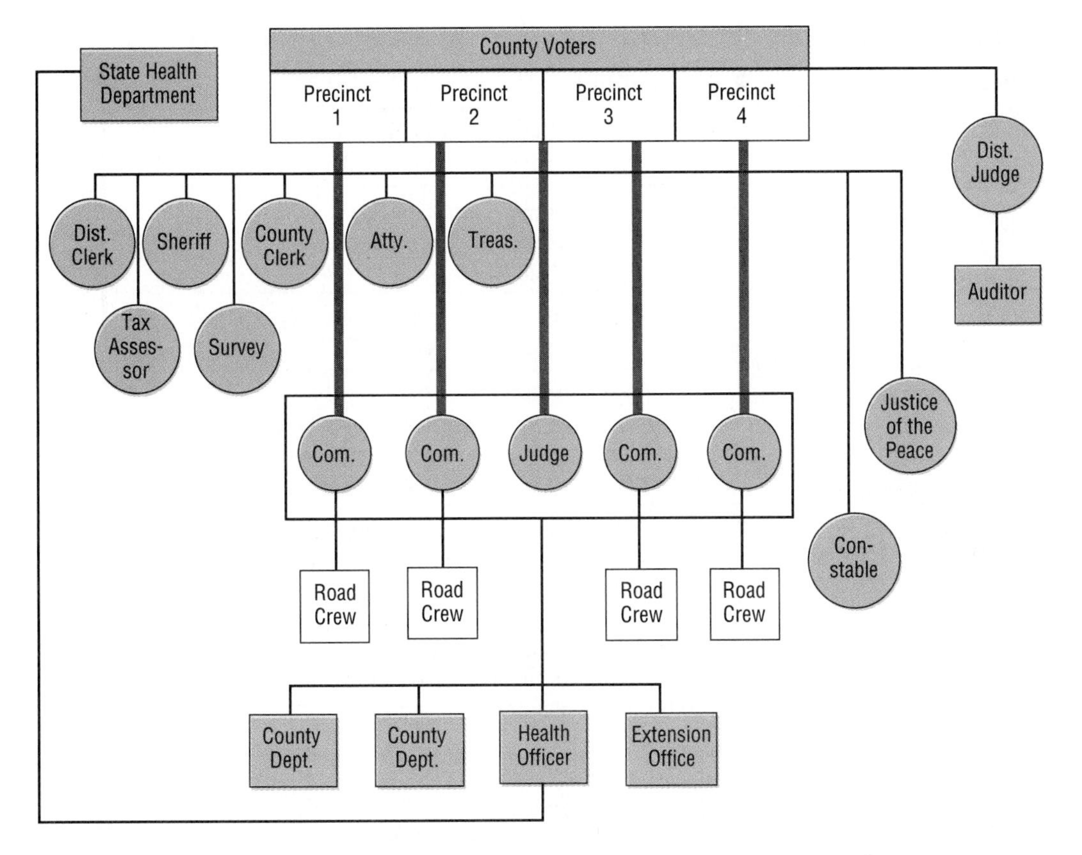

FIGURE 10.1 County Organization in Texas

Source: Robert E. Norwood, Texas County Government: Let the People Choose *(Austin: Texas Research League, 1970).*

because no individual or agency has clear authority over them, each operates with a surprising degree of independence.

The closest thing to an overall county governing body is the county **commissioners' court,** made up of the four county commissioners and the county court judge.[6] That body's power stems in large part from its budget authority: the commissioners' court determines how much money each agency has to do its job. The county agencies submit their budget requests to the commissioners' court. After reviewing all requests, the commissioners' court allocates funds to each agency, determines the size of the county budget, and sets the tax rate necessary to support the budget. The county court judge, the presiding officer of the commissioners' court, is the chief budget officer in most Texas counties, responsible for overseeing the implementation of the county budget.

County-government organization is complicated by the number of county agencies that are headed by elected officials (Table 10.1). These officials are

Table 10.1 Elected County Officials and Their Responsibilities

Office	Responsibilities
County judge	Presiding officer of the county commissioners' court and chief budget officer.
County commissioners	Members of the county commissioners' court; responsible for building and maintaining county roads and bridges in their pecinct.
Sheriff	Chief law enforcement officer in the county; responsible for managing the county jail.
County attorney	Provides legal counsel to the commissioners' court and represents the state in all criminal cases in the county court. In larger counties, a district attorney takes over these responsibilities.
County clerk	Provides staff support for meetings of the commissioners' court; keeps records on all legal documents affecting real property; issues marriage, hunting, and fishing licenses; provides staff support for the county courts (and the district courts in some counties); oversees the administration of elections; and maintains voter registration records in some counties.
District clerk	Provides staff support for the district courts in the county.
Treasurer	Manages funds for the county; prepares monthly financial reports for the commissioners' court. Larger counties often transfer many of the functions of this office to the county auditor's office. A 1993 constitutional amendment allows counties to abolish this office by a county referendum.
Tax assessor–collector	Collects taxes for the county and the state and handles voter registration in some counties.
County surveyor	Assists commissioners with their road and bridge work.
Justices of the peace	Hear small civil suits and misdemeanor criminal cases; responsible for determining the cause of death in cases of unattended death unless the county has a medical examiner.
Constables	Serve legal papers for the justice of the peace in whose precinct they work.

accountable to their own constituencies and may feel little obligation to support the county commissioners. The commissioners are in a much stronger position to influence the agencies with appointed heads.

Powers and Responsibilities

Texas is divided into 254 counties. The organization and powers of each of those counties is defined by the state constitution and the state law. To change that organization or those powers in any or all counties, a constitutional amendment or a state law—or both—must be passed. For example, in 1993, voters approved a constitutional amendment that authorized the legislature to set minimum qualifications for county sheriffs.[7] Without that authorization, the state legislature could not have acted. At times constitutional amendments put questions before the entire Texas electorate that apply only to a single county or group of counties. For example, it is fairly common for voters to be asked to approve a constitutional amendment abolishing the office of county treasurer in one or more counties. The duties of this office have been shifted to other officials in more populous counties. Although it would seem more logical to let local residents decide when they no longer need an office, because it is in the constitution, only a constitutional amendment—with a statewide vote—can abolish it.

Texas counties are required to provide certain types of services and are allowed to provide others. For example, counties are required by the state to build roads, enforce the law, and provide the other services listed in the first column of Table 10.2. Counties can provide the optional services listed in the table, but they are not required to do so. The fact that services are optional does not mean that they are not important. In fact the largest counties spend a major portion of their general revenue funds on hospitals and other optional services (Table 10.3).

Road building and maintenance. The state has assumed responsibility for the major roads in Texas, but the counties retain responsibility for the secondary roads. County commissioners supervise the building and maintaining of county roads and bridges, a responsibility that often consumes a major share of their time.[8] A law passed in 1947 allows counties to transfer the responsibility for roads and bridges to a county engineer. But in most counties, each county commissioner hires a road crew and oversees road and bridge construction and maintenance in his or her precinct.[9] Individual commissioners have not wanted to give up control of the payrolls and

Table 10.2 Functions of County Governments in Texas

Mandatory services	Optional services
• Building and maintaining roads	• Library services
• Preserving law and order	• Emergency medical services
• Conducting elections	• Social services
• Supporting the courts	• Parks and recreation
• Recording vital statistics	• Economic development
• Protecting public health and welfare	

Table 10.3 General Expenditures by Function in the Largest Texas Counties, 1991–1992*

	County					
	Bexar (percent)	Dallas (percent)	El Paso (percent)	Harris (percent)	Tarrant (percent)	Travis (percent)
Education and libraries	0.2	0.0	6.2	1.0	0.0	0.0
Public welfare	3.6	2.2	1.0	1.1	2.1	6.0
Hospitals	34.8	37.1	29.4	24.2	32.7	0.0
Health	4.8	6.6	9.5	3.5	6.7	12.2
Transportation	6.6	7.8	1.1	13.4	4.7	28.2
Public safety	13.6	15.4	17.1	17.7	16.6	20.6
Environment and housing	1.8	0.2	5.9	5.6	2.4	1.3
Government administration	13.5	16.6	22.8	15.7	17.0	19.6

*Counties with a population of 500,000 or more.

Note: Table includes only selected functions from the complete list.

Source: Calculated from U.S. Bureau of the Census, *County Government Finances, 1991–92* (Washington, DC: U.S. Government Printing Office, 1995), 50–53.

contracts that go along with building and maintaining roads—a valuable source of rewards for political allies.

Law enforcement. People who live in cities look to their local police for law enforcement. But people who live outside cities depend in large part on the county for basic law enforcement. The sheriff is the county's chief law enforcement officer. And depending on the proportion of rural area in a county, the sheriff's law enforcement duties can be significant.

In urban counties, counties where most of the territory falls within city lines, sheriffs spend much of their time overseeing the county jail. Because jails must meet both national and state standards in terms of inmate population and general conditions, most counties devote a considerable share of their resources to building jails and managing them.

Conducting elections. Several county authorities share responsibility for the conduct of elections (see Chapter 5). The county commissioners divide the county into election districts. The responsibility for registering voters and administering elections is assigned to the county tax assessor–collector, the county clerk, or an office of county elections administration (in some of the largest counties).

Keeping records and supporting the courts. The county government maintains the vital records of people in the county and of the county's operations.

Overseeing road crews such as this is still an important responsibility of most Texas county commissioners.

The county clerk files all legal documents that affect real property, records vital statistics, and issues licenses (marriage, hunting, and fishing). The clerk also provides staff support for the county courts and, in some counties, for the district courts.

The Challenge of Change

County governments in Texas face an enormous challenge. The central problems facing counties today are revenue, land-use planning, and employee management.

Revenue. The counties' chronic revenue problems in part reflect the limits imposed on them by the state. Counties derive their revenue from taxes and fees that the state authorizes them to collect. The primary source of revenue is the property tax. Working within limits established by the state, county commissioners set the county tax rate and, thereby, determine the revenue produced by the property tax. Counties also get revenues from fees and fines. For example, counties collect state motor vehicle registration fees and are allowed to keep some of what they collect. They also can assess an additional fee to support the construction of county bridges. And the county clerk collects a variety of fees for processing deeds and other legal instruments.

Counties must fund a number of programs that are required or authorized by the state. Their expenditures can be divided into several categories:[10]

- Salaries for county officials, including judicial officials
- The costs of building and maintaining roads and bridges
- Capital expenditures for the jail, the courthouse, and other county offices and buildings
- Health care, including expenditures for the indigent
- The costs of optional services, such as libraries, emergency medical services, and social services.

From the mid-1980s into the early 1990s, Texas counties had a hard time making financial ends meet. Poor business conditions in the state caused property values to fall and tax collections to shrink. Despite fewer resources, the demand for services continued and sometimes even expanded. Jails had to be enlarged, social service demands rose, and roads still needed building and maintaining. As a result, most large counties had to raise taxes or slash services. Rising property taxes were common. By 1995 the real estate market had revived, reducing the financial pressure on counties and allowing them to undertake deferred projects.

Land-use planning. The problem of land-use planning illustrates the difficulty some counties have in meeting their needs with the powers granted them by the state. Land use is a problem for county governments because the state has not given them the power to regulate development in unincorporated territories (areas outside city boundaries). In those areas, builders can decide where to build and what to build with little regard for the problems they impose on county and other governments. A new housing subdivision creates transportation needs, social service needs, and water and sewer needs.

Personnel management. The third major problem facing county governments in Texas has to do with the people who operate those governments. This is another case where counties do not have the necessary authority to meet their needs. Remember that a number of county officers are elected. But the constitution and the laws that mandate their election do not specify the qualifications necessary to do the jobs adequately. For example, a good sheriff probably needs law enforcement training, yet nothing in the selection process ensures that someone with training will be elected. A constitutional amendment passed in 1993 authorized the legislature to set minimum qualifications, and a sheriff must now get a license from the State Commission on Law Enforcement Officer Standards and Education no later than two years after taking office.[11] Justices of the peace serve as judges in Texas, but they are not required to be attorneys. In fact most county officers—tax assessor–collector, treasurer, or clerk—need some special knowledge or expertise that the law fails to address.

Another personnel problem many county governments face is the lack of a civil service system. All too often county governments hire and fire on the basis of partisanship and cronyism, not merit and performance. In many counties, personnel changes are common after an election, and there is no guarantee that the people hired are the best qualified for the jobs.

City Government

Cities and the State

Like counties, cities are political subdivisions of the state, and the degree to which they can control their own affairs depends on the policies adopted by the state. Some states restrict their cities; others delegate a substantial degree of authority to them. Until the late nineteenth century, most states limited the authority of their cities.

One way states control cities is by regulating the **city incorporation process** whereby new cities are formed. State laws commonly regulate the minimum geographic size and population of proposed cities and stipulate how many people must sign a petition to call an incorporation election.

States also control city governments through the charter process. A **city charter** is a city's constitution: it determines a city's powers and organization. By controlling a city's charter, a state controls the authority the city has over its own institutions and policies. For much of this country's history, states chartered only by **special act charter**: state legislatures passed special acts (statutes that apply to just one city) granting city charters. Moreover, to amend its charter, a city had to ask for another special legislative act.

In the late nineteenth century, states began to give up chartering by special act because they had more pressing legislative business. Gradually the states began to delegate the charter-writing process to the cities themselves through **home-rule charters.** City charters cannot contradict the state constitution or state law, but home rule gives the cities substantial discretion in deciding how to organize and what their government is authorized to do.

Texas liberally delegates power to its city governments. The U.S. Advisory Commission on Intergovernmental Relations rated Texas first among the states in granting local discretion to its cities.[12] One of the most significant steps the state has taken to give its cities independence was a home-rule amendment to the Texas Constitution approved in 1912. The amendment divides Texas cities into two classes: **home-rule cities** and **general-law cities.**[13] Cities of at least 5,000 people can become home-rule cities; those with fewer than 5,000 people are general-law cities. Home-rule cities can draft and enact their own charters. General-law cities fall under Dillon's Rule; they can exercise only those powers granted them in the constitution or by statute. In May 1996, 284 Texas cities held home-rule charters.[14] They ranged in size from under 5,000 people (they fell below the minimum after adopting a home-rule charter) to over 1.7 million people.

Although many Texans live in large cities, small towns are still an important part of Texas life. High-rise city skylines, such as this one in Houston, are the regular vista of most contemporary Texans.

Texas makes it relatively easy to form a new city. One significant restriction is the law governing the **extraterritorial jurisdiction (ETJ)** of existing cities.[15] ETJ is the jurisdiction an existing city has over a zone that surrounds it. Cities use this jurisdiction to enforce land-use controls along its boundaries. ETJ also prevents people who live on the outskirts of a city from incorporating themselves. It is almost impossible for one city to annex another. If a new city were to form at its boundaries, an existing city would not have room to grow and could well be cut off from a valuable tax base. If an area falls within an existing city's ETJ, a new city cannot be incorporated there.

Urban Development

Today Texas is an urban state: most of its residents live in big cities and their suburbs. Urbanization is a relatively recent phenomenon in Texas. The 1850 census, taken five years after Texas joined the Union, found only two places in the state that qualified as cities (incorporated areas of 2,500 or more people): Galveston and San Antonio. One hundred years later, the 1950 census was the first to find that a majority of Texans were living in urban areas. By the 1990 census, a majority of the residents of the state lived in the three largest metropolitan areas of the state: the Dallas–Fort Worth consolidated metropolitan statistical area (CMSA), the Houston-Galveston-Brazoria CMSA, and the San Antonio metropolitan statistical area (MSA). The U.S. Office of Management and Budget determines the categories used to describe metro-

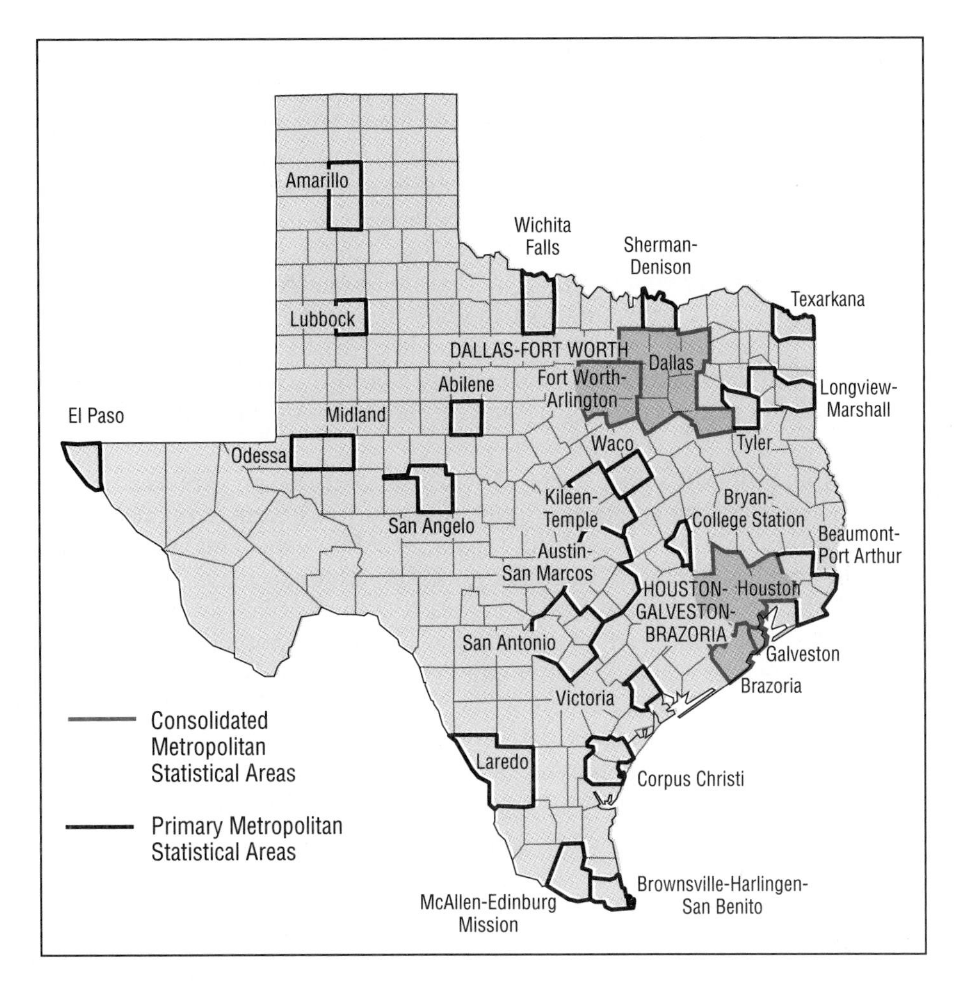

FIGURE 10.2 Metropolitan Areas in Texas
Source: Texas Almanac 1998–1999.

politan areas. **Metropolitan statistical areas** (MSAs) have as their core a county with at least 50,000 people. Adjoining counties that have a specified degree of social and economic interaction with that county are included to make up the entire MSA. **Consolidated metropolitcan statistical areas** (CMSAs) are large urban conglomerates containing more than one primary MSA.[16]

By the end of 1992, Texas had twenty-seven MSAs located throughout the state, and 83 percent of all Texans lived in those metropolitan areas (Figure 10.2).[17] In recent years, population growth has been concentrated in the state's most urban areas. Between 1950 and 1990, 95 percent of the state's population growth was in metropolitan areas.[18]

Organizing City Governments to Be Effective

When a city is formed, it must choose an organizational structure that will allow it to meet residents' needs effectively and efficiently. In this country there are three basic forms of city government: mayor–council, commission, and council–manager. Texas home-rule cities can choose any of these three forms; general-law cities must choose between the mayor–council and the council–manager forms.

The types of city governments in Texas were strongly influenced by the national Progressive movement in the late nineteenth and early twentieth centuries.[19] That movement stressed reform to make city governments honest and efficient. And that reform shaped both the choice of government forms available and ideas about which forms were most effective.

Mayor–Council. Until the early nineteenth century, all American cities used the **mayor–council form of government.** This form emphasizes the election of public officials and the separation of powers. The voters choose both the mayor (who is at least the nominal chief executive) and the city council (the city's legislative body). Figure 10.3 shows two variations on this form: the strong-mayor system and the weak-mayor system. In the *strong-mayor system,* the mayor is a true chief executive, the only or one of a few administrators elected. The mayor has the power to hire and fire major department heads and to formulate and present a budget to the council. In *weak-mayor systems,* the mayor usually must share authority with other elected officials, which dilutes the mayor's ability to exert real leadership in the community.

Commission. At the beginning of the twentieth century, Texas created the first alternative to the mayor–council system. The commission form was introduced after a hurricane destroyed the city of Galveston in 1900.[20] Initially intended as a temporary form of government to manage the rebuilding in Galveston, the commission form soon was adopted by many Texas cities. Houston, Dallas, and San Antonio were among the cities that began using the commission form in the period between the turn of the century and the end of World War II, a period of enormous change in the governments of major Texas cities.[21]

The **commission form of city government** merges legislative and administrative powers in the city commission. The voters choose several commissioners, who together function as the city's legislative body. The commission approves budgets, passes city ordinances, and exercises any other powers common to city councils. But each commissioner is also a department head, supervising part of the city bureaucracy (Figure 10.4). It seemed sensible to have the same people who formulated policies administer them.

The merging of legislative and administrative powers that initially was so appealing in the commission form turned out to be its fatal flaw. Instead of working together, individual commissioners began to build "empires," each thinking his or her department more important than the other depart-

a. Strong Mayor—Council Form of Government

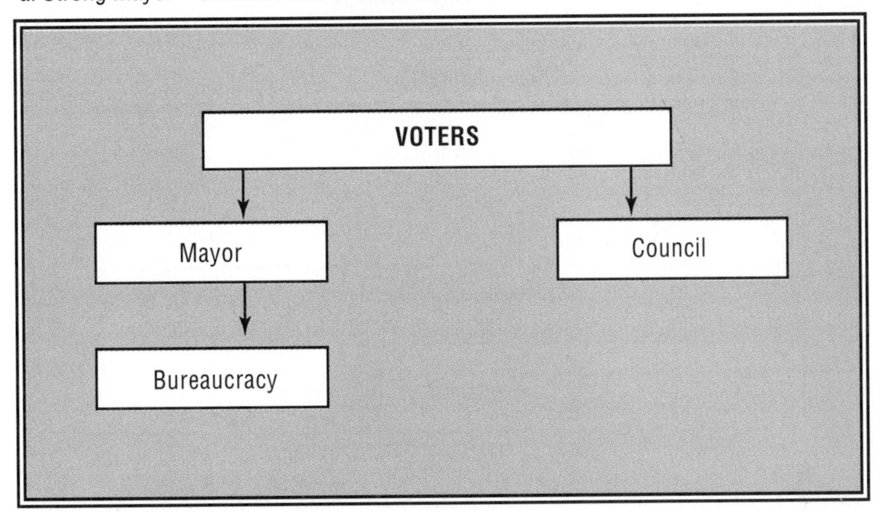

b. Weak Mayor—Council Form of Government

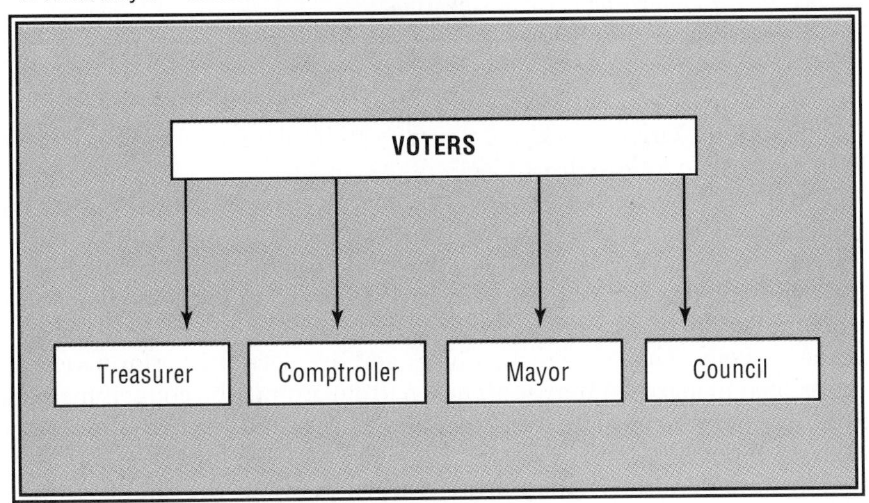

FIGURE 10.3 Mayor–Council Form of Government

ments. And there was no chief executive to control overall planning, to coordinate city policy, and to restrain the commissioners. Not surprisingly, cities began to abandon the commission form. Few cities use it today.

Council–Manager. As problems with the commission form became apparent, reformers developed a new structure, the council–manager plan (Figure

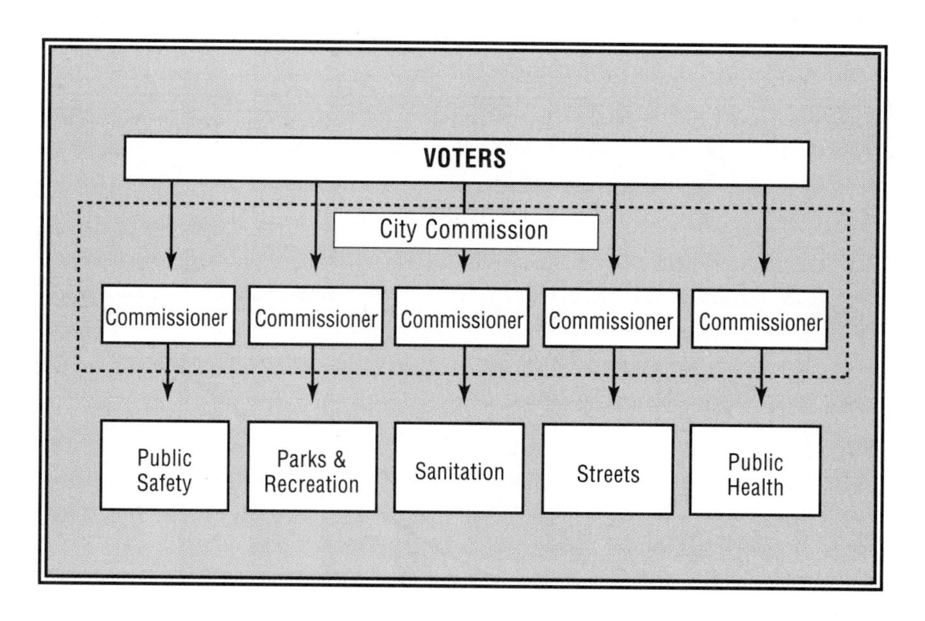

FIGURE 10.4 Commission Form of Government

10.5). Staunton, Virginia, was the first city to implement the plan, in 1908. Other cities soon followed.

The council–manager plan added one significant element to the structure of municipal government—the professional manager. Having learned that a city government needs a chief executive, reformers recommended hiring someone trained in the "science of administration." In the **council–manager form of government,** voters choose the members of the city council, the city's legislative body. The council then hires and oversees the performance of a professional manager. A mayor is chosen (from among the council members or by election) who presides over council meetings and serves as the ceremonial head of the city.

Corruption and mismanagement marked many of the country's major cities in the late nineteenth and early twentieth centuries. The reformers who promoted council–manager government were convinced that cities could be run by sound management principles and that politics would be eliminated from city government. They were only partially right. Council–manager government does not remove politics from city government; it only changes the form and style of city politics.

City governments in Texas. Although most major cities in Texas used the commission form of government at some point in their history, today few do. Texas cities now choose between the mayor–council form and the council–manager form. Most home-rule cities operate under the council–manager plan. Fewer than twenty-five home-rule cities use the mayor–council form.[22]

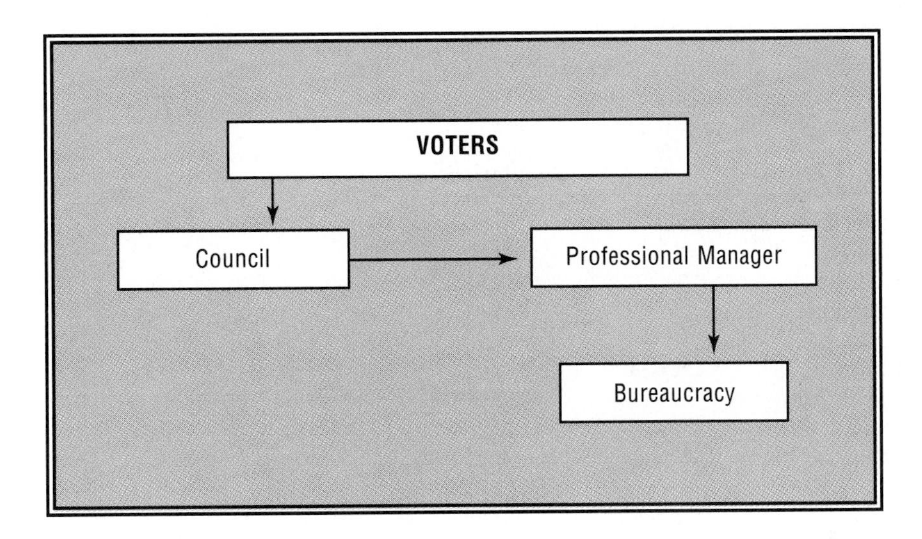

FIGURE 10.5 Council–Manager Form of Government

In contrast, most of the almost nine hundred general-law cities have opted for the mayor–council form.

Why do general-law and home-rule cities in Texas choose different forms of government? Remember that general-law cities are small. They do not need the expertise—or the expense—of a city manager. Nationwide, most cities with fewer than 10,000 residents choose the mayor–council form.[23] Texas home-rule cities choose the council–manager plan because of its emphasis on professional management. Nationwide, middle-sized cities (between 25,000 and 250,000 residents) commonly use the council–manager plan, but the biggest cities use the mayor–council plan.[24] In Texas, some of the largest cities—including Austin, Dallas, Fort Worth, and San Antonio—use the council–manager plan (Table 10.4). The only large Texas cities that use the mayor–council plan are El Paso, Houston, and Pasadena. The widespread preference for the council–manager form probably reflects the fact that the Texas cities were growing in an era when the reform movement was preaching the superiority of this city-government form.

Election Rules

Election options. Other important choices cities must make have to do with the rules for electing public officials. One important question is whether elections should be partisan or nonpartisan. In partisan elections, political parties nominate candidates who run for office under the party label. In nonpartisan elections, candidates "nominate" themselves and appear on the ballot without party affiliation. Cities also must decide whether council

Table 10.4 Population and Form of Government in the Largest Texas Cities 1996*

City	1996 Population
Council Manager Cities	
Abilene	108,476
Amarillo	169,588
Arlington	294,816
Austin	541,278
Beaumont	111,224
Brownsville	132,091
Corpus Christi	280,260
Dallas	1,053,292
Fort Worth	479,716
Garland	190,055
Grand Prairie	109,231
Irving	176,993
Laredo	164,899
Lubbock	193,565
McAllen	103,352
Mesquite	111,947
Plano	192,280
San Antonio	1,067,816
Waco	108,412
Wichita Falls	100,138
Mayor Council Cities	
El Paso	599,865
Houston	1,744,058
Pasadena	131,620

*Includes only those cities that exceeded 100,000 population in 1996.

Source: Population estimates from U.S. Census Bureau web site (**http://www.census.gov/population/estimates/metro-city/SCLOOK96.txt**). Form of government from *Texas Almanac 1998–99* (Dallas: A. H. Belo, 1997).

members should be elected from districts or at-large. In a **district election,** or ward election, each district in the city elects one member of the city council. In an **at-large election,** all candidates run in the city as a whole.

The choices governing election rules in cities were shaped by the same reform movement that promoted council–manager city government. Experience with the corrupt party organizations—often called **political machines**—that ran many of the country's largest cities in the late nineteenth century led many reformers to conclude that honest city governments could be achieved only by excluding political parties from city politics.

Reformers became disenchanted with ward elections because it appeared that council members elected from wards represented only the interests of their districts. No one seemed concerned about the interests of the city as a whole. Reformers argued that at-large elections would force council members to represent the city as a whole.

In recent years the realization that an electoral system affects the ability of minority groups to achieve fair representation has reshaped the debate over at-large elections. Reformers promoted at-large elections as a mechanism for protecting the interests of the whole city, but ethnic and racial minority groups argue that the system is a device that denies them representation. Research over the years has been mixed, but the best of the most recent studies support the conclusion that minority representation is affected by the system used to select council members.[25] The impact of at-large elections on African-American representation, although weaker than a decade ago, is still significant. The impact of at-large elections on Hispanic representation is less clear and varies from region to region.[26] In Texas, Hispanic representation on city councils is quite high in mixed systems; it is very low in at-large systems.[27]

In recent years, federal courts have supported the claims of racial and ethnic minority groups. Initially the U.S. Supreme Court required those challenging council districts to demonstrate discriminatory intent before an at-large system could be found unconstitutional.[28] In 1982, Congress amended the Voting Rights Act to allow challenges to the system based on outcome, not intent; and in 1986 the U.S. Supreme Court upheld that principle.[29]

The rules in Texas. Because most of the major cities in Texas were formed during the reform period, Texas cities overwhelmingly adopted both nonpartisan elections and at-large elections. The adoption of the reform package often was controversial; but business leaders pushed it through in Texas cities as they had in cities in other parts of the country to break the dominance of machines unfriendly to their interests.[30]

The experience in some Texas cities shows that nonpartisan elections ban only the major party organizations—the Democrats and the Republicans—from participation in city elections. Local groups are not prevented from forming and functioning much like political parties. In San Antonio, for example, the Good Government League grew up following World War II and strongly influenced city politics until 1974.[31] Born in the chamber of commerce president's home, the league quickly became the vehicle for defending reform government in San Antonio. The league's nominating committee put forward slates of candidates for council seats from 1955 to 1971, and those candidates won seventy-seven of the eighty-one council seats that were up for election.[32]

The amended Voting Rights Act and the U.S. Supreme Court decision upholding it have led the larger cities in Texas (and elsewhere in the country) to shift from at-large council elections to district elections. The battle over council districts in Dallas shows how designing a council election system

The Changing Face of Texas Politics

Minority Leadership Comes to Texas' Big Cities

On May 6, 1995, Dallas voters elected Ron Kirk their mayor. Kirk was the first African American to be elected mayor of a large city in Texas. Two years later, in December 1997, Lee Brown was elected mayor of Houston and became the first African-American mayor of Texas' largest city. How did these noteworthy victories occur and what are their implications?

Few people expected Kirk to win the 1995 election in Dallas, and most were surprised that he won more than 60 percent of the vote and avoided a runoff. How had he put together such a decisive victory? Former mayor Steve Bartlett opened the door for Kirk when he decided not to run for re-election. The absence of a well-known Anglo candidate in the race allowed Kirk to broaden his base of support and may have lowered the overall participation of whites in the election. Kirk had strong African-American support in the election. Turnout was higher than average in African-American precincts, which went overwhelmingly for Kirk. Estimates placed Kirk's support at about 97 percent among African Americans. But Kirk also did well among whites, polling about 42 percent of their votes.[1] Kirk also reached out across partisan lines. Although the election was formally nonpartisan, Kirk had known ties to the Democratic party. He reached out to Republicans by seeking the help of Carol Reed, a political consultant with known ties to the Republican party.[2] Finally, Kirk was able to outspend his opponents by more than two to one. All of this added up to a stunning success for Kirk.

Lee Brown's election in Houston was a longer and somewhat more bruising affair. Although he was endorsed by the city's popular retiring mayor, Bob Lanier, Brown did not manage a first ballot win. He was forced into a bitterly fought runoff with Rob Mosbacher, a wealthy Houstonian who previously had run as a Republican candidate for several state offices. The race took on a strong partisan tone, despite the formally nonpartisan nature of the city's elections. Brown got endorsements from well-known Democrats, including President Clinton. Mosbacher got Republican endorsements from equally well-known Republicans, including former President George Bush and his wife Barbara. The race also divided along racial ethnic lines, with African Americans supporting Brown, while Hispanic groups endorsed Mosbacher. Brown's ultimate victory

can ignite controversy.[33] In the 1970s, Dallas gave up at-large council elections and adopted a combination system called the 8–3–1 plan (eight council members elected from single-member districts, three elected at-large, and the mayor elected at-large). By the end of the 1980s, minority groups were pressing for single-member districts only, for the elimination of all at-large council members. Instead the city council put forward, and the voters approved the 10–4–1 plan (ten members elected from single-member districts, four elected at-large, and the mayor elected at-large). Although the plan called for district lines that would guarantee at least five minority seats on the council, dissatisfied minority groups appealed to a federal court.[34] The court was credited to high turnout in African-American precincts that bloc-voted for him. Hispanics had lower turnout and split their vote.[3] Both candidates were well financed in the race and total spending, $5.6 million, set a new record for Houston politics.[4] Thus, with the outgoing mayor's endorsement and strong African-American support, Brown claimed the victory.

What are the implications of these minority victories? Ron Kirk's victory in Dallas has contributed to easing tensions on a fractious city council. The switch in 1991 to single-member districts made the Dallas city council more representative, but not more harmonious. Kirk has played the mediator's role and this has helped ease tensions. In Brown's case, his election may add to racial/ethnic tensions in the city unless the mayor makes a concerted effort to reassure Hispanics. Throughout the election campaign, Hispanic citizens asked Brown if he was going to show racial favoritism in office. Although Brown denied that he would show favoritism in office, his actions must support that contention if he is to mollify the Hispanics in his community.

In terms of formal power, the Houston mayorship offers much more real power than does the Dallas mayorship. Houston is one of the few Texas cities with a strong mayor system. Thus, Brown will have real managerial power and responsibility in Houston. Kirk must operate in a council manager system that puts the day-to-day managerial responsibility in the city manager's hands. Kirk must rely more heavily on informal leadership opportunities that arise out of the visibility of the office. He has already demonstrated a capacity for that kind of leadership in both the arena and the Trinity River projects that were mentioned at the beginning of this chapter.

The election of African-American mayors in Texas' largest cities reflects the demographic changes taking place in the state's cities. Processes that have been observed in many older cities across the country are now reaching Texas cities as well. The flight of the white middle class to the suburbs has transformed big cities in Texas just as it has elsewhere, increasing the minority share of the vote in those cities. These victories in Houston and Dallas are likely to be the beginning of a change in city politics across Texas. ★

[1]Steve McGonigle, "Voters Cross Racial Lines to Elect Kirk," *Dallas Morning News*, May 8, 1995, p. 11A.

[2]Lori Stahl, "Kirk's Road to Office Had Twists and Turns but Stayed on Track," *Dallas Morning News*, May 20, 1995, p. 36A.

[3]Lori Rodriguez, "Assuring City's Hispanics Will be Brown's Challenge," *Houston Chronicle*, December 14, 1997, p. 1A.

[4]Bruce Nichols, "Brown Elected Houston's First Black Mayor," *Dallas Morning News*, December 7, 1997, p. 20A.

ordered the city to elect all council members from single-member districts; only the mayor would be elected at-large. This same plan had been narrowly rejected by the voters in a 1990 election that split along racial lines: minority groups supported it; whites opposed it. The city initially planned to appeal the court's decision, but ultimately city leaders realized that winning the suit could come only at the expense of racial relations in the city. The city dropped its suit; and the voters finally adopted the single-member district plan in May 1993.

Not long after the first council elected under the new plan took office, council members were questioning another element of the Dallas govern-

Lee Brown became the second African-American mayor of a large Texas city when he was elected in 1997.

ment: the city manager system. Council members complained that they could not respond to problems in their districts if major administrative decisions were in the hands of an appointed manager.[35] The city manager system survived in 1993, but the issue shows the problems that 1930s-style reform governments are having in today's racially diverse Texas cities.

The Financial Challenge

In a 1992 survey, the comptroller's office asked city officials what they considered their most urgent problems. The most striking finding of that survey was the preoccupation of city officials with fiscal and tax problems. As Table 10.5 shows, fiscal problems pushed transportation, racial problems, urban growth, and other urban problems down the priority list. Homelessness, the focus of much media attention, was forty-fourth on a list of forty-eight issues.[36] Texas cities could not address the broader social issues of city life until their financial situation improved.

The responses of city officials also indicate that they believe that state and federal authorities are contributing to cities' economic difficulties. On a list of fifteen specific issues considered important to the future of cities, city officials ranked compliance with state and federal mandates the number-one problem (Table 10.6). The quality of education and drug abuse came in second and third on this list. The federal mandates that cities find troublesome are

Table 10.5 Urban Issues Ranked by Texas City Officials, 1992

General issues	Score (5 = highest)
Fiscal and tax problems	4.5
Education	4.3
Infrastructure	4.2
Basic services	4.1
Public safety	4.0
Jobs and employment	4.0
Transportation	3.5
Racial and group problems	3.5
Intergovernmental relations	3.4
Political problems	3.5
Conservation and environment	3.3
Urban growth	3.2
Culture and recreation	3.0

Source: Texas Comptroller of Public Accounts, *Fiscal Notes,* September 1992, 9.

environmental measures—among them the Clean Water Act, the Solid Waste Disposal Act, and the Safe Drinking Water Act. The state mandates that create problems for cities include regulations governing landfill, wastewater, and sewers and solid waste. City officials want these mandates relaxed or financial help in meeting them.[37]

States influence the financial situation of their city governments not only by requiring them to conform to state mandates but also by limiting the ability of cities to raise money. The Texas Constitution authorizes cities to "levy, assess, and collect such taxes as may be authorized by law."[38] So the cities must depend on the state to grant them the authority to raise the financial resources they need to do their jobs.

Cities get their money from several sources, but most of it comes from taxes. Cities in Texas rely on two types of taxes: the property tax and the sales tax. Texas cities get nearly 50 percent of their revenue from these two taxes.[39] Historically, the property tax has been the backbone of local-government finances in Texas and elsewhere in the nation. Although the state no longer taxes property, cities in Texas do not have exclusive claim on the property tax: counties, school districts, and special districts also levy property taxes. The tax burden to most urban property owners, then, is the sum of the property taxes levied by these governments.

The administration of the property tax is now regulated by the Property Tax Code, which was passed by the legislature in 1979. The legislation controls the administration of the property tax in several ways:[40]

Table 10.6 Urban Issues Ranked by Urban Officials, 1992

Rank	Issue
1	State and Federal Mandates
2	Quality of Education
3	Drug Abuse
4	School Finance
5	Industrial and Commercial Development
6	Solid Waste, Sewage, and Landfills
7 (tied)	Streets and Traffic
7 (tied)	Roads and Bridges
9 (tied)	Increased Federal Regulations
9 (tied)	Sewage Collection and Treatment
11	Property Taxes
12	Drainage Facilities
13 (tied)	Juvenile Delinquency
13 (tied)	Crimes Against Persons and Property
15	Water

Note: City managers from forty-five Texas cities responded to the survey.

Source: Texas Comptroller of Public Accounts, *Fiscal Notes,* September 1992, 8–9.

- It created appraisal districts in each county to determine the taxable value of property. Counties, cities, and special districts must use appraisal district values for taxing purposes.
- A "truth-in-taxation" provision requires cities to calculate and advertise an effective tax rate so that residents can understand the effects of decisions made by the city government.
- A rollback provision allows residents to force a referendum if a city increases its effective tax rate by more than 8 percent.

Clearly, although the state delegates the power to tax property to the cities, it regulates and limits that power in significant ways.

The state also authorizes cities to levy a sales tax, subject to approval by the voters of the city. The Texas comptroller collects this tax, along with the state sales tax, and returns the appropriate amount to each city. Today virtually every city in the state levies a sales tax.[41]

The statute authorizes cities to use other taxes to supplement property and sales tax revenues. The hotel–motel occupancy tax, the bank franchise tax, the mixed-drinks gross receipts tax, and the bingo tax are all available for city use. Although each is used by some Texas cities, these taxes individually produce a much smaller proportion of city revenues than does the property tax or the sales tax.

In recent years, cities have turned to nontax sources of revenue to supplement tax revenue. User charges have become a common non-tax revenue source. Greens fees on municipal golf courses, court fees on public tennis courts, entrance fees at city swimming pools, and many other user charges have become common. Although reliance on these charges is a national trend, Texas cities make greater use of service charges than does the average city in the United States.[42] User charges now generate more revenue than the sales tax in some Texas cities.

Texas cities get some revenue from the state and national governments through grant-in-aid programs, but the amount is not what it once was. Federal aid to the ten largest cities in Texas dropped from a high of $360 million in 1980 to $183 million in 1990. Texas cities had to raise just 79 percent of their own revenue in 1981; they had to raise 90 percent of their own revenue by 1990.[43] Unfortunately, the state is not taking up the slack. As Figure 10.6 shows, in 1990 Texas ranked last among the ten largest states in per capita aid to local governments. Texas cities, then, are especially likely to think of this as an era of "fend-for-yourself" federalism.

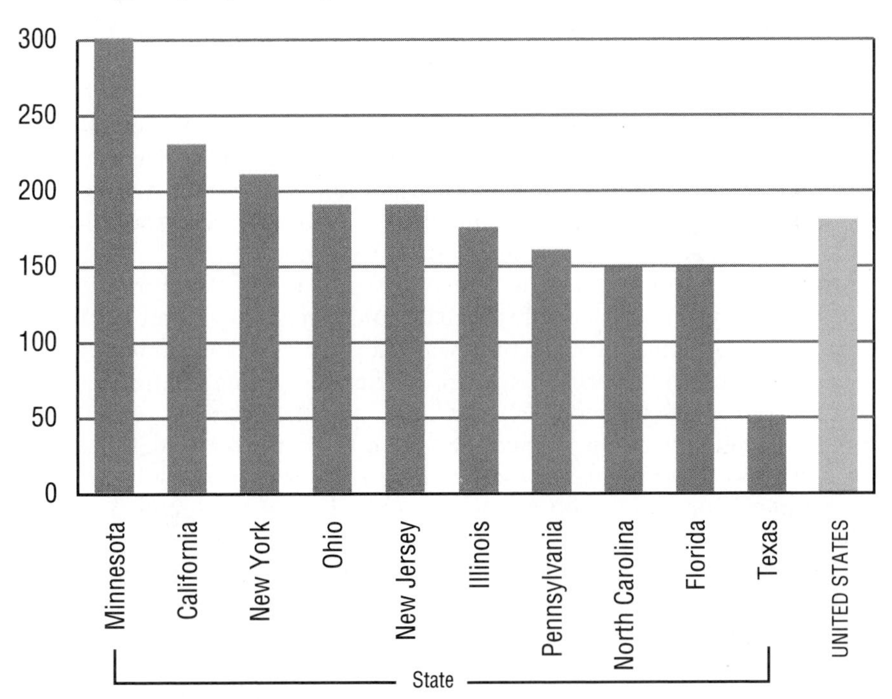

FIGURE 10.6 State Aid to Local Governments in the Ten Largest States, 1990*
**Excludes education and welfare*
Source: Texas Comptroller of Public Accounts, Fiscal Notes, *September 1992, 2.*

Special-District Governments

Special districts are the third type of local government used in Texas. Counties and cities are general-purpose governments; but special-district governments traditionally have been limited to a single function or a small set of related functions. Some special districts have managed to expand their operations to such an extent that one scholar called them "junior cities."[44] The tendency to expand has been especially apparent in districts used to provide urban-type services to housing developments on the outskirts of cities.[45] This means that the traditional distinction between special districts and other governments sometimes has blurred.

Reasons for Creating Special Districts

Why do states create special districts? If counties and cities already provide government services, what purpose do special districts serve? One reason states create special districts is to meet a need in a particular geographic area that no general-purpose government seems able to meet. For example, special districts called **municipal utility districts** (MUDs) often are used in Texas to provide water and sewer systems to housing developments in urban fringe areas. Cities usually do provide water and sewer systems. But remember that developers can choose to build on cheaper land outside the city limits. When they do, a special district often is set up to provide urban-type services.

Metropolitan transit districts are another example of special districts created to serve an area that cannot be served by existing governments. In several large metropolitan areas in Texas, neither the county nor the city can provide an areawide transportation system. In these cases, special districts take on responsibility for meeting transportation needs.

Another reason for creating special districts is to extract more tax revenues from a given tax base. If counties and cities already are taxing property at or near their limits, the only way they can raise additional revenue for a new service is by creating a special district and giving the new district its own power to tax property. For example, hospital districts sometimes are created to build hospitals that counties or cities cannot afford. Of course the system does expand the revenue available from a tax base, but layering governments on the same tax base runs the risk of producing a taxpayers' revolt.

Sometimes special districts are created to administer a program because it seems like a good idea to isolate the program from the politics of county or city government. This argument has been used often to justify the separation of schools from counties and cities. In fact special districts never eliminate politics from a program, but they can separate a program from the ongoing politics in a county or city.

Procedures for Creating Special Districts

Special districts, like other local governments, exercise power that is delegated to them by the state. This means that the state must authorize their creation or create them by legislative enactment. The Texas legislature has authorized the creation of certain types of special districts and has outlined the steps required to form those districts. For example, in 1971 the legislature passed a law permitting the Texas Department of Water Resources to create municipal utility districts (MUDs). Rapid growth in both the number of MUDs and the abuses in their use forced lawmakers to pass corrective legislation in 1973 that required proponents of new special districts to seek a special act from the legislature.[46]

Organizing Special-District Governments

Describing the organization of special districts is more difficult than describing the development of county or city government, in large part because special-district governments are so varied. Still, there are two aspects of special districts that are fairly standard (Figure 10.7). First, a governing board usually sets the budget, handles personnel decisions, and makes policy for the district. Second, the board usually hires a director to handle the day-to-day management of the district. The largest variation among special districts is the method for choosing the members of the governing board. In some districts—MUDs are a common example—board members are elected. In others, board members are appointed by officials of other governments or by some other group. In metropolitan transit districts, it is common for member

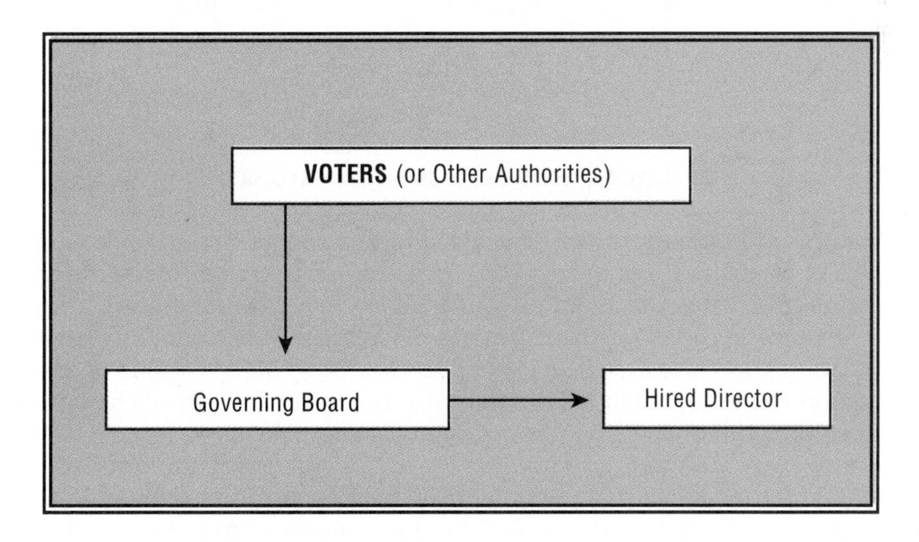

FIGURE 10.7 Organizational Structure of Special Districts in Texas

governments (a group of cities, for example) to appoint the members of the governing board. It should be noted that the director, or the board, or both may be chosen in a manner that does not make them directly accountable to the constituents through the electoral process.

An Evaluation of Special-District Governments

In some ways, special-district governments make sense. They are tailormade for the district they are expected to serve; they focus on one or just a few services instead of on a large number of services; and they are isolated from the politics of county or city governments.

But there are real limitations to this form of government as well. The people who manage special districts often are not accountable to the public through the electoral process or other mechanisms. Because their function is so narrow, special districts often operate without much public awareness—a situation that makes holding their managers accountable even more difficult.

Special districts often contribute to the lack of coordination among governments, especially in metropolitan areas. In fact they can create situations that impose burdens on nearby governments. The MUDs that make urban fringe developments possible often exempt those developments from meeting the nearby city's standards. If the city later annexes the area, it would be responsible for bringing the area into compliance with its standards.

Finally, special districts sometimes allow local groups to pursue their interests without regard for the surrounding area. Probably the most dramatic example of this comes from the MUDs in the Houston metropolitan area. That area has suffered in recent years from the problem of soil subsidence: the land is sinking because underground water is being removed faster than it is being replaced. The proliferation of MUDs, pumping water as needed to serve their constituents, has intensified the problem.[47]

The Future of Local Government in Texas

The forms of local government discussed in this chapter are all under some degree of stress in Texas today. The population of Texas already is concentrated in urban areas, a condition that is likely to continue into the future. The Texas comptroller's office estimates that almost 94 percent of the state's population growth between 1990 and 2026 will be in MSAs. Minority representation in metropolitan populations also is expected to grow. The comptroller's office estimates that minority groups will make up 62 percent of the population in MSA central counties by 2026.[48] Increased minority representation in city populations will likely increase conflict over equitable representation for minorities; and as minority representation is earned, the increased diversity on councils may impact decision-making. The projected growth in the state and the expectation that the state's financial problems are not likely to be resolved in the short term lead to the conclusion that the future will be a trying time in Texas cities, especially its largest cities.[49]

Texas local governments probably will find it necessary to continue to raise taxes and fees to increase revenues. Limited local resources make it likely that local officials will put more pressure on the state to increase funding to the cities and lighten the burden of local property taxes. Although such an effort failed in 1997, the pressure may build up in the future. State lawmakers are caught in the fiscal pinch too. They cannot solve the cities' financial problems unless they find a better revenue system for the state.

Another product of urban concentration of the population is likely to be tension between central cities and suburbs. Although cities and suburbs are linked socially and economically, they are separated politically in metropolitan areas. Continued squabbling in metropolitan areas over areawide problems—transportation and air and water quality, for example—seems probable.

County governments strain to make nineteenth-century political institutions serve the needs of urban Texas. They work with institutional arrangements that provide little central direction to county government. These governments often have to do things they were not designed to do. The biggest obstacle to change in county government is the large bloc of county officials who are tied to the existing system. Any reforms are likely to threaten the jobs of many of those officials—a strong motive for their commitment to the status quo. The job of county reform also is complicated by the differences among Texas counties. Texas has some of the most urban counties in the nation; it also has some of the most rural counties in the nation. Loving County, in West Texas, with an average of less than one person per square mile, does not have the same concerns that urban counties do. The differences among counties make it impossible for county officials to unify behind a program of statewide reform. Home rule would be a logical solution to the problem of diversity, but there seems to be little pressure for that now. Thus, major structural reform at the county level seems unlikely. Instead, Texas counties are likely to continue to search for innovative ways to meet the changing needs of residents.

The prospects for change do not seem any more likely for special-district governments. Although the independence of these governments clearly has created major problems in metropolitan areas, most special districts do an admirable job of providing their designated services.

Notes

1. Chalres Mahtesian, "The Stadium Trap," *Governing* (May 1998), p. 22.
2. Robert Ingrassia, "Record Bond Package, Trinity Place Approved," *Dallas Morning News,* May 3, 1998, 1A.
3. Rob Gurwitt, "Nobody in Charge," *Governing* (September, 1997) pp. 20–24.
4. Robert Ingrassia, "Suburban Success Story: Despite Some Problems, Many

Praise Plano as Model in Planning Growth," *Dallas Morning News,* December 30, 1993, 1A and 18A.

5. Quoted in Jefferson B. Fordham, *Local Government Law* (Mineola, NY: Foundation Press, Inc., 1975), 58.
6. Texas Constitution, Art. V, Sec. 18.
7. Texas Constitution, Art. V, Sec. 25.
8. Texas Department of Community Affairs, *Your County Government in Texas* (Austin, 1979), 5.
9. Texas Revised Civil Statutes, Art. 6702-1, Subchapter C.
10. For a discussion of county finances, see Texas Advisory Commission on Intergovernmental Relations, *An Introduction to Texas County Government* (Austin, 1980), 13–16.
11. Texas Government Code Sec. 415.053.
12. U.S. Advisory Commission on Intergovernmental Relations, *State and Local Roles in the Federal System,* Report A–88 (Washington, DC: Government Printing Office, April 1982), 151.
13. Texas Constitution, Art. XI, Secs. 4–5.
14. *Texas Almanac,* 1998–1999, (Dallas: A. H. Belo Corp., 1997), 436.
15. "Municipal Annexation Act," General and Special Laws of the State of Texas, Fifty-Seventh Legislature (1963), Chapter 160, 447–545.
16. See U.S. Bureau of the Census, *Patterns of Metropolitan Areas and County Population Growth* (Washington, DC: U.S. Government Printing Office, June 1989), 29.
17. Texas Comptroller of Public Accounts, "Texas Becoming More Urban: Metros Expand," *Fiscal Notes,* April 1993, 13.
18. Texas Comptroller of Public Accounts, *The Changing Face of Texas* (Austin, 1992), 21.
19. Amy Bridges, "Boss Tweed and V. O. Key in Texas," in *Urban Texas: Politics and Development,* Char Miller and Heywood T. Sanders, eds. (College Station: Texas A&M University Press, 1990), 58.
20. Bradley R. Rice, "The Galveston Plan of City Government by Commission: The Birth of a Progressive Idea," *Southwestern Historical Quarterly* 78 (April 1975): 366–408.
21. Bridges, "Boss Tweed," 58–71.
22. *Texas Almanac,* 1998–1999, (Dallas: A. H. Belo Corp., 1997), 436–443.
23. Thomas R. Dye, *Politics in States and Communities,* 7th ed. (Englewood Cliffs, NJ: Prentice-Hall, 1991), 277.
24. Dye, *Politics,* 277.
25. See Theodore P. Robinson and Thomas R. Dye, "Reformism and Black Representation on City Councils," *Social Science Quarterly* 59 (June 1978): 133–141; Richard L. Engstrom and Michael E. McDonald, "The Election of Blacks to City Councils: Clarifying the Impact of Electoral Arrangements on the Seats/Population Relationship," *American Political Science Review* 75 (June 1981): 344–354; and Arnold Vedlitz and Charles A. Johnson, "Community Racial Segregation, Electoral Structure, and Minority Representation," *Social Science Quarterly* 63 (December 1982): 729–736. For those finding no relationship, see Susan S. MacManus, "City Council Election Procedures and Minority Representation: Are They Related?" *Social Science Quarterly* 59 (June 1978): 153–161; and Albert Karnig, "Black Representation on City Councils," *Urban Affairs Quarterly* 12 (December 1976): 134–149.
26. Susan Welch, "The Impact of At-large Elections on the Representation of Blacks and Hispanics," *Journal of Politics* 52 (November 1990): 1050–

1076. Also see Charles S. Bullock III and Susan A. MacManus, "Structural Features of Municipalities and the Incidence of Hispanic Councilmembers," *Social Science Quarterly* 71 (December 1990): 665–681.

27. Welch, "Impact," 1067.

28. *Mobile* v. *Bolden,* 446 U.S. 55 (1980).

29. *Thornburg* v. *Gingles,* 106 S.Ct. 2752 (1986).

30. Bridges, "Boss Tweed," 62. For a discussion of the forces behind these reforms outside Texas, see Samuel P. Hays, "The Politics of Municipal Reform in the Progressive Era," *Southwestern Historical Quarterly* 55 (October 1964): 157–169.

31. John A. Booth and David R. Johnson, "Power and Progress in San Antonio Politics, 1836–1970," in *The Politics of San Antonio,* David R. Johnson et al., eds. (Lincoln: University of Nebraska Press, 1983), 3–27. The point made here is on pp. 19–25.

32. Booth and Johnson, "Power and Progress," 23.

33. Gregory Curtis, "Cutting Up Dallas," *Texas Monthly* 19 (May 1991): 5, 10, and 12.

34. *Williams* v. *City of Dallas,* U.S. District Court for the Northern District of Texas, Dallas Division, 734 F.Supp. 1317 (1990).

35. Jackson and Camia, "City Manager System," 1A.

36. Texas Comptroller of Public Accounts, *Fiscal Notes,* September 1992, 9.

37. Texas Comptroller, *Fiscal Notes,* 8–9.

38. Texas Constitution, Art. XI, Secs. 4–5.

39. Robert L. Bland, *Financing City Government in Texas* (Austin: Texas Municipal League, 1986), 16.

40. Bland, *Financing City Government,* 28.

41. Bland, *Financing City Government,* 69.

42. Bland, *Financing City Government,* 124.

43. Texas State Comptroller, *Fiscal Notes,* 2.

44. John C. Bollens, *Special District Government in the United States* (Westport, CT: Greenwood Press, 1957), 114.

45. See Virginia Marion Perrenod, *Special Districts, Special Purposes: Fringe Governments and Urban Problems in the Houston Area* (College Station: Texas A&M University Press, 1984).

46. Perrenod, *Special Districts,* 18.

47. Perrenod, *Special Districts,* 87–93.

48. Texas Comptroller, *Changing Face,* 24–25.

49. Texas Comptroller, *Texas Economic Quarterly,* September 1992, 2.

11 TEXAS PUBLIC FINANCE

CHAPTER OUTLINE

Finding the truth about state finances from public debate is often difficult. In the 1994 gubernatorial campaign, candidate George W. Bush stressed two public finance issues: funding for public education and the use of the state's lottery income. Bush pointed out that the state's share of funding for public schools had fallen and argued that the lottery income should have been dedicated to the schools. Moreover, he argued that most people had believed that the lottery funds would be going to education when they voted to allow a lottery in 1991. Governor Richards replied that no one had ever promised that lottery funds would be earmarked for education and that it would not be a good idea to make the schools dependent on an unstable source of revenue. She also pointed out that total funding for education had gone up during her years in office.

Both candidates appeared to be telling the truth. A school crisis was used to sell the lottery to the voters of Texas, but neither the amendment authorizing the lottery nor Governor Richards promised that lottery revenues would be earmarked for education. And although the percentage of public school funding provided by the state did fall by about 2 percent during the years of the Richards administration, funding for education did grow during those years.[1]

This story reveals several things about public finance in Texas. First, it plays a key role in Texas politics, especially in gubernatorial campaigns. Second, it often is confusing to the public: when the facts are presented in different ways, they lead to different conclusions. Third, public-finance issues often have to be resolved before other kinds of issues can be addressed. Money clearly is at the heart of the education problems Texas is facing today. All of these things point out the importance of understanding financial issues in Texas politics.

To further that understanding, this chapter explores several topics in Texas public finance:

- How is the Texas budget prepared?
- What are the trends and patterns of revenues and expenditures in Texas?
- What are the major problems facing Texas in the areas of budgeting and public finance?

Budget Politics in Texas

The taxing and spending patterns of the state are set by a budget process that involves many participants and takes months to complete. Understanding the rules of the game and the players is essential to understanding the decisions the Texas government makes about taxing and spending.

The Rules of the Game

The first rule is that the budget must be balanced (the **balanced budget rule**). A 1942 constitutional amendment prohibits the legislature from appropriating more money than the comptroller certifies will be available over a fiscal period.[2] Although the state can borrow money for the construction of buildings and other long-term capital projects, it cannot borrow money to cover its operating expenses. If revenue estimates fall short of estimated expenses, the legislature must trim the budget, pass a new revenue measure, or do both.

The second important rule is that each budget must cover a two-year period, a **biennium.** Only seventeen states operate on a two-year budget cycle.[3] The practice is necessary in Texas because the legislature meets in regular session only once every two years.

The third important rule is the **growth limitation rule.** It states that appropriations from tax revenue that is not dedicated by the constitution cannot grow faster than the estimated growth of the state's economy. For the 1998–99 biennium, the Legislative Budget Board calculated that this rule limited growth in the non-constitutionally dedicated part of the budget to $39.7 billion. The legislature actually appropriated $38.9 billion.[4]

External Factors and the Budget

Sometimes external factors beyond their control force the state's political leaders to raise taxes or appropriate more money. Three external factors have influenced Texas public finance in recent years: economic developments, court orders, and national government mandates. Change in world prices for goods or services produced in Texas and national economic changes (recessions, for example) are external economic developments. Decisions of the U.S. Supreme Court and federal courts and the rules laid down by the national government can force the state to provide additional services or can increase the cost of providing services.

Discretion in the Budget Process

Because of standing commitments and external factors, the choices of **nonrestricted appropriations** available to Texas budgetmakers in recent years have been limited. An analysis by the **Legislative Budget Board** (LBB) found that only $7.1 billion (13 percent) of the $54.1 billion appropriated for the 1998–1999 biennium from the General Revenue Fund was free to be allocated at the legislature's discretion (Figure 11.1). The balance already was committed before the legislature began working to items defined by the state constitution, state laws, and federal mandates. The budgetary battle, then, is fought over a relatively small proportion of the state's total spending.

Critical Stages and Key Players

Table 11.1 shows the steps in the Texas budget process. Several individuals and agencies are key players at critical junctures in that process. In the first two stages, the agencies prepare their strategic plan and their appropriations requests. The third stage—the budget proposal preparation stage—is critical.

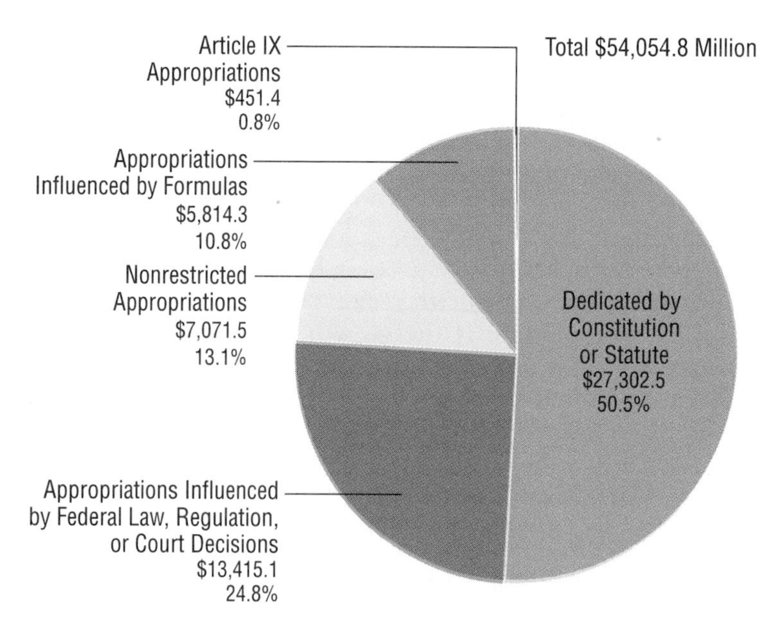

FIGURE 11.1 Restrictions on Appropropriations from the General Revenue and General Revenue-Dedicated Funds Budget for the 1998–99 Biennium (In Millions)
Source: Legislative Budget Board, Fiscal Size Up: 1998–99 *(Austin: LBB, 1998), pp. 1–8.*

In this stage initial decisions are made about the overall size of the budget and the funding for individual agencies. By law the LBB is responsible for formulating a budget proposal. In practice the speaker and lieutenant governor, who control the LBB, have enormous influence on this phase of the process. Through their spending priorities and their willingness (or unwillingness) to raise taxes to provide revenues, the presiding officers shape the basic contours of the proposed budget.

Once the proposal goes to the legislature, other players become important. The governor presents a policy budget in the early stages of the legislative session that endorses the LBB's recommendations or suggests alternatives to the LBB's plan. The popularity and political strength of the governor determine the weight the legislature gives the governor's recommendations. Most observers believe that the LBB's proposal generally has more influence on the budget that finally passes than does the governor's proposal.

The key budget committees in each house, the Senate Finance Committee and the House Appropriations Committee, take the budget proposals and, under the leadership of their chairs, draft the budget bills. Remember that the presiding officers choose the committee and their chairs, so the committees are not likely to stray far from what the leaders want.

Because floor consideration of budget bills usually comes near the end of the legislative session, there is not enough time for major changes on the floor. The house and senate almost never pass budget bills with exactly the

Table 11.1 Texas Budget Process

Stage	Timeline	Participants	Activities
Agency planning	March–June of even-numbered years	All executive-branch agencies and institutions of higher education	6-year strategic plan developed.
Agency requests	June–October of even-numbered years	All executive-branch agencies and institutions of higher education	Legislative appropriation requests (LARs) prepared.
Budget proposal preparation	October–December of even-numbered years	LBB and governor's budget office	Budget analysts review requests, public hearings are held, and LBB budget proposal is prepared.
Legislative consideration	January–May of odd-numbered years	LBB, governor, legislative leaders, key house and senate committees, and house and senate conference committee	LBB presents its proposal, governor makes recommendation, committees work out details of budget, each chamber passes a budget, and conference committee works out a compromise bill. Final passage by both chambers.
Gubernatorial action	May of odd-numbered years	Governor	Governor signs bill, using line-item veto to strike out some items.
Implementation	September 1 of odd-numbered years, for 2 years	All state agencies and institutions of higher education	Agencies spend in accordance with new budget.

same provisions, which means that a conference committee must work out a compromise between the house and senate versions of the budget. And because conference committee members are appointed by the speaker and the lieutenant governor, they, too, tend to protect leaders' interests.

Time plays a critical role at this point in the process. Usually the conference committee is working at the end of a legislative session. This means that the members of the house and senate have little choice but to approve the compromise budget. If they do not, the state would not have a budget. (Actually the governor would call a special session of the legislature to avoid a financial crisis.)

Once the legislature has finished, the governor gets another opportunity to influence the budget. Using the line-item veto, the governor can cut some spending from the budget—and most do. The governor receives the budget and makes veto decisions after the legislative session ends. So the legislature does not have an opportunity to override the line-item vetoes.

The Budget System

Texas, like other states, has tried several budgeting systems, hoping to improve the state's ability to manage its financial affairs. Until 1973 the state used **line-item budgeting,** each line (or item) in the budget describing the goods and services the agency would buy with the money (Figure 11.2). In 1973 Texas joined many other states in shifting to **zero-based budgeting** (ZBB), which required the agencies to prepare budgets at several funding levels so that the effects of funding at one level or another would be apparent. For the budget passed in 1993, the legislature switched to a new system, **strategic planning and budgeting.**[5] Under this system agencies submit plans that include goals, objectives, and strategies and must relate proposed expenditures to those goals, objectives, and strategies (Figure 11.3). Strategic planning and budgeting is based on performance; it focuses on measurable outcomes and rewards agencies for meeting or exceeding their goals. Because the new system of **performance budgeting** is organized around goals, objectives, and strategies—instead of the traditional line items—the system makes the governor's task of finding items to cut more difficult.

Revenue Patterns

Remember that the revenues available to the state can be affected by external forces. For example, the collapse of world oil prices in the mid-1980s created turmoil in the Texas oil industry and in its revenue system. Mainstays of the Texas revenue system—oil and gas taxes and sales taxes—produced far less revenue than was expected. National economic trends also affect Texas public finance. The national economy goes through periods of inflation (prices go up faster than revenues grow) and recessions (revenues fall faster than costs can be cut). A national recession in 1992 slowed economic activity and reduced tax collections in Texas. By contrast, the revival of the national economy in 1993 and 1994 bolstered the Texas economy. The state finished the 1994–1995 biennium with a sizable surplus in its treasury.

Sources of Revenues

Where does Texas get the money it spends? **Tax revenues** constituted about 50 percent of state revenues in the 1998–1999 biennium (Figure 11.4). Grants and other payments to the state by the national government made up about 29 percent of the revenues. Interest and dividends and income from other

Figure 11.2 An Example of Line-Item Budgeting

Texas Historical Survey Committee	For the Years Ending August 31, 1970	August 31, 1971
Out of the General Revenue Fund:		
Personal Services		
1. Executive Director	$ 17,000	$ 17,000
2. Director of Research	12,000	12,000
3. Director of Field Operations	13,500	13,500
4. State Archeologist	15,500	15,500
5. Salaries of Classified Positions	63,997	66,173
6. For necessary research to validate, investigate and authenticate historical and archeological sites, structures, archives and inscriptions, including salaries and wages, travel and other necessary expenses, to be expended by contractual relations with colleges, universities, historical societies or individuals, or by part-time and temporary employment	25,800	26,616
Total, Personal Services	$147,797	$150,789
Other Expenses		
7. To administer the National Historic Properties Act and prepare the Comprehensive Statewide Historic Survey, to be expended as follows: Architectural Restoration Consultant, $15,500; Secretary III (0135), $5,256—1970 and $5,436—1971; professional fees and services to validate and authenticate historical sites, structures, districts and archeological sites, including salaries and wages, to be expended by contractual relations with colleges, universities or individuals, or by part-time and temporary employment, $7,200; travel expenses, $4,800; consumable supplies and materials, current and recurring operating expenses and capital outlay, $3,428	$ 36,184	$ 36,364
8. Consumable supplies and materials, current and recurring operating expenses including maintenance and operation of motor vehicles, and capital outlay	37,564	41,164
9. For erecting memorials upon battlefields and placing medallions, inscription-plates, official Texas historical markers, gravestones and other markers at historical sites, structures and places, and necessary incidental expenses relating thereto	15,000	15,000

Figure 11.2 *Cont.*

Texas Historical Survey Committee	For the Years Ending August 31, 1970	August 31, 1971
10. For restoration of historic structures as provided for in H.B. No. 812, 59th Legislature and H.B. No. 1457, 61st Legislature:		
Gethsemane Lutheran Church	$ 53,275	
Carrington-Covert House		$ 80,000
11. For site development of Gethsemane Lutheran Church and Carrington-Covert House including landscaping and demolition of existing brick structure (Sunday School Annex)	43,500	
Grand Total, Historical Survey Committee	$333,320	$323,317

Source: House Bill 2, Sixty-first Legislature, 2d Called Session, 1969 (General Appropriations Act).

revenue sources—licenses, fees and fines, land, and the state lottery—made up the balance.

Although the biggest share of Texas revenues comes from taxes today, the percentage of revenue derived from taxes has dropped, from over 60 percent of state revenues in the 1988–1989 biennium to 50 percent in the 1998–1999 period. As Figure 11.5 shows, Texas has been generating a larger share of **non-tax revenues** in recent years.

What taxes produce state revenues? The sales tax accounts for about 55 percent of tax revenues (Figure 11.6). The sales tax, the motor fuels tax (which includes the gasoline tax), the vehicle sales and rental tax, the corporation franchise tax, and the oil and gas production taxes generate almost 90 percent of the state's tax revenues.

For a tax that is relatively young, the **sales tax** plays a pivotal role in Texas public finance, producing over half the state's tax revenues. Most states had adopted a sales tax in the 1930s, in response to the Great Depression. Texas finally adopted a sales tax in 1961. The state had managed to avoid a sales tax because revenues from oil and gas taxes were so high. Initially the sales tax played a modest role in state funding, producing just 10 percent of tax revenues in 1962. The first big jump came in the late 1960s, when the legislature increased the sales tax to fund rising education costs. In 1971 the tax went up again to meet mounting public assistance costs. As late as 1983, sales taxes generated about 40 percent of state tax revenue. The tax has been increased four times since 1983, and the range of items on which the tax is collected was expanded significantly three times. The legislature raised the sales tax to fund increased spending on education and to replace shrinking oil and gas revenues.[6] Texas now has one of the highest sales tax rates in the country.[7]

Figure 11.3 An Example of Strategic Planning and Budgeting

	For the Years Ending	
A. Goal: HISTORICAL PRESERVATION	**August 31, 1994**	**August 31, 1995**
Preserve our state's irreplaceable historic landmarks and artifacts for enjoyment by the public and the enrichment of future generations.		
A.1. Objective:		
Preserve landmarks through existing statutes and programs		
Outcomes:		
Of the Historic and Archeological Site Owners Assisted, the Percentage of Their Sites Preserved Annually	95%	95%
A.1.1. Strategy: OWNER ASSISTANCE		
Assist owners of historic properties in their preservation efforts through existing statutes and programs.	$ 258,416	$ 285,418
Outputs:		
Number of Historic and Archeological Sites/Owners Assisted	5,100	5,100
Efficiencies:		
Average Cost per Site/Owner Assisted	55.96	55.96
A.2. Objective:		
Preserve historic structures, archeological sites, and antiquities		
Outcomes:		
Percentage of Requests for Technical Assistance Served	90%	90%
Percentage of Needed Projects Implemented	100%	100%
A.2.1. Strategy: PRESERVATION ASSISTANCE		
Provide historical and financial assistance for the preservation of historic and archeological sites and collections.	$ 261,967	$ 261,967
Outputs:		
Number of Sites/Owners Provided with Technical Assistance	10,104	10,104
Efficiencies:		
Average Cost per Technical Assistance Provided	18.34	17.39
A.2.2. Strategy: MAINTENANCE AND REPAIR		
Provide for the repair, maintenance and compliance with the Americans with Disabilities Act of properties under Historical Commission jurisdiction, including the Governor's Mansion, Carrington Covert House, Gethsemane Church, and the Sam Rayburn House.	$1,161,158	$ 112,569
Outputs:		
Number of Construction Projects Completed on These Properties	8	8
Efficiencies:		
Average Cost for Bringing Historical Properties Under THC Jurisdiction into Compliance with Preservation Maintenance Standards	12,330	12,330

Source: Senate Bill 5, Seventy-third Legislature, Regular Session, 1993 (General Appropriations Act).

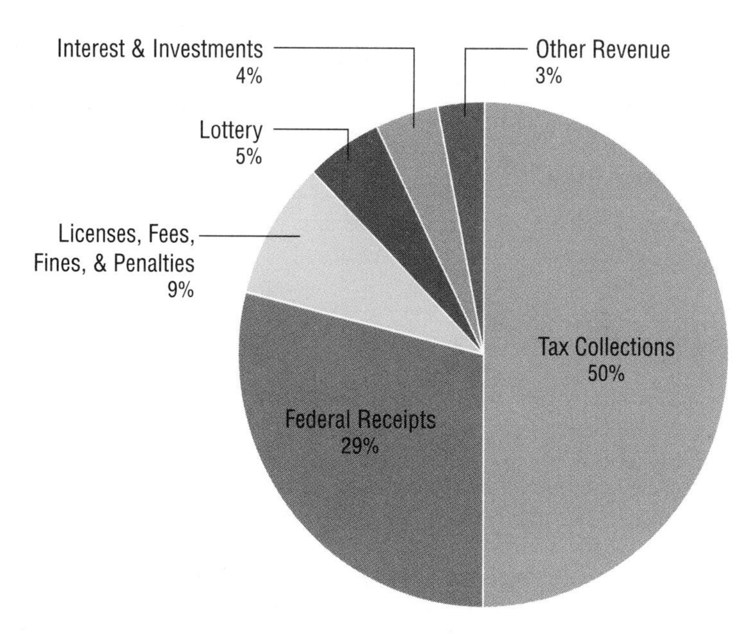

FIGURE 11.4 Estimated Revenue in Texas, 1998–99 Biennium
Source: Legislative Budget Board, Fiscal Size Up: 1998–99 Biennium, *p. 2-1.*

One type of tax is conspicuous by its absence in Texas: the individual income tax. Texas is one of only ten states that do not levy a personal income tax.[8] In fact in 1993, the legislature proposed and the public ratified a constitutional amendment that makes it impossible to pass a state income tax unless the public approves it in a statewide referendum.

Recent sessions of the legislature have produced other changes in the state's revenue system. When the Seventy-second Legislature met in 1991, the state's revenues for the 1992–1993 biennium were expected to fall over $4 billion short of the amount needed to maintain existing government services.[9] Acting to close the revenue gap, the legislature increased the gasoline tax $.05 cents per gallon; restructured the **corporation franchise tax;** shifting it from a tax on capital to a tax on corporate income; and proposed a constitutional amendment that would allow the state to establish a lottery. The voters ratified the lottery amendment in November 1991, and lottery revenues began to flow into the state treasury in 1992. By fiscal year 1994, the lottery was producing just over 4 percent of state revenues and was estimated to contribute about 5 percent in the 1998–99 biennium (see box).

The Burden of Taxes

How heavy is the burden Texas places on its taxpayers compared with other states? The Legislative Budget Board reported that, in 1998, Texas ranked

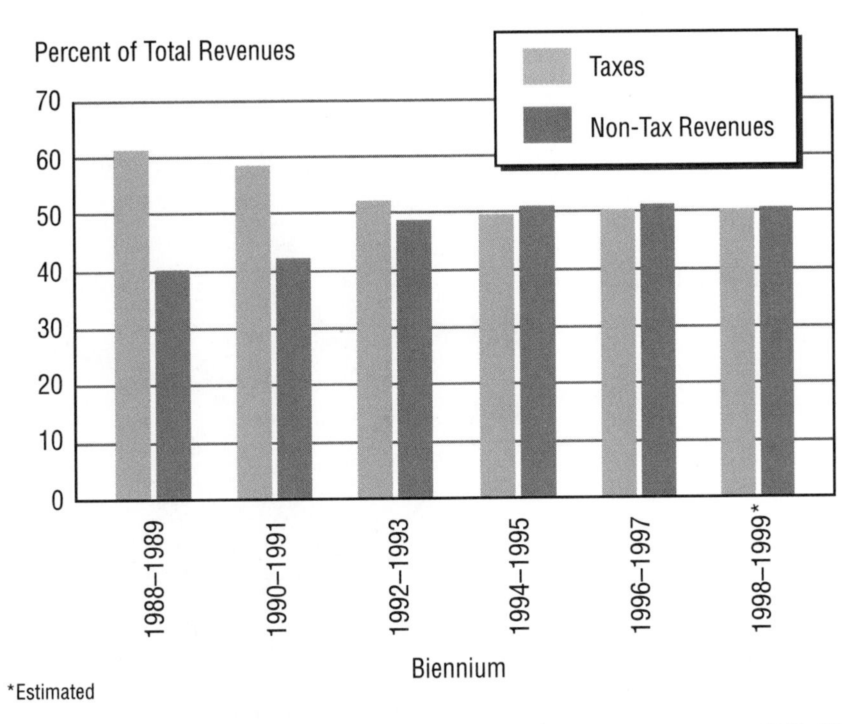

FIGURE 11.5 State Revenue Composition Taxes and Non-Tax Revenues 1998–89 Biennium through 1998–99 Biennium
Source: Legislative Budget Board, Fiscal Size Up: 1998–99, *2–3.*

forty-eighth on tax revenue as a percentage of income and last among the fifteen most populous states on **per capita tax revenue.**[10] The data indicate, then, that Texas does not impose a heavy tax burden on its citizens compared with other states.

Trends and Patterns in Expenditures

Total Expenditures

In 1983, total government expenditures in Texas were about $13.8 billion; by 1996, total expenditures had almost tripled, to over $39.9 billion. Texas politicians did not go on a reckless spending spree over that period. Population growth increased the demand for state services, and inflation pushed up the cost of those services. Figure 11.7 shows both the raw expenditure figures over the period and those figures adjusted for population growth and inflation. Given the pressure from external forces to increase expenditures, the gradual growth of the adjusted curve is proof of resistance in Texas to government spending. In fact, in per capita expenditures—that is, expenditures per person—Texas ranks last among the fifteen most populous states.[11]

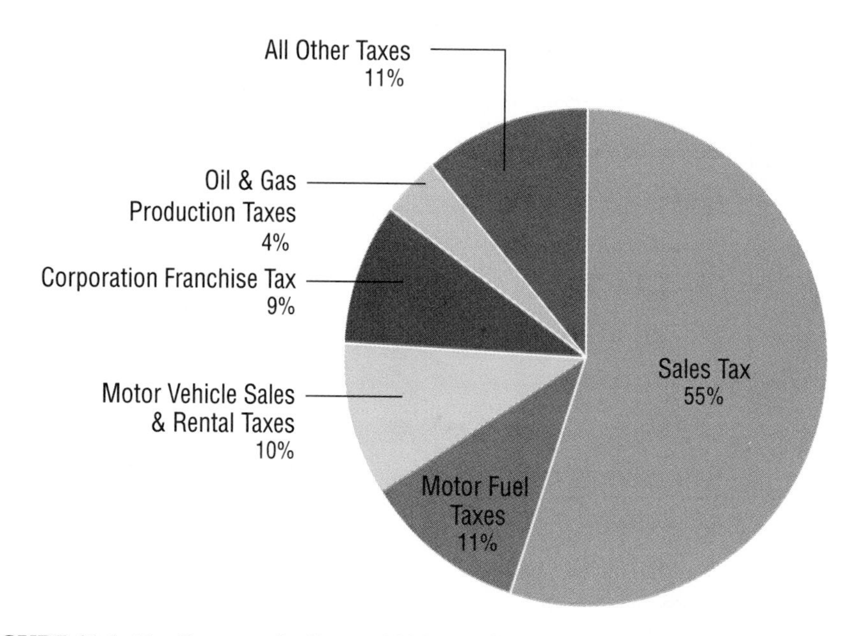

FIGURE 11.6 Tax Revenue in Texas, 1998–99 Biennium
Source: Legislative Budget Board, Fiscal Size Up: 1998–99 Biennium, *p. 2–2.*

Expenditures by Function

What programs get the largest share of the Texas budget? This question can best be answered by using information from the **all funds budget,** which appropriates money from the state's general revenue fund as well as from a number of earmarked funds and federal revenue. Revenue from an **earmarked fund** can be used only for the purposes specified in the statute or the state constitution. For example, revenue from the state's gasoline tax goes into a fund earmarked for highways and education. Because the all-funds budget includes all the revenues available to the state government, it gives the best overall picture of the state's expenditures by function.

A comparison of expenditures by function reveals that about 74 percent of the Texas budget goes to two functions: education and health and human services (Figure 11.8). Business and economic development (which includes highways), general government, public safety and criminal justice, natural resources, and all the other services the state provides share the remaining 26 percent of the budget.[12] The biggest percentage increase in the 1998–1999 budget was for the judiciary (a 21.7 percent increase over the 1996–97 biennium) to pay for salary increases for judges and prosecutors. The second largest increase went to education: expenditures in this area went up about 10.5 percent over the previous biennium.[13]

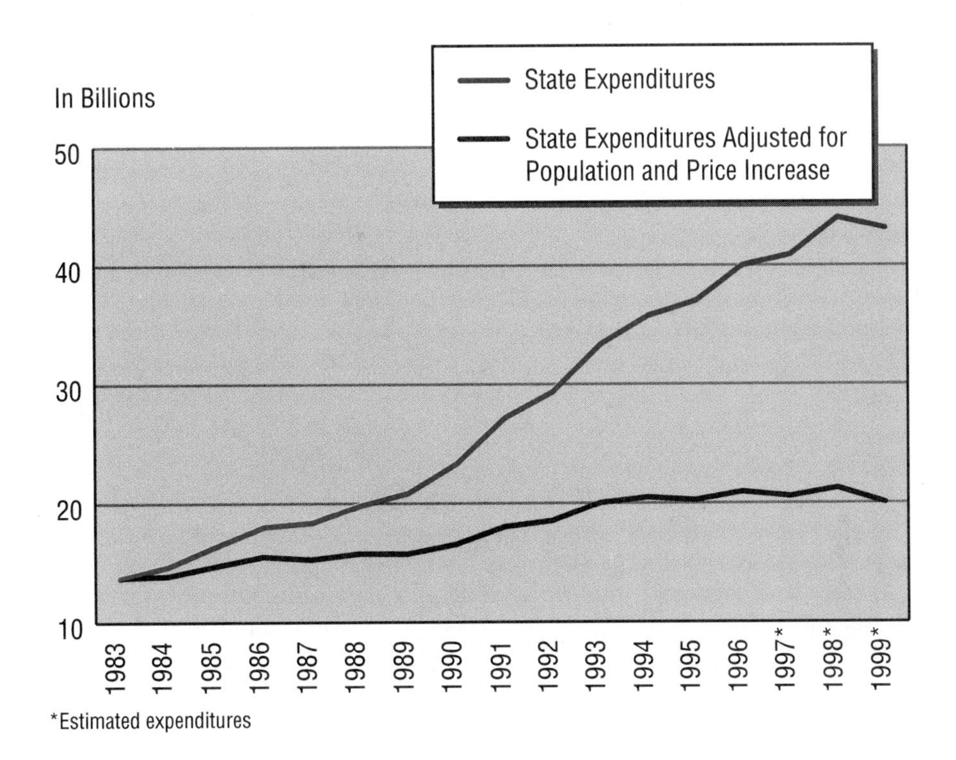

FIGURE 11.7 Trends in Texas State Expenditures, All Funds, Fiscal Years 1983–1999
Source: Legislative Budget Board, Fiscal Size Up: 1998–99, *1–9.*

Mandates and Expenditures

Mandates (i.e., orders from one level of government that another must provide a specific service) are responsible for some of the recent growth in Texas expenditures. Court orders have influenced Texas spending in three areas. In 1981, in a consent decree in *Ruiz* v. *Estelle,* the state agreed to operate its prison system at no more than 95 percent capacity.[14] To meet that agreement in the face of rising inmate populations, expenditures for prison construction rose dramatically. In 1981 the state also agreed to improve its mental health facilities to satisfy a complaint in federal court on behalf of residents of state mental hospitals and state schools for the mentally retarded.[15] In 1989 the Texas Supreme Court ruled that the state's system of financing public elementary and secondary schools was unconstitutional and ordered the legislature to equalize funding across school districts.[16] In each of these cases, the legislature had just one option: finding the financial resources to comply.

THE CHANGING FACE OF TEXAS POLITICS

The Texas Lottery: Good Revenue Source but No Panacea

When the Texas legislature convened in 1991, it faced a severe financial challenge. Revenue estimates showed that the state would be about $4 billion short of the amount needed to fund its current services budget—that is, to provide existing programs at the existing service levels. Having raised taxes several times during the 1980s, legislators looked for other ways to alleviate the budget crisis. Part of their solution was a constitutional amendment that would allow the state to set up a lottery. The voters approved that amendment in November 1991.

In May 1992 the state began operating a lottery. Scratch tickets were introduced first because they do not require an electronic network linking ticket vendors. But the major step came in November, when a big-prize lottery drawing was introduced. Participants try to match the six numbers that are drawn in each game. (Drawings are held twice each week.) Each entry costs players a dollar. The game begins with at least a $2 million payoff, which carries over to the next drawing if no one matches all six numbers. Thus excitement builds as payoffs grow with successive drawings.

The Texas comptroller's office set up the lottery and oversaw it through the establishment of the basic games and the electronic network necessary for retailers to enter numbers into the system. By October 1993 the lottery had set participation records for its games.[1] The lottery operation was a model of efficiency. Key to that efficiency, according to Comptroller John Sharp, is the use of private businesses wherever possible instead of a big bureaucracy. For example, the lottery uses a private firm to transport tickets to retailers; it has not built its own fleet. Sharp has noted that by 1993, he was getting calls from other states for advice on operating a lottery.[2] In December 1993, the comptroller's office had completed its charge—the lottery was off to a successful start—and control was transferred to the Texas Lottery Commission.

The lottery has exceeded all initial revenue projections. Net income from the lottery was $312 million in fiscal year 1992 (during which the lottery was operational for only a few months), $1.1 billion in fiscal year 1993, and $1.5 billion in fiscal year 1994.[3] (The fiscal year in Texas ends on August 31 of the calendar year.) Revenue forecasts predicted lottery revenues of $1.6 billion in fiscal year 1995 and $1.7 billion in fiscal years 1996 and 1997.[4]

Although lottery income has exceeded projections, it still makes up only a tiny fraction of the state's available revenues. In fiscal year 1993, the lottery provided 3.3 percent of the state's revenues; in fiscal year 1994, 4.3 percent.[5] The comptroller's office estimated that

Federal policy mandates are another source of influence on state expenditures. By altering eligibility rules for programs jointly funded by the national and state governments, the national government can force states to spend more money. An example: In 1991 the national government changed eligibility rules for Medicaid, requiring the states to provide medical services to the children of eligible recipients until they reach age nineteen. Texas had been providing services to poor children under the age of six, so it was the lottery would contribute 4.4 percent in 1995 and 1996 and 4.3 percent in 1997.[6]

Although the lottery is considered a success, it has not been without controversy. Those who initially opposed it argued that it would prey on the poor. The law setting up the lottery requires that participants be surveyed every two years. The first survey results were released by the comptroller's office in March 1993. The Center for Public Policy at the University of Houston (which conducted the survey) reported that those who play the lottery most earn between $50,000 and $75,000 a year, and that those who play the lottery least earn less than $10,000 a year.[7] The initial data, then, suggest that the lottery is not a "tax on the poor."

Another controversy surrounding the lottery has to do with the use of lottery earnings. Because there had been much talk of a financial crisis in the schools when the lottery was passed in 1991, many mistakenly believed that the lottery proceeds would be used only for education. The issue surfaced during the 1994 gubernatorial election, when George W. Bush charged that Governor Richards had misled the voters about the use of lottery funds. Richards vigorously denied saying that lottery revenues would be used only for education. And when legislation to earmark lottery revenues for the schools was introduced in the 1995 legislative session, it did not pass. The legislature passed legislation in 1997 dedicating lottery revenue to public education. Although lottery revenue cannot fund public education alone, at least the money is going where many thought it should.

Another concern raised recently is whether lottery revenues will hold up. Other states have seen earnings fall after the games have been in place for several years. Louisiana reported a decline in lottery revenues when its game was just two years old.[8] In early 1998, sales of lottery tickets were down sharply from the previous year, and it appeared unlikely that the lottery would bring in the $4.4 billion that the comptroller estimated for the 1998–99 biennium. The cause for the decline appeared to be the legislature's decision in 1997 to reduce the prize payout from 57 percent of sales to 52.5 percent. By trying to squeeze more revenue out of the lottery, the legislature may have undermined its attractiveness.[9]

[1]"Lottery Games Set National Records," *Dallas Morning News,* October 17, 1993, 30A.

[2]"Lottery Efficiency Saves $80 million, Sharp Says," *Dallas Morning News,* August 31, 1993, 19A.

[3]Texas Comptroller of Public Accounts, "Historical Data on Sources of Income," Texas Comptroller's web site.

[4]Texas Comptroller of Public Accounts, "Revenue Forecast," Texas Comptroller's web site.

[5]Texas Comptroller of Public Accounts, "Historical Data on Revenue Sources."

[6]Texas Comptroller of Public Accounts, "Revenue Estimates."

[7]"State: Lottery Doesn't Prey on the Poor," *Dallas Morning News,* March 10, 1993, 12D.

[8]Marsanne Golsby, "Louisiana Lottery Slumping," *Dallas Morning News,* December 12, 1993, 53A.

[9]Ken Herman, "Senators: Payout Drop Hurt Lottery," *Austin American-Statesman,* April 29, 1998, p. B1.

required to boost the maximum age for children one year annually until the new maximum is in place. This mandate means significantly higher Medicaid expenditures for Texas.[17] A 1994 report found that about 65 percent of the growth in total state expenditures between the 1990–1991 biennium and the 1994–1995 biennium was the product of federal initiatives—of court orders, laws, or regulations that require matching funds to receive federal aid.[18]

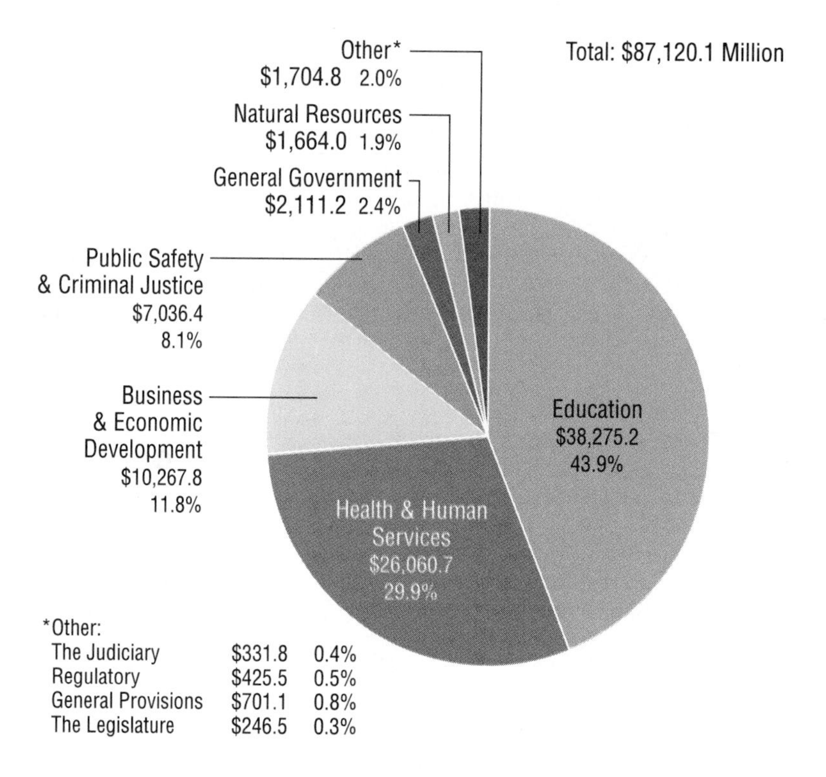

FIGURE 11.8 Texas All-Funds Budget by Function, 1998–99 Fiscal Period (In Millions)*

**Totals may not add due to rounding.*
Source: Legislative Budget Board, Fiscal Size Up: 1998–99, *1–2.*

State Finances and Local Finances

The finances of state governments and their local governments are closely linked. Some states choose to leave much of the taxing and spending to their local governments, whereas others centralized their finances by channeling more money through the state budget. The fiscal links between the two levels of government tend to derive from two conditions. First, states affect local finances by the amount of aid that they choose to give to local governments. Because a number of local programs are funded by a combination of local revenue and state aid, state decisions to increase or decrease aid will inevitably force local decision makers to respond. Most often, in such situations, local governments must either raise more revenue locally or cut back on the programs that they provide. The second way that state and local finances are linked is through the state's regulation of the taxing powers of local governments. States commonly stipulate what taxes local governments can impose and also regulate the rates that they can charge. Changes in these regulations may either provide opportunities for local governments to raise new revenue or limit them.

These children rejoice over their new school. School funding reform has produced more resources to assist local districts in building schools.

In recent years, the interaction between state and local finances in Texas has resulted in a sharp rise in local property taxes. Total local property tax collections nearly doubled in the years between 1984 and 1995, from $8 billion to almost $16 billion. School district property taxes more than doubled during this period, rising from about $4 billion to over $9 billion.[19]

How is the state responsible for these increases? The state contributed to these increases by cutting back on state aid. This is clearest with regard to school district aid. To avoid further state tax increases during some tight years for the state, the state share of funding for the public schools drifted from 46.9 percent in 1989 to 45.2 percent in 1994.[20] During the same period, wealthier school districts experienced a sharp decline in state support as the state tried to reduce the inequality in per pupil expenditure between rich and poor districts (see Chapter 13). The result was the doubling of school district taxes mentioned above.

The sharp rise in property taxes in the 1990s and the increases in state revenues prompted Governor Bush to propose a sweeping tax reform system that would have shifted more of the burden of public school funding to the state, thereby reducing property tax burdens. Much of the governor's program was not enacted, but the legislature did increase the homestead exemption from $5,000 of assessed value to $15,000 for school district property tax purposes.[21] Although that provides some relief from school property taxes, it does not address the rising county and city taxes. As the state attempts to hold the line on taxes, rising local taxes are a likely consequence.

A Final Assessment of the Texas Revenue System

Does Texas conform to good public-finance standards? The Select Committee on Tax Equity, created by the legislature in 1987, used four criteria to judge the state's tax system:[22]

- *Adequacy:* Does the tax system provide enough revenue to meet the state's needs?
- *Equity:* Is the tax system fair to all types of taxpayers?
- *Economic efficiency:* Does the tax system have any adverse effects on economic development?
- *Simplicity:* Is the tax system easy to administer?

Using these criteria, the committee identified several problems with the Texas tax system.

First, that system has not been consistently adequate to meet the state's financial needs. Whereas spending has grown as fast as—or faster than—the economy, tax revenues have not. So the legislature has had to scramble for new sources of revenue in some years. As noted above, in 1991 the legislature faced revenue estimates that fell over $4 billion short of what was needed just to maintain existing state services. By contrast, the state finished the 1996–1997 biennium with a $1.7 billion surplus of revenues over expenditures.[23] This does not mean that the state has solved its revenue problems. The surplus reflects a thriving Texas economy in the 1990s. A weaker economy would produce less revenue.

There are two **tax equity** problems with Texas taxes. First, taxes on individuals tend to be **regressive taxes**—that is, they fall more heavily on low- and middle-income taxpayers than on those with higher incomes. Citizens for Tax Justice reported in 1994 that the poorest one-fifth of Texas families paid more than 13 percent of their income in state and local taxes each year; the wealthiest 1 percent of the population paid just over 4 percent.[24] The regressive nature of the system is the product of the state's heavy dependence on the sales tax.

The second equity problem is that business taxes (primarily the corporation franchise tax) fall more heavily on some businesses than others. Specifically, the franchise tax is a tax on businesses that are organized as corporations—not those organized as partnerships or sole proprietorships. The legislature broadened the tax in 1991, when it changed the franchise tax from a tax on capital to a tax on income.[25] But the top ten corporations in Texas still pay 90 percent of all franchise taxes.[26]

Targeting the state's business tax toward corporations may have an adverse effect on economic growth, reducing the **economic efficiency** of the state's economy. Large corporations may see the franchise tax as an undue burden and choose to look for a more favorable climate elsewhere.

Finally, the Texas tax system fails the simplicity test. The rules governing the sales tax—which items are taxed and which are not taxed—are confusing, complicating matters for individual taxpayers and for administrators. In 1991, lawmakers did remove some of the exceptions to the sales tax, but administration of the tax still is complicated.

The revenue fixes of the early 1990s did not address the fundamental problems of Texas public finance. The tax system still fails the test of adequacy. And the system still places a heavier burden on low- and middle-income taxpayers than on upper-income taxpayers. In fact, a revitalized economy may prevent the state from confronting its public-finance problems. The sweeping overhaul of the revenue system that the state needs probably will not happen in the absence of a financial crisis in Texas. Although taxes in the state are not high, Texans have become resistant to tax increases. The legislature literally may be forced to let things get worse before they can get better.

Notes

1. Legislative Budget Board, *Fiscal Size Up: 1994–95* (Austin, 1994), 4–9.
2. Texas Constitution, Art. III, Sec. 49a.
3. U.S. Advisory Commission on Intergovernmental Relations (ACIR), *Significant Features of Fiscal Federalism* (Washington, DC: U.S. Government Printing Office, 1991), 1:4–5.
4. Legislative Budget Board, *Fiscal Size Up: 1998–99,* 1–12 through 1–13.
5. Texas Comptroller of Public Accounts, *Special Financial Report,* December 1993, 20–21.
6. Texas Comptroller of Public Accounts, *Fiscal Notes,* December 1991, 6–7.
7. Legislative Budget Board, *Fiscal Size Up: 1992–93,* 2–3.
8. *The Book of the States: 1998–99 Edition,* vol. 32 (Lexington, KY: Council of State Governments, 1998), p. 270.
9. Texas Comptroller of Public Accounts, *Fiscal Notes,* July 1991, 1.
10. Legislative Budget Board, *Fiscal Size Up: 1998–1999,* 3–4.
11. Legislative Budget Board, *Fiscal Size Up: 1998–99,* 3–12.
12. Legislative Budget Board, *Fiscal Size Up: 1998–99,* p. 1–2.
13. Legislative Budget Board, *Fiscal Size Up: 1998–99,* p. 1–2.
14. *Ruiz* v. *Estelle,* 66 F.2d 854 (1982).
15. *Lelsz* v. *Kavanagh,* 783 F.Supp. 286 (1991).
16. Texas Comptroller of Public Accounts, *Fiscal Notes,* April 1992, 5–8.
17. Texas Comptroller of Public Accounts, *Fiscal Notes,* April 1991, 3.
18. Cited in "Paying for Federal Mandates," *Fiscal Notes,* (April 1995), 1.
19. Legislative Budget Board, *Fiscal Size Up: 1998–99,* p. 2–9.
20. Legislative Budget Board, *Fiscal Size Up: 1998–99,* p. 6–5.

21. Legislative Budget Board, *Fiscal Size Up: 1998–99,* p. 2–11.
22. Select Committee on Tax Equity, *Rethinking Texas Taxes: Final Report of the Select Committee on Tax Equity* (Austin, 1989), 2 vols, 1:29.
23. Legislative Budget Board, *Fiscal Size Up: 1998–99,* 2-1.
24. Citizens for Tax Justice and the Institute on Taxation & Economic Policy, *Who Pays? A Distributional Analysis of the Tax Systems in All 50 States* (Washington, DC: Citizens for Tax Justice and Institute on Taxation & Economic Policy, 1996), p. 2.
25. Legislative Budget Board, *Fiscal Size Up: 1992–93,* 2-4.
26. "Inside the Franchise Tax," *Fiscal Notes,* January 1995, 6.

12

Social Welfare Policy in Texas

C H A P T E R O U T L I N E

Penny had been working and supporting herself. She faced her responsibilities and took care of herself the way people are generally expected to do. Then she discovered that she was pregnant. As a single woman without health insurance, her economic situation was suddenly overwhelming. At first she couldn't even afford to see a doctor. When she finally did, the physician told her the pregnancy was high risk and that she couldn't work. When she sought help from the state, at first she qualified for Medicaid (to help with the medical costs of the pregnancy), but was denied food stamps—and sometimes went hungry. After the baby was born, she qualified for a monthly cash payment and received other benefits. Altogether she spent two years on welfare.[1]

This story illustrates several points about economic well-being and social welfare policy. First, it reminds us that many people live at the very margins of economic existence. They are responsible, hard-working people, but their earnings provide no surplus as a buffer against economic disaster. A lost job or an unexpected pregnancy can plunge them into economic distress.

Second, this story points out that contemporary social welfare programs are actually a complex set of individual policies, each of which has its own eligibility rules. Qualifying for one benefit may—or may not—qualify one for another program.

Third, this story reminds us that once circumstances force someone onto welfare, it often takes time for them to get out of the system. National studies have found that although the median time on welfare was about eight months, about 30 percent of welfare recipients are on welfare for a two-year period.[2]

This chapter will try to answer several important questions about social welfare policy in Texas:

- What is social welfare policy and why is it needed?
- How did national social welfare policy evolve and how does it shape the way Texas deals with social welfare policy?
- How have Texas norms shaped the impact of national social welfare policies on Texans?
- How did the movement to reform social welfare policy evolve at the national level and in Texas?
- How are reform efforts working, and what are the prospects for the future?

What Is Social Welfare Policy and Why Is It Needed?

Social welfare policies provide what former President Reagan called the **social safety net.** That is, they protect those who fall on economic hard times from economic disaster by providing cash and services to tide them over until they can get back on their feet. For a long time, America was regarded as the land of opportunity, and individuals were expected to take care of themselves by thrift and hard work. Families, charitable or religious organizations, or (as a last resort) the local governments would take care of the few who could not take care of themselves; little government effort was expected to be necessary. Thus, organized social welfare policies of the state or national government were not given serious consideration.[3]

The **Great Depression** of the 1930s and the widespread economic hardship it brought with it began to change public attitudes toward those in economic need. By the time Franklin Roosevelt became president in 1933, a third of the national labor force was unemployed.[4] With so many ordinary good folk out of work, people realized that economic hardship was not just the result of laziness or personal ineptness—almost anyone could be touched by economic hardship. Moreover, it became apparent that the problem was too large for the local governments, or even the states, to handle. The magnitude of the problem would require the federal government's involvement.

The **self-reliance model** of economic thinking influenced Texans' notions about social welfare policy even more strongly than it had influenced the nation as a whole. Texans have historically been proud of the strength of their economy and the economic opportunities it offered. The Texas economy usually outperforms the national economy in creating jobs, and unemployment is usually lower in Texas than nationally.[5] Texans seem well-off compared to residents of other states. Its per capita gross state product in 1994 put Texas in seventeenth place among the states. In per capita personal income, Texas ranked twenty-sixth among the states.[6] Thus, Texas appears to be the land of economic opportunity, where there should be little need for state programs to assist the needy. People often point out that jobs and opportunities abound, so why should the government be taking care of people?

But, the Texas of abundant economic opportunity is not experienced by all. Some live in a different Texas where opportunities are fewer and farther between. Indeed, many Texans experience widespread poverty and need. In 1995, Texas ranked sixth among the states in the percent of its population living in poverty (17.4 percent). The percent of the population receiving food stamps (13.7 percent) put Texas in fifth place among the states. More than a fifth of Texas' school-aged children lived in poverty in 1995, putting Texas in tenth place in this category.[7] Thus, for many people Texas is a place of need and dependence.

Although poverty and need can be found in many places in Texas, they are especially prevalent in the Rio Grande valley (an area located between an imaginary line from El Paso to Corpus Christi and the Rio Grande River). (See Figure 12.1.) If treated as a separate state, this mythical "**State of South Texas**" has the highest poverty rate in the nation, with nearly one-third of the population living below the poverty line. The area also has a higher unemployment rate than any of the 50 states (9.6 percent). Its per capita income is lower than any of the 50 states ($15,570 compared with $22,536 for the rest of Texas).[8] In this part of Texas, economic need is a way of life.

Thus, while Texas opens the door of economic opportunity to many, some of its residents lag behind in the greatest poverty found in the nation. Because

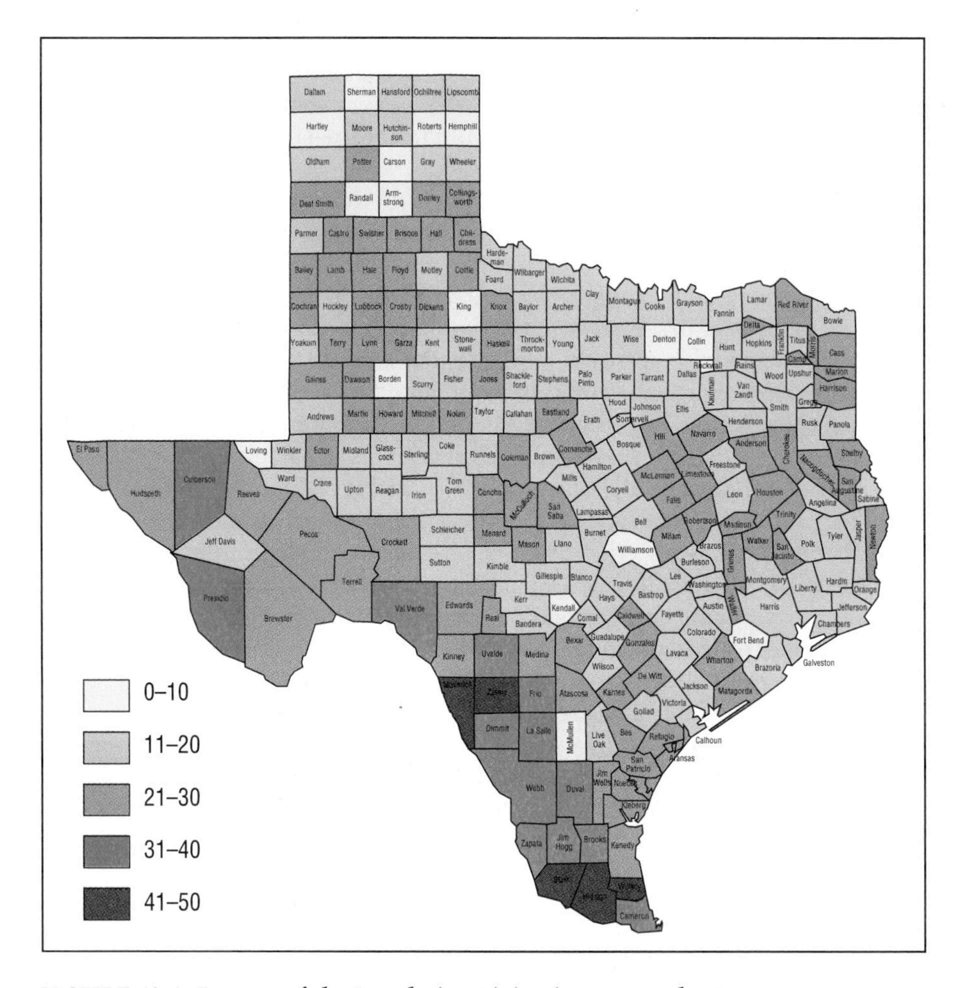

FIGURE 12.1 Percent of the Population Living in Poverty, by County, 1993
Source: Map generated from data made available by the U.S. Census Bureau on their web site **(http://www.census.gov).** See specifically, "State & County Income and Poverty Estimates, 1993."

many Texans do not participate in the benefits of a thriving Texas economy, finding a fair and equitable social welfare policy is a serious challenge to Texas.

Basic Elements of Social Welfare Programs

The basic structure of the welfare system was included in the **Social Security Act** passed by Congress in 1935. That law established a set of categorical aids (cash grants) to assist various types of needy people: dependent children, the aged, the blind, and the totally and permanently disabled. **Aid to Families with Dependent Children (AFDC)** became the largest of these programs, making payments to the most recipients. It was targeted to aid children no older than sixteen years of age who were "living in homes in which there was no adult person, other than the one needed to care for the child or children, who is able to work and provide the family with reasonable subsistence."[9] In reality, the program was intended to help female-headed households with dependent children. The program retained this focus for most of its history, but the law was later liberalized so that states could help needy two-parent families.

AFDC was a joint program of the national and state governments, with both levels sharing the cost of the program and the state governments administering the program. The states could also set benefit levels and set regulations for recipients, within the framework of the national law. Each state had to create the administrative structures necessary to screen applicants and pay benefits.

AFDC rules were modified several times after it was established. A 1961 change permitted (but did not require) states to pay benefits to families with an unemployed father. The Work Incentive (WIN) program was added in 1967 to provide training and assistance to help welfare recipients find work. In 1988 the Family Support Act required all able-bodied recipients with children aged three or older to participate in a program of education, training, and employment to enable them to become self-sufficient. By 1990, states were required to provide benefits to children in two-parent families who were needy because of unemployment.[10]

Although AFDC became the principal source of cash assistance to those in economic need, other programs of assistance were added through the years. To help poor families acquire food, Congress passed the Food Stamp Act of 1964. The **Food Stamp Program** is paid for by the national government, with the states handling administration. Eligible families receive an allocation of food stamps that can be used to purchase food in grocery stores.

Medicaid, which was created by the 1965 amendments to the Social Security Act, makes medical services available to the poor. Those who are eligible receive a Medicaid card that can be presented to doctors, hospitals, and other medical vendors for services. The vendors agree to collect their fees from Medicaid and not to bill the Medicaid patient. The national government and the states jointly fund Medicaid.

Another type of benefit available to some needy families is housing assistance. Through the public housing program begun in the 1930s, the national government made funds available to local governments to assist them in building publicly-owned housing units that could be rented to the poor at below-market rates. Many major American cities built large housing projects with these funds, many of which continue in operation today. Starting in the 1960s, the national government began to make rent-subsidy programs available to assist the poor with housing needs without consigning them to public housing projects.

As America entered the 1990s, the needy could be assisted by a package of benefits. AFDC was the principal source of cash. Additional services, such as food stamps, Medicaid, and housing subsidies were available to those who

Potential welfare recipients receive information from a caseworker.

qualified. Most AFDC recipients would be eligible for a bundle of services, such as food stamps and Medicaid. Some who were not eligible for AFDC cash grants might receive one or more of the other services provided, such as food stamps or Medicaid.

While rules of eligibility vary from one program to another, the one common feature of these programs is that they are **means-tested.** Eligibility for all of the programs for the poor takes into account the means (financial resources) of the recipient. In other words, an individual's income must fall below some stipulated level before help can be given from these programs. Additional requirements may exist, but the first hurdle to cross in getting assistance is income.

Historical Overview of Social Welfare Policy in Texas

National social welfare programs were designed as grant-in-aid programs that depended heavily on state administration. Thus, while the national government provided much of the money and set many of the eligibility rules, the states were assigned an important administrative role. Not only did they have to develop administrative structures to deliver the programs, but they also were given some discretion in many programs to shape the rules to suit their own resources and their own notions about how such programs should be run. Thus, to fully grasp the operation of these programs, state decisions must be taken into account. It is important, therefore, to comprehend the role of Texas government in shaping these programs.

The historical tendency in Texas welfare policy has been to impose stringent requirements for eligibility and to set low levels for benefits. The Texas Constitution specifically limits the share of the state budget that can be allocated to "assistance and medical care to needy aged, needy blind, needy children, and totally disabled" to 1 percent of the state budget.[11] This limit is not as restrictive as it sounds, because only the state's funds are counted. Many of the dollars spent in this area come from the federal government. In 1994, a single parent with two children could earn no more than $402 to qualify for minimum AFDC benefits. If such a family qualified for maximum benefits, it received $188 per month. This benefit level ranked forty-seventh among the states.[12] Of course, a family that received AFDC benefits was also eligible for food stamps and Medicaid. Counting a bundle of benefits that included an AFDC cash grant, food stamps, Medicaid, and an Earned Income Credit from the national income tax, a family's income would be raised to two-thirds of the income of one full-time minimum-wage job or 40 percent of the maximum income to be counted as living in poverty.[13] Thus, the Texas policy provided some relief for the needy, but fell far short of raising a family above the poverty line. The policy was apparently designed to ease the worst of poverty without making public assistance too comfortable.

Despite the comparatively low level of benefits provided by the state, the bite taken out of the state budget by such services is significant. As noted in Chapter 11, the budget category of health and human services, which includes the social welfare services discussed here, has been the second largest expenditure category in recent years. Much of the growth in this category has been attributable to growth in the cost of Medicaid services. The legislature appropriated $26 billion for services in this category for the 1998–1999 biennium, with $12.8 billion going to the Department of Health (which handles most Medicaid payments) and $7 billion going to the Department of Human Services (which administers AFDC and food stamp distribution).[14]

Change and Social Welfare Policy

By the 1990s, a consensus had emerged in American politics on the need for welfare reform. Both Democratic and Republican national leaders agreed that the existing welfare programs were no longer satisfactory. Many believed that the welfare programs fostered economic dependence and undermined individual initiative. Some thought they contributed to the problem of out-of-wedlock births because AFDC payments increased as the number of children increased. Some were simply concerned about the rising costs of social welfare programs. Others thought that welfare programs were insufficient to meet the needs of those whose job skills were too poor to get them jobs that could raise them out of poverty. As a result, welfare reform became a hot topic for debate.

The states began to experiment with welfare reform even before the national government. The governors of Michigan and Wisconsin, for example, made national reputations for themselves by promoting new approaches to getting people off welfare and into jobs.[15] In Texas, Governor Bush pushed welfare reform to the center of the public agenda in his campaign against Governor Richards in 1994.

State reform of shared programs like social welfare can be difficult. States that choose to try out new approaches to welfare, but who wish to continue receiving federal funds to assist with welfare costs, must get permission from the federal government. Specifically, states must apply for a waiver of federal rules if they want to try a different approach. This **waiver request** procedure can be slow, cumbersome, and frustrating to state political leaders.

Texas Welfare Reform

The Texas legislature began to work on restructuring welfare services in its regular session in 1993. This legislative session focused on restructuring the institutions that deliver social welfare services. Recognizing that social welfare programs were administered by a number of separate agencies, the legislature created the Health and Human Services Commission and made it responsible for coordinating the work of eleven agencies.[16] The Health and Human Services Commission was required to draft a strategic plan for health and human services and for developing a consolidated budget for agency appropriations.

Between the 1993 and 1995 sessions of the legislature, the office of the Texas Comptroller of Public Accounts was commissioned to do a study of social welfare programs and to make suggestions for reform to the legislature. That report, which was delivered to the legislature in January 1995, set five goals for welfare reform in Texas:

- Encourage personal responsibility and the preservation of families.
- Prevent at-risk Texans from depending on welfare.
- Prevent Texans from returning to welfare once they're off.
- Enable Texans with disabilities to leave public assistance.
- Cut the bureaucracy, reduce fraud, and improve services to save money.[17]

The report laid out a set of recommendations for the legislature's consideration as a plan for welfare reform.

The legislature pushed forward with welfare reform during its 1995 regular session. In the area of Medicaid services, the legislature instructed agencies to seek the national government's approval of a plan to enroll Medicaid recipients in managed care programs, such as Health Maintenance Organizations (HMOs) or Preferred Provider Organizations (PPOs) as an alternative to the traditional reimbursement-for-services program. Legislators believed that such a plan could provide more services to more people at no greater cost than the traditional Medicaid program.[18] Texas implemented several managed care pilot projects and started negotiations with the national government for a waiver permitting more widespread application of the managed care approach.

To reform the AFDC system, the legislature passed House Bill 1863, called the Welfare Reform Bill for Texas. Welfare applicants were required to sign a Personal Responsibility Agreement as a condition to eligibility. In the statement the applicant agrees to abide by program rules and work toward self-sufficiency. Recipients also agree to take part in programs, such as job training, schooling, or literacy training that will assist them toward independence. The state may impose penalties on those who break their agreement. Additional provisions included:

- requiring the Department of Human services to conduct a needs assessment for those welfare clients who are required to participate in employment services;
- setting a time limit on cash benefits, with the limit determined by a client's functional literacy and work experience;
- implementing additional fraud protection techniques, such as finger-print imaging of clients; and
- allocating the responsibility for job training programs and job placement activities to the Texas Workforce Commission.[19]

Parts of this bill could be put into place immediately but the most dramatic changes required approval of the national government to ensure that federal funds would continue. To get permission from the federal government to deviate from its welfare rules, Texas officials had to apply for a waiver from the national rules. Waiting on the waiver delayed implementation of the Texas reforms for a year. It took Texas officials until March 1996 to get the waiver, and the new program went into effect on June 1, 1996.[20]

National Welfare Reform

While Texas and other states were working on their own approaches to welfare reform, the U.S. Congress continued to be interested as well. After the Republican Party gained control of Congress in 1994, welfare reform was a major commitment of the new Republican leadership in the House of Representatives. The national welfare reform bill (the Personal Responsibility and Work Opportunity Reconciliation Act of 1996), which Congress passed and the president quickly signed into law in August 1996, overshadowed the Texas welfare reform program. The national law did not completely undo the state efforts. For Texas, the challenge was to find a way to make the national reforms fit the goals of state policy and to ensure that Texas got a fair share of national resources so that the state could deal effectively with those in need. States that had received waivers before August 22, 1996 (the date the president signed the bill into law), were granted the right to implement their own programs. But, if the state's program did not address a provision of the federal law, then the federal provision would have to be implemented. Texas chose to implement the provisions of the Texas Welfare Reform Act, which had been granted waivers in spring 1996.

The **Personal Responsibility and Work Opportunity Reconciliation Act of 1996** (PRWORA) made several significant revisions in national welfare policy that affected Texas and other states. AFDC was converted from an entitlement program to a block grant program called **Temporary Assistance to Needy Families (TANF).** As an entitlement program, AFDC committed the national government and the states to providing assistance to every qualified applicant. The national and state governments were essentially required to provide the funds necessary to pay cash grants to all those where were entitled to assistance. The new cash grant program, TANF, makes block grants of specific amounts of money to each state according to a formula contained in the national law. Each state is then responsible to meet the needs for public assistance out of the funds made available. TANF funds may be used for any purpose authorized under previously existing programs. Specifically, money can be spent for cash assistance, childcare, educational activities designed to increase self-sufficiency, job training, and work activities. Funds may not be used for medical assistance, except for pre-pregnancy family planning.

The amount of each state's TANF grant is based on 1994, 1995, or 1992–1994 average federal payments, whichever is highest. States are required to maintain 80 percent of their 1994 expenditures (or 75 percent if they meet requirements to put targeted proportions of their recipients to work). At the 80-percent-of-previous-expenditures level, Texas must spend $251.4 million annually. States with high population growth and/or low benefits receive a 2.5 percent increase over the basic formula amount. Texas' TANF Block Grant is set at $486.3 million through fiscal year 2002. Supplemental funding adds $12.7 million starting in fiscal year 1998 and increasing each year through 2001.

One of the key provisions of the TANF program was a time limit on eligibility for benefits. The national legislation limited eligibility to two years of continuous benefits and a five-year lifetime limit. Because Texas had already received a waiver to put its own reforms into effect, the benefit limits included in the Texas program were allowed to continue. As noted, the Texas limits take into consideration a person's education and work experience, and can vary from 12 to 36 months. (See Table 12.1.)

While the Food Stamp Program continues as an entitlement program with no spending cap, additional restrictions are placed on eligibility. Immigrants who are legal permanent residents ceased to be eligible for food stamps in August 1997. Able-bodied adults with no dependents between the ages of eighteen and fifty are limited to three months of food stamp benefits in a three-year period, unless they are working at least twenty hours per week or participating in a work training program for at least twenty hours per week. Lastly, the formula for determining food stamp allocations was lowered to

The Lone Star Card replaced printed food stamps as a means of providing food assistance to the needy in Texas.

100 percent (from 103 percent) of the cost of the Department of Agriculture's Thrifty Food Plan.

Texas Welfare Management Reforms

In addition to moving people from welfare to work, Texas has also been interested in ways to reduce welfare fraud. One early effort involved replacing food stamps with the **Lone Star debit card.** Instead of using the traditional printed stamps, Texas gave recipients a debit card credited with the appropriate benefit amount. The card acts like a debit card that can be run through the same scanners in grocery stores and elsewhere that have been used for years with credit cards and debit cards. This program was designed to allow the state to distribute food stamp benefits in a way that prevented their fraudulent use. It avoided the sale of the stamps in the black market, thus preventing the diversion of benefits into unauthorized use.

The Lone Star Image System, a statewide finger-imaging system, was designed to prevent recipients from collecting benefits in different places under different names. With the finger-imaging system, a person's correct identity can be quickly discovered. After a successful pilot project in Bexar and Guadalupe counties, the legislature provided funding to expand the project in 1997. It was expected to be fully implemented by the end of 1998.[21]

Table 12.1 Major Social Welfare Programs and Their Requirements in Texas, 1998

Program Name	Type of Benefits	Eligibility	Time Limits
TANF (Temporary Assistance to Needy Families)	Provides cash payments	• Child must be deprived of parental support due to death, absence, incapacity, or unemployment of one or both parents. • Child must be under eighteen. • Child must be a U.S. citizen or a legal permanent resident who was admitted before August 22, 1996. (All other legal permanent residents are barred from participation for five years after their entry.) • Family must be in financial need according to DHS guidelines. • Family must not have assets valued at more than $1,000. (The value of a car with Blue Book value under $4,650 is exempted.)	• twelve months for a caretaker with at least a high school diploma (or the equivalent) and at least eighteen months of work history. • twenty-four months for a caretaker who has completed three years of high school and six to eighteen months of work history. (Also eligible for twelve months of transitional benefits.) • thirty-six months for a caretaker who has completed less than three years of high school and has less than six months of recent work history. (Also eligible for twelve months of transitional benefits.)
TANF-UP (TANF Unemployed Parent)	Pays cash benefit	Children of two-parent households where the parents are working more than one hundred hours per month, yet meet the other income and resource guidelines for TANF.	Same as for regular TANF.
Food Stamps	Provides grant to buy food	• Household's gross family income must be at or below 130 percent of the federal poverty level ($16,050 for a family of four). • Net income, after taking allowable deductions, must also meet a means test.	Individual able-bodied recipients between ages of eighteen and fifty are limited to receiving food stamps for a total of three months in a thirty-six-month period unless they work at least twenty hours per week or participate in job training or community service volunteer program.

Table 12.1 *Cont.*

Program Name	Type of Benefits	Eligibility	Time Limits
Food Stamps (*cont.*)	Provides grant to buy food (*cont.*)	• Family must not have assets valued at more than $2,000. (The value of a car with Blue Book value under $4,650 is exempted.)	
Medicaid for Families and Children	Pays for medical care	• TANF recipients and children and pregnant women who are ineligible for TANF are eligible. • Caregivers and second parent of deprived children are eligible. • Immigrants who were admitted prior to August 22, 1996, are eligible.	
Medically Needy Program	Pays for medical care	• Children under 18 • Pregnant women • Caretakers of dependent children who are eligible	

Source: Compiled from information avialable on the web site of the Texas Department of Human Services (**http://www.dhs.state.tx.us**).

To help detect Medicaid fraud, Texas turned to neural-network technology. This technology had previously been found useful in detecting fraudulent uses of credit cards. Neural-network technology has the ability to look at large amounts of data simultaneously and detect patterns that look suspicious and warrant additional investigation. A pilot project produced good results, and the state legislature funded expansion of the project in 1997.[22]

Another innovation undertaken by the state was aimed at improving the processes used to determine eligibility for benefits. The state has been working on an integrated system to determine eligibility for welfare benefits. This project, called **TIES** (Texas Integrated Eligibility System), began as a result of legislation (HB 1863) passed in 1995. The Texas legislature ordered the Health and Human Services Commission to make eligibility processes more efficient and cost effective. The original plan included the possibility of contracting out the eligibility determination process to a private company. The Department of Human Services (DHS) entered into a contract with EDS for the development of the system, and EDS developed an alliance with Unisys to perform this work. The new eligibility system emphasized gathering and analysis of information and documents from potential clients by mail and telephone so that the information could be verified before the client came to a DHS office. This would permit eligibility specialists working for DHS to concentrate on client needs after eligibility information had already been verified.

Although the national government ruled that eligibility for government services could not be handled by a private company, the 1997 session of the legislature extended the project with new legislation (HB 2777) and the acronym took on new meaning: Texas Integrated Enrollment and Services.[23] The new legislation stipulates that the governor, the Legislative Budget Board, and appropriate federal officials must approve any plans for contracting with private companies. The new plans call for the development of specifications for an automated eligibility system to be developed by April 1998. A contractor would be selected by November 1998, and a pilot project begun in November 1999. Statewide implementation of the automated system was expected to take an additional two years.[24]

Welfare Reform: Policy Success Now and Later?

Although welfare reform has not been in place long, it is still helpful to evaluate the policy changes and assess their impact. Some effort must be made to see who is helped and who is harmed by reform.

Some people began to experience adverse effects almost immediately after the reforms went into effect. One such group were legal immigrants living in poor areas of the state. The national legislation cut off food stamps to legal immigrants. In Texas, about 121,000 legal immigrants were cut from the food stamp rolls in the fall of 1997. Many of them lived in depressed areas in South Texas. About 13,000 of those losing food stamp benefits were children.[25] To ease the blow, the state of Texas agreed to provide food benefits to legal immigrants, but only to those who were elderly or disabled. That still left thousands of children without this support.[26] Ultimately, the national government changed its mind on this issue. In June 1998, Congress restored food stamp aid, but only to those immigrants who had legally entered the country before August 1996. The new aid was further restricted to those immigrants who were children (under eighteen), elderly (over sixty-five), or disabled.[27]

Because the goal of all welfare reformers has been to get people off welfare, it is logical to examine the evidence to see how well this goal has been achieved. In this respect, the change has exceeded most expectations. Figure 12.2 shows that the average number of people receiving cash benefits through TANF (previously AFDC) awards has indeed dropped in recent years, and is projected to continue to drop through the end of this century. Thus, there is a strong temptation to conclude that the policy has been widely successful. But, Figure 12.2 also shows that unemployment dropped each year after 1992. While the number of TANF recipients dropped more slowly than did unem-

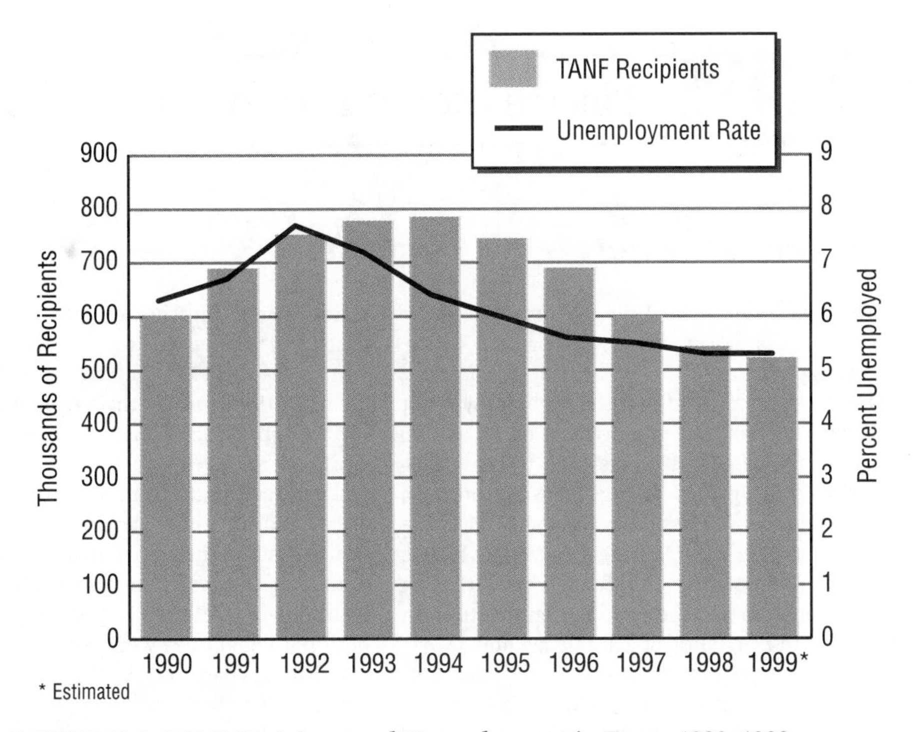

FIGURE 12.2 TANF Recipients and Unemployment in Texas, 1990–1999
Source: TANF recipient data from Legislative Budget Board, Fiscal Size Up: 1998–99 *(Austin: Legislative Budget Board, 1998), p. 5-2. Unemployment data from "State Economic Forecast, Fall, 1997," on Comptroller of Public Accounts web site (***http://www.cpa.state.tx.us/fest9731.html***).*

ployment, it seems apparent that a major part of the reduction in welfare recipients must have been the result of an improving economy.

Some critics have argued that the problems of welfare reform have been disguised by the buoyant economy and that the true problems would not be revealed until a recession occurs.[28] These critics point out that the current policies for caring for the needy work well when the economy is healthy and the number of recipients is falling naturally. The question for the future is, "How well will these policies perform should the economy go into a recession and unemployment soar?"

Another problem that has not been fully confronted is that of finding jobs for welfare recipients. Both the Texas law and the national law give first priority to the goal of moving people from welfare to jobs. In Texas the responsibility for helping people find jobs has been placed on the **Texas Workforce Commission,** created by the Texas welfare reform bill (HB 1863). As the box in this chapter explains, workforce development has been one of the weaknesses that limits economic development in Texas. Thus, the Workforce Commission has a difficult challenge: to train workers and find jobs for them. And, the Workforce Commission has been criticized for moving

The Changing Face of Texas Politics

Workforce Development: Can the Texas Workforce Commission Really Move People from Welfare to Work?

Gaining Ground, the 1995 performance audit of the Texas government, was critical of the existing program of workforce development.[1] The report concluded that the problem was not a lack of resources but a lack of focus. To sharpen the focus of Texas's job-training programs, *Gaining Ground* urged the creation of a single department to take responsibility for the state's diverse job-training programs. House Bill 1863, passed by the Texas Legislature in 1995, consolidated the state's programs to train workers in the hands of a single agency.

The legislation transformed the Texas Employment Commission into the Texas Workforce Commission. The commission retained its old responsibilities and added a division to manage workforce development programs. The agency is supervised by a three-member commission, appointed by the governor. The commissioners choose an executive director, who supervises the agency's operations. But, an organizational change alone is not likely to produce a well-trained workforce in Texas. Much depended on how well the agency followed through on the real challenge: to devise job-training programs that actually work, programs that train people well for jobs that really exist.

As a result of the welfare reforms passed by Texas in 1995, and by the national government in 1996, the Texas Workforce Commission was assigned an even greater challenge: moving welfare recipients from welfare to work. The agency came under severe scrutiny by state officials when the state failed to meet federally-mandated targets for moving welfare recipients into jobs by October 1, 1997 (a year after the national legislation went into effect). The federal officials had dictated that each state should move 25 percent of single-parent welfare households and 75 percent of two-parent welfare households into jobs or job-training programs by that date. Texas met the goal for single-parent households, but had placed only 47 percent of two-parent households by the deadline. Although most other states failed to meet the target also, Texas legislators grilled welfare officials about the failure.[2]

How had the Workforce Commission failed to meet its first big challenge? One oft repeated explanation was that the goals were simply

slowly in organizing for its tasks and for contributing to the state's failure to move welfare recipients into jobs quickly enough. At the end of the first year under national reform, Texas had failed to place the mandated proportion of welfare recipients in jobs.[29] It should be noted that this aspect of the reforms will be made even more difficult in times of economic recession. Indeed, the Workforce Commission has not yet been tested under those conditions.

A U.S. General Accounting Office study of job placement conducted for Congress found that while Texas was doing well at removing people from the welfare rolls, it was doing more poorly than other states in placing former welfare recipients in jobs. The report showed that Texas had cut the number unrealistic. Workforce officials pointed out that 170,000 Texans had left welfare rolls since the inception of the Texas program two years earlier and that welfare rolls had dropped by 26 percent.[3]

Although the bar may have been set too high by federal officials, part of the problem was the slow organization of the Workforce Commission. Much of the agency's real work of job placement is done through local workforce boards. The agency's plans call for a total of twenty-eight such boards. By April 1998, only nine of the proposed boards had submitted plans to be state and had become fully operational. Plans had been certified for an additional seventeen boards, but they were not yet operational. Two had not even submitted plans by this date. One of the two local boards that was not organized was in the Rio Grande Valley, where unemployment was running around 17 percent.[4]

There are some success stories. One of the first local workforce boards to get organized was in Dallas county. In December 1997, the Dallas officials reported that they had placed 400 welfare clients in jobs per month since June 1997.[5] Austin was also reported to have a successful program in 1997.[6]

The Texas Workforce Commission has been called upon to be the catalyst for change that allows welfare reform to succeed. So far, its results have been mixed. It is overseeing some successful programs in booming economies in Austin and Dallas. The real challenge, however, will be in finding enough adequate jobs in the more difficult situation in the Rio Grande Valley. There the results have been bleak. Reductions in the number of welfare recipients have been impressive, but they seem more attributable to good luck than to good programming. The challenge is in south Texas, and there the challenge is largely unmet. ★

[1]Texas Comptroller of Public Accounts, *Gaining Ground*, vol. 1 (Austin, 1995), Chap. 6.

[2]Bill Minutaglio, "Welfare Officials Grilled on Failure to Meet U.S. Guidelines," *Dallas Morning News* (October 29, 1997), p. 24A.

[3]David Herndon and Diane Rath, "Progress in Texas' Welfare Reform," *Austin American-Statesman* (September 30, 1997), p. A11. (David Herndon is the Chairman of the Department of Human Services and Diane Rath is Commissioner of the Texas Workforce Commission.)

[4]Rebeca Rodriguez and Suzanne Gamboa, "Review Mixed on Job-Training Plan," *Austin American-Statesman* (April 17, 1998), p. B1.

[5]Bill Minutaglio, "State Workforce Commission Falls Under Increased Scrutiny," *Dallas Morning News* (December 14, 1997), p. 1A.

[6]Rodriguez and Gamboa, "Review Mixed on Job-Training Plan."

of welfare recipients by 20 percent between 1995 and 1997, but had placed only about 13 percent of them in jobs. By contrast, Louisiana cut welfare rolls by 29 percent and placed 17 percent of former recipients in jobs. Wisconsin, an early pioneer in welfare reform, cut recipients by 52 percent and placed 48 percent of them in jobs.[30]

Several problems appear on the horizon. Now that the major cash assistance program has been converted from an entitlement program to the TANF block grant program, the federal government makes available a fixed and limited amount for cash assistance in any year. A severe downturn in the economy, such as Texas experienced in the mid-1980s, might exhaust the fund and make it impossible for the state to meet the needs of the poor. Given the fact that Texas has a significant proportion of its population in poverty, even in good times, how well can current policies be expected to perform under adversity? That is the lingering question still to be confronted.

One flaw in the Texas approach has been revealed under good conditions. Texas introduced the Lone Star card as an innovative way of delivering food stamp and cash benefits while reducing the opportunity for fraud. For this system to operate, the state needed an electronic network that could instantaneously let vendors know whether the cardholder still had unexpended benefits. Instead of creating the network itself, the state contracted this task out to a private company. Transactive, a subsidiary of Gtech, the same company that runs the state's lottery network, won the contract. The contract stipulated that the company would be reimbursed according to the number of transactions processed. By January 1998, the number of transactions had dropped by 39 percent since the program's inception in 1995. As a result, the fees paid to the company had dropped by about $1 million per month.[31] Transactive sold its contract to Citicorp Services of Illinois in February 1998.[32] It remains to be seen whether this privatized approach to benefit delivery will survive and how expensive it may ultimately become to the state, should the contact have to be renegotiated.

The lessons of the Lone Star Card also need to be considered as the state launches TIES, its ambitious program for integrated screening of potential beneficiaries of a variety of state programs. The state had originally intended to turn over the applicant screening process entirely to a private contractor. It was prevented from doing so by the national government, which refused to grant a waiver for this program. Still the development of the program has already involved substantial participation by two private companies, EDS and Unisys, and the operation of the program may involve dependence on private technology. The state will need to remember the lesson of the Lone Star card: private companies make a profit when the number of recipients is large. Because the state's goal is to reduce recipients, the conflict between its goals and the interests of private companies may continue to be problematic.

Thus, the problem with welfare reform in Texas thus far is that there is no way of knowing if it is a plan for all seasons and all regions. The ostensible success of the program may merely be the result of economic good fortune—not the solution to long-term economic problems. The reforms have not yet been tested in recession. In evaluating welfare reform, Texans must also remember that poverty is geographically concentrated in Texas (in the Rio Grande Valley). Welfare reform cannot be pronounced a success until the persistent problems of that region have been addressed. So far, reforms are clearly more successful in those areas of the state were the economy is booming. In high unemployment areas along the Rio Grande river, it seems almost inevitable that many will be pushed off welfare rolls without much prospect of self-sustaining employment. An approach for these more troubled areas has not yet been designed. Thus, the impact of welfare reform may be limited by time and place.

Notes

1. Jennifer Rankin, "Filling in the Gaps; Welfare Reforms Increase Burden on Local Charities." *Dallas Morning News*, January 22, 1998, p. 1A.
2. Martina Shea, *Dynamics of Economic Well-Being: Program Participation, 1991 to 1993,* U.S. Bureau of the Census, Current Population Reports, P70–46 (Washington, DC: U.S. Government Printing Office, 1995), p. 2.
3. Thomas R. Dye, *Politics, Economics, and the Public* (Chicago: Rand McNally, 1966). See especially Chapter 5.
4. Clarke E. Cochran et al., *American Public Policy: An Introduction,* 4th ed. (New York: St. Martin's Press, 1993), p. 219.
5. See, for example, Figure A1, "U.S. and Texas Employment Annual Growth Rates (1990 to 1997)," *Texas Economic Quarterly* (September 1997), p. 14.
6. *Texas: Where We Stand* (Austin: Texas Comptroller of Public Accounts, July 1997).
7. Ibid.
8. Jane Seaberry, "Texas Border a Stark Contrast to Rest of State," *Dallas Morning News* (December 29, 1997), p. 1D.
9. Lucy Komisar, *Down and Out in America: A History of Public Welfare* (New York: Franklin Watts, 1977), pp. 63–63.
10. U.S. House of Representatives, *Green Book: Background Material and Data on Programs Within the Jurisdiction of the Committee on Ways and Means* (Washington, DC, July 15, 1994), p. 341.
11. Texas Constitution, Article III, Section 51-a.
12. *Texas: Where We Stand.*
13. *A Partnership for Independence: Public Assistance Reform Options* (Austin: Texas Comptroller of Public Accounts, 1995), available on Comptroller's web site (**http://www.cpa.state.tx.us**).
14. *Fiscal Size Up 1998–99 Biennium* (Austin: Legislative Budget Board, 1997), see Chapter 5.
15. Irene Lurie, "State Welfare Policy," in *The State of the States,* 3d ed., Carl E. Van Horn, ed. (Washington, DC: CQ Press, 1996), pp. 209–230. The point made here is on p. 222.
16. The agencies placed under the supervision of the Health and Human Services Commission were the Department on Aging, the Texas Commission on Alcohol and Drug Abuse, the Commission for the Blind, the Commission for the Deaf and Hearing Impaired, the Interagency Council on Early Childhood Intervention Services, the Texas Department of Health, the Department of Human Services, the Juvenile Probation Commission, the Department of Mental Health and Mental Retardation, the Department of Protective and Regulatory Services, and the Rehabilitation Commission. *Fiscal Size-Up: 1994–95 Biennium* (Austin: Texas Comptroller of Public Accounts, 1993), 5–1.
17. *A Partnership for Independence: Public Assistance Reform Options* (Austin: Texas Comptroller of Public Accounts, 1995), cover letter from John Sharp.
18. *Fiscal Size Up: 1996–97 Biennium,* p. 5–2.
19. *Fiscal Size Up: 1996–97 Biennium,* p. 5–3.

20. "Family PathFinders: The Community Approach to Welfare Reform," *Fiscal Notes* (May 1996), p. 1.

21. "Texas Launching Finger Imaging System Statewide", *Government Technology* (December 1997), p. 12.

22. David Aden, "Neural Nets Nab Medicaid Fraud," *Government Technology* (October 1997), p. 10.

23. Lesley Kao, "Initiatives Push Privatization Envelope," *Government Technology* (September 1997), p. 48.

24. "State Proceeds with TIES Project," *Ties Wise* (October 1997), vol. 1.1 found at **http://www.hhsc.state.tx.us/ties97/wise.html.**

25. Bill Minutaglio, "Welfare Experts Say Cuts Threaten Texas Children," *Dallas Morning News,* January 13, 1998, p. 13A.

26. "Hungry for Assistance," *Austin American-Statesman,* January 16, 1998, p. A14.

27. Ellen Yan, "Legal Immigrants Aid Restored," *Newsday,* June 6, 1998, p. AO3.

28. Daniel P. McMurrer and Isabel V. Sawhill, "Planning for the Best of Times," *Washington Post* (August 16, 1997) p. A19.

29. Suzanne Gamboa, "Texas Falls Short on Welfare Goals; State Faces Loss of $25 Million," *Austin American-Statesman* (September 17, 1997), p. B1.

30. Reported in Christopher Lee, "Study Faults Texas' Job Help for Welfare Recipients," *Dallas Morning News,* June 28, 1998, p. 39A.

31. Ken Herman, "Welfare Case Drop Hits State Manager," *Austin American-Statesman* (January 9, 1998), p. B10.

32. Kathy Walt, "Lone Star Card Firm to Sell Out," *Houston Chronicle* (February 28, 1998), p. A29.

13

Education Policy in Texas

CHAPTER OUTLINE

As a campaign promise, "ending social promotions in schools" sounds pretty safe—almost like favoring motherhood and apple pie. But, making the promise brought more controversy to Governor Bush than might have been anticipated. Ending social promotions is an idea that almost everyone favors, at lease on some level. A Texas poll released in March 1998 indicated that 92 percent of Texans favored a plan that the state require school districts to make sure that no student leaves the third grade without the ability to read.[1] And, in fact, Texas law already outlaws social promotions. The law says "a student may be promoted only on the basis of academic achievement or demonstrated proficiency of the subject matter of the course or grade level."[2] But, social promotions have continued in Texas public schools because many educators fear dangers to the self-esteem of students held back and some are concerned about the problems of over-aged children in classrooms.

There is almost a consensus that social promotions are bad, but there is disagreement on the issue of who or what should determine whether a student has mastered the material in a particular grade or course. The specific plan that Governor Bush put forward in his 1998 campaign makes passing the TAAS (Texas Assessment of Academic Skills) test the determining factor. When asked what assessment tool should be used to determine whether a student has mastered the material or not, Texas Poll respondents were divided. Some favored reliance on a standardized test (44 percent), but others favored the teacher's evaluation (35 percent).[3] So far, only the Waco Independent School District has chosen to base promotion decisions on the outcome of the TAAS test.[4] For the rest of the state, the decision is likely to be made during the 1999 session of the Texas legislature.

The social promotion issue also raises the issue of local control versus state control, a point that has been emphasized by Governor Bush's 1998 opponent Gary Mauro. Mauro says that he, like almost everyone else, is opposed to social promotions, but does not want to base the decision about promotion on a state controlled and graded test.[5] Mauro has argued that imposing a state standard goes against the state's efforts in recent years to shift control from the state to the local school district.

This 1998 campaign issue calls attention to several issues about public education in Texas:

- Education is an important issue to Texans.
- Improving performance of schools and students is a continuing issue.
- There are significant differences of opinion about the means for improving education.
- The issue of state control versus local control is best an ongoing debate in education policy.

These issues make it clear that education is an essential government service to the people of Texas. Therefore, a knowledge of Texas educational policy is critical to understanding Texas government. To provide a foundation for understanding Texas educational policy, this chapter considers the following questions:

- How are educational services provided in Texas?
- What are the important educational issues confronting the state, and how has the state attempted to deal with them?
- What are the prospects for the future of education in Texas?

Two basic types of education services are provided by the state: public schools and higher education. The public schools are a joint venture of the state and over a thousand local school districts that provide free public education from kindergarten through grade 12. Higher-education services are provided through a set of state colleges and universities and a number of two-year institutions, including fifty community and junior college districts.

The Public School System

State policy governing the public schools is set by the Texas legislature and administered by the **Texas Education Agency** (TEA). The State Board of Education, an elected body, oversees the TEA. The governor appoints the commissioner of education (the chief executive of the TEA) subject to senatorial confirmation. The day-to-day management of the public schools is the responsibility of local school districts through school boards and superintendents.

The basic system for financing the public schools was defined in the **Gilmer–Aikin bills** passed by the legislature in 1949. Those bills created the **foundation school program** to guarantee each child an equal minimum educational opportunity. Funding was to come from local property taxes (20 percent) and the state (80 percent).[6] Because the state program was underfunded, the state share of public school funding gradually dropped over the years, and the reliance on local property tax revenues increased. By 1997 the state's share of public school funding was 45.0 percent.[7] The system's reliance on local-district resources is at the root of the recent school finance controversy.

School Districts

One essential type of special district in Texas is the school district. Like other local governments, the power exercised by school districts is delegated by the state. Unlike many other special districts, school districts are regulated by the state through the Texas Education Code, a compendium of regulations passed by the state legislature. The organization of school districts also is more standardized than that of other special districts.

Almost all public elementary and secondary schools in Texas today are operated by **independent school districts.** Those districts are governed by an elected board of trustees. Most boards have seven members; but small districts can have fewer, and large districts are required to have more. Districts with a school population of at least 66,000 must have nine members on their board.[8]

Members of school boards are elected in nonpartisan elections, usually at-large. Large school districts (again, with at least 66,000 students) must elect seven of their nine board members from single-member districts. In 1983 the legislature gave school districts the authority to switch to single-member districts or to a mixed system in which at least 70 percent of their members are elected from single-member districts.[9] One objective of using elected boards is to ensure that the schools are controlled by the people, not by professional educators. Most school boards in Texas are made up of local business and civic leaders.

As the governing body of the school district, the board of trustees has several important powers:

- It sets the district's property tax rate, thereby determining the amount of revenue that the school tax generates.
- It sets the budget for school operations, including salaries for school administrators and teachers.
- It makes decisions about incurring debt for the construction of school facilities.
- It enters into contracts with administrators and teachers.
- Within the framework of state laws and guidelines set by the Texas Education Agency, it determines local school policy.

The chief executive of the local school district is the superintendent. The superintendent is hired contractually by the board of trustees. Board members are supposed to be "average citizens"; school superintendents are supposed to be professionals. Most have been trained in educational administration at universities.

Public School Policy Problems

Over the last two decades, two policy problems have occupied the attention of those concerned with the public schools: educational equity and educational performance. The educational-equity battle has centered on whether the state's public school system offers equal educational opportunity to all of its children. The educational-performance issue emerged from widespread concern that the public schools were not doing an adequate job of educating the state's children.

In 1971, the ***Rodriguez* case** callenged Texas school finance policy in the federal courts. A federal district court found that there was so much variation in spending per pupil from one school district to another in Texas that the system violated the U.S. Constitution's Fourteenth Amendment requirement that states give "equal protection of the laws" to their citizens. Although the state won an appeal to the U.S. Supreme Court in 1973, policymakers

School districts with heavy minority enrollment were often the losers in the Texas school finance system before the courts forced change. While some school districts could afford to introduce modern technology into their classrooms, others used outmoded facilities and equipment.

recognized that there was a serious problem that had to be addressed. By 1977 the state legislature already had begun to alter state funding formulas for the public schools to shift more state aid to the poorest districts and to add equalization funds. Between 1977 and 1984, the legislature appropriated $1.1 billion in equalization aid.[10]

In 1984, a new suit was filed in a state district court alleging that the state's school finance system violated the state constitution. This suit was a reminder to the state's leaders that the problem of unequal funding for school districts was not going away.

In 1987 a State district court judge Harley Clark agreed with the plaintiffs in ***Edgewood* v. *Kirby*** that the state's school finance system violated the state's constitution. Judge Clark found too much disparity among the state's school districts resulting from what he called "the irrational accident of school district lines." Comparing the poorest school district with the richest school district, he noted that spending per pupil varied from $2,112 to $19,333 and that property tax bases ranged from $20,000 per pupil to $14 million per pupil.[11] In 1989 the Texas Supreme Court agreed with Clark's ruling and set a deadline for the legislature to correct the funding problem.[12]

Several efforts by the legislature between 1990 and 1992 failed to produce a solution to the problem. Various efforts were rejected by the state Supreme Court or by the voters. Finally, after proposing a constitutional amendment that was rejected by the voters in 1993, the legislature passed Senate Bill 7. This legislation adopted the Robin Hood spirit by requiring the wealthiest districts to transfer some property tax revenue to poor districts. In January

1995, the Texas Supreme Court ruled that Senate Bill 7 was constitutional in all respects.[13]

As specified in Senate Bill 7, the Foundation School Program (FSP) allocates funds to school districts through a two-tiered system. A basic allotment is granted under Tier One based on the number of students enrolled in regular education programs. In addition, weighted allotments are made for pupils enrolled in special programs. The purpose of Tier One is to guarantee "sufficient financing for all school districts to provide a basic program of education that meets accreditation and other legal standards."[14] To participate, a school district must levy an effective tax rate of $0.86 per $100 of taxable property. To the extent that the district's own tax base fails to produce the amount per pupil allotted by the state, the state makes up the difference.[15]

Tier Two of FSP permits each district to supplement Tier One funding at a level of its own choice. For Tier Two, districts are guaranteed that for each additional cent of tax levied, up to a maximum effective tax rate of $1.50 per $100 of assessed property values, they will receive $20.55 of revenue.[16] The state makes up the difference between the amount produced by a district's own tax base and the amount guaranteed by FSP.

To ensue that wealthy districts do not get too far ahead of poorer districts, each school district's taxable property values are capped at a level of $280,000 per student.[17] For districts whose taxable values exceed the cap, the law provides several means of transferring revenue to other districts.[18]

Finally, the state defined its responsibility under the constitutional mandate to provide "a general diffusion of knowledge."[19] The state outlined seven major goals of public education (see Figure 13.1) and it developed a system of assessment to measure school performance. Only districts that achieve the state's goals can achieve accreditation, and those districts that do achieve state accreditation are deemed to have achieved the constitutionally-mandated goal of education. The Texas Supreme Court concluded that to meet the constitution's requirements, a district must have equal access to the funds necessary to provide an accredited education. Thus, the court could conclude that although Senate Bill 7 did not guarantee revenue quality to districts, it did provide an efficient system of education for the state, as required by the constitution.

In 1995, for the first time, the new legislation committed the state to direct expenditures for school construction. The state committed itself to spend at least $170 million during the 1996–1997 biennium. The eligibility rules were written to favor low-wealth districts and small districts.[20]

The second persistant policy problem regarding Texas public schools has been the problem of poor performance by schools and their students. In 1982 Mark White was elected governor with the backing of teachers' organizations that was won, in part, by promising a substantial pay increase for teachers. Soon after taking office, Governor White responded to the recommendation of the Texas speaker and the lieutenant governor by appointing a commission (which came to be called the **Perot Commission**) to study Texas public schools and to make recommendations for reform. To chair the group, White

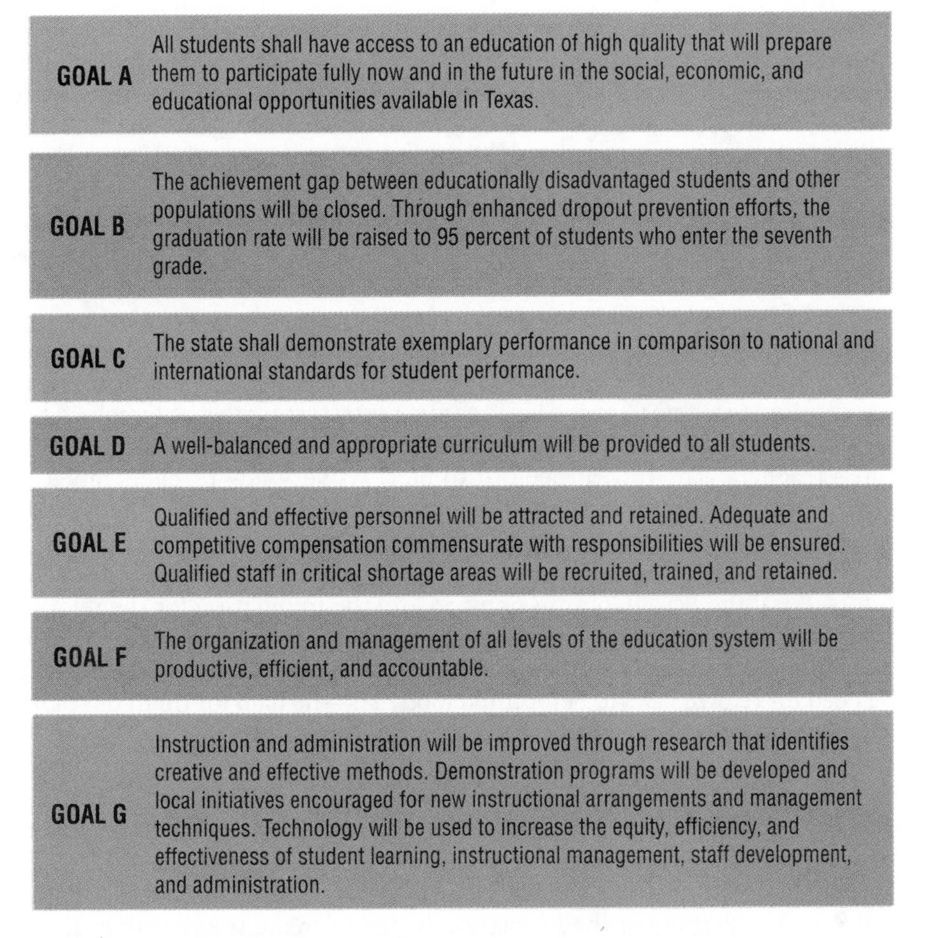

FIGURE 13.1 The Legislative Mandated Goals of Public Education
Source: Texas Education Code, Section 35.001.

chose Dallas businessman H. Ross Perot, who quickly became the dominant player in the commission's work and a vigorous advocate of school reform. The commission held hearings throughout the state and made its report in time for a special legislative session in 1984.

In 1984, responding to the recommendations of the Perot Commission and the pending lawsuit, the legislature passed a variety of reforms in House Bill 72. That legislation set stricter standards for accreditation of school districts by the State Department of Education, set limits on pupil–teacher classroom ratios, increased attention to the needs for bilingual education, provided Head Start–type programs for poor and non–English speaking students, and created programs for gifted and talented students. One of the more controversial provisions was the **no pass, no play rule** requiring that students must be passing all their courses at the end of each grading period to participate in band, football, and other extracurricular activities. A student failing a course could not become eligible for extracurricular activities until the end of the next grading period. This "no pass, no play" rule has been attacked many times since House Bill 72 was passed. In 1995, the legislature gave in to pressure and softened the rule by permitting a review of the student's status after three weeks had elapsed—instead of the full six weeks.[21]

To shake up the state's educational bureaucracy, the State Board of Education was abolished and a new board was created. Although the law provided that members of the new board would be elected, the governor was authorized to appoint the first members.

The bill included good news and bad news for teachers. On the positive side, it increased beginning teachers' salaries and created a career ladder that rewarded good teachers with merit raises. The bad news came was a provision that required teachers to pass a basic competency test to keep their jobs. That provision—a single test that put teachers' jobs on the line—infuriated the state's teachers. The test turned out to be easy; very few teachers failed it. But the teachers were angered by the state's willingness to put them in jeopardy.

The sweeping reforms of House Bill 72 were possible because of several factors. First, the Perot Commission had laid the foundation for the reforms by publicizing the need for change in the system. Second, the state's leaders (including the governor, the lieutenant governor, and the speaker) agreed on the need for reform. Third, Perot hired lobbyists—he paid for them out of his own pocket—to convince lawmakers that reform was necessary.[22]

In 1990, the legislature passed Senate Bill 1, which contained a number of changes designed to improve the performance of the schools. It created a special fund for innovative programs, with the stipulation that 70 percent of the revenue would go to programs to improve the academic performance of low-achieving students. It mandated a program of standardized testing for students. The drafters of the legislation hoped to make it easier to evaluate students and performance by using national achievement tests. To free teachers to teach, many of the rules and regulations imposed by the State Board of Education following the passage of House Bill 72 were eliminated. Specifically the bill eliminated all rules for local districts except those pertaining to curriculum, unless a local school board specifically adopted them.

In 1995 school reform was a key legislative issue once again. Governor Bush had made this a key element in his 1994 campaign, and legislative leaders had committed themselves to educational reform in the 1993 legislative session by creating a select committee to review the mission of the Texas Education Agency. The 1995 session produced Senate Bill 1, which made several changes in the school system. Underlying this reform effort was a desire to give more control of the local schools and school districts. Home-rule districts were one device for reducing state control. This provision authorizes districts to create charters that define many of their powers and free them from many state requirements. Creating such a system requires approval in a local election in which at least 25 percent of the registered voters participated. Since many local elections, including school district elections, commonly have much lower turnout rates, this may become a serious obstacle to creating home-rule districts. In addition, charters could be granted to open-enrollment schools that could draw enrollment across district lines, and special charter schools can be created within districts.[23]

The voucher system that Governor Bush supported during his campaign was not included in the final version of Senate Bill 1. The law does grant students in low-performing districts (i.e., those where average standardized test scores were below state norms), the right to transfer to another school.

After years of educational reform efforts, what results have been produced? The principal instrument for measuring educational performance in Texas today is the **TAAS** (Texas Assessment of Academic Skills) testing program, which is administered annually to students in grades three through eight and in grade ten. The test covers three skill areas: reading, writing, and mathematics. Individual scores on the test are used as indicators of individual achievement. Average scores for schools are used as measures of school performance.

The 1997 TEA *Interim Report on Public Schools* reported evidence of improvement. The percentage of students passing all tests rose from 56 percent in 1994 to 73 percent in 1997 (see Figure 13.2). Performance in

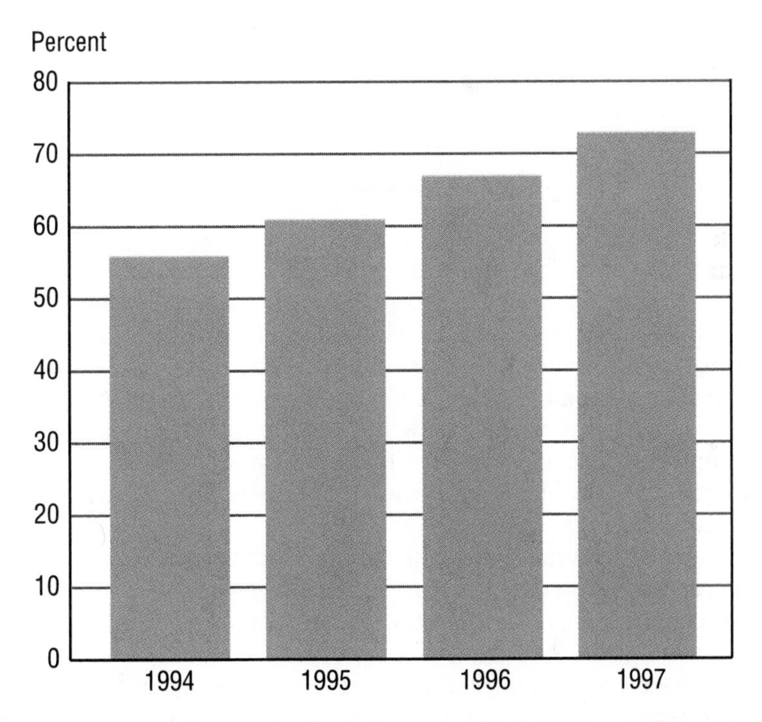

FIGURE 13.2 Percent of Texas Students Passing All TAAS Tests Taken, 1994–1997

Source: Texas Education Agency, 1997 Interim Report on Texas Public Schools *(Austin: TEA, 1997), p. vii.*

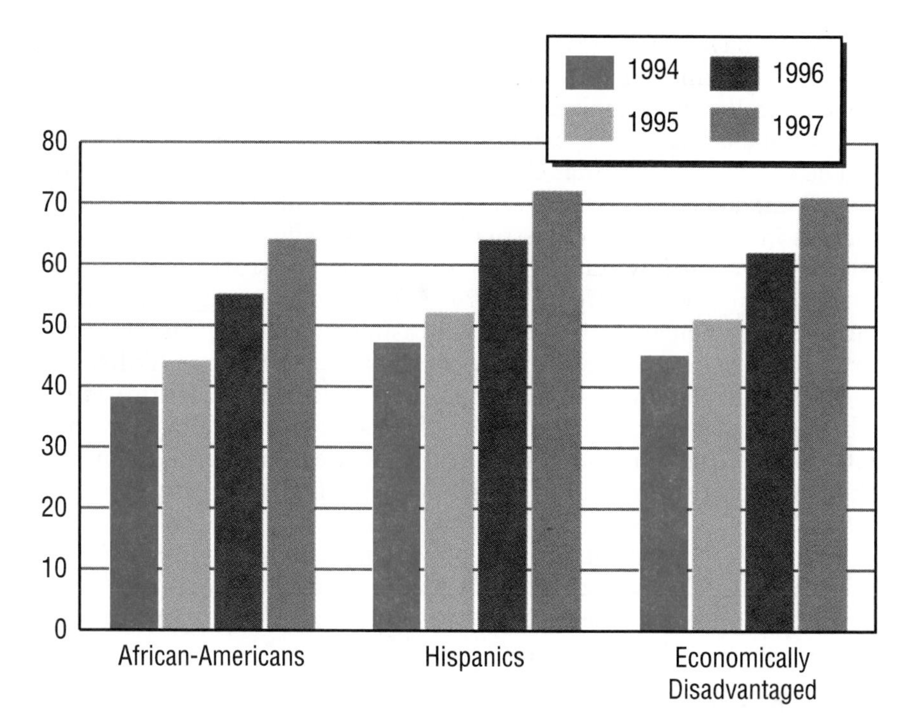

FIGURE 13.3 Percent of Texas Students Passing Mathematics TAAS Test, 1994–1997

Source: Texas Education Agency, 1997 Interim Report on Texas Public Schools *(Austin: TEA, 1997), p. vii.*

mathematics, which has typically been lower than on other tests, also improved. An encouraging aspect of that improvement is the evidence that minority students have improved as well (see Figure 13.3). Thus individual student test performance has improved in recent years.

Other information from the TEA's report is the encouraging evidence that schools are improving as well. Based on average test scores, schools are rated as "exemplary," "recognized," or "low-performing." The report notes that even as standards have risen, the number of **low-performing schools** has risen sharply (see Figure 13.4).

Another encouraging sign is the decline in the student dropout rate. The annual dropout rate declined from 6.7 percent in the 1987–1988 school year to 1.8 percent in the 1994–1995 year. The annual dropout rate held steady at 1.8 percent in 1995–1996.[24]

Thus, more schools, as well as more students, appear to be performing better in recent years. These indicators do not mean that Texas has solved all of its education problems. Standards could be raised even higher. And, minority students still have significant problems in test performance and in dropout statistics that must be addressed. But, this early evidence suggests some reasons to believe that recent reforms have had some positive effects.

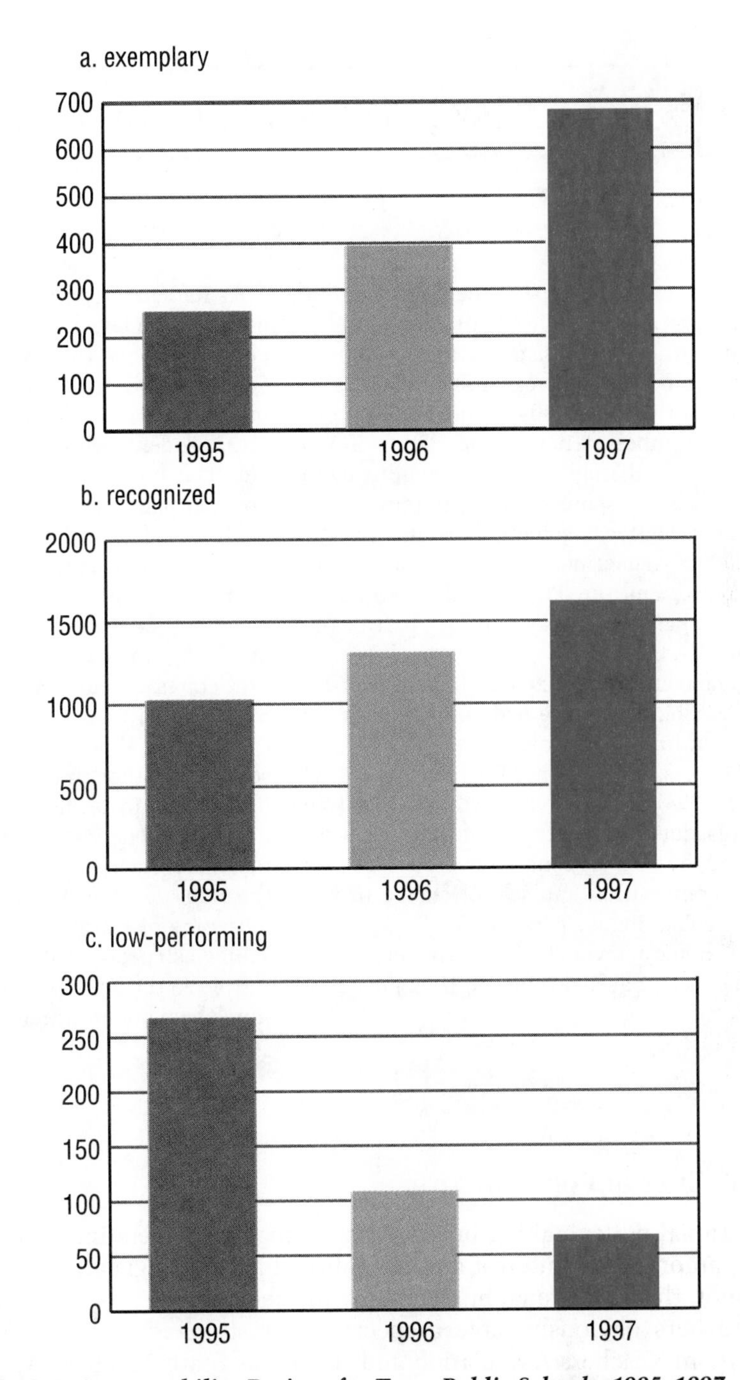

FIGURE 13.4 Accountability Ratings for Texas Public Schools, 1995–1997

Source: Texas Education Agency, 1997 Interim Report on Texas Public Schools *(Austin: TEA, 1987), p. viii.*

THE CHANGING FACE OF TEXAS POLITICS

Charter Schools: Education Reform Revisited

Education reform has a permanent place on the Texas political agenda. Ironically, the round of reform in the 1995 session of the legislature seemed to be a direct response to legislative reforms in the mid-1980s. Those reforms imposed a number of new standards on Texas education and made the Texas Education Agency (TEA) responsible for enforcing those standards on local school districts. By the 1990s, dissatisfaction with the schools was widespread, and the TEA had come to be regarded as part of the problem, not part of the solution.

Several factors mobilized the forces of reform in 1995. The legislature had committed itself to reexamining the role of the TEA after its 1993 session. Governor Bush had promised in the 1994 campaign to restore control to local districts. Moreover, Texans had been influenced by the national movement to use school competition and school choice to improve educational performance. (Actually school choice and voucher systems were issues that had been raised during the 1992 presidential race.)

As reform efforts developed, the two houses of the Texas legislature took somewhat different approaches to the issue of local control. Senate leaders originally favored a plan that included a voucher system that would have given students who attend private schools state aid. The house refused to go along with the voucher plan. Eventually the house and senate conferees focused their efforts on charter schools—an idea promoted by Governor Bush.

In endorsing charter schools, Texas joined eleven other states that had passed legislation providing for such schools. In January 1995, nine states actually had set up charter schools.[1] By 1998, thirty-two states and the District of Columbia had passed laws authorizing charter schools.[2] Although the term **charter schools** is used widely in discussions of education reform, no common definition of a charter-school system has emerged. The common denominator of the plans developed by the various states is the loosening of state restrictions on schools that achieve charter-school status.

In 1995 the legislature authorized the formation of open-enrollment charter schools that

The Politics of Policymaking

Educational policymaking brings a wide range of players into the political arena, among them interest groups, political parties, legislative leaders, the governor, the educational bureaucracy, and the courts.

Teachers obviously have a special interest in education policy. The Classroom Teachers Association and the Texas State Teachers Association are two of the most powerful groups in Texas politics. They have pressed the state to increase funding for education, raise teachers' salaries, and reduce the red tape strangling the education process. Teachers' unhappiness with some of the reforms in House Bill 72 and the governor's limited support of salary increases contributed to Mark White's defeat in 1986. The political clout of could accept students from anywhere in the state. The Texas Board of Education authorized twenty such schools for the 1995–1996 school year. Eleven of the charter schools created in this round were designed to serve at-risk students. Sixteen of the schools won special grants from the U.S. Department of Education. Nineteen of the twenty were operating and serving over 3,700 students in 1997—29 percent of whom were African American and 45 percent of whom were Hispanic.[3]

The legislature was sufficiently pleased with the results of the first charter schools that it authorized an additional one hundred charters. Procedures for allocating those charters were to be worked out in the spring of 1998. In addition, a number of universities were authorized to carry out a comprehensive evaluation of the program.[4]

One of the schools to attract some attention is the Raul Yzaguirre School for Success in Houston, one of the first charter schools approved. Its students are mostly poor, with 90 percent qualifying for the free or reduced-price lunch program. The school is small enough to give ample individual attention and has the freedom to choose a curriculum that it believes serves the needs of its students. The school emphasizes heavy parental involvement, with 95 percent of the parents directly engaged with the school. It has adopted a uniform for students to avoid competitive dress patterns. The school has been able to achieve a 98 percent average daily attendance with a student population that is almost 100 percent at-risk students. The one disappointment for this charter school, and all others, is that the state provides no support for facilities, making it difficult to acquire the kind of buildings the school needs. Although the school does not solve all problems, its proponents think it is an improvement over the indifferent treatment these students might have received in a traditional school.[5]

Although charter schools will not displace regular public schools, they have encouraged educational innovation as well as experimentation with new methods to help those students who did not perform well in more traditional schools. Thus, charter schools provide an additional strategy for educating the children of Texas without displacing the more traditional system. ★

[1]U.S. Government Accounting Office, "Charter Schools—New Model for Public Schools Provides Opportunities and Challenges," Letter Report GAO/HEHS-95-42, January 18, 1995.

[2]A New Chapter for Charters," *State Legislatures* (June 1998), p. 20.

[3]Texas Education Agency, *1997 Interim Report on Texas Public Schools* (Austin, TEA, 1997), pp. 47–48.

[4]Ibid., p. 47.

[5]"One School's Story," *State Legislatures* (June 1998), p. 21.

teachers' organizations comes from their perceived ability to deliver votes to endorsed candidates and to punish their enemies at the polls.

Ethnic groups also are important players in school policymaking. Realizing that they did not have the votes to demand the attention of the legislature, these groups took their concerns about school funding to the courts. And the courts forced lawmakers to act.

Political parties once would have been irrelevant to the politics of public schools. In recent years, however, the issue of school finance has divided the legislature along partisan lines. The staunch Republican opposition to reform legislation in recent sessions of the legislature reflects the fact that Republican legislators tend to represent constituencies with school districts that were destined to lose property tax revenues under the various **Robin Hood plans** pushed through the legislature. (Robin Hood plans is the term used for school reform plans that require wealthier districts to share their tax revenue with poorer districts.)

As they are in all areas of Texas politics, the legislative leaders—the lieutenant governor and the speaker of the Texas house—are big players in school policymaking. Their ability to structure key committees, to choose the chairs of those committees, and to appoint the members of conference committees has kept them in a position to shape the outcome of any legislative battle involving the public schools.

The governor's role in public school policy traditionally has been to mold public opinion and to broker the compromises that may be necessary to pass school legislation. Governor White clearly was a major player in the reforms in the early 1980s. In 1990, Governor Bill Clements used the threat of a veto to insist that the legislature give the governor the power to appoint the commissioner of education, a powerful tool in public school politics. Governor Richards was less successful in shaping policy alternatives. Her recommendations often were not followed by legislative leaders, and her efforts in 1993 to persuade the voters to approve a constitutional amendment that would have authorized the interdistrict transfer of property tax revenues were unsuccessful. Governor Bush helped build support for the 1995 legislative reforms by making school reform a key campaign issue in 1994.

The educational bureaucracy, specifically the TEA, more often is on the receiving end of policy changes than on the formulation end. The TEA is a bureaucracy without a large supportive clientele. Teachers, who might be expected to support the agency, are among its most vocal critics, pointing to the many rules and regulations that they believe limit their ability to do their jobs. As a result, the TEA often has been the whipping boy of recent school reform efforts.

Because of the legal and constitutional issues involved, the courts were a driving force in changing public school policy. This was a relatively new role for the Texas Supreme Court, which is known more for its involvement in claims against businesses than for its involvement in the broader issues of public law. The court's willingness to tackle the public school issue was partially due to the election of a number of fairly liberal Democratic justices. However, Republicans now hold a majority on the state supreme court, which has demonstrated a more conservative approach in the 1990s.

Higher Education

Policy Problems

Higher-education policy in Texas in recent years has focused on four areas: the organization of the system, regional equity, the adequacy of funding, and the question of mission.

Table 13.1 Public University Systems in Texas

Institution	Institution
Texas A&M University System, College Station	**The University of Texas System, Austin**
Prairie View A&M University	The University of Texas at Arlington
Tarleton State University	The University of Texas at Austin
Texas A&M International University	The University of Texas at Brownsville
Texas A&M University	The University of Texas at Dallas
Texas A&M University at Galveston	The University of Texas at El Paso
Texas A&M University-Commerce	The University of Texas-Pan American
Texas A&M University-Texarkana	The University of Texas of the Permian Basin
Texas A&M University, Corpus Christi	The University of Texas at San Antonio
Texas A&M University-Kingsville	The University of Texas at Tyler
West Texas A&M University	
Texas State University System, Austin	**University of Houston System, Houston**
Angelo State University	University of Houston
Lamar University-Beaumont	University of Houston-Clear Lake
Lamar University-Orange	University of Houston-Downtown
Lamar University-Port Arthur	University of Houston-Victoria
Lamar University Institute of Technology	
Sam Houston State University	
Southwest Texas State University	
Sul Ross State University	
Sul Ross State University Rio Grande College	

Source: Texas Higher Education Coordinating Board.

Organizational issues. Higher-education policy is set by the legislature. The **Texas Higher Education Coordinating Board** oversees higher education and recommends policies regarding it to the legislature. Each institution of higher education has its own administrative structure that is supervised by a local governing board or by the governing board of the system to which it belongs. For many years three major systems governed most colleges and universities: the University of Texas system, the Texas A&M University system, and the Texas state college and university system. Several large universities (for example, the University of Houston, Texas Tech University, and the University of North Texas) have operated independently of these systems, each with its own governing board of regents. The community and junior colleges also have their own local governing bodies.

In many ways it makes no sense to talk about Texas higher education as a system. *System* implies an underlying plan that guides related elements. California has a system of higher education: the various branches of the University of California focus on research and graduate instruction, the state colleges and universities emphasize undergraduate instruction, and the community colleges provide basic and vocational education. The mission of the institutions in each tier of the system is clear. No plan has guided the development of the higher-education system in Texas. New institutions and programs are the spoils of political battles, not part of a rational plan for higher-education services in Texas. Creating colleges or universities to reward powerful politicians was especially prevalent during the expansionary period of the 1960s. Texas now has four groups of colleges and universities that are designated as systems (see Table 13.1), but the four Texas systems do not have distinctive missions as do the various tiers of the California system. The gradual absorption of formerly independent institutions has simplified the structure of Texas higher education somewhat.

In an effort to bring order to Texas higher education, the legislature created the coordinating board in 1965. Although the coordinating board controls new programs, it still can find itself pressured by political realities in the legislature. For example, when the Seventy-first Legislature approved the addition of West Texas University to the Texas A&M University system and authorized the enrollment of freshmen and sophomores at the University of Texas at Dallas (previously an upper-level institution), it made those actions contingent on the coordinating board's approval. But because lawmakers already had acted, the coordinating board felt political pressure to rubber-stamp the plan. In 1997, the legislature acted again to expand UT-Tyler and UT-Brownsville to full undergraduate institutions by authorizing them to admit freshmen and sophomores.

Regional equity. The question of educational equity also has been raised in higher education. In 1987 the League of United Latin American Citizens, eight other groups, and fifteen Hispanic students filed suit in a Brownsville, Texas, district court.[25] The plaintiffs argued that the state had failed to provide equal educational opportunities to minority residents of communities in the Rio Grande Valley. Evidence in the trial showed that the 20 percent of the population living in the forty-one counties along the Texas–Mexico border received just 10 percent of the money spent on higher education and that 54 percent of the public university students in the area were Hispanic (compared with 7 percent in the rest of Texas). The state responded that money was distributed among educational institutions by formula, that there was no bias in the allocation of funds. The jury concluded that the state had not discriminated against the plaintiffs, but the district court judge set aside the verdict, ruled that the Texas higher-education funding system was unconstitutional, and gave the legislature until May 1993 to correct the problem.[26]

The state appealed the verdict to the Texas Supreme Court, but the legislature was forced to respond to the ruling before the high court rendered its decision. As a result, the higher-education funding passed in 1993 included a special **South Texas initiative** that directed more money to the institutions in that area. The legislature added over $60 million to the formula-based allocation and appropriated funding for program development in the targeted area. In addition, institutions in the area were authorized to issue $240 million in tuition revenue bonds to help underwrite construction

Texas university campuses have become more ethnically diverse.

and renovation programs.[27] In October 1993 the Texas Supreme Court overturned the lower-court decision, ruling that the evidence did not show that the state had discriminated against the residents of South Texas.[28] Nevertheless, the legislature has continued its efforts to upgrade the South Texas Universities.

Funding issues. One source of conflict in Texas higher education was the **Permanent University Fund** (PUF). This fund, which receives its revenues from oil leases on state lands, has been a valuable source of money for buildings, equipment, and library acquisitions. The problem was that the constitution restricted the distribution of revenues from the PUF to institutions in the Texas A&M University and University of Texas systems. Other colleges and universities had no continuing funding source to meet their construction needs. In 1983 the legislature proposed a constitutional amendment to set up a fund for the other universities; the voters approved the amendment in 1984. The **Higher Education Assistance Fund** (HEAF) serves twenty-six institutions outside the Texas A&M University and University of Texas systems. The legislature appropriates money for the fund. The fund distributes $175 million per year. In addition, the legislature began setting aside $50 million per year to build up an endowed fund. When the fund has accumulated $2 billion, annual appropriations will cease and the fund will begin to operate as an endowed fund. The amount of revenue to be distributed will be determined by fund earnings.

General funding for state colleges and universities is formula driven. The legislature simplified the formula system in 1997 so that most funding is determined by the number and types of students. The formulas also determine how much each institution should receive.

The Hopwood issue. A troublesome issue facing higher education at the end of the 1990s was minority enrollment in higher education. One of the ways that college admissions had worked to increase minority enrollment was through affirmative action programs. Affirmative action programs established special admission criteria for ethnic and racial minorities and targeted financial aid toward those historically underrepresented populations. In Texas, that system was challenged by a decision of the United States Fifth Circuit of Appeals court in the 1996 ***Hopwood* case.**[29] Arguing that she had been a victim of reverse discrimination when denied admission to the University of Texas Law School, Cheryl Hopwood sued the state of Texas. The federal court of appeals ruled that the law school's affirmative action program was indeed unconstitutional.

The impact of the *Hopwood* decision might have been narrowly applied to the UT law school situation, but that approach was ruled out by an opinion of the Texas attorney general. Attorney General Morales gave a sweeping interpretation that the *Hopwood* decision made it illegal to use race or ethnicity as a factor in Texas college and university policies concerning admission, financial aid, recruitment, or retention.[30] The result made it illegal for Texas colleges and universities to make special efforts to recruit minorities if they explicitly included race or ethnicity as a factor.

The effect of *Hopwood* is detrimental to the ability of Texas colleges and universities to recruit the best minority students because the precedent set by it does not apply to all states. Because it was a decision of the U.S. Court of Appeals for the Fifth Circuit, the decision applies only to states in the circuit: Texas, Louisiana, and Mississippi. And, because authorities in Louisiana and Mississippi have not given the decision the sweeping interpretation that Attorney General Morales has, the effect in those states is not so great as in Texas. Thus, Texas is disadvantaged in its efforts to recruit the best minority students. It cannot target financial aid or admissions policies to help those students, but neighboring states, whether they are in the Fifth Judicial Circuit or not, can. In hopes of leveling the playing field somewhat, the University of Texas was seeking a way to appeal the case to the U.S. Supreme Court in 1998.

In an effort to soften the expected impact on minority recruitment, the Texas legislature passed House Bill 588, requiring colleges and universities to broaden their admission standards. Under the law, institutions are required to automatically admit students who are in the top 10 percent of their high school graduating class. Boards of individual colleges were required to consider automatically admitting all students who are in the top 25 percent of their high school graduating class. In addition, the legislature created a new scholarship program targeted for economically and/or educationally disadvantaged populations.

It is too soon to determine the full effect of the Hopwood decision, but preliminary data indicated that the effect was greatest in professional schools in Texas; that is, in medical and law schools. Although acceptances of minority students were up for the 1998–1999 academic year over the 1997–1998 year, University of Texas law school officials still reported that Hopwood limited their efforts to recruit minorities. Minority students were expected to make up 21 percent of the first-year students in 1998–1999, up from 16 percent in 1997–1998.[31] At the undergraduate level the numbers looked better. UT reported that minority students would make up 37 percent of its freshman class in 1998–1999, as compared to 34 percent the previous year.[32] Thus, while some improvement was apparent, Texas colleges and universities were concerned about the effect of the Hopwood decision on efforts to recruit a representative student body.

The Politics of Policymaking

Who are the key players in higher-education policymaking? The politics of higher education involves a somewhat smaller set of actors than does the politics of public schools. In recent years, interest groups, the coordinating board, the governor, legislative leaders, and the courts have played a role in setting higher-education policy.

Ethnic groups have been especially important in recent higher-education policymaking. The LULAC suit temporarily focused higher-education spending on institutions along the Rio Grande Valley. There are groups that represent college and university faculty, but they do not have the power of public school teachers' organizations. College professors simply do not have the numbers that public school teachers do.

Although the authority of the Texas Higher Education Coordinating Board sometimes is limited by the legislature, the board tends to play a larger role in setting policy than the TEA does. Nevertheless, the Coordinating Board all too often finds itself responding to political decisions instead of setting policy itself.

The governor can influence higher education policy too. The governor makes policy recommendations to the legislature and to the public. Some governors have been strong advocates of higher education.

The Texas legislature is inevitably a powerful player in higher-education policy because it appropriates the funds for higher education. In recent years, however, the legislature has chosen to go well beyond controlling the purse strings to dictating elements of academic policy that might once have been left to the institutions or to the Coordinating Board. For example, the 1997 session of the legislature passed Senate Bill 148, which requires that a common core curriculum be developed by the Coordinating Board and mandates that the core be freely transferable among colleges and universities. In addition, the legislature passed Senate Bill 149 requiring colleges and universities to adopt a policy and procedures for evaluating tenured faculty members (those who have achieved a continuing commitment from the institution and are no longer subject to annual contract renewal reviews). Finally, the legislature imposed caps on the number of graduate and undergraduate hours students can accumulate and for which the state will provide formula funding to the college or university. These caps on hours were motivated by the belief of some legislators that students stayed too long in universities, drawing on state funding unnecessarily. What all of these pieces of legislation indicated was a belief among legislators that colleges and universities, and even educational bureaucracies, could not be trusted to efficiently manage their own affairs.

Education Policy and the Future

There have been many changes in Texas education policy in the last twenty years, and more change is likely. The problem of equalizing public school finance probably will remain on the public agenda for a few more years. In 1991 the Texas Supreme Court made the point forcefully in its second *Edgewood* decision that the problem with Texas public school finance is in the system itself, in its overreliance on local property tax revenue.[33] Although the plan adopted in 1993 forces the richest school districts to share their wealth, it does not alter the system fundamentally. The governor's attempt to reduce reliances on the property tax to fund public schools met with limited success in 1997.

One of the barriers to fixing the system of public school funding has been the state's economic situation. The state's revenue system could not keep pace with the growing cost of services. For much of the 1990s, instead of the state relieving local districts, the state shifted the burden to local school districts. An improved economy and increased tax revenues permitted the state to increase its support for the 1998–1999 biennium. But, the fundamental problem—heavy reliance on local property tax revenue—is still built into the system.

Whatever the outcome of the school finance issue, the public schools are likely to stay on the public agenda. If traditional reforms cannot solve the performance problem, Texas leaders will need to find new solutions. In the 1994 gubernatorial race, Republican candidate George W. Bush advocated school choice, a program that allows parents to choose the schools their children go to through some type of voucher system. A privately funded school-choice pilot project currently is operating in San Antonio.

The future of higher-education policy is also tied to the economic well-being of the state. Recent increases in funding have been made possible by a better economy. Remember that most of the budget cannot be changed because of statutory, constitutional, or court-ordered obligations. If the state's revenue declines again, higher education will become a target of budget cuts again. Although those cuts may well be shortsighted and a threat to the state's economic future, politicians in Texas continue to be convinced that avoiding new taxes is their highest priority.

Notes

1. Kathy Walt, "Non-Readers Shouldn't Go to the 4th Grade," *Houston Chronicle,* March 9, 1998, p. 13A.
2. Texas Education Code, Section 28.02(a).
3. Kathy Walt, "Non-Readers Shouldn't Go to the 4th Grade," p. 13A.
4. Kathy Walt, "TAAS No Pass Rules Will Apply; Waco Makes Summer School Preparations for Kids Who Fail Tests," *Houston Chronicle,* May 31, 1998, p. 1A.
5. Max B. Baker, "Leave Promotion Choices to Teachers, Mauro Says," *Fort Worth Star-Telegram,* February 27, 1998, Metro Section, p. 4.
6. Legislative intent is explained in *Carrollton-Farmers Branch Independent School District et al., appellants* v. *Edgewood Independent School District and Alvarado Independent School District et al., appellees,* 826 S.W.2d 489 (1992), at 495.
7. Legislative Budget Board, *Fiscal Size Up: 1998–99 Biennium* (Austin, 1998), 6–5.
8. *Texas Education Code,* Chap. 23.
9. *Texas Education Code,* Chap. 23.
10. Texas Comptroller of Public Accounts, *Fiscal Notes,* March 1988, 8.
11. *Edgewood* v. *Kirby,* No. 962516 (259th District Court, Travis County, TX, June 1, 1987).
12. *Edgewood* v. *Kirby,* 777 S.W.2d 391 (1989).
13. *Edgewood Independent School District et al.* v. *Meno,* No. 94–0152 (Supreme Court of Texas, January 30, 1995).
14. *Texas Education Code,* Section 16.002(b).
15. *Texas Education Code,* Section 16.254.
16. *Texas Education Code,* Section 16.254.
17. *Texas Education Code,* Section 36.002.
18. *Texas Education Code,* Section 36.003 and Section 36.004.
19. *Texas Constitution,* Article VII, Section I.
20. Senate Bill 1, 74th Legislature, 1995, Sec. 12.
21. Senate Bill 1, 74th Legislature, 1995, Sec. 33.081.
22. William P. Hobby, Jr. and Billy D. Walker, "Legislative Reform of the Texas Public School Finance System, 1973–1991," *Harvard Journal on Legislation 28* (Summer 1991), 379–394. The point made here is on p. 391.
23. Senate Bill 1, 74th Legislature, 1995, Sec. 12.
24. Texas Education Agency, *1997 Interim Report on Texas Public Schools* (Austin: TEA, 1997), p. 19.
25. James Pinkerton, Clay Robison, and Todd Ackerman, "Judge Rules for Change in Higher Ed; Jury Verdict Set Aside as Hispanics Claim Win," *Houston Chronicle,* January 21, 1992, 1A.
26. Ibid.
27. Texas Higher Education Coordinating Board, *Report,* July–September 1993, 6.
28. *Ann Richards, Governor of the State of Texas, et al., Appellants* v. *League of United Latin American Citizens (LULAC) et al., Appellees,* 868 S.W.2d 306 (1993).
29. *Hopwood* v. *Texas* 78F.3d 932 (1996).
30. Opinion of the Attorney General of Texas, L097-001, February 1997.
31. Christy Hoppe, "Hopwood Ruling Hindering Minority Recruitment,

UT Says," *Dallas Morning News,* May 27, 1998, p. 28A.

32. Christy Hoppe, "Early Figures Show Slight Increase in UT Minority Enrollment," *Dallas Morning News,* May 20, 1998, p. 16A.

33. *Edgewood* v. *Kirby,* 804 S.W.2d (1991), at 496.

14 Texas Environmental Policy

Chapter Outline

In 1992 in Brownsville, a city in the Rio Grande Valley, babies were being born without brains eight times more often than the nationwide rate.[1] Although a study by state and national investigators failed to identify the specific cause of the phenomenon, many believe that it had something to do with pollution. American industries had built several factories—called ***maquiladoras***—on the Mexican side of the Rio Grande to take advantage of favorable tariffs, cheap labor, and Mexico's weaker environmental-protection laws. Many suspect that the brainless babies were affected by air and water pollution from these factories. An out-of-court settlement in 1996 resulted in a payment of about $25 million to Brownsville families. A new suit was brought to court in 1997 involving Mexican families.[2]

Between 1988 and 1995, Texas reduced emission of toxic substances into the air, water, and land by 38 percent, a reduction rate bested only by Louisiana. But even with that achievement, Texas still ranked first among the states in total toxic emissions in 1995.[3]

By 1998, the failure of the state's metropolitan areas to meet national air quality standards threatened to trigger the application of more stringent procedures to reduce air pollution in these cities.

Stories such as these illustrate the variety and magnitude of environmental problems in Texas. How the state responds to those problems has implications both for the state's economy and for the quality of life there. This chapter addresses several questions:

- What types of environmental problems is Texas facing, and how serious are they?
- What policy steps has the state taken to address these problems?
- What political forces are important in environmental policymaking?
- What does the future hold for environmental policy in Texas?

The Challenge to Change: An Introduction

The principal force instrumental in bringing about change in Texas environmental policy is the national government's environmental policies, which mandate certain state actions. The environmental protection movement produced major national legislation in the 1960s and the 1970s. The Clean Air Act was passed in 1963; the Water Quality Act, in 1965; the Clean Water Restoration Act, in 1966. The Environmental Protection Agency (EPA) was created in 1970 to coordinate national environmental policies. The Federal Water Pollution Control Act was strengthened in 1972; the Clean Water Act was passed in 1972; and the Resource Conservation and Recovery Act was passed in 1976.[4] Congress amended some of these laws after they were passed, often setting new deadlines for state and local governments to meet (Table 14.1). Particularly noteworthy were the 1990 amendments to the Clean Air

Table 14.1 Selected National Environmental Mandates and Their Impact

Legislative Mandate	Requirements	Deadlines	Effect
Clean Air Act Amendments (1990)	Set new schedule for addressing remaining air pollution threats.	The amendments set a series of new deadlines between 1995 and 2010 and require non-attainment areas to take additional steps to reduce air pollution.	Many areas will be required to have automobile emissions testing. Traffic reduction and alternative fuels may be required in some cases.
Clean Water Act of 1972	Prohibits polluted discharges into rivers, lakes, and bays.	Most cities were required to comply with sludge-handling standards by February 1994; those needing new equipment had to comply by February 1995.	Many cities had to upgrade sewage treatment facilities.
Resource Conservation and Recovery Act (1976)	Sets national rules for landfills.	April 1994.	Many existing landfills had to be closed. New landfills must meet more stringent construction requirements.
Resource Conservation and Recovery Act (1976)	Sets new EPA standards for underground storage tanks.	By 1998, older tanks must be equipped with devices to prevent spills and overflows.	Local governments must buy insurance or otherwise guarantee that money will be available to clean up spills and compensate third parties for damages.
Safe Drinking Water Act (1974, 1986)	Sets national standards for health-threatening contaminants in drinking water.	National standards are in effect for 84 potential contaminants. Large cities must install corrosion control and water treatment equipment by January 1997; medium-sized cities (fewer than 50,000 customers), by January 1996; and small cities by January 1998.	Cities that do not meet lead and copper standards must install corrosion control equipment and new water treatment equipment.

Source: Adapted from "State and Local Environmental Agenda," *Governing* 8 (February 1995): 50–51.

Act, which renewed the nation's commitment to improving air quality in its cities.

In the movement to clean up the environment, the national government's primary role was to set standards. The states and their local governments were made responsible for implementing those standards. So Texas (along with all the other states) had to improve air and water quality or face the threat of federal intervention.

Organizing to Manage Environmental Policy

Until recently the formulation and implementation of environmental policy were allocated to several Texas agencies: no agency was responsible for coordinating that policy. The Texas Air Control Board was responsible for air quality. The Texas Water Commission handled water quality. The Texas Railroad Commission regulated the environmental aspects of mining. The Department of Health was responsible for municipal solid waste and several other environmental matters.

In 1991 the legislature created the **Texas Natural Resource Conservation Commission** (TNRCC) to oversee the state's environmental policy. When it began its work on September 1, 1993, the TNRCC absorbed the Texas Water Commission, the Texas Air Control Board, the Water Well Drillers Board, the Texas Board of Irrigators, and the solid waste, sewage and wastewater treatment, and radioactive waste disposal programs of the Department of Health. The new agency is headed by three full-time commissioners, appointed by the governor with the consent of the senate. The commissioners hire an executive director who is responsible for most day-to-day administrative tasks.

The TNRCC is a major step forward in coordinating the state's environmental policies, but some environmental responsibilities remain with other agencies. For example, the Texas Railroad Commission still is responsible for many environmental concerns related to mining; and the General Land Office still has responsibility for coastal management and cleanup. Consolidation has started, but further consolidation may be needed to finish the job.

Environmental Policy Problems in Texas Today

Air Pollution

The basic standards for air quality are set forth in the national Clean Air Act (originally passed in 1963, reenacted in 1977, and amended in 1990). In response, Texas passed its own clean air act in 1971 and has amended it on several occasions.[5] Federal law requires that local areas be evaluated on six pollution categories: ozone, sulfur dioxide, carbon monoxide, lead, nitrogen dioxide, and particulate matter. Based on the standards in the amendments to the Clean Air Act, Texas currently has sixteen counties in four metropolitan "nonattainment areas": Dallas–Fort Worth, Beaumont–Port Arthur, El Paso, and Houston–Galveston (Table 14.2). All of these areas have been cited for ozone problems; El Paso also has been cited for carbon monoxide and

Table 14.2 Clean Air Act Nonattainment Areas in Texas

Nonattainment Area	EPA Classification
Dallas–Fort Worth	Moderate
Beaumont–Port Arthur	Serious
El Paso	Serious
Houston–Galveston	Severe

Source: Legislative Budget Board, *Fiscal Size Up: 1998–99* (Austin, LLB, 1998), p. 9–10.

particulate-matter problems. As Table 14.2 shows, the problems in each area have been classified by their severity. In addition, Austin, San Antonio, Corpus Christi, and the Longview-Tyler-Marshall area are considered marginal or near **nonattainment areas.**

The TNRCC's Office of Air Quality developed a program to encourage compliance with federal standards for air quality. If the state's efforts fail to produce compliance, the EPA could step in, leaving the state with no control over its air-quality program.

Because **ozone** has been the most common air-quality problem, and because ozone problems are related directly to automobile exhaust emissions, Texas nonattainment cities have worked to reduce automobile emissions. The cities also worked to reduce the number of automobiles in their downtown areas. **High-occupancy vehicle (HOV) lanes** have been constructed on major thoroughfares to cut down the number of single-occupancy vehicles. Houston became the "HOV Capital of the World." In the Dallas area, the Dallas Area Rapid Transit system (DART) manages a bus and a light rail system as part of its metropolitan transportation system.[6]

In another step to reduce emissions, the legislature required transit authorities to begin switching their fleet vehicles to liquefied natural gas or other clean-burning alternative fuels. Over a period of three years (1998 to 2000), 30 to 70 percent of each transit authority's fleet must be using alternative fuels.[7]

In January 1998, the Commissioner of TNRCC announced that although there had been dramatic improvements in the ozone levels in Texas, the progress was not fast enough. Consequently, the commissioner outlined a series of new steps that the state was considering.[8] One possibility was the widespread use of **reformulated gasolines** that burn cleaner than regular fuels. In 1997, the Dallas/Fort Worth and Houston metropolitan areas were already using this gasoline. The new proposal would extend the covered area to include most of the central and eastern half of Texas. Similarly, the commission was considering expanding the area in which the use of vapor-trapping equipment for deliveries of gasoline to retailers is used to prevent the escape of the ozone-producing vapors into the air. A third step under consideration

This picture of Houston rush hour traffic shows the problem of automobile traffic that has contributed to the city's problems in meeting federal air quality standards.

was the imposition of tighter regulations on larger business and major industrial sources of pollution in all of eastern and central Texas. Finally, TNRCC encouraged automobile makers to move forward with the development of a National Low Emission Vehicle (NLEV) and to bring those cleaner-burning automobiles and trucks to the Texas market by 2001. Although these recommendations had not been transformed into an official plan by spring 1998, it was clear that meeting federal standards would force the state to undertake more strenuous efforts to reduce air pollution at the end of the 1990s.

Water Pollution

Texans depend on two sources of water: surface water and groundwater. About 39 percent of the state's water supply comes from surface water, the water in rivers, streams, and lakes. **Surface water** is the principal source of water in East Texas. Farther west, cities, farms, and industry rely on the water held in underground aquifers (Figure 14.1). About 61 percent of the state's water supply comes from **groundwater.**[9]

The purpose of water policies is to ensure that the state has an adequate supply of water and that the supply is protected from pollution by bacteria or poisonous chemicals. The national government took the lead in dealing with water pollution when it passed The Clean Water Act in 1972. Amendments in 1987 extended the act through 1994. Following federal guidelines, the

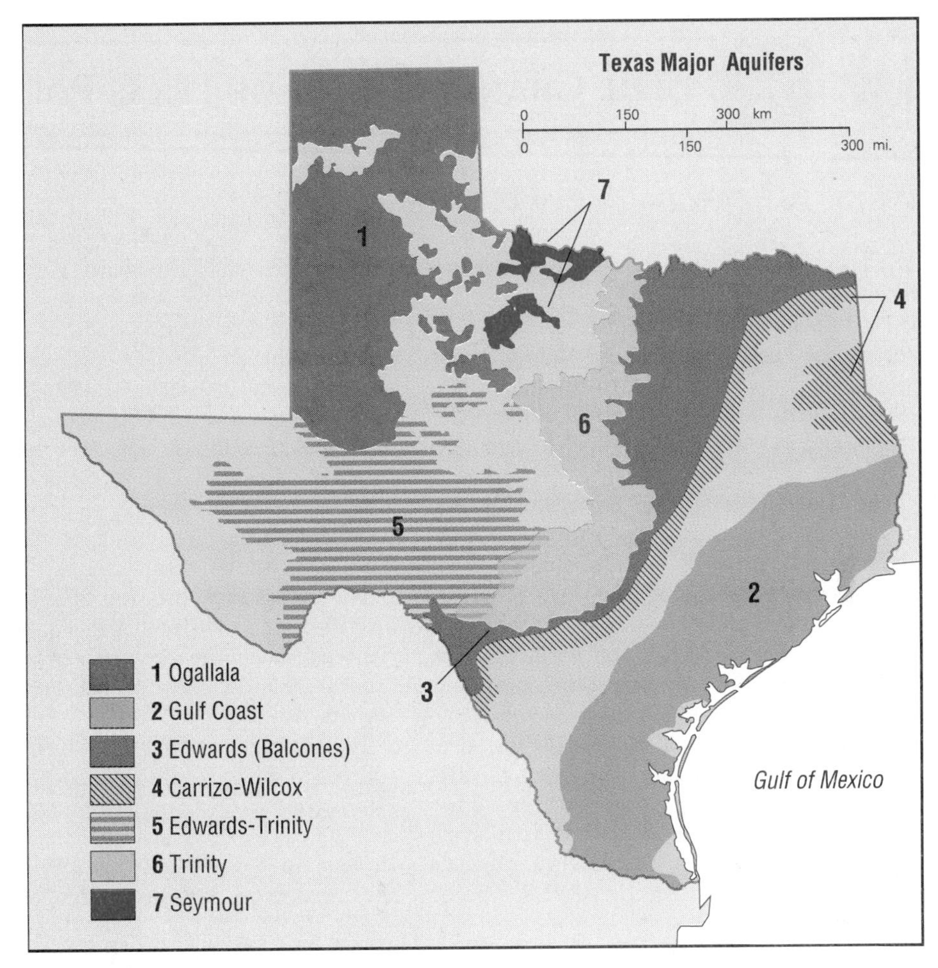

FIGURE 14.1 Major Aquifers in Texas
Source: Texas Comptroller of Public Accounts, Forces of Change *(Austin, 1994), 2: pt. 1, 419.*

Texas Natural Resource Conservation Commission sets standards for water quality. Water supplies are designated for specific uses, such as drinking, swimming, or fishing. Water-quality standards vary with the designated use. In 1997, the legislature passed Senate Bill 1 charging the **Texas Water Development Board** with developing a comprehensive water plan. The plan would ensure the availability of sufficient water at a reasonable cost to maintain public health, safety, and welfare; to support further economic development; and to protect the agricultural and natural resources of the entire state.[10]

A 1992 report concluded that most surface water in Texas is clean. The report found that 72 percent of stream miles, 89 percent of reservoir waters, and 66 percent of bay waters support their designated uses.[11] Some areas that had serious problems in the past have made significant improvement in

THE CHANGING FACE OF TEXAS POLITICS

Water for Texas—Today and Tomorrow

The Texas environmentally-related agency that received the biggest budget increase for the 1998–1999 biennium was the Texas Water Development Board. The agency's appropriation more than doubled, from $42 million for 1996–1997 to $86 million for 1998–1999. What is this agency and why did it receive such a big budget increase?

The Water Development Board was created in 1957 and given broad responsibility for developing and conserving water supplies in the state. Among its planning responsibilities, the agency prepares and periodically updates a 50-year water plan entitled *Water for Texas—Today and Tomorrow.*[1] In addition to planning, the agency has distributed funds to local governments to assist with the construction of water systems and wastewater removal systems. To fund those operations, the board has periodically been given authority to borrow money by selling bonds. The voters approved a constitutional amendment in 1997 providing more flexibility to the board in the use of the funds to develop water infrastructure.

So why did an agency that has traditionally operated out of the limelight get its budget doubled by the legislature in 1997? For the most part, the reason was the legislature's passage in 1997 of Senate Bill 1.[2] The very number of the bill signals that the Texas Senate considered this an important piece of legislation—the number one has been assigned in the past to major educational reform legislation and even to the state's appropriation bill. That number also indicated that the legislation was high on the legislative priorities of the lieutenant governor—the most powerful person in the Texas Senate.

Two forces converged to bring water resources to the top of the legislative list in 1997. First, the state experienced a devastating drought in 1996. At that time, Texas was one of three states (New Mexico and Wyoming were the other two) without a drought plan. The

recent years. The Houston ship channel is a notable example. Before regulations were implemented in the 1970s, there were no fish in the channel. Today, there are fish again, but they are not fit for consumption because of chemical pollution.[12]

A continuing water pollution problem in Texas comes from the discharge of sewage into water supplies. Municipal sewage—not manufacturing or agricultural waste—is the largest source of water pollution in the state. The Rio Grande River area has some of the most severe problems from sewage pollution. Cities on the Mexican side of the river dump raw sewage directly into the river, creating serious health hazards.[13]

Colonias are settlements in Texas that have serious water pollution problems and the health problems that go along with them. ***Colonias*** are created by subdividing and selling land without improvements or basic services. The land is cheap, and buyers build on the land using whatever drought of 1996 was a wake up call. The other force driving Senate Bill 1 was the realization that the state's population would double in the next fifty years, but that the amount of water available will not. Thus, planning to ensure an adequate water supply became a critical issue for Texas legislators.

Senate Bill 1 makes development of a water plan the responsibility of the Texas Water Development Board and sets a deadline of 2001 for completion of the plan. After that, the plan must be updated every five years. In addition, the legislation calls for regional water development boards to develop plans consistent with the state's plan. The Texas Water Development Board is authorized to make grants to local governments for developing water plans, as well as for developing water and wastewater infrastructures.

One of the more controversial aspects of this legislation authorizes the Texas Natural Resource Conservation Commission to establish "interbasin transfers." In simple terms, this allows the TNRCC to authorize transfer of water from lakes on one river to lakes on another river. The transfer of water from one area of another, especially during a drought, is always a touchy issue.

The law also requires groundwater districts to monitor pumping from aquifers—the other source of water in Texas. The use of the Edwards Aquifer near San Antonio has been an ongoing debate in recent years. The new law recognizes that other underground water supplies will need to be monitored as well.

The passage of Senate Bill 1 makes it clear that the state must plan for the development of water supplies and for the rational allocation of water as the population outruns water supplies and as drought heightens the risk in some areas more than in others. Moreover, the law makes it clear that water supply will be a critical issue for Texas—along with water quality. This is a politically explosive issue, and Senate Bill 1 does not resolve all of its ramifications, especially those regarding pumping rights to water in underground aquifers. But, at least the law obligates the state and its public agencies to work toward an equitable solution to the problem of water supply. ★

[1] Texas Water Development Board, *Water for Texas: A Consensus-Based Update to the State Water Plan* (Austin: Texas Water Development Board, 1997).

[2] Senate Bill 1, 75th Legislature, 1997. This lengthy bill was a major rework of the Texas Water Code.

materials they can afford. These developments are found in the unincorporated areas of counties where building codes and zoning ordinances are minimal or nonexistent. A 1990 national government study found that 60 percent of Texas *colonias* had access to public water supplies but less than 1 percent had sewerage systems.[14] A survey by the Texas Water Development Board in 1992 identified 1,193 *colonias* with an estimated population of 280,000. Most of these settlements are along the Texas–Mexico border.[15] Because of the primitive conditions in the *colonias,* diseases spread by waterborne bacteria (such as tuberculosis, dysentery, gastroenteritis, and hepatitis) occur at two to three times the national rate.[16]

To address the problems in the *colonias,* Texas passed two constitutional amendments authorizing the sale of bonds to raise money for water projects. The 1989 amendment earmarked $100 million for projects in the *colonias.* A 1991 amendment allocated an additional $150 million.[17]

Because Texas has a significant number of chemical industries, industrial pollution like this from factories along the Houston ship channel contributes to the problems of air quality.

Vast areas of Texas, including central and western areas and the Panhandle, depend on groundwater for most uses. **Aquifers** are subject to some natural pollution from deep saline water and minerals. But about 80 percent of the groundwater pollution problems in Texas come from underground petroleum storage tanks. Industrial hazardous wastes, the byproducts of oil and gas production, and industrial and municipal wastewater account for the remaining problems.[18]

A major cause of declining groundwater quality is overpumping. When aquifers are drained faster than they can replenish themselves, higher concentrations of mineral sediments and seepage of saltwater will lower water quality. This is a special problem in the Panhandle because of heavy agricultural use and the Gulf Coast area because of heavy urban pumping. Conflict between farmers and the city of San Antonio that threatened water quality in the Edwards Aquifer caused the legislature to create the Edwards Aquifer Authority in 1993 to regulate withdrawals from that source.[19]

Solid Waste

In 1991 Texans generated 18 million tons of municipal waste—about one ton per resident. Governments can deal with trash in four ways: bury it in landfills, burn it in incinerators, recycle it, or reduce the source. Most solid waste goes to **landfills.** Requirements in the national Resource Conservation and Recovery Act that took effect in 1993 may force many existing landfills to close.[20]

The environmental hazards of Texas colonias have threatened the health of their residents.

Because of the vast open spaces in West Texas, the state is an attractive site for **megafills,** huge landfills in rural areas that take trash from cities on a fee basis. One site near Sierra Blanca (in Hudspeth County just east of El Paso) will receive 240,000 tons of processed sludge from New York City as part of a six-year, $168 million agreement. Not surprisingly, residents of rural areas in Texas are not excited at the prospect of having huge trash dumps nearby.[21]

To divert solid waste from landfills, state and local governments have begun to encourage **recycling.** In Texas, the General Land Office has a legislative mandate to raise public awareness of recycling possibilities and to develop new markets for recycled goods.[22] Several Texas cities have passed ordinances prohibiting citizens from putting grass clippings in their trash. The Recycling Bill, passed in 1991 by the legislature, set a goal of recycling at least 40 percent of the state's municipal solid waste by 1994. By 1997, all but six states had set recycling goals. Cities had to establish programs to collect waste paper, plastic, glass, aluminum cans, used oil, lead-acid batteries, and yard waste. The chairman of the TNRCC reported in 1994 that this goal would not be met in 1994, and it still had not been met in 1997. Results varied widely from city to city, with some coming close to the 40 percent recycling goal.[23] The biggest problem with recycling programs is that the supply of recyclable materials often exceeds demand. To stimulate demand, Texas has established guidelines for state agencies that encourage the purchase of materials with recycled content.[24]

Some Texas cities have developed innovative ways of dealing with solid waste. Both Austin and Houston operate programs to turn sludge into fertilizer. Using a process that dries sewage at high temperatures, Austin converts sewage into "Dillo Dirt"; Houston produces "Hou-Actinite."[25] Austin also has restructured its solid-waste collection system to create incentives for residents to reduce waste. A "pay as you throw" garbage collection system charges each household by the size of the garbage cart it chooses. In addition the city encourages recycling by collecting recyclables on the same day it collects garbage.[26]

Hazardous Waste

Hazardous materials are inherently dangerous to handle or eliminate because they are explosive, ignitable, radioactive, or toxic. This is a significant problem in a state with a large number of chemical and petrochemical plants. Texas leads all the states in the amount of toxic chemicals released or transferred by major manufacturers.[27]

Most toxic wastes end up in landfills, where they contaminate the soil or leach out and contaminate groundwater. In 1993, for example, the state health commissioner issued a warning against eating fish from Clear Creek (near Houston) because the fish may have been contaminated by the nearby Brio hazardous-waste site.[28] In 1994, planning for a hazardous-waste landfill near Dryden, Texas, included the restriction that all materials added to the landfill be in solid form.[29]

Hazardous waste has been a central concern in the Rio Grande Valley. *Maquiladoras* in Mexico are required to ship hazardous wastes back to the United States, along with the goods they manufacture. But Texas authorities suspect that only about 60 percent of the waste is being returned, that the balance is being dumped illegally.[30] Before a hazardous-waste tracking system came on line in 1992, an EPA official estimated that only 29 percent of American-owned *maquiladoras* returned their waste to the United States.[31] An environmental agreement with Mexico (the La Paz Agreement) that was a prelude to entering into NAFTA in 1993 was intended to help solve some of these problems. Senate Bill 843, passed by the legislature in 1997, requires the TNRCC to study the cost and effectiveness of an electronic system to track the amount of hazardous waste returned to the United States under the La Paz Agreement.

Clean Industries 2000 was cited by the chairman of TNRCC as a success story in reducing hazardous waste generation in Texas. The program gives companies flexibility in the means used to achieve their goal, but they must install sophisticated pollution-monitoring equipment that transmits data directly to state officials.[32] To be admitted to the program, a business pledges to reduce its generation of hazardous waste by 50 percent or to reduce toxic pollutants released into the environment by 50 percent, or both by 2000. By 1997, the members of the program had reduced hazardous waste generation by 15.3 million tons.[33]

Radioactive material is a special problem. Low-level radioactive material—which is produced by nuclear power plants, hospitals, universities, and industry—must be disposed of in sites licensed by the TNRCC. In 1992 the megafill in Sierra Blanca was approved for low-level radioactive waste, mostly from nuclear power plants. The location was chosen because its groundwater is very deep and, therefore, is less likely to be contaminated. In 1993 the state agreed to accept low-level radioactive waste from Maine and Vermont.[34]

High-level radioactive waste, which is produced by reprocessing spent nuclear fuel, remains radioactive for thousands of years. One source of that waste is the Pantex nuclear weapons assembly plant near Amarillo, in the Panhandle region. In 1992 the U.S. Department of Energy announced that the plant temporarily would store tons of plutonium from dismantled nuclear weapons. Critics fear that the Pantex plant has become an unofficial permanent storage site for nuclear waste.[35]

Cleaning Up the Environment

Cleaning up damage that already has been done is also a vital part of protecting the natural environment. Materials that are harmless in their appropriate use can be major environmental threats when they spill or leak into other environmental settings. In 1990, for example, an oil tanker collided with two barges in the Houston ship channel, releasing as much as 700,000 gallons of oil into Galveston Bay and threatening marshes and birds and other wildlife.[36] An elaborate cleanup effort—microbes were released to eat up the oil—was required.[37] In response to the crisis, the state legislature enacted a new law in 1991 that made the General Land Office responsible for preventing coastal oil spills and responding to them. It further created the Coastal Protection Fund to pay for prevention and cleanup activities.[38] In 1995 another collision off Galveston released about 47,000 gallons of oil, and the state launched another clean-up effort.[39]

The 1991 legislation made the General Land Office responsible for developing a **coastal management plan.** As late as 1995, Texas was one of only two coastal states without an approved coastal management plan. Approval of the plan by the federal government in 1997 opened the door for some federal coastal improvement grants.[40]

Spills are a serious problem in Texas. Between September 1992 and May 1993, 4,500 spills were reported to the state. Cleanup was completed at over 3,000 sites. In 1993, Texas had 29 sites either on or proposed for federal superfund cleanup.[41] Congress established the **Superfund,** which is funneled through the EPA, to pay for cleaning up hazardous-waste sites. The Texas sites were created by a variety of pollutants, including oil, mercury, pesticides, lead, creosote, and paint solvent.[42]

Also in need of cleanup are abandoned landfills or storage tanks. The TNRCC's Petroleum Storage Tank Division is responsible for cleaning up leaking underground storage tanks and preventing further pollution from them.[43] Estimates were that it could take another thirty years to clean up all these tanks.[44]

Another cleanup task results from abandoned oil and gas wells. The state has provided funds for plugging wells since 1984, but the legislature significantly increased that funding in 1991. The program, which is supervised by the Texas Railroad Commission, gives highest priority to wells that are leaking in a sensitive area, that have been cited in a complaint, or for which a surety bond has been forfeited. Another program supports the cleanup of oil-field pollution. That program is supported entirely by fees, fines, and other payments collected from the oil and gas industry.[45]

Who Pays for Environmental Protection?

Environmental protection is costly. An important question, then, is "Who pays?" Usually the polluter pays. In Texas, for example, recent legislation imposed charges on the oil and gas industry to support storage tank and oil-field cleanup. Ultimately, of course, industry passes these costs along to its customers, the price of products reflecting environmental costs.

Making the polluter pay works when the polluter can readily be identified. But what happens when instead of one major polluter, there are many small polluters? This is the case with the air pollution in Texas cities that is caused by thousands of cars. Where pollution stems from many sources, the cost of prevention and cleanup generally must be borne by a broad group—the residents of a city, a state, or the nation. Citizens pay the costs of environmental protection through fees and taxes.

What level of government pays for environmental protection? Cities bear much of the environmental burden because they traditionally are responsible for drinking water, garbage collection, sewage treatment, and solid-waste disposal. Texas cities are affected more than cities in other states because the state gives its cities relatively little help in meeting environmental mandates.[46]

Environmental Politics

At the national level, the making of environmental policy usually involves a struggle among coalitions of interest groups. At the state level, the key player in environmental policymaking is often the national government. Since the 1960s, the states generally have not been allowed to choose whether they want to enact environmental policies; they are required to meet federal guidelines. Texas environmental policymaking, then, has tended to be a response to federal mandates, especially in the areas of air and water pollution. And sometimes Texas policy has been a response to rulings in the federal courts. The Edwards Aquifer bill, which was enacted by the Texas legislature in 1993, settled an environmental protection suit that had been filed by the Sierra Club.

In Texas, as elsewhere, environmental protection and economic growth commonly are seen as conflicting goals. And business interests usually oppose environmental regulations, claiming those regulations obstruct economic development. Environmental problems in the state have been concentrated along the Gulf Coast, where oil, gas, and petrochemicals are key parts of the economy. Lobbyists for those industries have been the principal opponents of environmental legislation in Austin. Although contemporary environmentalists increasingly argue that economic growth and environmental protection can be pursued simultaneously, to date Texas leaders have remained concerned about the economic efforts of environmental regulations.

One political struggle in the 1995 legislative session illustrates the kinds of coalitions that have commonly fought over environmental policy in Texas. At issue was a bill authorizing a private waste disposal company to seek a license to dispose of mixed nuclear and hazardous waste at a site in Andrews county (near the New Mexico border) where the company was already authorized to dispose of hazardous waste.[47] The waste disposal company and officials of Andrews County supported the bill. The proponents of the bill sought its passage because of the economic benefits, billions of dollars of Department of Energy and Department of Defense contracts for the waste disposal company and jobs for sparsely populated Andrews County. Opponents wanted the bill killed because of potential environmental hazards, because private companies had not established a reputation for reliable disposal of such material, and because Texas had established a policy of disposing of low-level radioactive materials only in a state-run dump (Sierra Blanca).[48] The waste disposal company was able to hire some high-powered lobbyists to push the bill: Kent Hance (former member of the Texas Railroad Commission and former gubernatorial candidate) and Carl Parker (former state senator). Initially the bill seemed headed for passage, sailing through the senate in record time. It met more opposition in the house, however, and ultimately was defeated there. When a member objected that it did not conform to the rules of the Texas House or to the Texas Constitution, the speaker upheld the objection. Because the end of the session was near, the bill could not be further considered. The bill illustrated the clash between economic motives and environmental concerns that has been characteristic of this kind of policy.

Political leaders in Texas usually have not taken an aggressive role in environmental politics. No recent governor of either political party has made the environment a key campaign issue or has tried to build a significant record of environmental protection. Legislative leaders also have been reluctant to take highly visible positions on environmental regulation. Texas politicians have found that it makes good political sense to tell the public that "the federal government made us do it."

The Future of Texas Environmental Policy

Most observers agree that Texas has changed its policies toward environmental protection and that environmental quality in the state has improved. The air and water are cleaner. Environmental hazards left behind by the oil industry are being cleaned up.

Certainly improvements have been made, but Texas still faces formidable environmental challenges. Ensuring an adequate supply of good-quality water is still an important challenge, especially in the western part of the state. Air quality in metropolitan areas—where most of the state's population lives—is an ongoing problem. Years of work remain to clean up environmental hazards left behind by the state's oil industry. Abandoned wells need to be capped, storage tanks need to be removed, and old drilling sites need to be reclaimed. Cleaning up the Rio Grande Valley is a special challenge because it demands the cooperation of the Mexican government. And solid-waste disposal will become increasingly problematic unless the state can find ways of diverting more waste from landfills.

The future of environmentalism in Texas depends in part on the actions of the national government. It seems doubtful that Texas would have made the progress it has in environmental protection without the prodding of national environmental standards or the incentives from federal grants. The national government, though, has been sending mixed signals to the states. On the one hand, national mandates are being enacted and enforced aggressively. On the other, the national government has reduced the amount of aid it provides for environmental cleanup. This means that state and local authorities, especially city officials, are faced with the growing burden of unfunded mandates (see Chapter 10).

The lobbying efforts of proponents and opponents of environmental protection also will shape the future of Texas environmental policy. Here, too, in the absence of public awareness and the commitment of environmental groups, lobbying efforts by business interests that want to ease the economic burdens of environmental regulation are likely to be more successful.

The future of environmental progress in Texas depends on a number of contingencies. Because environmental concerns historically have not ranked high on the political agenda in the state, it is not hard to imagine a scenario that would lead to environmental backsliding. In fact, some thought that the 1995 session of the legislature already demonstrated that tendency.[49] Thus, Texas does not yet seem to have established a firm commitment to environmental protection.

Notes

1. Dan Fagin, "Border Town Mystery: Why Are So Many Brownsville Babies Being Born Brainless," *Newsday,* July 12, 1992, 5.

2. "Hazardous Trades Bring Pollution and Health Fears Down Mexico Way," *Financial Times* (London), June 6, 1997, p. 6.
3. Environmental Protection Agency, *1995 Toxic Release Inventory* (Washington, DC: EPA, 1995), pp. 23 and 120.
4. Texas Comptroller of Public Accounts, *Forces of Change* (Austin, 1994), 2: pt. 1, 435.
5. Texas Health and Safety Code, Sec. 382.
6. Texas Comptroller of Public Accounts, *Fiscal Notes,* February 1994, 4–5.
7. Texas Comptroller, *Fiscal Notes,* February 1994, 4.
8. Press release from Texas Natural Resource Conservation Commission dated January 27, 1998. Available from TNRCC web site (**http://www.tnrcc.texas.gov**).
9. Texas Comptroller, *Forces of Change,* 2: pt. 1, 453.
10. Texas Water Code, Section 12.051.
11. Texas Comptroller, *Forces of Change,* 2: pt. 1, 453.
12. Texas Comptroller, *Forces of Change,* 2: pt. 1, 454.
13. Texas Comptroller, *Forces of Change,* 2: pt. 1, 454.
14. Cited in F. Andrew Schoolmaster, "Free Trade and the Environment: A Case Study of the Texas Colonias," *Great Plains Research* 3 (August 1993): 321–35. The point made here is on p. 324.
15. Cited in Schoolmaster, "Free Trade and the Environment," 325.
16. Texas Comptroller, *Forces of Change,* 2: pt. 1, 454.
17. Schoolmaster, "Free Trade and the Environment," 329–330.
18. Texas Comptroller, *Forces of Change,* 2: pt. 1, 458.
19. Texas Comptroller, *Forces of Change,* 2: pt. 1, 459–460.
20. Texas Comptroller, *Forces of Change,* 2: pt. 1, 444.
21. Texas Comptroller, *Forces of Change,* 2: pt. 1, 444.
22. Texas Health and Safety Code, Sec. 361.424.
23. Quoted in Bill Dawson, "Recycling Program Lags Despite Its Solid Support," *Houston Chronicle,* March 12, 1994, 1A.
24. Texas Comptroller, *Forces of Change,* 2: pt. 1, 451.
25. Texas Comptroller, *Forces of Change,* 2: pt. 1, 452.
26. Texas Comptroller, *Forces of Change,* 2: pt. 1, 448.
27. Texas Comptroller, *Forces of Change,* 2: pt. 1, 461.
28. Ruth Rendon, "State Warning: Don't Eat Clear Creek Fish," *Houston Chronicle,* November 19, 1993, 33A.
29. Texas Comptroller, *Forces of Change,* 2: pt. 1, 463.
30. Texas Comptroller, *Forces of Change,* 2: pt. 1, 464–465.
31. Cited in James Pinkerton, "Living on the Edge: Toxic Waste Data in Short Supply," *Houston Chronicle,* October 20, 1993, 21A.
32. Bill Dawson, "New Way to Fight Pollution," *Houston Chronicle,* February 16, 1994, 25A.
33. "Clean Industries 2000," (**http://www.tnrcc.state.tx.us**).
34. Texas Comptroller, *Forces of Change,* 2: pt. 1, 465–466.
35. Texas Comptroller, *Forces of Change,* 2: pt. 1, 466.

36. "Galveston Bay Spill Could Hit 700,000 Gallons," *Los Angeles Times,* August 4, 1990, 17A.
37. "Microbes Appear to Work on Oil Spill," *Fort Worth Star–Telegram,* June 17, 1990, 8A.
38. Legislative Budget Board, *Fiscal Size Up: 1992–93 Biennium* (Austin, 1991), 10-8.
39. "Oil Spill is Reaching Beach," *Houston Chronicle,* February 27, 1995, 11A.
40. "State to Get Coastal Funds," *Houston Chronicle,* January 11, 1997, p. 30a.
41. Legislative Budget Board, *Fiscal Size Up: 1994–95 Biennium,* 10-14.
42. Texas Comptroller, *Forces of Change,* 2: pt. 1, 464.
43. Legislative Budget Board, *Fiscal Size Up: 1994–95,* 10-14.
44. Texas Comptroller, *Forces of Change,* 2: pt. 1, 459.
46. Texas Comptroller of Public Accounts, *Fiscal Notes,* June 1992, 12.
46. Texas Comptroller, *Forces of Change,* 2: pt. 1, 472–473.
47. George Kuempel, "Waste Bill Dies Again in the House," *Dallas Morning News,* May 27, 1995, 30A.
48. R. G. Ratcliffe, "Nuclear Dump Finds New Life in the Senate," *Houston Chronicle,* May 25, 1995, 33A.
49. Christy Hoppe, "95 Session Proves Tough for Environmentalists," *Dallas Morning News,* May 15, 1995, 1A.

Appendix A

Keeping Up with Texas Politics

The goal of this book is to help students become informed citizens so that they can participate effectively in Texas politics. To that end, the book provides background on the structure and processes of politics in the state. But being an informed citizen means keeping up with Texas politics long after this book is finished. In this appendix are suggestions about resources that can help students stay current with the changing issues and processes in Texas politics. The intent here is not to list every available resource—just those that the author has found especially valuable. The notes at the end of each chapter also list important sources of information.

A word of caution: No one source can keep users up to date on all the different types of information available on politics in Texas. This appendix, then, not only lists resources; it also describes the type of information the resources are likely to contain. Four types of resources are discussed here: periodicals, reference works, government sources, and Internet resources. Each offers different kinds of information about Texas government.

Periodicals

Newspapers are one obvious source of contemporary information about Texas government and politics. All newspapers report news about Texas government because they all subscribe to the large news services like the Associated Press. But those services provide just the basics. For in-depth coverage—for probing behind the headlines—students should turn to the big-city papers. Among the major regional papers that do a good job of reporting on Texas government are the *Dallas Morning News,* the *Fort Worth Star-Telegram,* the *Houston Chronicle,* and the *Austin American-Statesman.*

Finding political news in a newspaper can be a difficult task. Front pages tend to be filled with news of national and local crises. Political news typically makes its way onto front pages when politicians are campaigning, when the legislature is in session, or when a scandal breaks in state government. At other times, state political news is buried in the inside pages. Figuring out where that news is demands some experience with the format of individual papers.

Students of state politics also can use newspapers to research political happenings. Most college and university libraries keep back issues of major newspapers on microfilm. And modern technology in the form of CD-ROM has made major Texas newspapers even more accessible. The software makes it possible to search for stories that contain a specific word (like *governor*) or a string of words (like *governor and budget*). Many college and university libraries have several newspapers on CD-ROM, as do major-city libraries. The major Texas newspapers also maintain web sites that provide current information. A few newspapers offer access to archives on-line.

In addition to local newspapers, national newspapers like the *New York Times* and the *Wall Street Journal* also can be a valuable source of news about Texas politics. The advantage here is perspective. When they write about politics in Texas, these papers are likely to compare what's happening in Texas with what's going on in other states. For example, a story about welfare payments in Texas is likely to compare them with welfare payments elsewhere. National papers are commonly available in major libraries, in the same formats as local papers.

Magazines are another source of information about Texas government and politics. Although it is not a newsmagazine as such, *Texas Monthly*'s reports on the state's legislative sessions are well known, filled with an entertaining list of the best and worst legislators in the session and behind-the-scenes reporting on how major deals were struck. *Texas Business* also reports on state and local politics. Although it speaks from a business perspective, it is a good source of information about the state's political affairs. It also does a good job of reporting business news that can help readers assess the state's progress in economic development. National newsmagazines—for example, *Time, Newsweek,* and *U.S. News & World Report*—occasionally report on developments in Texas. Like national newspapers, their stories are valuable for comparisons with other states.

Reference Works

The *Texas Almanac,* which is published every two years, is the standard reference work on Texas. Its sections on politics and government list election statistics, the names of state agencies and officeholders, and information about local governments. Along with the tabular information are informative essays. In addition, the *Almanac* is one of the few readily available sources of the wording of the Texas Constitution (with amendments up to the date of publication). Because of its length, the Texas Constitution is not nearly as easy to find as a copy of the national constitution. The *Almanac* can be purchased for a modest price from most bookstores; it also can be found in libraries.

A new reference work on the Texas legislature has recently become available: *The Texas Legislative Almanac.* The first edition of this work was published for the 1997 legislative session by Texas A&M University Press, edited by Harvey J. Tucker and Gary M. Halter. It provides information about the legislature's structure and procedures, and includes a biographical page on each member of the legislature. It should quickly become a standard reference work in libraries.

For comparative information about the states, the *Book of the States,* published biennially by the Council of State Governments, is an excellent source. In addition to valuable information in tables, each volume contains original essays on major policy problems being addressed by the states. These essays can help readers evaluate whether Texas is leading or following other states in addressing important problems.

For statistical data that allow comparisons of Texas and other states, the *Statistical Abstract* (published by the U.S. Census Bureau) is useful. The *Abstract* provides a range of demographic information about the states, including education levels, income, and even voting patterns.

Government Sources

Texas government agencies publish a substantial amount of information about themselves and their work. The comptroller's office has a tradition of getting information out in readable form. In a periodical called *Fiscal Notes,* the office provides information, not only about the state's financial affairs, but also about important economic and social trends that are affecting the state. Many libraries keep *Fiscal Notes* on their shelves; and with a written request, the comptroller's office will send it free of charge. The comptroller's office also publishes the recommendations of its *Texas Performance Review* before each legislative session and, from time to time, reports on state issues. These publications can be read in libraries or purchased from the comptroller's office for modest prices. For example, the three-volume *Forces of Change* report cited throughout this book was priced at about $20.

The Legislative Budget Board also publishes useful and readable information about Texas. One very helpful publication is *Fiscal Size-Up,* which is published after each legislative session. It contains not only the best analysis of budget actions taken by the legislature, but also summaries of important pieces of legislation that will affect major state programs and agencies. There is no better summary of legislative activity than *Fiscal Size-Up.*

Internet Resources

An exciting new source of information is the information superhighway: the Internet. The Internet is an international communications network that gives millions of computer users access to all sorts of information. There are several ways to access the Internet. Most colleges and universities are linked to the Net and provide access to some or all of their students. Many commercial services sell access for a monthly charge.

Today, the World Wide Web, a branch of the Internet, is growing in popularity. The Web displays both text and graphics. An important tool for using the Internet is a network browser, software that allows the user to search for information and retrieve it in usable form. Netscape and Internet Explorer are the two most popular browsers. Many commercial services include a browser in their service package. To access a Web page, the user must know its address. Addresses can be found by accessing one of several search services. In addition, the University of North Texas political science department maintains a home page (**http://www.psci.unt.edu**) with links to many important information sources about Texas.

There are several very useful sites for information about politics in Texas. The general home page for Texas government (**http://www.texas.gov**) provides access to information about and the addresses of Texas agencies. The comptroller's home page (**http://www.cpa.state.tx.us**), called the Window on Texas Government, is a good source of information about the state's revenue sources and expenditures. In addition, the comptroller's office makes performance reviews, policy recommendations, and other reports available on the Web. The Texas Constitution can also be accessed in electronic form. (One advantage of electronic access to the constitution is the ability to carry out word searches to find the provision of interest.) The Texas Legislature Online provides a wealth of information about the legislature and its work (**http://www.capitol.state.tx.us**). Available are a list of members and their addresses and a list of committees and their members. Also included is the wording of bills that are pending or that have been passed by the legislature. The Legislative Budget Board, which can also be reached through this site, makes budget information, including full text of all appropriations bills, available. For lists of elected officials and recent election statistics, the secretary of state's home page (**http://www.sos.state.tx.us**) contains up-to-date information.

By using the sources described in this appendix, students of Texas politics can have up-to-date information. With the basic concepts of Texas government and politics learned from this book, and with the means to keep current outlined in this appendix, students will have gone a long way toward preparing themselves to be informed and active citizens of Texas.

Appendix B

Using the Internet to Gather Information About Texas

Internet Exercises

Chapter 1: Context of Texas Government
Use the World Wide Web to find out the population of your home community. (Hint: Go to the state web site—**http://www.texas.gov**—then choose counties, and then choose Texas Community Profiles. From there you should be able to obtain the population by filling out the appropriate blanks in the form.)

Chapter 2: Legal Environment of Texas Politics
Use the online copy of the Texas Constitution found at **http://www.capitol.state.tx.us** to determine what part of the state constitution guarantees equal rights to all without regard to sex, race, color, creed, or national origin.

Chapter 3: Political Parties
Using the secretary of state's web site—**http://www.sos.state.tx.us**—find out what proportion of the vote went to each major party's candidate in the most recent gubernatorial election.

Chapter 4: Interest Groups in Texas
Using the Texas Ethics Commission's web site found at **http://www.ethics.state.tx.us,** identify a contract lobbyist and list five of his or her clients.

Chapter 5: Elections, Campaigns, and Voting in Texas
Using the secretary of state's web site at **http://www.sos.state.tx.us,** find out what percent of the voters voted during the early voting period in the last gubernatorial election.

Chapter 6: Texas Legislature
Using the Texas Legislature Online site at **http://www.capitol.state.tx.us,** find out who the members of the House State Affairs Committee were in the most recent legislative session.

Chapter 7: Texas Governorship
Use the governor's web site at **http://www.governor.state.tx.us** to find out what mailing address should be used to send a letter to the governor.

Chapter 8: Texas Bureaucracy
Use the Texas Department of Insurance's web site at **http://www.tdi.state.tx.us** to get a profile of your automobile insurance company. If you do not have an insurance company, just choose a name that you recognize and print out the profile.

Chapter 9: Texas Judiciary
Using the Texas Judiciary On-Line site at **http://www.courts.state.tx.us,** go to the section on the Texas Supreme Court and print out the biographical sketch for one of the justices.

Chapter 10: Local Government in Texas
Determine whether your city or county has a web site. Give the address (URL) for the site, then print out the opening page for the site.

Chapter 11: Texas Public Finance
Using the state comptroller's site—**http://www.cpa.state.tx**—find out how much money the comptroller estimated would be available for the current budgetary period.

Chapter 12: Social Welfare Policy in Texas
Using the Health and Human Services Commission's web site at **http://www.hhsc.state.tx.us,** find out what the latest developments are on the integrated enrollment system (TIES). Print out the information that you find.

Chapter 13: Education Policy in Texas
Using the Texas Education Agency's web site at **http://www.tea.state.tx.us,** see what you can find out about the latest TAAS test scores. Has the state average improved? Print out the information you find.

Chapter 14: Texas Environmental Policy
Using the Texas Natural Resource Conservation Commission's web site at **http://www.tnrcc.state.tx.us,** find out what the agency is featuring under its "Hot Topics." Print out the information on one of the items listed in this category.

Glossary

Accelerated agenda clearing (141) The period from the 127th day of the legislative session through its end, when the legislature acts on a large number of bills at a fast pace.

Administrative oversight (135) A responsibility of the legislature to make sure that executive agencies are following the law.

Aid to Families with Dependent Children (AFDC) (298) The major cash grant program of the welfare system until 1996.

Agenda-building stage (141) The first sixty days of a legislative session when bills are introduced for legislative consideration.

All funds budget (286) The comprehensive state budget that includes all state funds as well as those funds received from the federal government.

Amendment (35) A procedure for changing one part of a constitution.

Angry white males (62 [box]) Men who are dissatisfied who believe that the programs of the Democratic party are unfavorable to them.

Appellate jurisdiction (213) A court's right to hear a case on appeal from a lower court.

Aquifers (346) Underground water sources that are heavily relied on in Central and West Texas and that are often endangered by overpumping.

Association lobbyist (77) A lobbyist who represents an association for whom he or she works.

At-large election (260) A type of city election in which all council members are elected by the city as a whole—not by districts.

Balanced budget rule (276) Constitutional requirement that the legislature not appropriate more money than the state comptroller says will be available for a budgetary period.

Bicameralism (128) A way of organizing a legislative body that creates two chambers in the legislature, called the House and the Senate in Texas.

Biennial sessions (128) A system in which the legislature meets once every two years in regular session.

Biennium (277) The two-year budgetary period used by the state of Texas.

Budget execution power (165) Power of the governor (with the consent of the LBB) to change agency authorizations between legislative sessions.

Bureaucracy (185) The set of executive agencies responsible for operating state programs or enforcing state regulations.

Calendar (139) A listing of bills that are scheduled for legislative consideration.

Campaign finance reports (111) Reports on the collecting and spending of money that Texas law requires all candidates to file with the Texas Ethics Commission.

Campaigning (103) The procedures used by a candidate to persuade people to vote for him or her.

Caucuses (150) Party organizations through which the members of each party plan their party's strategy concerning major pieces of legislation.
Cause lobbyists (77) Individuals who lobby for cause groups to which they belong, such as Common Cause.
Charter school (326) A special type of open-enrollment school first authorized by the legislature in 1995. Charter schools are free to determine curriculum and methods largely without regard to state regulations.
City charter (253) The city's constitution; the charter describes the organization and powers of city government.
City government (246) Created principally as instruments of local self-government; i.e., to serve the interests of a local group of people and give them the legal powers necessary to meet their needs.
City incorporation process (253) The legal process set out in state law by which a city can be created.
Civil cases (212) Disputes between private individuals or groups over contracts, marriages, divorces, or injuries one party has allegedly caused another.
Closed primary (49) A party nominating election in which only members of a political party can participate.
Coastal management plan (349) A plan submitted to the national government by the Texas General Land Office setting forth procedures for protecting the public coastal areas.
Colonias (344) Rural settlements, primarily in South Texas, that lack basic water and sewer systems. They provide very cheap housing for low-income workers.
Commission form of city government (256) A form of city government invented in Texas in which elected city commissioners serve both as the city council and as city administrators.
Commissioner's court (247) County commission composed of county judge and county commissioners. Derives most of its power from its control of the county budget.
Committee assignments (143) The process by which the presiding officers place legislative members on various standing committees.
Company lobbyist (77) A lobbyist who represents the business he or she works for.
Complementary interest group system (88) An interest group system in which interest group power is balanced by the participation of several other significant types of political actors.
Concurrent jurisdiction (213) When two courts have the right to hear a particular type of case.
Conference committee (140) An ad hoc committee created by the legislative leaders to attempt to reconcile House and Senate versions of a bill that has been passed by both houses, but with different provisions.
Consolidated metropolitan statistical area (CMSA) (255) A federally-defined term that applies to metropolitan regions where several MSAs are located adjacent to each other.
Constitution (25, 35) A document that organizes the government, setting forth its basic structures and operating principles.
Constitutional Convention of 1974 (34) A special meeting of the Texas Legislature serving as a constitutional convention, which was charged with revising the Texas Constitution.
Constitutional reform (30) A process that involves a major rewriting of a constitution.

Constitutional Revision Commission (34) A study group appointed in 1973 to recommend changes to the constitution.

Contract lobbyist (76) A lobbyist who represents several groups on a fee basis.

Corporation franchise tax (284) The principal business tax, which is levied on businesses organized as corporations.

Council–manager form of government (258) A form of city government in which an elected council serves as the city's legislative body and also hires a professional manager who serves as the city's chief executive officer.

County executive committee (55) A county-level permanent organizational structure that is made up of the county's entire precinct chairs.

County government (246) Traditionally created by states to perform tasks at the local level that the state needs to have done.

County party chair (55) Presiding officer of the county executive committee, who is elected by participants in the party's primary election.

County convention (53) The second level temporary party organization, which elects delegates to the state convention. Also **senatorial district convention.**

Court of record (215) A court in which a full transcript of case proceedings is kept.

Criminal cases (212) Actions brought by the government against individuals who are charged with violating criminal laws.

Dealignment (42) A period in electoral history when all of the major parties lose support.

Demographic trend (8) A change over time in the size and/or the composition of the population.

Demonstrations and protests (79) An interest group strategy in which groups stage marches or protest activities to dramatize the group's position.

Dillon's Rule (246) A legal principle that has traditionally defined powers of local governments by stipulating that local governments have the powers expressly delegated to them by the state, those necessary or fairly implied, and those essential to carrying out stated objectives.

District election (260) A type of city election in which each council member is elected from a specific territorial district.

Dominant interest group system (88) An interest group system in which interest groups play an overpowering and persistent role in policymaking.

Early voting (103) A procedure in Texas that allows people to vote from the twentieth day through the fourth day prior to a scheduled election.

Earmarked fund (286) A state fund whose revenue can only be used for a purpose specified in state law or in the state constitution.

Economic efficiency (293) A principle for assessing taxing systems that asks whether the taxes deter economic growth in the state.

Edgewood* v. *Kirby (319) A Texas court case in which the Texas Supreme Court ruled in 1989 that the state school finance system violated the Texas constitution and was unconstitutional.

Electioneering (77) An interest group strategy that involves trying to get individuals elected who will support the group's interests when in office.

Electoral accountability (201) A system that depends upon the voters to evaluate agency heads and base their votes for or against them on the performance of the agencies they head.

Exclusive jurisdiction (213) When a particular type of court is the only one authorized to hear a particular type of case.

External factors (171) Events occurring outside the state that may affect the governor's potential for leadership.

Extraterritorial jurisdiction (ETJ) (254) State-granted jurisdiction granted to each city over a territorial zone surrounding the city.

Factionalism (44) A tendency for a political party to contain groups that compete for dominance of the party's activities.

Federal preemption (24) A national standard, or policy, which displaces a state standard or policy.

Federalism (21) A system of government that divides governmental authority between a national government and a set of component regional governments (states).

Felonies (212) Serious crimes punishable by long prison sentences or death.

Filibuster (140) A tactic used sometimes in the Texas Senate whereby prolonged debate is used to try killing a bill.

First primary (100) The Texas primary elections that are now held in May of even-numbered years.

Food Stamp Program (299) A system for providing needy families and individuals with stamps that can be used to buy food.

Foundation school program (317) A program that was intended to guarantee each child an equal minimum educational opportunity.

Functional organization (203) A criterion used to assess organizational structures. The criterion emphasizes that agencies doing similar work should be grouped together in one organizational structure so that their work can be coordinated.

General elections (100) Elections held in November in which state and county officeholders are elected in Texas.

General-law cities (253) Cities with a population less than 5,000 whose powers and organization are determined by the General Law of Municipalities.

Geographic integrity (21) A protection afforded the states by the U.S. Constitution, which prohibits Congress from subdividing states or combining them without the consent of the states.

Gilmer-Aikin bills (317) Legislation passed in 1949 that created the foundation school program concept.

Government (2) Regulates the lives of citizens and produces and distributes services to them.

Government lobbyist (77) Lobbyist who represents local governments.

Governor E. J. Davis (26) Governor of Texas during Reconstruction whose abuses of power influenced the drafting of the constitution of 1876.

Grant-in-aid conditions (24) Conditions attached to monetary grants to the states to which the state must conform if it wishes to receive full federal funding.

Grass roots mobilization (78) An interest group strategy in which the group tries to mobilize some segment of the public to contact public officials and send them messages that will support the group's interests.

Great Depression (297) The economic crisis of the 1930s that was the longest and most severe economic crisis experienced by the United States.

Groundwater (342) Water in underground pools that is pumped out to provide water for drinking and irrigation in many Texas areas.

Growth limitation rule (277) A constitutional requirement that appropriations from non-dedicated tax revenues not exceed the rate of growth in the state's economy in a budgetary period.

Hierarchical jurisdiction (212) The place that a court occupies above or below other courts in the judicial system.

High-occupancy vehicle (HOV) lanes (341) Lanes on urban freeways that are dedicated to the use of vehicles with two or more persons. These lanes, which are especially prevalent in Houston, are intended to encourage car-pooling and other high-occupancy vehicle strategies that will limit the number of cars on the road.

Higher Education Assistance Fund (HEAF) (331) A fund created to provide funds for capital projects in non-PUF universities and colleges.

Home-rule charter (253) A charter that is drawn up by an eligible city and determines that city's organization and powers.

Home-rule cities (253) Those cities with a population of at least 5,000 to whom the right to draw up a home rule charter is granted.

Homestead policy (4) An early Texas policy to encourage settlement of the land and to place as much land as possible into private ownership.

Hopwood case (332) A case decided by the Court of Appeals of the Fifth Judicial Circuit that outlawed the use of race or ethnicity as a criterion in admissions, financial aid, or other university programs.

Ideological labeling (105) A campaign strategy that involves attaching an undesirable political label to a candidate. In Texas, the ideological label to be avoided is "liberal."

Ideology (65 [Fig. 3.3]) A related set of political attitudes and beliefs that cause one to be positioned along a political continuum ranging from liberal to conservative.

Impeachment (161) The procedure whereby a governor can be removed from office by the legislature for official wrongdoing.

Impeachment process (136) The process by which the Texas House of Representatives may bring charges against a public officeholder. The Texas Senate would try the charges.

Independent school district (317) The governmental entity that runs the public and elementary schools in Texas.

Indictment (236) A formal criminal charge against an individual made by a grand jury. Also called **true bill.**

Individual lobbyist (77) A lobbyist who is motivated by his/her own personal beliefs to influence public policy.

Initial agenda clearing (141) The period from the 61st day through the 126th day of a session when the legislature begins to take action on bills.

Institutional factors (170) Factors in state law or the constitution that grant authority or withhold authority from the governor.

Interest group (73) An organization of individuals who share a common interest and who work together to advance that interest.

Intergovernmental power (167) Power of the governor to represent the state in dealings with the national government.

Interim committee (149) Committee of the legislature that meet between sessions to conduct studies and formulate proposals.

Jacksonian Democracy (164) A nineteenth century political movement that popularized (among other things) the idea of having state executives elected by the people, instead of appointed by the governor.

Judicial decrees (22) Court decisions that require states to take certain actions.

Jurisdiction (212) The area(s) in which a court has the right to make decisions.

La Raza Unida (46) A third party that emerged in the 1970s supported primarily by Hispanic voters.

Land-based economy (5) An economy which relies primarily on agricultural employment. The first stage of Texas' economic development.

Landfills (346) Systems for burying trash from municipalities.

Leadership (170) Using available resources to get others to cooperate in solving problems.

Legislative address (136) A procedure by which the Texas legislature can remove judicial officers.

Legislative Budget Board (LBB) (153, 277) Legislative agency that formulates a proposed budget for the legislature and provides staff assistance to the legislature during the legislative session.

Legislative Council (152) A legislative support agency that provides bill drafting services and does background research on issues before the legislature.

Legislative districts (131) The territorial districts into which the state is divided for purposes of electing members of the legislature.

Legislative Redistricting Board (134) The constitutionally created body that is responsible for redrawing legislative districts after a national census, if the legislature has been unable to carry out the task.

Legislative Reference Library (153) A legislative support agency that maintains a library of materials that might be helpful to legislators and the staff.

Legislative regulations (23) Laws passed by the U.S. Congress that require the states to meet nationally set requirements for certain activities.

Lieutenant governor (143) The presiding officer of the Senate.

Line-item budgeting (280) A budgeting system in which each line (or item) in the budget describes goods or services that would be bought with the money appropriated.

Line-item veto (140, 165) A constitutionally granted power of the Texas governor to veto specific items in appropriations bills instead of just signing or vetoing the entire bill.

Litigation (80) An interest group strategy in which a group brings test cases to the courts in hope of achieving a favorable change in policy.

Lobbying (74) Formal or informal attempts to influence policy decisions through direct contact.

Lobbyist (76) A person designated by an interest group to represent it for the purposes of influencing public policy in the group's favor.

Lone Star debit card (305) An electronic means of distributing food purchasing power used instead of distributing actual stamps.

Low-performing school (324) A school in which the average TAAS scores fall below a minimum level set by the state.

Mandate (287) An order by one level of government that another provide a specified service. Mandates commonly cause expenditures to go up.

Maquiladoras (338) American factories built inside Mexico to take advantage of cheaper labor and weaker regulations.

Mayor–council form of government (256) A form of city government in which an elected mayor is the chief executive officer and the elected council is the legislative body.

Means-tested program (300) A social welfare program with eligibility rules requiring that a person's income and economic resources fall below some level to receive benefits.

Medicaid (299) The program that provides medical assistance to the poor.

Megafills (347) Very large landfills developed in some open spaces in West Texas.

Message power (166) Power of the governor to address the legislature and to call upon them to take action on certain issues.

Metropolitan statistical area (MSA) (255) A term defined by the federal government that designates a specific level of population concentration.

Misdemeanors (212) Less serious crimes for which punishment is limited to shorter jail sentences or fines.

Modified one-party system (47) A political party system in which one party wins most of the time, but is periodically beaten by an opposition party.

Municipal utility districts (MUDs) (268) A commonly used type of special district in Texas that provides water and sewer services to housing developments located outside any city.

National government powers (21) Powers delegated to congress by Article I, Section 8 of the U.S. Constitution.

Negative campaigning (105) A campaign that includes personal attacks on opponents to undermine voters' confidence in them.

No bill (236) A decision by a grand jury not to charge an individual with a crime.

No pass, no play rule (321) A principle adopted in 1984 stating that students must be suspended from participation in extra-curricular activities for six weeks if they did not pass all of their courses. The suspension period was later shortened to three weeks.

Nonattainment areas (341) Metropolitan areas in Texas that have been unable to meet federal air quality standards.

Non-restricted appropriations (277) That part of the budget that the legislature is free to appropriate because there are no constitutional or statutory limitations.

Non-tax revenue (282) Money collected by the state as payments for fees, fines, etc. or money earned by the state on funds held in reserve.

Oil-based economy (5) The second phase of development of the Texas economy in which the economy depended heavily on jobs in oil and gas production.

One-party dominance (43) A period in Texas political history when the Democratic party dominated, almost without opposition.

One-party system (47) A political party system in which one party consistently wins all or almost all state offices.

Open primary (49) A party nominating election in which any qualified voter can participate.

Original jurisdiction (213) A court's right to hear a case on its first hearing.

Ozone (341) A form of chemical pollution in the air that is prevalent in Texas cities. Ozone is produced by interaction of gasoline fumes from automobiles and bright sunlight, so it is a problem in Texas summers.

Partisan choice (115) The choice that voters make when they choose one party's candidate over another party's candidate.

Party activists (57) The individuals who staff a political party's political structures.

Party identification (61) A sense of attachment to a political party.

Party platform (53) The statement of a party's position—adopted by the state convention-on the key issues in an election year.

Per capita tax revenue (285) The amount of tax revenue collected per person. Often used as a measure of relative tax burden when comparing states.

Performance budgeting (280) Requiring agencies to submit performance measures with budgets and rewarding agencies for achieving performance targets.

Performance measures (202) Quantifiable measures of performance developed by the Legislative Budget Board and used to indicate how well an agency is doing its job.

Permanent party structures (50) Party structures—committees and officers—that continue throughout the year and carry out the party's activities.

Permanent University Fund (PUF) (331) A special state fund that gets revenue from leases on state-owned lands. Revenue from the fund is available only to universities in the University of Texas or Texas A&M systems.

Perot Commission (320) A group appointed by Governor Mark White in the 1980s to recommend school reforms.

Personal factors (171) Aspects of the governor's personality that affect his or her potential for leadership.

Personal Responsibility and Work Opportunity Reconciliation Act of 1996 (304) The federal welfare reform law.

Political action committee (PAC) (77) An organization created by interest groups or corporations as a means of channeling campaign contributions to friendly candidates for office.

Political consultants (104) Individuals who provide campaign advice and/or other campaign-related services for a fee.

Political factors (171) Variables in the political environment that affect a governor's potential for leadership.

Political machines (260) City political party organizations that dominated many American cities in the late 19th century and often were characterized by corruption.

Political outsider tactic (105) A campaign strategy in which a candidate emphasizes that he or she is *not* a politician.

Political party (41) Any group seeking to elect government officerholders under a given label.

Politics (2) Includes all of the processes by which citizens attempt to control or influence the decisions of the government.

Poll tax (97) A voting requirement that demanded a person to pay a tax before becoming eligible to vote. Such a requirement is now unconstitutional.

Precinct chair (54) The permanent party officer at the precinct level.

Precinct convention (51) The lowest-level temporary party organization which meets every two years and elects delegates to the county or senatorial district convention.

Presidential coattail effect (100) The effect produced when a presidential candidate's popularity boosts the number of voters received by his or her party's candidates for state or local offices.

Primary election (99) An election that selects a political party's nominees.

Property qualification (97) A once common requirement for voting requiring that a person own property before he or she would be granted the right to vote.

Public relations techniques (79) An interest group strategy in which the group tries to build a favorable image of itself in the mind of the public.

Realignment (42) A turning point in electoral history when one party gains support and the other loses support.

Recycling (347) An approach to municipal waste that emphasizes channeling waste into other uses instead of burying it in landfills.

Referendum (101) A type of election in which voters themselves decide policy issues—such as approving constitutional amendments.

Reformulated gasoline (341) A cleaner burning gasoline that is required in some nonattainment areas in Texas.

Region (8) A part of the state that is distinguishable from other regions by its distinctive geography, race, ethnicity, or economy, or by some distinctive combination of such factors.

Registration of Lobbyists Act (90) A Texas statute that requires lobbyists to register and to report on their financial activities.

Registration requirements (98) A voting requirement that demands an individual to establish his or her eligibility to vote by following a state-prescribed procedure.

Regressive taxes (292) Taxes that take a higher percentage of income from low income groups than from higher income groups.

Residence requirement (97) A voting requirement stipulating that a person must have lived in a political jurisdiction for a certain period of time before becoming eligible to vote.

Retention elections (232) A type of election used for judges in some states in which a judge's name is put on the ballot and voters vote for or against retaining that person in office.

Robin Hood plans (328) Plans for school finance reform that required wealthier districts to share their tax revenue with poorer districts.

***Rodriguez* case** (318) A case that was decided by the U.S. Supreme Court on appeal in 1973, in which the Court said that the Texas school finance system did not violate the national constitution.

Ruiz* v. *Estelle (238) The federal court case in which the state of Texas was ordered to reduce the crowding in its prisons.

Runoff primary (49, 100) A primary election in which the top two vote-getters from the first primary compete. Runoff primaries are held only if no candidate receives a majority of the votes cast in the first primary.

Sales tax (282) The principal source of tax revenue in Texas. A tax collected as a percentage of the value of certain types of sales designated in state law.

Secretary of state (101) The chief elections officer of the state, who is responsible for seeing to it that local authorities follow state law when administering elections.

Self-reliance model (297) The model for personal behavior that believed people should take care of themselves by hard work and thrift.

Senatorial district convention (53) See **county convention.**

Separation of powers (27) A constitutional principle that allocates the three basic powers of government-executive, legislative, and judicial-to different institutions: the governor, the legislature, the courts. This principle is explicitly stated in Article II of the Texas Constitution.

Service sector (6) A rising part of the contemporary Texas economy in which workers provide services, instead of producing goods.

Sharpstown banking scandal (31) A scandal that opened the door to constitutional revision in Texas because so many high-ranking Texas officials appeared to have been involved in official wrongdoing.

Social safety net (296) The set of government programs intended to help those unable to generate sufficient income to take care of themselves and their families.

Social Security Act (298) Law passed by Congress in 1935 that established the framework for the social welfare system in the United States.

South Texas initiative (330) A special state program to build up colleges and universities in the Rio Grande Valley area.

Speaker of the house (143) The presiding officer of the House of Representatives.

Special act charter (253) A city charter that is granted by a special act of the legislature and applies only to one specific city.

Special elections (101) Elections called by the governor to fill vacancies caused by death or resignation of state officeholders.

Special session power (166) Power of the governor to call the legislature into special session and to determine the issues that can be addressed during a special session.

Special-district government (246) Created to perform specific tasks that are not appropriate for county or city governments; usually to provide a single type of service or small related set of services.

Staff (155) Legislative employees who work either for individual legislators or for one of the standing committees.

Standing committee (146) A continuing committee in the legislature. Each standing committee is responsible for bills dealing with a particular subject.

State executive committee (56) The state-level part of the county's permanent organization. It is made up of one man and one woman from each of the state's senatorial districts. State executive committee members are elected at the state convention.

"State of South Texas" (297) The region of Texas located between the Rio Grande River and an imaginary line from El Paso to Corpus Christi in which high levels of poverty are present.

State party chair (56) The chief executive office of the party's permanent organizational structure. The party chair is elected at the party's state convention.

State powers (21) Powers reserved to the states by the Tenth Amendment to the U.S. Constitution, which stipulates that "powers not delegated to the United States by the Constitution, or prohibited by it to the States, are reserved to the States respectively, or to the people."

Statute (135) A law made by the Texas legislature.

Straight ticket (102) A requirement of Texas law that requires ballots to provide a single procedure—a single box or a single lever—by which voters can vote for the candidates of one political party for all the races on the ballot.

Strategic planning and budgeting (280) The current Texas budgeting system that requires agencies to submit strategic plans, goals, and objectives, and to show how spending requests are related to their plans.

Subject-matter jurisdiction (212) The types of subjects about which a court has the right to make decisions.

Subordinate interest group system (88) An interest group system in which interest groups usually have less influence than other types of political actors.

Suffrage (97) The right to vote.

Sunset legislation (136) Laws that enable the legislature to terminate or reauthorize agencies or programs.

Sunset reviews (202) A system for evaluating bureaucratic agencies periodically to determine whether their work justifies their continued existence and to determine if improvements can be recommended. A certain number of agencies are scheduled for review at each legislative session.

Superfund (349) A fund set aside by the U.S. Environmental Protection Agency to assist states with cleaning up hazardous waste.

Surface water (342) Water in streams, rivers, and lakes that provides much of the drinking water in parts of Texas.

Swing voters (116) Those voters who switch from one party to the other from election to election, instead of consistently voting for the candidates of one party.

TAAS (323) Texas Assessment of Academic Skills: a testing program used to determine the progress of students and the performance of schools.

Temporary Assistance to Needy Families (TANF) (303) The block grant program to provide cash assistance that replaced AFDC.

Tax equity (292) A principle for assessing taxing systems that asks whether the burden is fairly allocated among citizens.

Tax revenue (280) Money collected by the state as payments for specific taxes.

Temporary party structures (50) Party structures—usually conventions—that come into existence only in election years and adjourn as soon as their function has been fulfilled.

Terrell Act (99) The Texas law that requires most political party nominations to be made by primary elections.

Territorial jurisdiction (212) The geographic area for which a court has the right to make decisions.

Texas Education Agency (TEA) (317) State agency responsible for supervising public elementary and secondary education in Texas.

Texas Election Code (99) A compilation of the rules governing registering and voting that have been passed by the Texas legislature.

Texas Ethics Commission (91, 111) A state agency that is responsible for enforcing the law requiring lobbyists to register and file financial reports. The agency receives and monitors reports.

Texas Higher Education Coordinating Board (329) The state body responsible for coordinating higher education programs and preventing needless duplication of programs among colleges and universities.

Texas Natural Resource Conservation Commission (TNRCC) (340) Agency created in 1991 to coordinate environmental policy in Texas.

Texas Performance Review (185) A review of the operations of state government carried out every two years by the comptroller's office to recommend ways that the government can work more effectively and/or efficiently.

Texas Triangle (10 [in Fig. 1.4 caption]) A triangular region containing 60 percent of the state's population with one corner at the Dallas-Fort Worth metropolitan area, one corner at the San Antonio metropolitan area, and the third corner at the Houston metropolitan area.

Texas Water Development Board (343) Texas agency charged with developing and implementing a state water plan.

Texas Workforce Commission (192, 309) The Texas agency charged with helping welfare recipients move into jobs.

TIES (307) Texas Integrated Eligibility System—the automated system for gathering eligibility information for which Texas has contracted with EDS.

Tort reform (240) Changes in the rules concerning civil suits for damages.

Trial courts (214) Courts of original jurisdiction.

Trial *de novo* (215) A re-hearing of a case that starts anew with a full presentation of the evidence because the lower court was not a court of record.

True bill (236) See **indictment.**

Two-party system (47) A political party system in which two political parties compete and have roughly equal chances of winning elections.

Veto (140) An action that may be taken by the governor to kill a bill passed by the legislature.

Veto power (166) Power of the governor to reject any bill passed by the legislature. The governor's veto can be overridden by a two-thirds vote of each house of the legislature.

Voter turnout (113) The percentage of eligible voters who actually participate in an election.

Voting Rights Act (98) A federal law that forced some states, including Texas, to eliminate restrictions that prevented minorities from registering and voting.

Waiver request (302) A petition submitted by a state requesting that it be allowed to deviate from some federal rules in the administration of its welfare programs.

White primary (98) A type of nominating election in which only whites were allowed to vote.

"Yellow dog Democrats" (116) A type of voter who is so committed to the Democratic party that he or she would vote for the party's candidate even if it were a yellow dog.

Zero-based budgeting (280) A budgeting system that required agencies to prepare budgets for several funding levels so that the effects of budgeting at one level or another would be apparent.

Index

Photo Credits

P. 3: **Adam Jahiel/Gamma Liaison**; p. 4: **Curt Wilcott/Gamma Liaison**; pp. 8, 13, 36, 41, 52, 54, 76, 79, 84, 115, 129, 130, 131, 177, 197, 251, 254, 346: **Bob Daemmrich**; p. 45: **R. Maiman/Sygma**; pp. 29, 75, 211, 331: **Bob Daemmrich/Stock Boston**; pp. 102, 121, 167: **AP/Wide World Photos**; pp. 144, 166, 305, 319: **Bob Daemmrich/The Image Works**; pp. 194, 264, 300, 342: **Paul S. Howell/Gamma Liaison**; p. 225: **Black/Gold Photography**; p. 227: **Courtesy of State Bar of Texas**; pp. 238, 347: **Alan Pogue/TexaStock**; p. 291: **David E. Kennedy/TexaStock.**